THE
RECONSTRUCTION
PRESIDENTS

THE
RECONSTRUCTION
PRESIDENTS

Brooks D. Simpson

University Press of Kansas

© 1998 by the University Press of Kansas
All rights reserved

Published by the University Press of Kansas (Lawrence, Kansas 66049), which was
organized by the Kansas Board of Regents and is operated and funded by Emporia State
University, Fort Hays State University, Kansas State University, Pittsburg State University,
the University of Kansas, and Wichita State University

Library of Congress Cataloging-in-Publication Data

Simpson, Brooks D.
   The Reconstruction presidents / Brooks D. Simpson.
    p.   cm.
   Includes bibliographical references and index.
   ISBN 0-7006-0896-6 (cloth : alk. paper)
   1. Reconstruction.   2. United States—Politics and
government—1865–1877.   3. Presidents—United States—History—19th
century.   4. Lincoln, Abraham, 1809–1865.   5. Johnson, Andrew,
1808–1875.   6. Grant, Ulysses S. (Ulysses Simpson), 1822–1885.
7. Hayes, Rutherford Birchard, 1822–1893.   I. Title.
E668.S58   1998
973.8—dc21   98-4772

British Library Cataloguing in Publication Data is available.

Printed in the United States of America

10 9 8 7 6 5 4 3 2

For Jean

CONTENTS

PREFACE

Perhaps Michael Perman was merely being mischievous when he argued that Eric Foner's *Reconstruction: America's Unfinished Revolution, 1863–1877,* published in 1988, raised the unsettling question "What is left to be done?" It did not seem so funny at the time. Perman's query was especially unsettling for those of us just starting out in the field, sometimes with advance contracts in hand. Foner's majesterial work, integrating social, political, and economic history in a forcefully argued narrative, was frankly intimidating, and no more so than to those of us who preferred to explore politics and policy on the national level, for his account emphasized the grassroots struggle for emancipation and equality waged by black Americans and their white allies, erstwhile and earnest alike. If one followed Perman, the very success of Foner's book as a definitive synthesis implied that while the revolution itself remained unfinished, the scholarship tracing that revolution had come to a stopping point, a sure case of unintended consequences. To the extent that it established an agenda for future research, it called upon scholars to elaborate on its chief theme. In a profession known for its admiration of the fashionable and the "hot" topic, where innovation is followed by imitation, it seemed that historians who had chosen to explain the actions of political leaders who lived and worked in Washington were in trouble.

This book, appearing as it does ten years after the publication of Foner's work, will doubtless strike some readers as an anomaly, a curiously old-fashioned study. Yet presidents, national politics, and policy matter. An understanding of them is essential to comprehending Reconstruction. History from the top down still has its merits, and no one knew this better than the southern blacks themselves, who looked to Washington for protection from violence and for assistance in building a future. How the four occupants of the White House confronted this challenge and others and why they responded as they did in addressing the issues of Reconstruction form the heart of this book. The interpretation it offers is based partly on original research, but even more so on an effort to bring together the work of several fine scholars who have written extensively on the politics of Reconstruction and the presidents who played such a pivotal role in shaping federal policy toward the South.

Over the last several decades, a number of historians have redefined our understanding of Reconstruction politics and policy. Phil Paludan offered what remains the most satisfying account of Lincoln as president, while LaWanda Cox and David Donald highlighted his political skills and his pragmatism. Albert Castel's examination of Andrew Johnson's administration reinforced impressions I received while working on the papers of the seventeenth president; Hans L. Trefousse's scholarship repeatedly reminded me of the Radical Republicans' commitment to equality. My understanding of Reconstruction politics owes much to the work of Michael Les Benedict and Michael Perman; even though I disagree with several of William Gillette's arguments, I found his study of Reconstruction under Grant and Hayes refreshing and challenging. Although most people are drawn to Eric Foner's discussion of the opening years of postwar Reconstruction, his treatment of the 1870s is equally compelling. Mark Summers's scholarship provoked thought while his prose tickled me; even when I grew exasperated with some of the assumptions in William B. Hesseltine's work, I admired his willingness to take Grant seriously as a politician. Finally, Ari Hoogenboom's writings on Rutherford B. Hayes presented a wealth of insight into that often overshadowed presidency.

In some cases, the interpretations of these scholars provided the framework for my inquiry; in other instances, the publication of their findings as I worked on this manuscript forced me to revisit some issues and rethink some interpretations, although in general I was pleasantly surprised to see that there was much consensus and convergence. Thus, this book owes much to the work of others, even as it reflects one historian's efforts to wrestle with various interpretations in arriving at the following perspective on presidents, policy, and politics during the Reconstruction era. If the result spurs discussion, it will have proved a worthwhile endeavor.

One of the ironies of preparing acknowledgments is that authors, regardless of the admonishment that they alone are responsible for all errors that remain, implicate others by thanking them for their contributions to the final product. What is thus in one sense a sincere effort to give thanks is therefore also payback time: the reader is left to figure out which is which.

At various stages of my professional training, Michael Holt, Richard Sewell, and Allan Bogue did much to cultivate my understanding of Reconstruction politics; all three will detect traces of their handiwork in what follows. In addition, every one of the scholars listed above whom I have met has provided encouragement and challenged my thinking as it evolved. Albert Castel offered sound advice in many letters; Ari Hoogenboom, Charles Dellheim, and Roger Bridges read portions of the manuscript. Once again Mark Summers shared his opinions and challenged me to do better; his detailed critique embodied the best qualities of scholarship and friendship we all treasure in the profession. For the University Press of Kansas, Phillip Shaw Paludan went over the entire manuscript with care and highlighted areas in need of repair or reassessment.

Essential to the preparation of this volume were grants from the National Endowment for the Humanities, the American Philosophical Society, and the Faculty Grant-in-Aid Program at Arizona State University.

Several people at the University Press of Kansas have been cheering me on (although a few kept peering over my shoulder) as I wrote, revised, and postponed deadlines. The idea for the book was sparked by an inquiry from Kate Torrey, who in migrating from Lawrence to Chapel Hill simply traded one set of overdue obligations for another. Cynthia Miller offered reassurance and encouragement, then left for Pittsburgh, raising in my mind the possibility that this project would outlast the press's staff. Mike Briggs and Susan Schott took up where Cynthia left off, providing welcome advice and support, while Rebecca Knight Giusti oversaw the production process. It was thus left to Fred Woodward to play the role of Maxwell Perkins in cajoling a manuscript from me, using whatever it took to achieve his end. He may attribute the result to his tenacity, but I prefer to think that good things come at the right time to those who wait.

Finally, three lively women waited patiently for their turn while I wrote about four dead men. Rebecca and Emily thought the prime reason for my sabbatical was to enable me to join them in watching the Phoenix Coyotes battle through the 1996–1997 National Hockey League schedule. I wish they were right. Jean has made my life better and richer in countless ways, although I don't always tell her so. The dedication is small remuneration indeed for all she's done for me.

INTRODUCTION

It is difficult to be dispassionate about Reconstruction, an era of American history in which myth vies with the historical record in shaping our vision of the past. Americans who believe that they are immune to political terrorism overlook what happened in the South in the dozen years after the Civil War; old stereotypes, shaped by white supremacist assumptions, still exert influence on the popular imagination in some parts of the country. Scholars concerned with the present state of race relations often cast a critical eye at the efforts of white policy makers to achieve a more egalitarian nation, preferring to arraign the past rather than confront the continued intractability of such issues today. Rather than attempt to understand Reconstruction, many Americans prefer simply to pass judgment on it.

Never is this tendency to view history in terms of moral judgment more evident than in assessments of how presidents approached Reconstruction. Americans once cherished an image of Abraham Lincoln as both the Great Emancipator and the apostle of forgiveness toward the defeated South. Older accounts, which approved Lincoln's skepticism about racial equality, sometimes by wrenching statements out of context, have given way to a far more critical view offered by people who find such sentiments unacceptable. These scholars challenge portrayals of Lincoln as a humanitarian liberator, while the proponents of a more positive perspective continue to endeavor to establish his claim to greatness. Once celebrated as a staunch defender of constitutional rights and sectional reconciliation, Andrew Johnson is now roundly denounced as a racist, as if that in itself explains what happened during his presidency. Ulysses S. Grant, castigated by early historians of Reconstruction for his commitment to Republican Reconstruction, is now chastised for lacking a commitment to black freedom and equality. One historian, who claimed in 1955 that Grant was in the pocket of the Radicals, in 1981 stated that Grant was sympathetic to Johnson's conservative approach—although in each case the saving consistency remained the scholar's unremitting hostility to Grant.[1] Rutherford B. Hayes has come under fire for consigning the freedpeople to their fate at the hands of white southerners; others celebrate him as a "statesman of reunion."

Such judgments tell us at least as much about the attitudes of the critics as they do about the preferences and policies of the presidents under discussion: in some instances it seems as if critics are seeking some sort of validation for their own views on race by offering their observations on what presidents believed and did in matters of race. These appraisals are often based upon the simplistic assumption that how each president approached Reconstruction can be attributed in large part to his attitudes toward race: political action, according to these arguments, is a function of personal beliefs. Occasionally, moralizing judgment replaces analysis, assessment, and understanding.

Undoubtedly, part of the historian's task is to pass judgment, explicitly or implicitly; the topics a historian chooses to explore and the very words he or she uses to describe or characterize someone or something reflect personal preferences. But such judgments, in the end, should rest upon first achieving an understanding of historical actors and the world they lived in, an ability to put oneself in their place and see matters as they saw them in all their complexity and context. Present-day concerns about civil rights and race relations have led many historians to emphasize the same aspects in their examination and assessment of Reconstruction. They often criticize their predecessors for offering accounts of policy making during Reconstruction infused by a preference for sectional reconciliation or the assumption that blacks were incapable of meting the challenges of emancipation and citizenship. And yet it is important that we today do not allow our current commitment to racial equality to overwhelm our ability to understand the past. A complete understanding of Reconstruction policy must recall that the issue of how best to reunite the nation was at least as important to most white Americans as was defining exactly what freedom and equality meant for black Americans. The central dilemma for most Republican policy makers was how best to promote both sectional reconciliation and justice for black Americans, a matter complicated by differing opinions on exactly what would constitute racial justice and what role government would play in securing it. Of the four presidents under study, only Andrew Johnson lacked any sincere commitment to helping black Americans, although historians may disagree on the extent to which Lincoln, Grant, and Hayes possessed such a commitment or were willing to act on it. In framing policy and in reacting to events, presidential action is shaped in part by personal preferences and beliefs but not solely (and rarely overwhelmingly) by them. A more informed assessment of presidential policy rests upon viewing the framing and implementation of policy in larger contexts of governmental institutions, political circumstances, and popular support.

How one goes about realizing one's objectives can prove as important as what one seeks to accomplish. Process was extremely important to these four men, perhaps even more so at a time when many of the principles of representative government were being tested. Abraham Lincoln, for example, sought to secure emancipation through constitutional means; as a result, he pursued several paths, depending upon the situation he confronted. In the electoral crisis of 1876–1877, Ulysses S. Grant realized the importance of seeking a resolution through means the contending factions recognized as legitimate. In both cases, the chief executives, by exercising restraint, strengthened their claim to authority; in contrast, Andrew Johnson's vigorous exercise of his prerogatives led to his impeachment. Moreover, federal authority in nineteenth-century America was rather limited—and most Americans wanted it that way. If the Civil War and Reconstruction offered opportunities for federal action, they were also exceptional, and the principles of federalism continued to constrain a president's ability to shape events.

Concentrating on the individuals who wielded presidential power often comes at the cost of overlooking the various contexts in which one exercises those powers. The institutional bases of presidential power provide the chief executive with certain policy-making tools, each with its own advantages and disadvantages. Patronage offers a way to build support, reward friends, and punish enemies, but in using it a president often offends those not chosen. The veto can block legislative initiatives and force congressional majorities either to craft acceptable alternatives or forge veto-proof majorities, but its limits as a creative tool are obvious. Political circumstances also shape the context in which a president governs. Lincoln and Grant enjoyed Republican majorities in Congress during much of their time in office, yet intraparty divisions proved troublesome; Johnson and Hayes (as well as Grant during his last two years) confronted either divided or eventually hostile Congresses. In three instances presidents assumed power in difficult circumstances. Lincoln entered upon his responsibilities just as the Union confronted the crossroads of its continued existence; Johnson took the oath of office in the wake of the assassination of his predecessor; Hayes's inauguration was overshadowed by the controversy over who had the better claim to the presidency in 1877. Lincoln, Grant, and Hayes had to work within the limits of northern electoral politics concerning issues of race; Johnson eagerly sought to exploit racist sentiment. All four men struggled with mixed results to build support in the South for their policies. The breadth and depth of support for presidential policies fluctuated over time and according to circumstances. Not all leadership styles are equally appropriate for all circumstances: a preference for confrontation over accommodation and compromise, for example, may lead to triumph or tragedy, depending on what the situation requires, as does one's willingness to innovate or press against the boundaries of the possible.

A study of four presidents' approaches to Reconstruction seems to offer a promising opportunity for comparative analysis. The nature and use of presidential power, the relationship between making and implementing policy, the interplay between policy and partisan advantage, and the impact of personal characteristics, style, and beliefs are concerns common to an examination of these four presidencies. However, the persistence of such themes by itself is not sufficient to engage in a disciplined comparative analysis: what impresses the historian who examines these presidencies collectively is the specificity of context in each case. Each president came to office facing different circumstances, each posing its own challenges. During most of his presidency, Lincoln had to give priority to winning a war for reunion; in contrast, Johnson assumed office just as that conflict wound down to a close. Grant entered the White House with what on the surface seemed overwhelming advantages, yet they soon dissipated—and were bound to do so—while Hayes succeeded him under conditions that might have crippled a lesser man or politician. Although all four men can collectively be termed the Reconstruction presidents, the Reconstructions over which they presided and which they helped shape also differed in important ways as the process evolved over time. And in confronting the problems of Reconstruction, each president kept in mind the experience of his predecessor. Thus a comprehension of chronology, circumstance, and context is essential to informing one's assessment of presidential performance, for such considerations delineate the boundaries of the possible.

"Politics is the art of the possible." This statement, appealing in its (sometimes deceptive) simplicity, is more often cited than understood. Before assessing presidential performance, one must first ascertain what was possible. Those historians who are critical of the performance of these four men for not achieving more for black Americans find it rather difficult to offer a historically viable alternative that improves markedly on what happened, even with the immense advantages offered by hindsight. Much of the counterfactual speculation about what might have happened in 1865—complete with images of landowning blacks participating in politics—hinges upon eliminating Andrew Johnson altogether as a factor in the policy process. What Lincoln, Grant, and Hayes could have accomplished was limited by circumstances not easily altered, especially in the context of nineteenth-century notions of federalism, limited government, and presidential power, to say nothing of the broader circumstances of politics and society. If their actions do not always meet with present-day approbation, it remains to be said that each of these three Republicans could have done far less when it came to the fate of black Americans. Only in the case of Andrew Johnson's ascension to power is it possible to envision markedly different results with a different man (one elected by Republican votes) in office, and even then it is wise and prudent not to exaggerate how different the result might have been.

Lest this lead one to adopt a deterministic view of Reconstruction, it remains important to understand what each chief executive did and why he chose as he did. Presidents are not total prisoners of their environment, and they themselves help determine what is, in fact, possible. It may prove difficult to envision exactly how postwar Reconstruction would have evolved had Abraham Lincoln served out his second term, but not to conclude that he would have led in different ways and for different ends than Johnson did. One might be critical of Grant's performance as president, but what would have happened had Horatio Seymour taken the oath of office on March 4, 1869? Moreover, one test of presidential leadership is the president's ability to reshape what was possible and to take advantage of changing circumstances to push his agenda. Lincoln once asserted that he did not control events, but a hallmark of his leadership was his ability to turn them to his advantage with a fine sense of timing. By realizing both that politics is the art of the possible and that presidents help determine what is possible, we may gain a better understanding of how presidents governed (and the extent to which they did or could) in the nineteenth century.

Although in thinking, reading, and writing about these four men I have been influenced by studies of presidential and political leadership, I have deliberately eschewed explicit model building. I offer an approach to understanding and assessing presidential policy making that emphasizes the environment in which a president governs and the nature of the challenges facing him (and, someday, her) as well as issues of personality and character. One can judge a president's performance better if one does not rest content with passing judgment on that president's character and motivation from the lofty heights of the ivy tower. A scholarship grounded in seeking out moral shortcomings may assuage a scholar's conscience, but in the end it marks no improvement upon a search for flawless heroes. To avoid making such judgments is impossible, but it is debatable whether passing judgment is the scholar's primary goal. Better to understand a person in the context of his or her times and circumstances as a way to render more judicious and informed assessments, so that we can better understand not only our past but ourselves.

PART ONE
ABRAHAM LINCOLN

1

"BROKEN EGGS CANNOT BE MENDED"

Throughout Abraham Lincoln's presidency his main concern was the preservation of the Union. That Union, and the Constitution which framed it, was essential to the propagation of American principles of representative government, equality before the law, and equal opportunity: to him it was axiomatic that it must be preserved. How best to do this was not always clear to him, and over time his thinking evolved in response to events and opportunities; in turn, he developed a better understanding of what saving the Union meant. How and why he waged war, sought peace, or addressed the issues of slavery and emancipation were all part of this evolving understanding. So was his keen sense of constitutional, institutional, and political contexts in which he framed and implemented policy. No one knew better than he that presidents could not simply transform personal preferences into public policy and be successful. Lincoln the war leader, Lincoln the emancipator (whether hesitant or eager), Lincoln the peacemaker, Lincoln the politician, Lincoln the constitutionalist, and Lincoln the private individual—all simultaneously inhabited the body and mind of Abraham Lincoln, president, conversing on what to do.

Although Lincoln heeded constitutional limitations on his authority, within those limits he often skillfully shaped his conception of the Constitution to fit the situation at hand, justifying his actions on practical grounds followed by "assurances and proofs that the Constitution permitted it anyhow."[1] He could use constitutional reasoning rather deftly to serve his purposes and never so much as when he cited his war powers. As he groped for ways to promote emancipation within existing institutional frameworks, he came to see a disciplined definition of his war powers as offering him one way to strike a blow at slavery while remaining true to his desire to save the Union and representative government.[2] What restrained him here and elsewhere was his pragmatic sense of political reality. To move too far in advance of public opinion might well mean the loss of the popular support and electoral majorities that made the exercise of political power possible. His experiences as a politician in Illinois had educated him about working within such limits. The state, stretching from the Wisconsin border to the juncture of the Ohio and Mississippi Rivers, contained a spectrum of opinions about race and slavery representative of the nation as a whole. Lincoln knew that what might please staunch opponents of slavery in Chicago might not go down so well with the rabid racists who inhabited Cairo. His comprehension and exploitation of the interplay among various considerations and conditions was politics at its best, and it made Lincoln one of its most skillful practitioners. Contemporaries noted that he "sought to measure so accurately, so precisely, the public sentiment, that, whenever he advanced, the loyal hosts of the nation would keep step with him."[3]

Lincoln the politician realized that Lincoln the private person could not always translate his personal beliefs into policy. Whatever one might make of his attitudes toward blacks, there is no mistaking his deep hatred of the institution of slavery. Moreover, Lincoln believed that if the Union was to be truly preserved for all time, white Americans would have to devise some way of putting slavery on the road to extinction; as long as slavery continued, the Union remained tenuous. But that was not the issue immediately at stake in 1861. The struggle was to foil secession and reunite the country, not inaugurate a social revolution or a crusade for human liberty. It would be left to secessionists to point out that if Lincoln adhered to his principles, especially his steadfast opposition to the spread of slavery, his presidency would endanger the peculiar institution without launching a direct assault upon it. They argued that if slavery did not expand it would eventually die; they were not going to wait for it to expire. Whether Lincoln grasped this perspective remains unclear; whatever his comments about the future of slavery before his election, in public he did not explicitly connect the containment of slavery with its ultimate implosion, in part because to do so would exacerbate the difficulties facing him. First things first: he was preoccupied with perpetuating the American republic. It would not be until the war was well under way that Lincoln and others would realize that in order to save the Union, one might well have to transform it. Only through revolutionary change could the republic be reconstituted on a solid foundation. To save the Union without destroying slavery now would merely postpone the ultimate confrontation over who would define the American legacy and how. In short, even as war threatened the existence of the Union, it eventually offered Lincoln the opportunity to guarantee its preservation by striking at the underlying cause of conflict.

Lincoln considered the reactions of southern whites, whether residing in the Confederacy or in that treacherous area of tenuous loyalty known as the border states, as he contemplated how best to restore the Union and strike at slavery. He understood that the most lasting reconstruction would be on terms accepted voluntarily by southern whites, and he harbored hopes that they might initiate such measures. The concerns and prejudices of border state unionists also shaped his approach to reconstruction, for he could not risk those states falling into the Confederate column. Finally, he realized that the Republican party, while it might have achieved majority status in the North, remained a minority in the country as a whole. The very reuniting of the country would endanger the party's hold on power. He explored ways of building a southern wing to the Republican party, grounded on notions of economic development and opportunity and offering an alternative to plantation slavery.

Personally Lincoln abhorred the enslavement of human beings; politically, he had to consider the ramifications of decisions concerning the peculiar institution. Would War Democrats and conservative Republicans support a war for abolition as well as reunion? Might he lose the support of the border states if he lashed out at slavery? Would Confederate resistance intensify? In short, would emancipation make winning a war for reunion easier or more difficult? During Lincoln's first two years in office, he was far more concerned about the reaction of whites to emancipation than he was about the fate of emancipated blacks. In adopting a policy of emancipation based upon gradualism, compensation, and colonization, he sought to assuage white concerns and meet their objections. But whites in the border states and the Confederacy rejected these attempts at compromise. The determined Confederate war effort, the timid behavior of southern unionists, and the resistance to change of border state slaveholders, rather than increasing pressure from antislavery enthusiasts or the fear of European intervention, forced Lincoln to take more extreme measures, culminating in the issuance of the Emancipation Proclamation on New Year's Day, 1863.

Political reality and personal belief merged in Lincoln's embrace of emancipation. "In taking the various steps which have led to my present position in relation to the war," he commented in September 1864, "the public interest and my private interest, have been perfectly parallel, because in no other way could I serve myself so well, as by truly serving the Union."[4] But he also realized that how slavery was destroyed would shape the prosecution of the war and determine the prospects for both a lasting reunion and the emergence of a southern wing for the Republican party.

If one defines Reconstruction as the process of rebuilding, in one way or another, the United States, then it commenced during the secession crisis of 1860–1861. Some of the problems that surfaced again and again over the next two decades first appeared at this time. Having secured the presidency upon a platform opposing the expansion of slavery, Republicans—Lincoln most of all—had to ponder whether to surrender the party's principles to the blackmail of secession. To accede to southern demands was as sure to destroy the American political system as to reject them, for it would exhibit for all to see the collapse of legitimate politics. Threats of secession had been bandied about, but they had withered away or encouraged the construction of compromises that defused the tension. The decision of southerners to commence the actual process meant that the American republic would never be the same.

Lincoln understood the implications secession held for the republican experiment in self-government. "We have just carried an election on principles fairly stated to the people," he wrote one Pennsylvania congressman. "Now we are told in advance, the government shall be broken up, unless we surrender to those we have beaten, before we take the offices. In this they are either attempting to play upon us, or they are in dead earnest. Either way, if we surrender, it is the end of us, and of the government." During the presidential contest he reaffirmed his opposition to expanding slavery and disclaimed any intention to interfere with the peculiar institution where it already existed. But he soon tired of requests to reiterate his stance for public consumption. "Those who will not read, or heed, what I have already publicly said," he told one Tennessean, "would not read, or heed, a repetition of it." He maintained this position after his election, despite various efforts to draw some statement from him. "I am not at liberty to shift my ground—that is out of the question," he warned one Missouri newspaper editor. To fellow Republicans he was just as blunt. "Let there be no compromise on the question of *extending* slavery," he told Illinois senator Lyman Trumbull. "If there be, all our labor is lost, and, ere long, must be done again. . . . Stand firm. The tug has to come, & better now, than any time hereafter."[5]

This stand placed Lincoln in opposition to virtually all of the compromise proposals brought before Congress during the secession winter of 1860–1861, for each involved concessions allowing slavery the opportunity to expand into the territories. Several staunch antislavery Republicans, concerned that the president-elect might heed the call for compromise, hurried to Springfield, as Joshua Giddings told Charles Sumner of Massachusetts, "to strengthen his faith and nerve him to the business at hand." They need not have worried. Repeatedly Lincoln reminded southerners that he stood firmly against the expansion of slavery. "On that, there is a difference between you and us," he told John A. Gilmer of North Carolina, "and it is the only substantial difference. You think slavery is right and ought to be extended; we think it wrong and ought to be restricted."[6]

Elsewhere Lincoln reiterated his position on other issues concerning the South and slavery. He would not recommend abolition in the District of Columbia or the cessation of the interstate slave trade, let alone touch slavery where it already existed. He advocated complying with the Constitution's provisions regarding the recovery of fugitive slaves, although he urged revision of the Fugitive Slave Law of 1850. "In one word," he concluded, "I never have been, am not now, and probably never shall be, in a mood of harassing the people, either North or South." Moreover, from the moment of his election he attempted to balance the need to maintain the party's core principles with an effort toward extending the Republican party southward. James A. Garfield, an Ohio Republican, believed that the latter goal was possible: "If the new administration shall treat [southern whites] justly, firmly, and uncompromisingly I believe that the reaction, which had already begun, will raise a strong Union party in even the cotton states."[7]

In constructing his cabinet Lincoln sought to achieve a balance between radical and conservative, Whig and Democrat antecedents, and northerner and border state residents to keep open such opportunities. He first offered the post of secretary of state to William H. Seward, his chief opponent at the 1860 convention. Ironically, many Republicans had preferred Lincoln to Seward because of the New Yorker's reputation for radicalism, embodied in his notions of "a higher law" and the "irrepressible conflict." Yet it was Seward, not Lincoln, who had shown signs in the past year of wavering in the face of southern threats of disunion. He had already contacted several southern unionists to discuss peaceful solutions to the crisis and now entertained thoughts of forging a new majority, more conservative in nature than the Republican party and bisectional in nature. Such a proposal might not only forestall war but restore Seward to the position of party leadership lost to Lincoln at Chicago.

Seward urged Lincoln to name several southern unionists to his cabinet. Lincoln had pondered such a course for some time. In the *Illinois State Journal* he planted an editorial inquiring whether such men were willing to accept an offer and whether they would give in to Lincoln on any differences in southern policy. These questions emerged in more concrete form when Lincoln and Gilmer corresponded on the possibility of Gilmer's joining the cabinet. Gilmer told Lincoln that if he presented a moderate stance on slavery-related issues, "You may divide from your many party friends, but by the preservation of the peace of the country, you will nationalize yourself and your party."[8] But the price Gilmer asked was too high. Lincoln maintained his earlier refusal to "shift the ground upon which I have been elected." Eventually Gilmer declined the opportunity for a cabinet post because he refused to oppose the expansion of slavery into the territories.[9]

Hope persisted that Lincoln, working with Seward, would abandon antislavery in favor of a realignment based on union versus disunion. Some southerners, especially those who lived in the Upper South or the border states, expressed hopes that the rumors would prove true. Claiming that Lincoln and Seward were realists, the Richmond *Whig* believed that "political necessity will constrain them to abandon not only the extreme dogmas of their party, but also to adopt a new name significant of the policy of the new party, and this name must be the UNION PARTY." But Lincoln's subsequent cabinet choices revealed that southern unionists would have to join the administration on his terms. Edward Bates of Missouri, who had contended for the 1860 nomination, became attorney general; Montgomery Blair of Maryland, who embraced Andy Jackson's admonition that the Union must be preserved at all costs, was named postmaster general. Both men opposed slavery's expansion; neither liked Seward, nor did renowned radical Salmon P. Chase, soon to head the Treasury Department. He cautioned Lincoln against "the disruption of the Republican party through Congressional attempts at compromise."[10]

No compromises were achieved during the winter session, leaving the new administration to confront the challenge of secession. Concerned that he would not be able to sway Lincoln toward a negotiated settlement, Seward threatened not to enter the cabinet. To some extent, the ploy worked. The incoming president made some concessions, notably a softening of his inauguration address in line with Seward's suggested revisions intended to present a more conciliatory policy toward the South; in turn Seward agreed to accept his appointment to the cabinet. How much influence he would wield remained to be seen. "I can't afford to let Seward take the first trick," Lincoln told his secretary.[11]

On March 4, 1861, Abraham Lincoln took the oath of office as the sixteenth—and perhaps last—president of the United States. He reiterated his pledge not to disturb slavery where it already existed and reminded his audience that he would enforce the Fugitive Slave Law. Reaffirming his opposition to secession, Lincoln nevertheless added that he would not initiate hostilities but simply execute the laws according to his oath of office. "In *your* hands, my dissatisfied fellow countrymen, and not in *mine,* is the momentous issue of civil war," he warned. "The government will not assail *you.* You can have no conflict, without being yourselves the aggressor."[12] There was no doubt, however, that as much as Lincoln wanted to avoid war, he would accept it as an alternative to disunion. Although he was willing to honor present guarantees protecting slavery, he would have nothing to do with securing its future; left unsaid was any hint of how he might go about placing it on the road to extinction. It was not time to discuss that possibility; it was not an immediate priority. For the moment, he wanted to make sure that no more states would join the seven Deep South states in forming the breakaway republic christened the Confederacy.

Discussion about the status of slavery in the territories quickly gave way to the issue of whether Lincoln should hold on to Fort Sumter, located in Charleston Harbor, South Carolina, and Fort Pickens, near Pensacola, Florida. Both military installations lay offshore Confederate territory, and the Confederates would not long tolerate the continued presence of their former countrymen. Evacuation would remove an opportunity for conflict, at the cost of appearing to give way to the insurgents. As president-elect, Lincoln had made it known that if President James Buchanan gave up the forts, he would retake them. On becoming president, however, Lincoln learned that Sumter's garrison required reprovisioning to avoid starvation or evacuation. Seward then urged that Fort Sumter be abandoned. There were sound military reasons for such a course: the fort was but partially finished, its garrison could do little more than annoy South Carolina, it was located in a very vulnerable position, and it would require continuous resupply. Although he enlisted his old political associate, general in chief Winfield Scott, in support of evacuation, military considerations were the least of Seward's concerns. Giving up the fort voluntarily would signal the peaceful intentions of the new administration, strengthen southern unionist sentiment, and allow the passions of secession to fizzle out. He had kept open lines of communication to Virginia's unionists and had held before them a possibility of a swap—a fort for a state. Within days of Lincoln's inaugural, in which he had pledged to hold on to Sumter, Seward was letting it be known that the fort's abandonment was all but an accomplished fact.[13]

Blair and, to a lesser extent, Chase opposed Seward's plan. It was time to draw the line, Blair argued: to vacate Sumter would display weakness and embolden secessionists. It was an odd alliance between colonizationist and abolitionist, but they were both old Democrats with sufficient reason to suspect the motives of that old Whig Seward. To counter the advice of Scott, Blair had consulted with his brother-in-law and naval officer Gustavus Fox about a plan to reprovision Sumter. That the issue was political and not military was revealed in the responses of Seward and Blair to Lincoln's request for the opinions of his cabinet as to the proper course of action to pursue. Seward revealed anew his concern with retaining the border states. To reinforce the garrison would be to inaugurate war "after which reunion will be hopeless." Blair, betraying his worship of Andrew Jackson's response to a similar situation—an example sadly ignored by Buchanan—believed that only firmness inspired respect. Lincoln himself weighed the political impact of withdrawal versus standing firm, noting that while withdrawal would demonstrate the moderation of the administration, it would demoralize the party and might be interpreted as weakness.[14]

Seward's last bid to direct administration policy came in the form of a memorandum delivered April 1 to Lincoln. *"Change the question before the Public from one upon Slavery,* . . . for a question upon *Union or Disunion,"* he beseeched the president. He offered the prospect of a foreign war as a means to reunite the country against a common enemy and volunteered himself as prime minster in charge of administration policy. Lincoln deftly brushed this proposal aside and once more reviewed the alternatives. He had lost faith in the willingness of southern unionists in the Upper South to defy secessionist sentiment outright. He now realized that the majority of Virginia's unionists were conditional unionists, defining the Union on their terms. Nor was there any guarantee that Virginia would remain in the Union if Fort Sumter was evacuated: the best Virginia unionists would offer was an assurance that if Fort Sumter was evacuated, then Virginia *probably* would not secede. This position was not good enough. Southern unionists had to make the first move in order to prove their sincerity. Reports from several envoys dispatched south to test the strength of unionism in the seceded states suggested that the time for reconciliation had past. The Deep South was, in the words of one emissary, "irrevocably gone."[15]

Pessimistic about compromise, Lincoln chose to resupply Sumter's garrison, informing South Carolina governor Francis Pickens of his decision. In so doing he accepted the chance of war but held fast to his pledge that he would not fire the first shot. Confederate president Jefferson Davis accepted that responsibility, believing that to do so would not only inspire present members of the Confederacy but also attract several states still wavering on the verge of secession. He believed that by firing on Sumter he would force Lincoln to call for troops, lest he look as if he was backing down. Once Lincoln made such a call, the remaining states, protesting such coercion, would break away. These calculations proved correct. The Confederates opened fire on Fort Sumter early on the morning of April 12, 1861, and the fort surrendered after a day of bombardment. On April 15, Lincoln called 75,000 militia into national service for ninety days. Two days later, Virginia seceded, to be followed by Arkansas, North Carolina, and Tennessee.

Lincoln's behavior between his election and his call for troops was that of a thoughtful leader who, after some hesitation, moved quickly to impress his stamp on events. Far from setting out "almost from the moment he was elected" to destroy the very party that had elected him, as Michael F. Holt has asserted, he endeavored to shore up party ranks during the secession winter of 1860–1861.[16] The price of satisfying southern unionists was too high. Efforts to garner their support threatened to divide the very coalition that had elected him and might cripple the new administration. In forgoing Seward's advice and resupplying Sumter, Lincoln made clear that party unity was more important than realignment. His efforts to transform a sectional Republican majority into a national unionist majority would emerge only with the commencement of hostilities.

The outbreak of war transformed the nature of the problems facing Lincoln. In the twenty months after the outbreak of hostilities, he worked to retain the loyalty of the four border slave states (Delaware, Maryland, Kentucky, and Missouri) who ultimately did not join the Confederacy and to build unionist support in the seceded states in an effort to undo secession, all the while struggling with the question of slavery and emancipation. All three issues were interdependent in various ways, and the waging of war promised to complicate matters still further.

The coming of war augmented Lincoln's presidential powers considerably. His conception of the constitutional prerogatives of the president as commander in chief was a broad one. His opposition to James K. Polk's efforts to bring about a military confrontation with Mexico in 1846 had alerted him to the possibilities inherent in wielding presidential war powers. While he might have had qualms about the use of those powers in bringing on a war with a foreign power, such reservations vanished when it came to subduing a separatist insurrection. In Maryland he acted decisively to keep the state in the Union; he also encouraged firm measures in Missouri. Lincoln used his war powers broadly to retain control over the issue of slavery and emancipation, to justify reconstruction measures as war measures, and to build unionist coalitions in the insurrectionary states. Nevertheless, he sought to justify his actions by reference to the Constitution as he understood it, demonstrating a commitment to constitutional restraints as well as an adroit interpretation of war powers that maximized his influence while serving to restrain others.[17]

Lincoln's belief in the eventual resurgence of southern unionism persisted through the early months of the conflict. Only in South Carolina did he acknowledge that secessionists held a majority. "There is much reason to believe that the Union men are the majority in many, if not in every other one, of the so-called seceded States," he asserted. Believing as much, he pledged to Congress in July 1861 that he would simply act on the principles laid forth in his inaugural address, which included an acceptance of slavery where it already existed. As much as possible, he was committed to a policy of restoration, not transformation. It was not time to discuss the future of slavery; first the Union must be saved. Congress reinforced this notion when it passed the Johnson-Crittenden Resolutions. Sponsored by Senator Andrew Johnson of Tennessee and Representative John J. Crittenden of Kentucky, the resolutions, approved by Congress in the aftermath of defeat at Bull Run, declared that the war "is not waged upon our part in any spirit of oppression, or for any purpose of conquest or subjugation, or purpose of overthrowing or interfering with the rights or established institutions of those States." The sole goal of the war was to restore the Union "with all the dignity, equality, and rights of the several State unimpaired," and that with this achieved "the war ought to cease." Several passionate antislavery Republicans—most notably Charles Sumner and Thaddeus Stevens—were absent at the time of the vote. Nevertheless, the extensive support Republicans gave the resolutions—only Senator Lyman Trumbull of Illinois and two Republican representatives voted against it—suggested that abolition as a war aim was premature.[18]

Lincoln strove to stanch the wound of secession before it spread to the border states. His behavior during the secession crisis reaffirmed his intention not to abandon party principles in order to lure southern unionists to his party. The price was simply too high. But Lincoln did not number immediate abolition among those party principles. "I have no purpose, directly or indirectly, to interfere with the institution of slavery in the States where it exists," he informed the Virginia secession convention on the day that Sumter fell. "I believe I have no lawful right to do so, and I have no inclination to do so."[19] Whatever his personal sentiments on the issue of enslaving fellow human beings, he chose to work within the bounds of the possible even as he sought to enlarge those boundaries.

In taking this position, Lincoln rejected the arguments of those who saw the conflict primarily as a war for abolition. He was astonished by the fervor of some antislavery advocates, remarking that they seemed "bewildered and dazzled by the excitement of the hour." Even such a conservative Republican as Senator James Rood Doolittle of Wisconsin informed Lincoln that "this war is to result in the entire abolition of slavery." In August, Congress passed confiscation legislation that freed slaves employed in the Confederate war effort. But the president's immediate priority remained saving the Union; he declared that he was set on "proving that popular government is not an absurdity. We must settle this question now, whether in a free government the minority have the right to break up the government whenever they choose."[20]

Lincoln's interest in emancipation was also tempered by his desire to retain the border states, especially Maryland, Kentucky, and Missouri. These areas were crucial militarily and politically. Both the Johnson-Crittenden Resolutions, composed by two border state representatives, and Lincoln's July 4 message were designed in part to assuage border state concerns about a war for abolition. Lincoln's forceful actions early in the war had saved Maryland; secession in Missouri had been thwarted, although only because the strong response of unionists in the state had transformed a standoff into a bitter conflict. That still left Kentucky. Divided into unionist and secessionist factions, with the legislature favoring the former while the governor, Beriah Magoffin, leaned toward the latter, the state had declared that it would remain neutral.

At first Lincoln and his opposite number, Jefferson Davis, respected the status of the Bluegrass State, afraid of forcing it into the enemy camp, even as both men sought to gain an advantage in anticipation of the collapse of neutrality. Lincoln allowed recruiting of unionist forces in Kentucky, brushing aside the objections of Governor Magoffin by remarking that he saw no sign that the state executive "entertain[ed] any desire for the Federal Union." But he took no steps to compel Kentuckians to defend the Union, waiting for the Confederates to first violate the state's neutrality. As the hesitancy of these border state unionists grew longer, Lincoln's patience with them became shorter, and he told some Kentuckians that "professed Unionists gave him more trouble than rebels."[21]

But Lincoln had no other choice than to treat Kentucky rather gingerly. When General John C. Frémont issued a proclamation in Missouri that, among other things, amounted to an emancipation edict, the president revoked it, fearing its detrimental impact on the loyalty in the border states: "I think to lose Kentucky is nearly the same as to lose the whole game. Kentucky gone, we cannot hold Missouri, nor, as I think, Maryland. These all against us, and the job on our hands is too large for us." The measure would "alarm our Southern Union friends, and turn them against us." Nor would the president allow generals to wrest from him control of policy concerning slavery. Fortunately for him, the precipitate action of Confederate general Leonidas Polk in seizing Columbus, Kentucky, tipped the scales in favor of the state remaining in the Union. Still, by not sanctioning Frémont's directive, Lincoln incurred the wrath of some members of his party. "Our President is now dictator, Imperator—what you will," Sumner impatiently explained; "but how vain to have the power of a God if not to use it God-like."[22] Lincoln was willing to take such criticism if he could also have Kentucky.

As 1861 drew to an end Lincoln had to contemplate the three problems of retaining border state support, establishing loyal governments in areas occupied by Union forces, and formulating an approach to the possibility of emancipation. The need to retain the support of border state unionists and northern conservatives dictated a cautious approach to the question of slavery, but he also had to contend with members of his own party who were convinced that abolition should be an enumerated war aim. "There is but one way in which peace can be restored here," Charles Sumner declared, "and that is by the removal of slavery." He told Lincoln that emancipation was essential "*in order to save the country.*"[23]

Acknowledging the historian George Bancroft's wish for "an increase of free states," Lincoln replied that he treated that issue "in all due caution, and with the best judgment I can bring to it." In groping for a solution, he took into consideration political and social realities. Unconditional and immediate emancipation, however appealing it might be to someone who hated slavery as Lincoln did, promised political disaster. It would intensify Confederate resistance, alienate many whites in the critical border states, and anger those northerners who recoiled at the idea of fighting to free blacks. He approached the problem of ending slavery with white sensibilities foremost in mind when it came to determining means. To soften the economic impact of emancipation, he advocated some form of compensation for slaveholders. To quiet fears about the future of a free black population in the United States, which reinforced his own doubts about the willingness of white Americans to accept blacks as an equal part of a democratic polity and society, he promoted colonization.[24] Together these measures would ease emancipation's impact on whites by making it more acceptable economically, socially, and politically. In reaching such conclusions Lincoln came close to accepting the idea of slavery as property whose taking must be compensated while ignoring the claims of many blacks that they, too, were Americans. But this approach should not be attributed primarily to Lincoln's own racism, for it was at least equally a reflection of his understanding of the racism of most white Americans.

The first sign of Lincoln's solution appeared within days of his reply to Bancroft's plea. He offered a Delaware unionist several drafts of a bill for compensated emancipation to be introduced in the state legislature. Should such a bill pass, Lincoln would work to secure federal appropriations to achieve its objective; it also recognized that the fate of slavery in states which had not left the Union was in the hands of those states. No one ever introduced the bill. Undeterred, he used the occasion of his first annual message to elaborate on this beginning, outlining a plan for colonizing freed slaves (and those blacks already free). To overcome whatever reservations Congress might have about taking such a step, Lincoln pointed out that his plan concerned the future of the nation. "In considering the policy to be adopted for suppressing the insurrection, I have been anxious and careful that the inevitable conflict for this purpose shall not degenerate into a violent and remorseless revolutionary struggle," he contended. "I have, therefore, in every case, thought it proper to keep the integrity of the Union prominent as the primary object of the contest on our part, leaving all questions which are not of vital military importance to the more deliberate action of the legislature."[25]

To some people, talk of colonization was merely a way to avoid contemplating the consequences of emancipation; for others, it was simply a tactic to allay the racist fears of American whites, North and South. There was something to these arguments, although it would be hard to claim that Lincoln was simultaneously deluding himself and consciously deluding others. However, he had long advocated colonization, recommending it at times when discussions of slavery and emancipation were not at white heat. He did not have to share the bitter racism of Francis P. Blair and his son Montgomery, both of whom spoke passionately of the necessity for colonization, to wonder whether blacks and whites could live together harmoniously in a free society. Perhaps he grasped the fact that only by addressing the concerns of many whites about the shape of postemancipation society could he induce them to consider emancipation. Questions about Lincoln's sincerity forget that the president clearly distinguished between how to end slavery and what was to come after it. If he struggled with the best way to achieve the former, he was nevertheless committed to it in the abstract; he was much more unsure about what would follow. That he was aware of the possible political benefits of urging colonization as a way to pave the way for the acceptance of emancipation does not mean that he also sincerely saw it as one way to address the intractable problems of race relations that were sure to ensue. Like many other white Americans, he had yet to focus his attention on answering the question of what freedom meant.[26]

Compensation and colonization remained the cornerstones of Lincoln's early emancipation policy. In March 1862, he asked Congress to consider a program whereby the federal government would offer to fund state programs of emancipation, suggesting that "gradual, and not sudden emancipation, is better for all." He explained that whatever hopes Confederate leaders entertained of inducing the border states to join their cause would be dashed by such a measure, adding that compensation would be far less expensive than prosecuting the war. But the president also warned that if the war continued, "it is impossible to foresee all the incidents, which may attend and all the ruin which may follow it. Such as may seem indispensable, or may obviously promise great efficiency toward ending the struggle, must and will come." Many northern newspapers enthusiastically endorsed the proposal, confirming his belief that his plan would render emancipation palatable to whites. He assured border state representatives that he would not try to coerce them to accept his proposal.[27]

Many Republicans in Congress were ready to take more forceful action against slavery. The Johnson-Crittenden war aims resolution dropped from sight: Congress directed military commanders not to return refugee blacks to their owners, then addressed the issue of abolishing slavery in the District of Columbia. Lincoln expressed hope that in framing legislation Congress would incorporate his twin principles of compensation and colonization. The bill's authors did so, and in signing the act into law in April 1862, Lincoln made sure to publicize these facts in a message.[28] Two months later Congress also barred slavery from the territories.

By that time Lincoln had to make sure yet again that his commanders in the field did not anticipate administration policy. Since November 1861, Union forces had worked to secure a foothold on the shores of South Carolina, Georgia, and part of Florida. Many fugitive slaves sought protection behind Yankee bayonets. On May 9, 1862, General David Hunter, acting under martial law, proclaimed free all slaves in these three states. Ten days later, Lincoln, determined to retain control over such matters, revoked the order. Reminding people of his March message on compensated emancipation, he urged the slave states to take advantage of his offer. "You can not if you would, be blind to the signs of the times," he remarked, implying that before long changed circumstances might lead to new policies.[29]

Lincoln had been pondering an alternative approach for some time. Foremost among his considerations was the desire to keep control of the slavery issue rather than abandon the initiative to Congress. He wanted to devise a plan that met constitutional tests of presidential authority, finding such justification in the expansive notion of war powers. Finally, he wanted to frame a proposal that somehow might entice white southerners to return to the Union. Thus what form emancipation took and what warranted it remained important elements of his thinking. For the moment, practical concerns stayed his hand. To declare for emancipation would surely jeopardize the continuing allegiance of the border states. Many army officers, led by George B. McClellan, commander of the Army of the Potomac, strongly opposed the measure. When Sumner pressed him to issue "an edict of emancipation" on Independence Day, Lincoln replied, "I would do it if I were not afraid that half the officers would fling down their arms and three more states would rise."[30] It was not yet time to act.

Lincoln labored hard to establish some form of government for areas that fell under Union occupation. Early on he encouraged the establishment of a unionist government in Virginia headed by Francis H. Pierpoint.[31] Pierpoint and his supporters, representing the western third of the state, had set up shop in the aftermath of Virginia's secession. Early Union military successes secured the area, and western Virginians, tired of being overruled by the tidewater and piedmont areas of Virginia, instigated a movement for the creation of a new state. By the middle of 1862 they had framed and ratified a constitution, secured approval from Pierpoint and his legislature for a division of the state under the provisions of the U.S. Constitution, and were seeking admission by Congress. That was not quite what Lincoln had anticipated, for the carving of a new state from an old one raised constitutional questions.

However, circumstances in Virginia were unusual. Elsewhere, Lincoln attempted to reestablish loyal civil governments under the supervision of provisional military governors. Military success bred opportunities to act. In March 1862, following the Confederate withdrawal from western Tennessee in the wake of Ulysses S. Grant's victories at Forts Henry and Donelson and the evacuation of Nashville, Lincoln appointed Andrew Johnson as military governor with instructions to rebuild a unionist state government. Johnson arrived in Nashville pledging to restore the Volunteer State "to the same condition as before the existing rebellion." Before long Lincoln, anxious to accelerate the process of reconciliation in Tennessee, began prodding Johnson to hold elections. Such efforts proved embarrassingly premature; a secessionist candidate won a contest for a Nashville judgeship in May 1862, and Confederate raiders disrupted other elections. Nevertheless, the president persisted. "If we could, somehow, get a vote of the people of Tennessee and have it result properly it would be worth more to us than a battle gained," he urged Johnson in July. Unfortunately, the area under Union control encompassed the region where secessionist sentiment was strongest; it would not be until the fall and winter of 1863 that Union forces, again under Grant's command, finally ousted Confederates from East Tennessee. Nor, as Lincoln would soon find out, was Johnson willing to consider emancipation without some serious prodding from Washington.[32]

Tennessee offered the model Lincoln initially sought to follow elsewhere. In May 1862, he appointed Edward Stanly military governor of North Carolina after Union forces under the command of Ambrose E. Burnside had established a foothold on the coast of the Tarheel State. Stanly, a prewar Whig, went to work to forge a coalition of loyal planters as the foundation for a unionist government—exactly the sort of coalition that would protest emancipation most vociferously.[33] Louisiana provided another opportunity to experiment with executive reconstruction. In April 1862, New Orleans fell to a combined army-navy expedition. Planters, many of whom had not been enthusiastic supporters of secession, and New Orleans merchants and businessmen sought reunion as a way to commence business operations. In June Lincoln appointed Colonel George F. Shepley, already serving as mayor of New Orleans, as military governor. Unlike Johnson and Stanly, Shepley was not a native of the state, and the dominant force there remained Benjamin F. Butler, whose rigorous rule offended many residents. Still, prospects for self-reconstruction in Louisiana looked good as the year wore on, although several conservatives made it clear to Washington that they did not welcome emancipation. The president was much less successful in Arkansas, where an effort to establish a government under Missourian John S. Phelps fell stillborn due to the failure of Union forces to penetrate into the center of the state.[34]

Many congressional Republicans spoke out against Lincoln's approach to reconstruction. Lyman Trumbull protested that the appointment of a military governor without the approval of Congress was unconstitutional. Charles Sumner affirmed that only Congress could establish such governments, "call them provisional, territorial, or what you will," which was not a disinterested suggestion on the part of the Massachusetts senator. Congress could "affix terms of restoration, or, if it please, by special legislation trample Slavery out & keep the territory in pupilage until the discipline is finished." Lincoln indicated that he found acceptable proposals for some form of temporary civil government approved by Congress, but Congress failed to enact appropriate legislation.[35]

Lincoln would have been far more reluctant to surrender control over the issue of emancipation, using it as he did to try to keep the border states in line while wooing white southerners to return to the Union. If he proved a hesitant emancipator to some critics, it was due to his insistence that emancipation be weighed against the broader context of the war effort. From North Carolina Stanly warned that whites would not stand for emancipation: "Unless I can give [them] some assurance that this is a war of restoration and not of abolition and destruction, no peace can be restored here for many years to come."[36] Similar feedback came from other border state spokesmen. As the war continued through 1862, with ultimate Union victory not yet in sight, Lincoln began to wonder if he would have to take that step or else lose the whole game. He moved cautiously and circumspectly, well aware of the consequences of such a momentous decision, yet all the while moving in the direction of emancipation.

For several months Lincoln had warned all who would listen that events would force his hand in this matter. In so doing he hinted that he would use his war powers to strike against slavery if the military situation so dictated—a shift from his earlier argument that he could not act unilaterally in emancipating slaves. Whatever notion remained of a short war, one with minimal impact on American society and institutions, melted away that summer in the wake of George B. McClellan's failure to capture Richmond. The defeat accelerated efforts to escalate the conflict. Nevertheless, it was not pressure from Republicans anxious to strike at slavery that induced Lincoln to consider far-reaching measures. That pressure had always been there; there was just as much pressure not to adopt a more radical course. What made Lincoln willing to move more aggressively against slavery was the intensity and durability of Confederate resistance, the quiescent state of southern unionism, and the failure of the border states to adopt gradual, compensated emancipation programs. So long as there was the chance of a compromise solution, Lincoln sought it. But it takes two to craft a compromise.

Lincoln was reminded of this fact when he met with a delegation of border state congressmen on July 12, 1862. Pointing out that the border states had failed to embrace compensated emancipation, he suggested that before long what they had dreaded—emancipation—might well happen. Slavery would be "extinguished by mere friction and abrasion—by the mere incidents of the war. . . . How much better for you, and for your people, to take the step which, at once, shortens the war, and secures substantial compensation for that which is sure to be wholly lost in any event." Antislavery advocates, angered at his revocation of Hunter's order, were pressing him to move in their direction. He could ill afford to lose their support, but he had nothing to show to them to ease the pressure of their demand for emancipation.[37]

If Lincoln thought that this time his listeners would heed his warning words about escalation, he was to be disappointed. The majority of the border state men proved unmovable, claiming that the measure would strengthen secessionist sentiment without lessening abolitionist pressure. Although Lincoln went ahead and transmitted to Congress the draft of compensation legislation, he was deeply disappointed at his failure to win enough converts to his cause. The stubborn refusal of border state leaders to contemplate emancipation—even though several of them admitted that slavery was a dying institution in their state—once again foiled a compromise solution.[38]

That events were moving in directions hostile to slavery was evident when Lincoln sat down to contemplate a new confiscation act passed by Congress on the same day he sent off his compensation bill. It confiscated the property and slaves of secessionists and authorized Lincoln to employ blacks in support of the war effort, move forward on colonization, and issue proclamations of amnesty and pardon. Obviously the provision freeing the slaves of secessionists, whether they resided in the Confederacy or in the loyal border states, promised to have the most far-reaching impact. Orville Browning warned Lincoln that the bill would damage the party in the border states and rejuvenate the Democrats; he argued for a party of the center, asserting that the decision would show "whether he was to control the abolitionists and radicals, or whether they were to control him." But it was not the provision for emancipation that disturbed Lincoln but some of the bill's other features, notably the forfeiture of property "beyond the lives of the guilty parties." He thus prepared a veto, informing some congressmen of the substance of his objection in a last effort to reach common ground while asking Congress to stay in session a few days longer. Immediately congressional Republicans passed a joint resolution clarifying the terms of their legislation, whereupon Lincoln signed the Second Confiscation Act into law, although he also released for publication the draft of his intended veto message.[39]

By this time Lincoln was close to completing a first draft of an emancipation proclamation. He shared his thinking with two of his cabinet members on July 13, the day after his interview with the border state delegation. Emancipation was "a military necessity, absolutely essential to the preservation of the Union. We must free the slaves or be ourselves subdued." Although Lincoln had been working on such a document for months, the short statement he finally presented to his cabinet on July 22 reflected events of the past week. It simply called attention to the clauses of the Second Confiscation Act providing for the emancipation of slaves owned by Confederates; reiterated his commitment to gradual, compensated emancipation, in line with his proposal of July 14; and concluded that as a military measure he would declare free all slaves (regardless of the loyalty of the owner) held in areas still in rebellion.[40] Only Blair spoke out against the proposal, citing its political costs. Lincoln, having already considered that aspect of the question, was undeterred. He was far more willing to accept Seward's suggestion to delay the issuance of such a document until Union fortunes improved on the battlefield.

Lincoln's first attempt at an emancipation proclamation sought to induce reconstruction. If rebel slaveholders did not immediately return to the fold, their property, including slaves, was vulnerable to confiscation. And if all slaveholders in the Confederacy, including those who professed to remain loyal to the Union, did not act to regain their place in the Union by the end of the year, their slaves would be emancipated under the justification of military necessity. Tired of southern loyalists who thus far had failed to act, Lincoln now gave them an incentive to do so or else lose their slaves. He was willing to make emancipation as painless as possible by providing that they be compensated for the loss of their slaves and that the emancipation process be a gradual one. Elsewhere he also had made clear that he would do what he could to quell concern about free blacks by recommending colonization, which was about as far as one could go toward achieving eventual black freedom while catering to white prejudices. But it would be up to southern whites to accept or reject it.

Lincoln had lost patience with the promises of southern unionists. "This appeal of professed friends has paralyzed me more in this struggle than any other one thing," he complained. When Reverdy Johnson of Maryland warned him that Louisiana unionists were losing heart because of rumors concerning abolition, Lincoln's response betrayed his exasperation. "The people of Louisiana—all intelligent people every where—know full well, that I never had a wish to touch the foundations of their society, or any right of theirs," he reminded Johnson. "They very well know the way to avert all this is simply to take their place in the Union upon the old terms. If they will not do this, should they not receive harder blows rather than lighter ones?" He questioned "the *wisdom* if not the *sincerity* of friends, who would hold my hands while my enemies stab me." And, in yet another warning of things to come, he added, "I shall not surrender this game leaving any available card unplayed."[41]

Within days Lincoln penned more letters making much the same points. If a majority of Louisianans did not support secession, he asked one loyalist, "Why did they not assert themselves? Why stand passive and allow themselves to be trodden down by a minority? . . . The paralysis—the dead palsy—of the government in this whole struggle is, that this class of men will do nothing for the government, nothing for themselves, except demanding that the government shall not strike its open enemies, lest they be struck by accident!" If unionists were as good as their word, Lincoln continued, then they would assert their faith rather than scramble for safety; instead, they clamored for the rights of loyal citizens without exercising the responsibilities that came with those rights. What did they want? "What would you do in my position? Would you drop the war where it is? Or, would you prosecute it in future, with elder-stalk squirts, charged with rose water? Would you deal lighter blows rather than heavier ones?" If southern unionists failed to cooperate now, Lincoln concluded, he would "do *all* I can to save the government, which is my sworn duty as well as my personal inclination." Another warning went out to New York War Democrat August Belmont. "Broken eggs cannot be mended," he pointed out. The sooner southern unionists acted, "the smaller will be the amount of that which will be broken. This government cannot much longer play a game in which it stakes all, and its enemies stake nothing. . . . If they expect in any contingency to ever have the Union as it was, I join with the writer in saying, 'Now is the time.'"[42]

Having encountered border state opposition to his compensation proposals, Lincoln next discovered that black leaders cared little for colonization. Meeting with a delegation of blacks in August 1862, he stated that whites' racial prejudices were of such intensity and durability that perhaps it would be best for blacks to leave the United States. But most blacks rejected Lincoln's argument. In the words of one Philadelphia black, "This is our country as much as it is yours, and we will not leave it."[43] Certainly colonization might make emancipation more palatable to many whites, but Lincoln believed that colonization, although preferable, had to be voluntary. If presidential power is the power to persuade, then he had failed to exercise it successfully when it came to gathering the support of border state whites for emancipation or of blacks for colonization.

Lincoln shrewdly prepared the ground for his proclamation of emancipation in a series of public statements that made him appear unwilling to undertake the very step he contemplated. On August 4 he told a number of westerners that because of the impact of such a step on the border states he could not as yet recommend the arming of blacks as soldiers "unless some new and more pressing emergency arises." Nevertheless, he would implement recent legislation on "emancipation and confiscation." This statement implied that circumstances determined policy. Several weeks later came his famous reply to Horace Greeley's "The Prayer of Twenty Millions," a public letter critical of Lincoln's slowness in implementing confiscation legislation. In his reply Lincoln brushed aside Greeley's accusations to make the point he wanted to make. "My paramount object in this struggle *is* to save the Union, and is *not* either to save or to destroy slavery," he forcibly reminded the New York *Tribune* editor. "What I do about slavery, and the colored race, I do because I believe it helps to save the Union; and what I forbear, I forbear because I do *not* believe it would help to save the Union." Nevertheless, he pointed out, "The sooner the national authority can be restored, the nearer the Union will be 'the Union as it was'"; he then struck out what by now was a familiar phrase: "Broken eggs can never be mended, and the longer the breaking proceeds the more will be broken." He pledged to "do *more* whenever I shall believe doing more will help the cause . . . and I shall adopt new views as fast as they shall appear to be true views." In closing, he reminded Greeley that whatever his official position, "I intend no modification of my oft-expressed *personal* wish that all men every where could be free." Once again Lincoln held out the possibility of change according to circumstances as he distinguished between public policy and personal principles.[44]

Lincoln even took time from watching military events unfold in Maryland and Kentucky in September to reiterate his position to a delegation of Chicago Christians. "What *good* would a proclamation of emancipation from me do, especially as we are now situated?" he asked. "I do not want to issue a document that the whole world will see must necessarily be inoperative, like the Pope's bull against the comet!" But circumstances might change, and if so, he would change his position, "for, as commander-in-chief of the army and navy, in time of war, I suppose I have a right to take any measure which may best subdue the enemy." Thus the way toward emancipation remained open. "I view the matter as a practical war measure," he added, preparing the ground for precisely his justification to act, "to be decided upon according to the advantages or disadvantages it may offer to the suppression of the rebellion." Nevertheless, he reassured his visitors that he had not "decided against a proclamation of liberty to the slaves, but hold the matter under advisement," adding: "The subject is on my mind, by day and night, more than any other."[45]

Lincoln had made up his mind to issue the proclamation, although he waited until news came that Robert E. Lee's Confederates had withdrawn from Maryland after barely holding off the Army of the Potomac at Antietam Creek on

September 17. Realizing that this victory was about as much as he could expect from the overly cautious McClellan and afraid that the moment might be lost if the Confederates achieved success in their offensives in northern Mississippi and Kentucky, Lincoln used it as the occasion to release his proclamation of emancipation. Once again he announced that the ultimate aim of the war was reunion; once more he endorsed compensated emancipation. Unlike the July document, he reiterated his support for colonization, and he reminded military personnel of congressional legislation touching fugitive slaves and confiscation of slaves held by secessionist slaveholders. He even promised that in the future he would recommend that loyal slaveholders should be compensated for their losses, including slaves, at war's end. But the heart of the document lay in Lincoln's pledge to declare free all slaves held in areas in rebellion on January 1, 1863. He would determine exactly which areas were still in rebellion; should citizens in the eleven Confederate states elect representatives to the U.S. Congress, the residents of those districts represented might be excluded from the ramifications of the proclamation.[46]

Scholars have spend much time and energy exploring the reasoning behind Lincoln's decision to issue his proclamation. Some point to the threat of foreign intervention, arguing that the proclamation helped to diffuse it. But what really helped dissuade English and French authorities from intervention was the failure of Confederate arms to secure victory in September 1862. To be sure, the news of the proclamation emboldened Union supporters and deprived Confederate sympathizers of the claim that the war had nothing to do with slavery, but had the Confederate offensives of 1862 achieved great successes, the proclamation would have been viewed as a last gasp ploy, insufficient to deter intervention.

Some scholars argue that the increasing support for emancipation in the North, especially in his own party, forced Lincoln's hand. To be sure, some Republicans were intent on doing just that. As Lincoln made his final decision for emancipation, he was aware of rumors that Massachusetts governor John A. Andrew, having met with his fellow New England governors, had arrived at a meeting of those governors armed with a call for emancipation and the enlistment of black soldiers, if need be, in a separate army under the command of John C. Frémont. Edward Stanly came away from a conversation with Lincoln convinced that the president had issued it "to prevent the Radicals from openly embarrassing the government in the conduct of the war."[47] But to take this position is to overlook the political balance sheet, something Lincoln never did. Although the proclamation pleased passionately antislavery Republicans, it was not without its political costs in the North. Democrats jumped on it to reinforce their claim that it was a black man's war but a white man's fight; some conservative Republicans, believing that emancipation complicated the task of reunion and lessened the chances of a return to the prewar Union, were less than enthusiastic. In short, whatever gains Lincoln secured in increased support from abolitionists and Republicans committed to destroying slavery were offset by losses in the conservative camp and the intensification of Democratic opposition, although there was little that Lincoln could do to woo or at least placate members of the opposition party.

Three factors shaped Lincoln's decision for emancipation: the persistence of Confederate resistance, the failure of southern unionism to assert itself, and the refusal of border state leaders to accept his earlier proposals. It was now clear to him that the war would be of some duration: Confederate resistance would not be easily overcome. Southern unionists had proven both less numerous and less courageous than he had anticipated (with a few notable exceptions), rendering illusory the hope of an overthrow of the Confederacy from within by whites. Stubborn to the end, border state leaders would not cooperate with Lincoln on the issue of emancipation, no matter how sugarcoated, leaving him to seek new allies. Emancipation, while it still might further intensify Confederate resistance, would also intensify antislavery support for the war, free military commanders from protecting slavery, and make available a new source of manpower with which to subdue the rebellion. By omitting the border states from the provisions of the proclamation Lincoln bought himself more time to work out arrangements to secure abolition there as he simultaneously cut the props out from under slavery elsewhere, forcing them to reconsider their position. Besides, the Confederate invasions of Maryland and Kentucky had demonstrated the weakness of Confederate sympathy in those areas.

Although most people viewed the proclamation as one of emancipation, it also offered southern unionists one last chance to avoid it through voluntary self-reconstruction by proving their loyalty at the ballot box. This time Lincoln chose not to place his energy into reestablishing state governments but in advocating the holding of congressional elections in areas under Union control, enhancing the prospects for a revival of loyalist sentiment under the protection of federal bayonets. Only a week after issuing the proclamation, Lincoln pressed North Carolina's Stanly to hold elections prior to the New Year's Day deadline. Within the next two months he sent the same message to the military governors of Louisiana, Tennessee, and Arkansas. "In all available ways give the people a chance to express their wishes at these elections," he urged. "Follow forms of law as far as convenient, but at all events get the expression of the largest number of the people possible. All see how such action will connect with, and affect the proclamation of September 22nd."[48] He kept a close eye on these elections, as they represented the last gasp of southern unionism before emancipation took place. Eventually portions of Louisiana and Virginia held elections and chose representatives to Congress, while attempts in Tennessee were broken up by Confederate raids.

Other elections were also on Lincoln's mind: the midterm elections of 1862. Democrats fiercely attacked the Emancipation Proclamation; they also assailed the administration's conduct of the war. These charges had their effect. Republicans lost the governorships of New York and New Jersey and state legislatures in New Jersey, Illinois, and Indiana, and the Democrats picked up a net gain of thirty-four seats in the House of Representatives. Although the degree of the Republican setback is often exaggerated—the party maintained control of the House, and Republican-controlled state legislatures replaced several Democrats elected in 1856–1857 with Republicans, resulting in a gain of five Senate seats—most observers saw very little for the administration to celebrate, and Lincoln concurred.[49] It was hard to maintain that the president had derived much of a net political benefit from his proclamation.

Lincoln took the occasion of his annual message to Congress in December to once more outline his approach to emancipation and reconstruction. This time he proposed a constitutional amendment calling for gradual, compensated emancipation and government-supported colonization, supporting it with a long discussion of why it represented a successful compromise solution. Of most interest was his reasoning in favor of colonization. He dismissed several racist arguments against increasing the number of free blacks through emancipation, denying that they would undercut whites in the labor market or would overwhelm white communities in the North. Left unaddressed but significant because of its omission was white racism, pure and simple, as a reason for colonization. In justifying this proposal, he expressed his doubts that a better one existed. "It is not 'can *any* of us *imagine* any better?' but 'can we all do better?' The dogmas of the quiet past, are inadequate to the stormy present. The occasion is piled high with difficulty, and we must rise with the occasion. As our case is new, so we must think anew, and act anew. We must disenthrall our selves, and then we shall save our country."[50] These words, often quoted out of context, are usually contrasted with the words of his first annual message in which he expressed his determination that the war "shall not degenerate into a violent and remorseless revolutionary struggle" as a demonstration of the broadening scope and revolutionary impact of the struggle. Yet in both cases they were used to justify compensated emancipation and colonization.

As the New Year's Day deadline approached, Lincoln struggled to retain the support of Republicans who were increasingly impatient with the pace of prosecuting the war. He waited until the elections had passed to remove from command Don Carlos Buell and George B. McClellan, suggesting that he would no longer support generals who did not support the administration. But when Republicans sought to extend the purge into Lincoln's cabinet in the aftermath of the bloody Union setback at Fredericksburg in December, the president stood firm, thwarting efforts to secure the resignation of Seward. Moreover, he still labored to get southerners to hold elections. As late as New Year's Eve he was still awaiting news about congressional elections in southeast Virginia, although he noted, "Time nearly up." The Virginians made the deadline in the nick of time.[51]

Virginia matters also confronted the president in quite a different shape as 1862 drew to a cause. West Virginia's quest for statehood was reaching its climax. On December 10, the House approved its application, including a constitutional provision for gradual (but uncompensated) emancipation. At first Lincoln appeared "distressed" at the notion of separate statehood for West Virginia, asking his cabinet for opinions as to its constitutionality and expediency. The six members split down the middle on both issues, with Seward, Chase, and Secretary of War Edwin M. Stanton in support of statehood and border staters Blair and Bates, along with constitutional conservative Gideon Welles, the secretary of the navy, opposing it. The matter was left in Lincoln's hands. Reasoning that it was not the fault of the Pierpoint government if most of the population chose not to participate in a statewide referendum, and that its admission would spur on "the restoration of federal authority throughout the Union" and "turns that much slave soil to free," he signed the act on New Year's Eve, 1862.[52]

On January 1, 1863, Lincoln issued the Emancipation Proclamation. Justifying it "as a proper and necessary war measure," he exempted Tennessee (a coup for Andrew Johnson, who wanted to manage the slavery issue himself) and those portions of Louisiana and Virginia (including West Virginia) under Union control where elections had taken place. The document also called for the enlistment of black soldiers, turning into reality white southerners' nightmarish vision of armed blacks bent on revenge. It was a dry document, bereft of celebration aside from a brief comment characterizing it as "an act of justice, warranted by the Constitution, upon military necessity"—an apt expression of Lincoln's reasoning. There was no mention of compensated emancipation or colonization.[53]

Lincoln maintained that the sole justification for the Emancipation Proclamation was as a war measure responding to military necessity. He would not go beyond that. When Salmon P. Chase pressed him to expand the proclamation's scope, Lincoln snapped back that to act on no other justification than what was politically expedient and morally correct would abandon "all footing upon constitution or law" and leave him "in the boundless field of absolutism." And in the long run such a measure would damage the administration. Democrats, with reason, would charge tyranny: "Would not many of our friends shrink away appalled? Would it not lose us the elections, and with them, the very cause we seek to advance?"[54]

Having taken this momentous step, Lincoln encountered critics who maintained that it created another obstacle to reunion. "I struggled nearly a year and a half to get along without touching the 'institution,'" he reminded General John McClernand, a War Democrat from Illinois. The paucity of response following the issuance of the preliminary proclamation in September underlined his point that southern whites were determined to continue the fight. Now what had been done could not be undone. "Broken eggs cannot be mended," he told McClernand. He would not retract the proclamation. But that did not mean that Lincoln remained committed to immediate and unconditional emancipation. If southern whites proposed gradual emancipation, Lincoln was willing not only to consider such plans but to support them with federal aid. So intent was he on securing both emancipation and the acquiescence of southern whites in the process that he was willing to be flexible about means. Thus emancipation remained a means to an end, at least in his mind; abolition could take many forms.[55]

Lincoln explored this option through 1863. "Those who shall have tasted actual freedom I believe can never be slaves, or quasi slaves again," he observed. "For the rest, I believe some plan, substantially being gradual emancipation, would be better for both white and black." But gradualism should apply only to those already enslaved; no one else should be born into slavery. For Louisiana he envisioned "some practical system by which the two races could gradually live themselves out of their old relation to each other, and both come out better prepared for the new." However, his thinking did not go beyond these vague generalities, nor was it clear exactly what form gradual emancipation would take or who would oversee it.[56]

By the summer of 1863 Lincoln could confidently state that the Emancipation Proclamation and the enlistment of blacks constituted "the heaviest blow yet dealt to the rebellion." To those northern whites who still resisted emancipation Lincoln insisted that it brought victory one step closer. And when that victory came, he remarked, "there will be some black men who can remember that, with silent tongue, and clenched teeth, and steady eye, and well-poised bayonet, they have helped mankind on to this great consummation; while, I fear, there will be some white ones, unable to forget that, with malignant heart, and deceitful speech, they have strove to hinder it."[57]

Emancipation had transformed the nature of reconstruction. There was no going back. When Maryland senator Reverdy Johnson tried to turn back the clock in late 1863, John Hay shook his head. "Blind and childish groping after a fact which has been buried," he confided to his diary. "Puerile babble over a ghost of an institution which is as odorously defunct as was Lazarus." And this time the Lord's work demanded that it be kept that way.[58]

2

"MUCH GOOD WORK IS ALREADY DONE"

Although Abraham Lincoln's decision to accept emancipation freed him to strike aggressively at slavery, it broadened and complicated the task of reconstruction, for the war to reunite the Union now most avowedly would transform it. Emancipation also introduced new issues and raised new questions. What would be the contours of black freedom in the wartime and postwar South? What role would the federal government play in the transformation from slavery to freedom? What of slavery in areas not covered by the proclamation? If emancipation was a war measure, what would happen at war's end? How Lincoln chose to answer these questions would be as important as the answers he offered. He had to strike for the right pace at the right time. "I hope to 'stand firm' enough to not go backward," he told Republican senator Zachariah Chandler, "and yet not go forward fast enough to wreck the country's cause."[1]

In walking this tightrope the president struggled to maintain unity among Republicans. In his efforts to build support for emancipation, he had encountered criticism from party members who thought him lacking in his commitment to the cause of human freedom. Those Republicans who pushed for more extreme measures against slavery and did so with some impatience soon became identified as Radicals. Efforts to offer ironclad definitions of this group's ideology, membership, and voting behavior once consumed much scholarly energy and tended to obscure common values cherished by the vast majority of Republicans. As a matter of course, however, Radical Republicans, whatever their disagreements among themselves on how best to achieve their agenda, believed that if reconstruction was to be successful, it had to achieve fundamental change in southern society. Emancipation was not enough: any settlement had to secure for blacks basic civil rights—and, according to many, political rights, including some form of suffrage. Other Republicans were less

36

sure of these objectives or wanted to achieve them without upsetting current institutional frameworks of governance; in turn, Radicals were far less concerned about achieving reconciliation with southern whites than were their more moderate colleagues.

Lincoln enjoyed an uneasy relationship with the Radicals. Although he abhorred slavery, he was more conscious of achieving emancipation through accepted avenues of change, and he remained determined to entice white southerners back to the Union and make them willing partners in the destruction of slavery. He still believed that the transition from slavery to freedom would be a gradual and time-consuming one and thought much more about how to achieve emancipation than defining what it would mean for blacks. Moreover, he realized that in demanding that Congress be a partner in establishing policy, Radicals were not alone, for many Republicans thought that Congress should play an equal if not leading role in determining the terms of reconstruction. In employing presidential war powers, Lincoln established the basis for autonomous action. However, he knew that Congress had to be part of the reconstruction process, for it would decide whether to seat the delegations sent to Washington by the loyal state governments established with his blessing and support.

Lincoln struggled to establish loyal governments in several southern states in 1863. He looked for great results from Tennessee and its military governor, Andrew Johnson. He cajoled or flattered Johnson as the situation required and granted him extensive powers to assist him in his task. But Johnson's behavior tended to promote division rather than reconciliation. Before the war, he had been a polarizing figure in Tennessee politics. His unrepentant loyalty and his hatred of secession were fused in speeches and proclamations that resembled fire-and-brimstone sermons on good and evil. This behavior complicated an already difficult task, for the parts of Tennessee that first came under Union control were areas of secessionist strength; what loyalty remained in these areas was eroded by the prospect of emancipation, even though Johnson had persuaded Lincoln to exclude the entire state from the Emancipation Proclamation. Not until Federal forces drove the Confederates out of East Tennessee in the fall of 1863 could Johnson count on much support at home. And if Johnson's unionism was unquestioned, the same could not be said for his commitment to emancipation. Johnson, himself a slaveholder, originally claimed that the Union provided the best protection for slavery. Only with the passage of time did he reluctantly accept emancipation, and even then he saw it primarily as a means to cripple the political power of aristocratic slaveholders, not as a means to secure black freedom.[2]

In Louisiana Lincoln found it difficult to weave his way through competing factions. He refused to cooperate with Louisiana's conservatives on a plan of reconstruction commencing with a fall election under the state's prewar constitution, pointing out that Louisianans were preparing to call for a constitutional convention. In rejecting their offer, he repudiated their desire to reinstate slavery as part of the old order. Early efforts at establishing a loyalist regime, however, proved inconclusive, in part because Lincoln wanted Louisianans to take the matter in hand. "While I very well know what I would be glad for Louisiana to do," he told General Nathaniel Banks, "it is quite a different thing for me to assume direction of the matter." As much as possible, he wanted whites to shape their own world in accordance with the principles of union and emancipation. But Louisiana whites could not agree on a vision or how best to achieve it. Conservatives continued to drag their feet in an effort to salvage slavery, encouraged by the fact that areas under Union occupation as of January 1, 1863, were exempt from the Emancipation Proclamation. Their hesitation in adopting emancipation or in constructing a framework of post-emancipation race relations frustrated Lincoln. Employing Banks as his representative on the scene, he did what he could to encourage the reestablishment of loyal civil government as he balanced the different aims of Louisiana radicals, moderates, and conservatives.[3]

Elsewhere Lincoln fostered reconstruction efforts. After Union forces had gained control of much of central Arkansas by mid-1863, he suggested that the state take immediate measures to end slavery, accepting the possibility of gradual emancipation. When bluecoats made their way into Texas, he appointed Andrew J. Hamilton, a staunch unionist of Democratic antecedents, as that state's military governor. Such measures reflected Lincoln's anxiety to establish civil governments as quickly as possible. But the president would not accept just any state government. Against the need for prompt action he weighed the necessity of ensuring that loyal men controlled those governments, for to allow secessionists to control the result would destroy all that had been achieved. "Let the reconstruction be the work of such men only as can be trusted for the Union," he instructed Johnson in September 1863. "Exclude all others, and trust that your government, so organized, will be recognized here. . . . Get emancipation into your new State government—Constitution—and there will be no such word as fail for your case." Similar advice went out to Banks in November, when Lincoln, "bitterly" disappointed at the slow pace of restoration in Louisiana, instructed him "to lose no more time" in presenting Lincoln "with a tangible nucleus which the remainder of the State may rally around as fast as it can, and which I can at once recognize and sustain as the true State government." It was important to act now. "It is something on the question of *time,* to remember that it cannot be known who is next to occupy the position I now hold, nor what he will do," he reminded Johnson.[4]

The president also sanctioned efforts to woo back southern whites. He soft-pedaled confiscation as mandated by the Second Confiscation Act, believing that the threat of confiscation might help rekindle loyal sentiments as a matter of economic self-interest. More controversial was his decision to allow speculators to buy cotton from southern planters. Grant and William T. Sherman objected to what they saw as trading with the enemy, arguing that it prolonged the war by allowing the Confederates to purchase weapons, munitions, and other essential supplies. Lincoln acknowledged the force of their complaints but asserted that such trade weakened Confederate will and allegiance in other ways. So did the policy of leasing plantations to provide work for the freedmen, although at times the freedmen wondered if the resulting working conditions differed significantly from slavery. Lincoln, however, responded to other priorities. Planters, having confronted the unpleasant fact that the Confederate government could no longer protect them, became attracted to the idea of doing business with the Yankees. The cotton that thus became available eased shortages in the North and in England.[5]

These limited efforts represented Lincoln's evolving notions of the course emancipation and reconstruction should take, seeking when possible the voluntary acquiescence of southern whites. But executive action could do only so much. Lincoln might encourage movements for emancipation in the border states, but he could not mandate abolition. In the Confederate states he might push for unionists to call conventions, elect representatives, end slavery, and provide for some sort of transition between slavery and freedom, but he had failed to outline a coherent procedure, in part because he had tailored his approach to fit local circumstances. It was time to establish uniform procedures and policies and to recognize the formal role Congress would play in any policy of reconstruction when it decided whether to seat a state's representatives.[6]

On December 8, 1863, Lincoln announced his reconstruction policy in two documents. He issued a special proclamation that outlined procedures for amnesty and pardon and for reconstruction. In order to obtain pardon, persons had to take an oath pledging future loyalty and acceptance of emancipation. All property, except slaves and redistributed property, would be restored to those people. Certain classes were excluded, including Confederate civil officials, generals and high-ranking naval officers, those who resigned U.S. judicial or military commissions or seats in Congress, and those found guilty of mistreating prisoners of war, black or white. In each state, once the number of people taking the oath who met the qualifications for voting in 1860 equaled 10 percent of the votes cast in that state in the 1860 presidential contest, that state could reestablish its government. Lincoln hoped these new state governments would make provision for emancipation and the education of the freedmen. He would not object to any "temporary arrangement" in regard to labor, by which he meant some form of an apprenticeship system. Finally, he admitted that "while the mode presented is the best the Executive can suggest, . . . it must not be understood that no other possible mode would be acceptable."[7]

Lincoln offered some clarifications in his annual message. Any state, having met the requirements he had set forth, would receive protection from the federal government. But to expect Confederates to be part of that process was "simply absurd." He sought "a test by which to separate the opposing elements, so as to build only from the sound," although that included those who renounced their identity as Confederates by taking the oath. Pledged "not to retract or modify the emancipation proclamation," he had acquiesced in any temporary arrangements states might make about the freedpeople to reduce "the confusion and destitution" resulting from "a total revolution of labor." By outlining a plan, he hoped to remove another obstacle to delay by providing a "rallying point" that had already received presidential sanction; yet "saying that reconstruction will be accepted if presented in a specified way, it is not said it will never be accepted in any other way."[8]

Lincoln sought to offer a policy as congruent as possible with current constitutional provisions. Citing the guarantee clause as the basis for his exercise of executive power, he conceded that at least in some form the states were still in the Union. He was still willing to leave the decision for emancipation, at least in principle, to white southerners (although if they failed to accept it Lincoln would not recognize the result, thus creating a powerful incentive for white southerners to abolish slavery and qualifying the "voluntary" nature of emancipation). In so acting Lincoln wanted to ensure emancipation as part of reconstruction and to circumvent questions about the continued applicability of the Emancipation Proclamation, for once white southerners reestablished loyal state governments, they could argue that the principle of military necessity that justified the proclamation no longer applied. State action would also render immaterial questions about the proclamation's constitutionality, for no one denied that a state could abolish slavery. Charles Sumner grasped that fact when he declared that the president's proposal "fastens emancipation beyond recall." Lincoln also preferred to make white southerners partners in shaping the terms of emancipation. Better to conciliate than to coerce; the president wished "to avoid both the substance and the appearance of dictation." Others recognized Lincoln's motives. From Louisiana Banks sent word that amnesty offered "an escape to many classes of people in the South."[9]

The election of 1864 also weighed on Lincoln's mind, and he wanted to set up as many free state governments as possible prior to the fall contests. In months to come, critics of his policy would claim that Lincoln's primary motive in doing so would be the establishment of "rotten boroughs" whose electoral votes would enhance his chances for reelection. This accusation made some sense when the critics were Republicans, for they believed that Lincoln was trying to assure the presence of loyal administration delegations at the 1864 Republican convention (just as Lincoln's rival, Salmon P. Chase, was trying to build support for his own candidacy in Louisiana). However, Lincoln's desire to accelerate the process of reconstruction was linked far more clearly to his concerns about the consequences of his defeat in the fall contest—especially the fate of emancipation under a Democratic administration—than to a desire to increase his probability of winning the Republican nomination.[10]

Most Republicans praised Lincoln's message. "The president seems to have made friends among the radicals and conservatives with his new plan of reconstruction," announced the Springfield (Mass.) *Republican*. "Henceforth, the Republican party is a unit, and no quarrels between radicals and conservatives will be in order." Administration observers agreed. "It seemed as if the millennium had come," John Hay remarked. "Chandler was delighted, Sumner was beaming, while at the other political pole Dixon & Reverdy Johnson said it was highly satisfactory." Sumner's approval was especially gratifying. "It satisfies his idea of proper reconstruction without insisting on the adoption of his peculiar theories," Hay recorded. "The President repeated what he has often said before that there is no essential contest between loyal men on this subject if they consider it reasonably. The only question is who constitutes the state? When that is decided the solution of subsequent questions is easy."[11]

Sumner minimized the significant differences that remained, most notably over the constitutional status of the seceded states. For some time he and others, including Representative Thaddeus Stevens of Pennsylvania, had offered a different view of reconstruction based upon the assumption that through secession the Confederate states had forfeited their status as states—thus allowing Congress a free hand in governing them as territories (Sumner) or conquered provinces (Stevens). Lincoln's plan, Sumner asserted, was little different. "How this differs from what is called 'the territorial theory' I am at a loss to perceive, except that it is less plain and positive," he claimed. "In short the

President's theory is identical with ours, although he adopts a different no-menclature." But, as Lincoln "makes Emancipation the corner-stone of Re-construction," Sumner was pleased.[12]

Anxious to find common ground with Sumner, Stevens, and other congres-sional Republicans, Lincoln glossed over possible areas of disagreement. He contended that all he had done was to offer "a rallying point—a plan of ac-tion"; his plan did not exclude others. As for the question of the status of the states in rebellion, Lincoln believed that the difference over this issue was "one of mere form and little else." This statement was disingenuous; Lincoln had found issues of form to be ones of constitutionality when it came to the rela-tive power of the president and Congress to press for abolition. Far more important was to discover a way "to keep the rebellious populations from overwhelming and outvoting the loyal minority."[13] Committed to government by consent, Lincoln realized that the needs of reconstruction clashed with majority rule. How could one create a viable unionist majority?

Lincoln's proposal was in part a wartime expedient, a way to sap Confeder-ate morale by offering a comparatively painless way for southern whites to reenter the Union. However, it also pointed the way to the process of restor-ing civil governments for the postwar world. The relative weight of these two priorities fluctuated over time and in response to other concerns; the presi-dent did not always address the tensions and sometimes contradictions be-tween these two objectives, for expediency and reliability did not always go hand in hand. At the same time, he sought to faciliate emancipation by mak-ing it appear to be upon the initiative of white southerners. The president did what he could to bolster the status of blacks in territory under Union military control, prodding the leaders of his wartime regimes to support the advance-ment of blacks, although he always left the final decision in the hands of the people on the scene. Should voluntarism fail, Lincoln was willing to move more forcefully. When Louisiana leaders hemmed and hawed about the prospects for emancipation in 1863, Lincoln directed Banks to use his power to per-suade them to see the light. In Arkansas, General Frederick Steele received instructions from Washington directing him to nullify any election that re-sulted in the elevation of proslavery candidates to office.[14]

Lincoln, reported John Hay, was "deeply interested" in the problems of establishing a policy to provide for the transition from slavery to freedom: "He considers it the greatest question ever presented to practical statesmanship." But he was not yet ready to embrace an economic revolution. He encouraged planters to contract with former slaves to revive their plantations and enter-tained notions of apprenticeships for blacks. More momentous was his changing position on suffrage. He began to consider the possibility of limited black suffrage, whereby proof of literacy or military service would qualify the freedmen to vote.[15]

The state that presented Lincoln with the most challenges was Louisiana. Its white unionist element had failed to erect an alternative government in 1862, convincing Lincoln that perhaps his faith in the eventual revival of loyalty was a frail one. Hereafter he would exercise a more active role in shaping the contours of a new state government, whatever his reservations about doing so, in his eagerness to see something done. In December 1863, he had urged Banks to "give us a free-state reorganization of Louisiana, in the shortest possible time," and throughout the next year he did what he could to hasten the emergence of a unionist government that embraced abolition.

Haste had its costs. Banks thought that the best way to achieve success quickly was to work with moderates and conservatives who were eager to minimize the amount of change they were willing to accept. Aware that such groups did not willingly embrace emancipation on their own, Banks announced that Louisiana whites would accept abolition if it was imposed from without, thus allowing them to tell fellow whites that there was nothing to do but to comply. The general observed to Lincoln that "revolutions which are not controlled and held within reasonable limits produce counterrevolutions." Insisting upon the election of state officials prior to the convening of a constitutional convention, Banks got his way, and the moderates swept to victory in elections held in February.[16]

Radicals, seeking more substantial changes, expressed uneasiness about the speed with which Louisiana erected a new state constitution. As one remarked, "There is no middle ground in revolution." They understood how expedience might lead to missteps, as did the substantial number of free blacks who sought suffrage for themselves. Two of them, armed with a petition urging black suffrage, visited Washington in March 1864. The encounter proved an educational one for Lincoln, in large part because the spokesmen themselves were sufficient testimony as to the preparedness of at least some blacks for full citizenship. The president declined to grant their request, reminding them that "having the restoration of the Union paramount to all other questions, he would do nothing that would hinder that consummation, or omit anything that would accomplish it"—a comment that brought to mind his August 22, 1862, letter to Horace Greeley. In adding that "he did nothing in matters of this kind upon moral grounds, but solely upon political necessities," he was careful to separate personal preference from a sustainable justification for policy.[17]

However, the encounter did inspire the president to do something. In keeping with his desire not to mandate but to suggest, Lincoln prodded the new governor of Louisiana, Michael Hahn, to consider extending the suffrage to some blacks, suggesting that at least the "very intelligent" and those who served in the Union army should vote. But he would only "barely suggest" such a step, and he advanced it in private correspondence—trusting Hahn to reveal the letter to delegates at the constitutional convention. Although the constitution eventually framed by the convention did not allow blacks to vote or hold office, in other areas, including public education, militia service, and civil rights, it did not make racial distinctions. Many white Louisianans were not ready for more: the pressures to put a government in place forced local radicals to compromise their principles.[18]

Perhaps conditions in Louisiana were exceptional. After all, free blacks had been an integral part of prewar New Orleans, suggesting that some form of a biracial society could actually prosper there. Lincoln himself recognized that the opportunity offered in Louisiana was unique, for he did not urge other states to follow the blueprint drafted there. Nor should one mischaracterize the division between Louisiana moderates and radicals. Both sides accepted limited black suffrage in principle, although they disagreed over how extensive it should be; both desired abolition. The question was how best to go about achieving these aims. The moderates had the votes. Lincoln made sure that everyone in Louisiana knew that he backed ratification and would remember those who opposed it. In September the constitution was ratified by voters in Union-held areas, who also elected representatives to Congress.[19]

Elsewhere reconstruction moved at a slower pace. Lincoln's attempt to erect a unionist regime in Florida on the heels of a Federal military penetration of the state proved flawed. In January 1864, he sent John Hay to the state with instructions to lay the foundation for a loyal civil government "in the most speedy way possible." The president's private secretary soon concluded that the idea was premature. Critics lambasted the mission, arguing that Lincoln had launched an invasion for the purpose of constructing a "rotten borough" committed to his renomination and reelection. That the Union military operation intended to reclaim that state proved an abject failure added fuel to these attacks. Events in Arkansas seemed more promising. In January Lincoln instructed Steele to hold an election for governor, adding that the state constitution could be modified to abolish slavery by military mandate as a consequence of the gubernatorial election. When news came that some Arkansans were proceeding to frame a new state constitution that abolished slavery, the president sought to "harmonize the two plans into one," eventually giving way to the Arkansas initiative in his eagerness to advance the cause. He was anxious to point somewhere other than Louisiana for evidence that something was in fact happening.[20]

Louisiana radicals, defeated at home, looked to Congress to undo moderates' handiwork. They argued that under the current regime black rights enjoyed insufficient protection, and Banks's labor policy lent credibility to these complaints. In attempting to frame measures that served short-term wartime interests, including the revival of the local economy, the wooing of white planters, and a prevailing desire for order, the general also was defining a rather limited notion of freedom. He defended his policies, arguing that they accorded with the desires of rural blacks for safety, education, and wages and would eventually lead to the acquisition of land by blacks. But opponents charged that they embodied a compromise that fell far short of full freedom and equality and as such forecast an unsatisfactory blueprint for a truly reconstructed free society. The protests proved effective. Before long, Republicans began to question Lincoln's reconstruction policy as they saw its fruits in several southern states.[21]

Many Republicans doubted that Lincoln's policy provided a sound foundation for southern Republicanism, fearing it would facilitate the return of southern conservatives to power. In order to assure a lasting peace, they claimed, federal policy must remake the South by infusing it with the virtues of free labor. "The whole fabric of southern society must be changed, and it can never be done if this opportunity is lost," proclaimed Thaddeus Stevens, renowned for his advocacy of a harsh war followed by a rigorous peace. Some, like Charles Sumner, went so far as to advocate enfranchising blacks. "I see no substantial protection for the freedmen except in the franchise," the Massachusetts senator declaimed. "And here is the necessity for the universality of the suffrage: every vote is needed to counter-balance the rebels."[22]

There was no need for a hasty reconstruction. Better to suspend (if not altogether eliminate) state governments so that Congress could establish a firm foundation for extensive change. Patchwork solutions shaped by wartime expedience and a desire to reconcile white southerners might well harden into permanent compromises that would constrict the true meaning of emancipation. Some Republicans winced at Banks's labor policies; others squirmed at signs that moderates had seized control of the movement for a free state constitution. Congressional Republicans agreed that it was up to Congress to take the lead in framing these measures. "The executive ought not to be permitted to handle this great question to his own liking," Ohio's Ben Wade remarked.[23]

Republican critics of the president were of two minds regarding his exercise of presidential power. They questioned the use of executive power in reconstruction, insisting on a partnership with Congress if not legislative supremacy, yet they empowered him to strike at the roots of southern society. In legislation concerning fugitive slaves in military zones, confiscation of property, emancipation, and the enlistment of blacks in military service, Congress staked out radical positions yet called on the president to implement them.[24] In attacking Lincoln's exercise of executive power, these critics were seeking institutional grounds upon which to attack his policy. Had Lincoln used his powers to serve ends approved by his critics, they would have remained silent about the means so long as the ends were achieved.

The debate over Lincoln's exercise of executive power was linked to the desire of many Republican leaders in Congress to turn to someone else to head the party's ticket in the 1864 presidential contest. They suspected that Lincoln was too eager to conciliate white southerners and Democrats in pursuit of a centrist policy. Salmon P. Chase offered himself as an alternative: to Radicals he seemed far more sound on the issue of black rights. The treasury secretary had no qualms about the vigorous exercise of executive power toward that goal. When it came to the ends of policy, there was more divergence. Reconstruction seemed the best issue on which to unify Lincoln's Republican opponents behind a Chase candidacy.[25]

Lincoln easily forestalled the Chase movement. His ability to cultivate support among party loyalists paid off as Republican-controlled state legislatures passed resolutions calling for his renomination. Chase's advocates were stampeded into responding prematurely in the form of a circular letter, only to discover that few outside Washington shared their dissatisfaction. Chagrined, the cabinet minister disavowed encouraging such a movement and eventually withdrew formally after Frank P. Blair Jr., who had taken a seat in Congress at Lincoln's behest, blasted him for corruption in the Treasury Department.[26]

Lincoln drew another link between his quest for reelection and his policy of reconstruction when Republicans met in Baltimore in June to select a ticket for the presidential contest. Lincoln's own renomination was a foregone conclusion; having fended off Chase, he was relieved to discover that the new general in chief, Ulysses S. Grant, would not heed cries to take the White House as he had taken Vicksburg. Although the president claimed that he did not want to interfere with the convention's deliberations, he was well aware of the maneuvering going on for the second slot. Whether he worked for Andrew Johnson's nomination, however, has long been a matter of dispute: the lack of concrete evidence for either case makes it difficult to offer more than a reasonable surmise.[27]

Lincoln knew that a War Democrat as his running mate would broaden his support in the critical mid-Atlantic and midwestern states and counter the impact of possible defections among those Republicans who thought the president lacked an earnest commitment to emancipation. A border state man would also help the Republican cause in those states where the opposition had shown great strength. Lincoln also planned to allow the reconstructed citizens of Tennessee, Louisiana, and Arkansas a chance to vote in the November election, and delegations from these states had been seated at the Baltimore convention. It is hard to believe that he did not know something about the sentiment for Johnson, and he offered no objection to having the Tennessean on the ticket. To come out against Hannibal Hamlin, the current vice president, however, would have served only to alienate New England Republicans. Johnson's selection was a tacit recognition of the progress of reconstruction in Tennessee and suggested that plans for a postwar southern wing of the party composed primarily of centrist whites remained very much alive.

Congressional Republicans had yet to present their own version of reconstruction. Several of them had not given up on the idea of unseating Lincoln, while others realized that they still had not come up with an alternative to Lincoln's policy. Their dissatisfaction grew when the House of Representatives on June 15 failed to pass a proposed constitutional amendment to abolish slavery throughout the United States. Making things worse was the failure of Republicans in both houses to agree upon a proposed federal agency to supervise southern blacks' transition from slavery to freedom. These setbacks reminded congressional Republicans that if they did nothing, Lincoln's plan would remain in force, complete with what they deemed its unsatisfactory safeguards for blacks. Radicals' grievances mounted when on July 1 Lincoln unexpectedly accepted Chase's resignation as treasury secretary in the wake of a patronage dispute.

By the beginning of July, Republicans had fashioned a bill, cosponsored by Benjamin F. Wade and Henry Winter Davis, that attracted majority support. Several sacrifices had to be made, the most prominent of which was the decision to drop black suffrage. In other ways, however, this finished product was at odds with Lincoln's plan. Once a state in rebellion ceased resistance to United States authority, a provisional governor, appointed by the president, would open the voting registers to all adult white males. When a majority of those enrolled took the oath of allegiance, the governor would hold an election to reorganize that state government, in which only those southern whites who had been continuously loyal to the United States could vote. The members of the reorganization convention had to amend the state constitution to abolish slavery, bar prominent Confederates from voting or running for the state legislature or governor, and repudiate the Confederate debt. Efforts to go beyond these limits were defeated by the House of Representatives, and the Senate passed the bill on July 2, 1864.

The final version of the Wade-Davis Bill commanded wide support among congressional Republicans in large part because it did not mandate black suffrage. The bill's supporters wanted to establish some guidelines for creating loyal governments in part to remind Lincoln that the president and Congress were partners in reconstruction. Proclamations were not legislation, they argued, and some of Lincoln's actions reflected such a broad notion of the president's war powers that they came close to usurping what many congressional Republicans believed were matters better left to Congress. Republicans in Congress also sought to achieve emancipation through legislation by insisting upon it as a prerequisite for readmission, whereas the Emancipation Proclamation had left slavery intact in Union-occupied areas and Tennessee. They believed that such action would protect emancipation against court decisions by presenting it as the decision of white southerners, just as Lincoln's amnesty proclamation required repentant Confederates to renounce slavery before receiving amnesty. The failure of the House to pass an amendment abolishing slavery in June only added to the pressure to find some way to make sure that emancipation did not fall a casualty to peace. Congressional Republicans could argue that they shared Lincoln's goals while offering more secure means.[28]

Other features highlighted larger differences between executive and congressional approaches to reconstruction. Congress sought civil governments while the president, aware of his powers as commander in chief, opted for military supervision. Lincoln's plan had been designed with wartime imperatives in mind; the Wade-Davis Bill was first and foremost a postwar policy, based upon the assumption that the cessation of hostilities did not automatically result in immediate reunion. The bill distinguished between those white southerners willing to take an oath of *future* allegiance with those white southerners who had *always* been loyal—seeking to achieve both a white majority as the basis for action in restoring civil government while restricting the process of restoration to those people whose loyalty was unquestioned (only those whites who could swear to continuous loyalty—past as well as future— could participate in reconstruction as voters or officeholders). While any constitution resulting from a convention elected under such rules would reflect loyal principles, it would not necessarily enjoy a broad base of support. These considerations would work against Lincoln's goals of reconciliation and the cultivation of renewed loyalty from former Confederates, for they offered no positive incentive to undergo a reconversion to unionism.

Lincoln refused to embrace the congressional alternative. On July 4, as the session drew to a close, Sumner, Zach Chandler, George Boutwell, and other prominent Radicals crowded into the President's Room at the Capitol to see whether Lincoln would affix his signature to the bill. Chandler began to badger the president, but Lincoln cut him off: "Mr. Chandler, this bill was placed before me a few minutes before Congress adjourns. It is a matter of too much importance to be swallowed that way." When Chandler defended the bill by pointing out that it called for the termination of slavery as a prerequisite for admission, Lincoln replied, "That is the point on which I doubt the authority of Congress to act." This caught Chandler by surprise. "It is no more than what you have done yourself," he pointed out. But Lincoln held fast, citing his commitment to constitutional principle: "I conceive that I may in an emergency do things on military grounds which cannot be done constitutionally by Congress."[29] With that he made it clear he would pocket veto the bill, failing to sign it after Congress had adjourned for the summer, thus avoiding an attempted override.

Why did Lincoln veto the Wade-Davis Bill? First, its passage would have threatened Lincoln's efforts to encourage reconstruction in several southern states, notably Louisiana, Tennessee, and Arkansas. The conditions under which reconstruction would be initiated by the provisions of the bill represented a death sentence for the Lincoln governments; if the legislation became law, it would smother attempts to undertake the reconstruction of loyal state governments during the war by establishing preconditions that would be nearly impossible to meet while hostilities persisted. The president also sincerely believed that emancipation could not be achieved merely through legislation. It was one thing for Congress to confiscate the property of secessionists, including slaves, as a war measure; it was quite another simply to order emancipation across the board by legislative fiat. The Supreme Court had knocked down earlier efforts by Congress to restrict slavery's expansion; it could just as well declare the Wade-Davis Bill unconstitutional. Lincoln held fast to his belief that there were only three ways to place emancipation upon a lasting foundation: by justifying it as a war measure, by inducing southern whites to abandon slavery voluntarily through individual or state action, and through constitutional amendment. The Emancipation Proclamation embodied the first approach; the December proclamations complied with the second, as had previous proposals for gradual, compensated emancipation. The third was not yet possible, as the June vote in the House of Representatives demonstrated.

Also at stake was the question of who controlled reconstruction. Although always conceding that Congress had a role to play in the process of restoring the seceded states to their proper relationship to the Union, Lincoln insisted that while the war continued he, too, had a part in the process. For some time he had tried to finesse the question of the precise status of the seceded states, asserting that the question "as to whether certain States have been in or out of the Union" was "a merely metaphysical one and one unnecessary to be forced into discussion." Most congressional Republicans disagreed. They based much of their claim for Congress's authority to supervise reconstruction upon the notion that somehow the act of secession impaired the rights and standing of the seceded states in the Union. Nor is there much doubt that Lincoln knew that in taking such a step he risked offending the more radical members of his party. Having just accepted Chase's resignation, he doubtless believed he was strong enough to withstand the criticism that was sure to follow the rejection of the Wade-Davis Bill. Anticipating such attacks, he elaborated his position in a proclamation issued July 8. Standing behind the progress already made in Arkansas and Louisiana, and questioning Congress's authority to legislate abolition, he nevertheless offered the plan as an alternative to his own, should southern whites want to take it.[30]

Wade and Davis found this explanation insufferably arrogant. Of course southern whites would embrace Lincoln's plan in preference to their own, in large part because it asked so much less of them. On August 5, 1864, their protest appeared in the New York *Tribune*. Angered at least as much by Lincoln's proclamation explaining the veto as by the veto itself, Wade and Davis launched a no-holds-barred attack. They characterized the governments of Louisiana and Arkansas as "mere creatures of his will," not products of truly voluntary self-reconstruction or representative of the majority of citizens in either state. These manifestations of executive despotism failed to guarantee emancipation: Lincoln's veto and proclamation together struck "a blow at the friends of his Administration, at the rights of humanity, and at the principles of Republican Government." Wade and Davis reminded Lincoln "that the authority of Congress is paramount and must be respected . . . and if he wishes our support, he must confine himself to his Executive duties—to obey and execute, not make the laws—to suppress by arms armed rebellion, and leave political reorganization to Congress."[31]

Many Republicans criticized the Wade-Davis manifesto as ill-timed, ill-tempered, and ill-advised, but few denounced it as wrongheaded. It highlighted some of the weaknesses in Lincoln's policy and raised serious doubts about whether it would assure either emancipation or loyalty in the South. Lincoln's plan encouraged repentance by offering a way to return; the Wade-Davis Bill required broad-based repentance as a prerequisite and excluded the repentant from matters of voting and governing, cutting down the incentive for former Confederates to repledge their loyalty. Nor was it yet clear how well Lincoln's governments would protect the rights of the newly freed. Nevertheless, as even Wade and Davis had to admit, with the collapse of efforts to replace Lincoln as the Republican standard-bearer, it was better to endorse the current occupant of the White House than risk his replacement by a Democrat. For the moment—and only for the moment—it was best to put differences aside.

The concerns of war, peace, and politics dominated Lincoln's thinking during the election year of 1864. Democratic critics charged that the president was cutting short the prospect for a negotiated peace by refusing to abandon his commitment to emancipation as a prerequisite for reunion. These claims gained an audience when it became clear that the chances for a quick military victory were evaporating. Union armies remained stalled outside Richmond, Petersburg, and Atlanta, and a Confederate raid northward in July had reached the outskirts of Washington itself. Even Republicans were tempted by the thought of some sort of peaceful agreement. Horace Greeley took it upon himself to act as a conduit between Lincoln and several Confederate agents stationed at Niagara Falls, only to find out that the Richmond representatives would not accept Lincoln's demands of reunion and abolition. Of course, that was exactly what the Confederates had anticipated; they could now confirm that the president insisted upon emancipation as part of any settlement. Another editor-turned-adviser, Henry J. Raymond of the New York *Times,* looked to nullify the propaganda advantage gained by the Democrats. He urged Lincoln to offer Jefferson Davis the opportunity to negotiate peace based upon reunion alone, foregoing abolition.

Raymond's proposal had its advantages. Davis had sought to damage Lincoln in the eyes of those northern voters who retained their racist attitudes by reminding them that the president was willing to sacrifice white lives for black freedom. Now Lincoln could turn the tables and encourage growing evidence of Confederate dissent by ostensibly removing slavery as an obstacle to reunion, safe in the knowledge that Davis would not abandon his dream of national independence. At the same time Lincoln would counter claims that his commitment to abolition was prolonging the bloodshed, for northerners would be reminded that the Confederates would reject any peace that did not incorporate disunion. A sign of the proposal's appeal was that Lincoln actually drafted a document embodying Raymond's recommendations in order to consider its merits more closely. He did not doubt that he was in a desperate situation. As August drew to a close he thought that he would lose his bid for reelection, leaving the problems of war and peace in the hands of his Democratic successor.

In the end, however, Lincoln decided against accepting Raymond's recommendation. The president would not renege on his commitment to abolition, although he remained flexible as to how it was realized. To ask blacks to fight for the Union cause—especially when they were needed—without guaranteeing their freedom would be an unconscionable betrayal. And to adopt Raymond's proposal would raise questions in Republican minds about Lincoln's commitment to freedom and equality in the aftermath of the veto of the Wade-Davis Bill. Of course, a Democratic victory might render such considerations moot. With that in mind, Lincoln urged Frederick Douglass to devise some way of increasing opportunities for slaves to escape Confederate control while the Emancipation Proclamation remained in effect, for the door to freedom might well slam shut next March should President McClellan take office.[32]

Union battlefield triumphs rescued Lincoln's political fortunes. On September 2, Sherman entered Atlanta. Several weeks later, Phil Sheridan scored the first in a series of dramatic victories in the Shenandoah Valley. Meanwhile, Grant maintained his bulldog grip on Lee. These triumphs strengthened Lincoln's hand, quelled efforts to replace him as the Republican nominee, and allowed him to mend party divisions in part by securing the resignation of Postmaster General Montgomery Blair, whose conservative views on race and reconstruction infuriated Radicals. The death of Chief Justice Roger B. Taney in October gave Lincoln another chance to woo Radicals, for Salmon P. Chase had long lusted to wear the robes of the nation's top judge. For the moment the president let the prize dangle in front of the Ohioan's eyes in order to ensure that he stayed in line through the election.

Elsewhere the signs that Lincoln would indeed win reelection were improving. Republican margins in the October elections were sufficient to forecast what would happen in November, although Lincoln at first continued to be pessimistic. Soon it became clear that the voters would try the rail-splitter for four more years. The president's majority in the electoral college was overwhelming, for the Democratic candidate (none other than George McClellan) carried only three states. But McClellan had polled some 45 percent of the popular vote, an impressive total given the recent improvement in Union military fortunes, nor could observers overlook the fact that the Confederate states had not participated in the contest. In a reunited nation, the Republicans would continue to be a popular minority, unless something could be done to build a southern wing. Whether that structure would be erected upon a foundation of black votes remained to be seen.

With Republican control of the White House secure, reconstruction surfaced again as a divisive issue. As before, matters in Louisiana sparked the debate. Whatever his qualifications as a politician, Nathaniel Banks's shortcomings as a general terminated his tenure in the Bayou State in the spring of 1864. His successor, Edward R. S. Canby, did not share Banks's vision of reconstruction; if Banks's approach to securing black rights irritated Radicals, Canby's conservatism infuriated them. More reports of the consequences of Banks's labor policy, in which he sought to regulate black labor and used the army to "encourage" them to contract with plantation owners, filtered north to Washington, reaffirming Radical concerns that more had to be done to secure equality as well as emancipation. Lincoln preferred to focus on what had already been achieved. Pleased with the Louisiana constitution, he pointed out that in regard to blacks it was better than that of Illinois. "Much good work is already done," he told Canby, "and surely nothing can be gained by throwing it away."[33]

Radicals disagreed. They raised the old issue of which branch of the federal government would shape policy toward the South. As Congress assembled, Sumner wrote Lincoln "to suggest, whether the whole subject of 'terms' and of 'reconstruction' does not properly belong to Congress. . . . I make this remark with no other object than to secure that harmony and unity in our public counsels, which will render the Govt. irresistible."[34] But the president was not willing to make peace on Sumner's terms and took far more interest in a compromise measure brokered by Representative James M. Ashley. Congress would accept what had been done in Louisiana if it could have its way elsewhere, thus reviving the Wade-Davis Bill. In addition, Ashley wanted some form of black suffrage in the states reconstructed under the congressional plan.

For a time it seemed as if this proposal might suffice. Sumner swallowed hard and accepted it. Lincoln noted reservations about blacks as jurors and voters but observed that its passage would result in the admission of Louisiana. He still harbored serious doubts about whether Congress could mandate emancipation through legislation. These were not minor points: they struck at key features of the bill. Lincoln did not think the legislation laid down "a cast iron policy"; Banks thought that congressional Republicans wanted to reassert their role in the reconstruction process.[35]

Ashley amended his proposal to meet Lincoln's objections, although the new bill would enfranchise those blacks who had served in the military. At first, it seemed that the bill might still survive, in part because Sumner did not scrutinize it carefully enough in concluding that it eliminated color as a barrier to voting. Nor was it clear where the bill left the Lincoln governments in Tennessee and Arkansas as well as what passed for a loyal government in Virginia. But when Congress reconvened in January, Ashley offered new amendments that significantly impinged upon current understandings. One explicitly guaranteed civil equality under the law; the other demanded that Louisiana and Arkansas conform to the provisions of the bill.

Slowly the deal unraveled. Moderate Republicans backed away. Radicals became more critical of the Louisiana government and outspoken in favor of black suffrage. Ashley tried to salvage the situation with yet another set of amendments that would have allowed the Lincoln governments in Louisiana, Arkansas, and Tennessee to persist provided that they incorporated in their constitutions the principles of reconstruction set forth for the other states. These included the exclusion of Confederate officeholders from voting or holding office, color-blind equality, and the repudiation of Confederate debts. However, Ashley reverted to his insistence upon black suffrage. This and subsequent modifications revealed that Republicans could not reach a consensus strong enough to overcome Democratic determination to defeat all such measures. Radicals and Democrats torpedoed moderate proposals; moderates and Democrats terminated Radical propositions. All Sumner could do was to block recognition of Louisiana and Arkansas by denying seats to their elected representatives.

Lincoln, frustrated, asked Senator Lyman Trumbull, "Can Louisiana be brought into proper practical relations with the Union, sooner, by *admitting* or by *rejecting* the proposed Senators?" But Sumner had his way. By failing to recognize the Louisiana regime, he thought he had bought time for public discussion and the acceptance of black suffrage: "We shall need the votes of the negroes to sustain the Union, to preserve tranquility and to prevent repudiation of the national debt." Viewing the enfranchisement of the freedmen as a practical necessity as well as a principled measure, the Massachusetts senator explained that "without their votes, we cannot establish stable govts. in the rebel states. Their votes are as necessary as their musquets." Otherwise white southerners, under color of law, would resume control of their states and, in alliance with northern Democrats, try to gain back in peace much of what had been lost in defeat. Moreover, he continued to insist that "the rebel region must for a while pass under the *jurisdiction of Congress,* in order to set up the necessary safeguards for the future."[36]

In the absence of a congressional alternative, Lincoln remained in control for the moment. He could point with pride to the fact that slavery was now dead in Louisiana and Arkansas, even if it was not clear yet what emancipation meant. Nor were these his only successes. West Virginia had adopted a plan of gradual emancipation in 1863; in October 1864, voters in Maryland ratified a new state constitution that ended slavery; Missouri embraced emancipation in January 1865; the next month, Andrew Johnson, in one of his last acts as military governor before heading to Washington, declared the triumph of abolition in the Volunteer State.

Republicans pursued other ways to secure emancipation. One was through the creation of a federal agency to oversee the transition from slavery to freedom. Mistrustful of the efforts of state governments and military personnel to shape this process, congressional Republicans thought it better to take these matters into their own hands. An initial proposal fell short in 1864; now in March 1865, with the end of the war in sight, they passed a bill establishing the Bureau of Refugees, Freedmen, and Abandoned Lands. Lincoln saw nothing wrong with the idea. Perhaps he realized that with such an agency in place, Republican concerns about how the reconstructed governments managed such affairs would diminish, easing their path to full recognition.[37]

The best way to achieve emancipation on a lasting basis throughout the nation was through constitutional amendment. Lincoln strongly advocated this approach but remained uncertain of the impact of the Emancipation Proclamation. Would it survive a court test? What would happen to those slaves still under Confederate control at war's end? Would not the justification of military necessity vanish in such circumstances? Democrats charged that such an amendment was itself unconstitutional; other critics noted that much depended on whether ratification would be contingent on the votes of several states currently affiliated with the Confederacy. Perhaps Lincoln anticipated the latter reservation, for in that case it behooved congressional Republicans to recognize his makeshift regimes in order to gain their votes.

Although Republican majorities in the 1864 elections meant that the next Congress would pass an abolition amendment, Lincoln decided to press for ratification with the very Congress that had rejected it in 1864. There were good reasons for this choice. It was not clear how long the war would go on, and Lincoln thought that an amendment might hasten its conclusion by contributing to the erosion of Confederate hopes. "I am very anxious that the war be brought to a close at the earliest possible date," he told one Missouri Democrat. However, he believed that the Confederates would continue to fight "as long as those fellows down south can rely on the border states to help them." An amendment, especially one that enjoyed support in the border states, would help Confederates to "see that they could not expect much help from that quarter."[38] And the passage of an abolition amendment would render moot questions about the status of the Emancipation Proclamation, a measure justified by military necessity, once that necessity evaporated with war's end—a concern never far from the president's mind.

In his annual message Lincoln urged Congress to frame such an amendment, reminding Democrats that its eventual passage was inevitable. Administration supporters offered House Democrats incentives to facilitate the passage of the amendment either by supporting it or by abstaining. Most Democrats realized that to continue to pose as the defenders of slavery would be to risk political opprobrium. Together, these considerations proved sufficient. On January 31, 1865, the House of Representatives reversed its action of the previous June and voted to send to the state legislatures a thirteenth amendment ending slavery in the United States. The president, elated, declared that "this amendment is a King's cure for all the evils. It winds the whole thing up."[39]

Congressional passage of the amendment came just in time for Lincoln to use it as a weapon of war in the cause of peace. As the measure moved to a final vote, rumors circulated throughout Washington that Confederate commissioners were ready once more to discuss peace terms. Lincoln denied that any such envoys were coming to Washington, neglecting to add that three men *were* at City Point. It was not the first time since the election that Lincoln had contemplated negotiating an end to the war. He had not been fooled by the offer to treat for peace at Niagara Falls, although his response proved counterproductive. After the fall of Atlanta he had taken a good deal of interest in rumors that Governor Joseph E. Brown of Georgia was pondering the wisdom of taking his state out of the Confederacy; there was talk that Zebulon Vance of North Carolina was contemplating the same course. If Jefferson Davis refused to listen to Lincoln, perhaps these men would be more amenable to conversation, especially in the wake of Lincoln's reelection.

The sticking point proved to be slavery. Although Lincoln had said in his annual message that Confederates could "have peace simply by laying down their arms and submitting to the national authority under the Constitution," such a promise did not clarify the fate of the peculiar institution. All remaining questions, the president asserted, would be answered "by the peaceful means of legislation, conference, courts, and votes, operating only in constitutional and lawful channels." Although in peace the scope of presidential power would contract, Lincoln would maintain control of "pardons and remissions of forfeiture." The door remained open. "But the time may come—probably will come—when public duty shall demand that it be closed; and that, in lieu, more rigorous measures than heretofore shall be adopted." Privately Lincoln assured Orville H. Browning and self-appointed go-between James W. Singleton that he did not insist upon immediate abolition as a prerequisite for reunion. Perhaps he did not need to: although in the short term slavery might persist, in the long term it would be doomed, especially after the passage of the Thirteenth Amendment. More curious was the effort of Francis P. Blair Sr. to craft an armistice followed by a joint blue-gray expedition to Mexico to overthrow Maximilian's French-supported regime. Davis saw his opportunity, claiming he was willing to commence negotiations to arrange a temporary peace between the Union and the Confederacy. Of course, this approach was not what Lincoln wanted: he would only talk about "securing peace to the people of our one united country."[40]

Davis, determined to remind his people that the cost of peace was the sacrifice of their dream for independence, appointed three commissioners to meet Lincoln to discuss terms. The delegation was headed by Vice President Alexander H. Stephens, who was joined by Virginians Robert M. T. Hunter and John A. Campbell. The three men made their way to Grant's headquarters and sought an audience with the president. They got one, not because Lincoln initially desired it but because Grant urged him to meet with them.[41]

By the time Grant's telegram arrived in Washington, Congress had passed the Thirteenth Amendment. Now Lincoln was ready to talk. On the morning of February 3, he and Seward met the Confederate trio at Hampton Roads, offshore Norfolk, Virginia. Lincoln insisted upon reunion; he also pledged not to retract the Emancipation Proclamation or reenslave any blacks freed during the war. Nevertheless, he was willing to be flexible on how emancipation was completed, even if he remained committed to its achievement. Most interesting, if Stephens is to be believed, was a suggestion that Confederate state legislatures "prospectively" ratify the Thirteenth Amendment so as to put it into effect in 1870—an odd notion that had no standing in constitutional law. Lincoln did reiterate his willingness to compensate slaveholders. Such an infusion of capital would go far to help rebuild the economy of the former Confederate states. It all sounded quite promising, even generous, but negotiations quickly floundered when it became evident that the Confederate commissioners were unwilling to embrace what they already privately had come to expect, the end of their experiment in independence. Lincoln went so far as to draw up one final proposal for compensated emancipation, only to have the cabinet act in rare unanimity in rejecting it.[42]

Nevertheless, the president had accomplished much since he had issued the Emancipation Proclamation. Having highlighted several paths to emancipation, he was now seeing the fruition of his labors. Maryland, Arkansas, Louisiana, and Tennessee had all abolished slavery through state action; the advancing Union armies had freed still more slaves; and now the nation had before it a constitutional amendment that would terminate the peculiar institution once and for all. Yet much remained to be done. Lincoln was still not sure exactly what the postemancipation South would look like, especially in how it addressed the transition from slavery to freedom, nor was it clear how the seceded states would take their place in a reunited nation. The president was willing to trust former Confederates with a role in that process, but congressional Republicans remained skeptical of the wisdom of that approach. In turn, Lincoln, aware of the persistence of racism and still unsure whether the former slaves were ready to become full members of the body politic, was reluctant to push for extensive black participation in these new regimes. These questions, overshadowed by the need to win victory on the battlefield, became more pressing as it became evident that the Confederacy was doomed.

On March 4, 1865, Abraham Lincoln took the oath of office as president of the United States for a second time. Observers read much into the fact that the Capitol dome, under construction four years before, was now completed, topped by a statue representing freedom and liberty. Other signs of reunion were less auspicious. Andrew Johnson had arrived in Washington still suffering from illness. Seeking a quick cure, he downed several glasses of whiskey. The effect was all too evident as the new vice president staggered through his own swearing-in ceremony, capped by a ludicrous attempt at speech making that left listeners astonished if not horrified. In the last act of his first term, Lincoln directed others to make sure Johnson kept his mouth shut.

The ceremonies continued on the east front of the Capitol, where a special platform had been erected. The audience waited to hear what the president would say. Those who anticipated a celebration of victory were disappointed, for Lincoln chose to use the opportunity to set the mood for how he thought Americans should approach reconstruction. He suggested that many Americans, North and South, were to blame for what happened, although he was quick to add that not everyone was equally at fault. Somehow, he added, slavery was at the heart of the dispute, but he did not say how. He hoped for a quick end to the fighting but asserted that somehow the sanguinary struggle was God's way of assigning retribution. In conclusion, Lincoln called upon his audience to heed the better angels of their nature:

> With malice toward none; with charity for all; with firmness in the right, as God gives us to see the right, let us strive on to finish the work we are in; to bind up the nation's wounds; to care for him who shall have borne the battle, and for his widow, and his orphan—to do all which may achieve and cherish a just, and a lasting peace, among ourselves, and with all nations.

Reconciliation, forgiveness, binding up wounds—there had been enough hatred and enough bloodshed to satisfy anyone's thirst for revenge. And yet Lincoln's primary audience was white. Yes, slavery had been an injustice done to blacks by whites; the war itself was somehow punishment for it—for whites. But what of the future? What would freedom mean? The war might well be retribution for white sin, but how would it remedy the injustice done to the slaves? To be sure, the address was eloquent and moving, but it was also incomplete.[43]

For the next five weeks Lincoln's primary concern was managing the war to a successful conclusion. He made sure that his generals understood that he retained control over political questions arising out of surrender negotiations, informing Grant of that fact in a stiffly worded dispatch (written in the third person and signed by Stanton) on inauguration eve. Yet he soon came to realize that how the war ended would help shape how peace started. Whether he liked it or not, he would have to entrust Grant and Sherman with roles that were as much political as they were military. With that in mind he conferred with them at the end of March aboard the *River Queen* offshore Grant's headquarters at City Point. He impressed upon them both his dread of more bloodshed and his desire for liberal and generous terms as essential foundations for a lasting peace—although he did not go so far as to dictate terms. In so doing he misread the temper of his two generals. The images of Unconditional Surrender Grant and the firestorm of Sherman's marches blinded Lincoln to the fact that both men made hard war but advocated a lenient peace. As they pointed out to the president, much of what would happen depended upon how the Confederate armies behaved. They could seek decisive battle; their generals could decide to disband their commands and commence guerrilla operations. When and how the war ended was not totally controlled by Union leaders.

The conversation proved a timely one. As Sherman returned to his command in North Carolina, Grant launched an offensive designed to compel Lee's army to surrender. On the night of April 2, Confederate forces evacuated Petersburg and Richmond; Grant's energetic pursuit trapped them a week later at Appomattox Court House. With Lincoln's words still fresh in his mind, Grant offered Lee most generous terms, designed to spare the former foe any unnecessary humiliation and to send him home to start life anew. Among the key clauses were the terms of Grant's parole, which protected the surrendered Confederates from prosecution by federal authorities so long as they obeyed the law. It would later be used to shield Lee, among others, from being tried for treason—just the sort of act that would sow new bitterness in the souls of many white southerners. Lincoln beamed as he read the terms. He could not have done better.[44]

Even with military victory imminent, Lincoln tinkered with ways to close out the conflict. Upon entering Richmond on April 4, he encountered John A. Campbell, one of the Confederate commissioners from the Hampton Roads Conference. Over the next two days Campbell and Lincoln worked out an agreement whereby the members of the Virginia state legislature would meet to take the Old Dominion out of the Confederacy. The idea seemed a little far-fetched, even to Lincoln, and soon involved him in matters he would have done better to avoid. Grant, as the president admitted, was doing a good job of securing the withdrawal of Virginia from the war; after Appomattox there was no reason to continue these discussions. Campbell's decision to overlook the distinction Lincoln had made between "the gentlemen who have acted as the legislature of Virginia" and the actual state legislature gave the president the opportunity to wash his hands of the whole affair by claiming that he did not intend to recognize Confederate civil governments. He did so after coming under criticism from Stanton and others who worried about what sort of precedent the president might set, especially as the administration had long recognized another government in Virginia as legitimate.

As hostilities drew to a close, a new era in reconstruction policy opened. Gone was the old goal of weakening the Confederacy by providing dissenters with viable alternatives. Gone, too, were the incentives to move cautiously on emancipation in part to woo those dissenters. With the war over, many white southerners would seek protection from change by flocking back to the Union. Lincoln did not intend to let them off the hook so easily. As he pointed out in his December 1864 annual message, he had held the door open for a year. Appomattox signified that the time had come to close the door.[45]

Nor was it clear that Lincoln alone could reopen the door. With the end of hostilities came an end to the war powers of the president. In peace he would have to forge a partnership with congressional Republicans. That had not been easy in the past, as the case of Louisiana demonstrated. Lincoln might prolong his period of autonomy (as he had at the outset of the war) by refusing to call Congress into session and by continuing to recognize the existence of a state of war, but sooner or later he would have to deal with the fellows at the other end of Pennsylvania Avenue.

Nevertheless, Lincoln resolved to keep his options open. On the day following Lee's surrender he told Virginia's wartime governor, Francis Pierpoint, "that he had no plan for reorganization, but must be guided by events," in part because he really did not know what to do.[46] He had been so absorbed by the need to win the war that he had spent little time pondering what to do next. But he knew that it was time to begin. Determined to choose his words carefully, he declined to respond to a serenade on April 10 but invited his audience back the next evening, thus guaranteeing that listeners would pay especial heed to his remarks.

"We meet this evening, not in sorrow, but in gladness of heart," Lincoln announced as he began to speak on April 11. But he did not dwell on the Union's military triumph. Instead, he wanted to remind Americans that now the problem of reconstruction "is pressed much more closely upon our attention." No agreed-upon plan existed. The president retraced his own actions, termed the question of whether the seceded states were in or out of the union "a merely pernicious abstraction," and once more made the case for his regime in Louisiana. None of this demonstrated new thinking. What the audience could not have known was that Lincoln was addressing his remarks in part to the new chief justice, Salmon P. Chase, who that morning had favored the president with his opinions in such a way as to alert Lincoln to the possibility that while he had removed Chase from the cabinet, he had not eliminated him as a critic and as a rival. Nevertheless, there were some ideas made public for the first time. Lincoln remarked that he favored suffrage for those blacks who had served in the Union military as well as the "very intelligent," although he did not mandate the measure. He admitted that in light of the varying circumstances across the southern states, it might be unwise to pass one uniform plan since it could create complications and entanglements. Finally, he promised that at some future date he would outline an approach to postwar reconstruction, although he said nothing about what he might say or when he might say it.[47]

It was time for new beginnings. Lincoln would not be the sole judge of them, a fact emphasized when he brought his negotiations with Campbell to an end after he encountered serious opposition in his cabinet. This situation left him wondering how best to preserve order in the postwar South in the short term. "Civil governments, he was accustomed to say, must be introduced at once to prevent anarchy and punish crime," recalled Gideon Welles, who nevertheless objected to the Campbell scheme and reminded Lincoln of the Pierpoint government. Yet Lincoln now wondered whether the rapid reintroduction of civil government was altogether wise, which became evident on April 14 at a cabinet meeting devoted to that issue. "We can't undertake to run State governments in all these Southern States," he observed. "Their people must do that,— though I reckon that at first some of them may do it badly." Just as he had stood behind his experiment in civil government in Louisiana three days earlier, he argued that any postwar planning had to take into consideration that existing loyal government in Virginia—and, by implication, the other wartime state governments. Yet he proved willing to consider Stanton's plan for temporary military regimes in the occupied South. Grant, who might have to help administer such a scheme, was present at the meeting; absent was Andrew Johnson, who could offer his own testimony about the practical workings of Reconstruction.[48]

In later years both conservatives and Radicals cited this meeting as indicating Lincoln's basic adherence to their views. Welles recounted the president's adherence to the principles of leniency and the restoration of civil government. Others saw something different. "He never seemed so near our views," Attorney General James Speed later told Chase, adding that the president admitted that he "had perhaps been too fast in his desires for early reconstruction."[49] These conflicting assessments reflected Lincoln's own uncertainty as to what to do next. In such circumstances, it was understandable that he was glad that Congress was not in session. For the moment it was time to relax and to think. Perhaps a night at the theater would put him in the proper mood.

John Wilkes Booth ended Lincoln's life that evening. He did so in part because he was convinced that the president would push for black suffrage, a conclusion he reached after listening as Lincoln spoke on April 11. But Booth's bullet did not end speculation about what the president intended to do. It is fascinating yet futile to ponder what Lincoln might have done had he lived, in part because Lincoln himself did not know what he was going to do. In years to come contemporaries, eager to wrap themselves in the mantle of the martyred president, highlighted those aspects of Lincoln's thoughts, remarks, and actions that tended to support their own vision of Reconstruction. Historians have engaged in the same guessing game, constructing programs to serve their own purposes. Complicating matters further is the dependence of scholars upon the testimony of contemporaries about Lincoln's intentions, for this testimony often is rendered suspect by the motive of the witness to situate Lincoln's position in comparison to the witness's own preferences about what should have happened during Reconstruction.

In the quest to discover what Lincoln would have done had he lived, we overlook what Lincoln did while he lived. The sixteenth president was always governed by his recognition of the importance of process and context in shaping policy. The war presented unprecedented problems; its course meant that the situation Lincoln confronted was fluid and ever changing. Lincoln often made clear that his primary purpose was to preserve the Union, but he soon realized that in order to achieve that goal he would have to address the root cause of its disruption. In devising ways to do this, he was aware of the importance of institutional and political limitations upon his freedom of action. How he acted was as important as what he did; as he once pointed out to Salmon P. Chase, to declare free those slaves already in areas under Union occupation (and thus not coming under the umbrella of military necessity) would make him the dictator his enemies charged him with being. Thus he sought constitutional justification for his actions and whenever possible sought to make emancipation a voluntary or consensual act by whites.

"I claim not to have controlled events, but confess plainly that events have controlled me." So Lincoln once asserted. Nevertheless, he always looked to cultivate the opportunity for change even as he waited for it. As newspaper editor John Forney observed, "He always moves in conjunction with propitious circumstances, not waiting to be dragged by the force of events or wasting strength in premature struggles with them."[50] His achievements during the war, especially in handling the thorny issue of slavery and emancipation, testify to this skill.

Nevertheless, Lincoln's wartime reconstruction policies carried with them implications that lasted far beyond the war itself. In opening the door to a rapid restoration of civil rule under military supervision, he empowered whites who were at the fringe of southern politics and society. In many cases their commitment to emancipation and equality was suspect if not altogether lacking. How could Lincoln compel their voluntary adherence to his principles?

What would happen to these governments once the war was over? What standing would they have with other southern whites? Nor was it yet clear what would happen to blacks in this world or the degree to which blacks would be allowed to determine their own future. Lincoln may well have embraced the principle of what Gabor Boritt has called "the right to rise," but what exactly did blacks need in order to exercise that right? What sort of opportunities would they enjoy? To what degree would they be able to shape their own destiny? An assassin's bullet may have spared Lincoln from addressing these matters, but they still confronted Americans in April 1865.

PART TWO
ANDREW JOHNSON

3

"THERE IS NO SUCH THING AS RECONSTRUCTION"

The course of Reconstruction changed in fundamental ways during April 1865 with the collapse of the Confederacy. Justifications of wartime expediency gave way to postwar concerns about how best to achieve a lasting reunion. The assassination of Abraham Lincoln removed from the political scene a master politician who tried to balance conciliation with justice and understood how to frame policy in accordance with circumstances. But Lincoln's death in itself cannot explain what happened to the course of Reconstruction between 1865 and 1869. Just as important was the man who became president on April 15, 1865, Andrew Johnson. No other single individual contributed more to the shaping of the contours of reconstruction policy. "To day you occupy a position more potent for good or evil, than any man on the face of the earth," offered the abolitionist George Stearns.[1] Of the four presidents who occupied office during Reconstruction, Johnson enjoyed the most freedom of action and the greatest opportunity to leave his mark on determining its course.

Tired of Lincoln's pleas for leniency and moderation, Radical Republicans initially were delighted with his successor, who pledged condign punishment for traitors and claimed he was the freedmen's friend. "Hostility towards Lincoln's policy of conciliation and contempt for his weakness were undisguised," observed Congressman George Julian. "The universal feeling among radical men here is that his death is a god-send." Yet Democrats were cheered by the prospect of having one of their own in the White House. As he entered upon his new duties, Andrew Johnson seemed all things to all people.[2]

Had observers wanted to learn something more concrete about the new chief executive, they needed to look no further than his career as military governor of Tennessee. Johnson encouraged them to do so: "You can judge my policy by the past," he announced to a delegation of Republicans on April 16. However, those who examined Johnson's wartime record to discover portents of his presidential policy found it susceptible to various interpretations. Although he had moved quickly to reopen civil courts, appoint officials, and hold elections, all with Lincoln's encouragement, he showed no such energy when it came to destroying slavery. At his behest, Lincoln excluded Tennessee from the Emancipation Proclamation, leaving the propriety and timing for answering that question to the Volunteer State's leaders, who waited until 1865 to abolish slavery.[3]

Johnson swore vengeance against secessionist leaders. "The tall poppies must be struck down," he claimed, and he was just the man to wreak such revenge: "Treason must be made odious, and traitors must be punished and impoverished. Their great plantations must be seized and divided into small farms, and sold to honest, industrious men." Nor would Johnson necessarily stop there: the leaders of the rebellion, "the instigators, the conscious intelligent traitors, they ought to be hung." Such language seemed to confirm Johnson's Radical credentials. Calls for punishment and property confiscation were part of the creed. Excessive leniency, he had warned Lincoln, would only "keep alive the rebel spirit in fact reconciling none."[4]

Johnson believed that in acting as he did he enjoyed Lincoln's approval, and never more so than when he succeeded in displacing Hannibal Hamlin as the president's running mate in 1864. On the eve of his departure for Washington the next winter, he declared slavery at an end in Tennessee, telling blacks that he was their "Moses," guiding them to freedom. Illness plagued him as he came east; on the eve of his inauguration as vice president, he turned to alcohol to assuage his aches and steady his nerves. The result was a disastrous embarrassment: intoxicated when he took the oath of office, he delivered a rambling discourse on the glories of democracy before Hamlin pulled him away. For nearly a month Johnson kept a low profile, reemerging in the public eye during the last week of the war in Virginia. Nevertheless, he had but little idea what was on the president's mind about reconstruction. When the two men met on April 14, Johnson complained about Grant's generous terms at Appomattox. The next morning he took the oath of office as president.

Radicals' wooing of Johnson commenced almost immediately. "Johnson, we have faith in you," Benjamin Wade told the new president. "By the gods, there will be no trouble now in running the government!" They had anticipated a continuing struggle with Lincoln over the terms of reconstruction. "Had Mr. Lincoln's policy been carried out we should have had Jeff Davis, Toombs and co. back in the Senate at the next session of Congress," Zachariah Chandler growled. "Johnson is all right now thinks just as we do and desires to carry out radical measures and finish treason and traitors but much depends on his surroundings."[5]

Chandler's conclusion seemed reasonable. To a delegation from Indiana, Johnson proclaimed, "The time has come when the American people should understand what crime is, and that it should be punished, and its penalties enforced and inflicted." Treason "is the highest crime that can be committed, and those engaged in it should suffer all its penalties." Not only must traitors be punished, "but their social power must be destroyed." Details were unnecessary; people wanting to find out what Johnson planned to do needed only to refer to his record. "You may look back to it as evidence of what my course will be. . . . Mine has been but one straightforward and unswerving course, and I see no reason now why I should depart from it." He believed that "my past is a better foreshadowing of my future course than any statement on paper that might be made." The record was a harsh one. "President Johnson is not disposed to treat treason lightly," Secretary of the Navy Gideon Welles observed, "and the chief Rebels he would punish with exemplary severity."[6]

Only the careful listener would have noticed that despite his fiery rhetoric, Johnson also delineated the limits of his radicalism. The rebellious states were not to be reduced to territorial status: they remained states within the Union. "Their life breath has only been suspended," and Johnson intended to revive them as quickly as possible. Moreover, it would be up to southerners to complete the work of restoration (although for the moment he did not add that the southerners in question would be white). He reminded his audience that "while I have opposed dissolution and disintegration on the one hand, on the other I am equally opposed to consolidation, or the centralization of power in the hands of a few." His responsibility was to restore the constitutional order, not to transform it.[7]

Democrats courted the new chief executive. His emphasis on states' rights and past principles seemed to indicate that he would gravitate toward his roots. "Your old Democratic associates feel a revival of their ancient regard for you," Senator James Dixon of Connecticut told his old colleague. "It would not surprise me at all, if you should find them among the warmest of your supporters." Pennsylvania Democrats moved quickly to avow their support, convinced that Johnson would "bring things back to the balmy days of Andrew Jackson." Conservative Republicans, including Dixon and Wisconsin senator James Rood Doolittle, also rallied to the side of the president. Montgomery Blair, Lincoln's postmaster general and host to Johnson in the aftermath of the inauguration day debacle, predicted that Johnson would break with the Radicals "on the fundamental questions of states rights and negro suffrage."[8]

Radicals persisted in believing that the new president embraced two cornerstones of their approach to reconstruction: the punishment of traitors and the enfranchisement of blacks. They pointed to Johnson's speeches calling for the breaking up of southern plantations and the redistribution of land and his declaration that he would be blacks' "Moses leading them from slavery to freedom" as evidence of his Radical credentials. He had proclaimed so many times that the crime of treason had to be punished and traitors impoverished that it had become his mantra. Not to be outdone, Democrats and conservative Republicans looked to Johnson's choice of advisers, including Blair and Secretary of State William H. Seward, as proof of his conservative leanings. Indeed, Blair and Seward, implacable foes, were far more worried about each other than they were about Radical chances of influencing the president. Nevertheless, no one was sure of the president's position. As Julian later recalled, "He had suddenly become the central figure of American politics, and both radicals and conservatives were as curious to know what line of policy he would follow as they were anxious to point his way."[9]

Two Radicals who were intent on winning Johnson over were Chief Justice Salmon P. Chase and Massachusetts senator Charles Sumner. Both men had long thought Lincoln had lagged behind in the battle for black rights; days before Lincoln's death Chase had taken it upon himself to press the president to enfranchise blacks. In light of his previous difficulties with Lincoln, Chase welcomed the chance for a fresh start with the new chief executive, believing that Johnson "seems thoroughly in earnest and much of the same mind with myself." The two Radicals were convinced that the president believed that "all loyal people, without distinction of color, must be treated as citizens, and must take part in any proceedings for reorganization"; however, Johnson added that motions for black suffrage "should appear to proceed from the people." Chase offered to spread Johnson's preferences as he traveled along the south Atlantic coast in May. The president, according to Sumner, agreed, authorizing Chase "to do everything he can to promote organization without distinction of color." As the Radicals prepared to depart, the president reassured them, "There is no difference between us."[10]

Chase and Sumner overlooked the importance Johnson attached to means as well as ends. The president had declared repeatedly that since he did not recognize the viability of secession as constitutional doctrine, the rebellious states remained in the Union, with all the rights of states, including determining who should exercise the right of suffrage. Johnson would welcome black suffrage provided it came as an initiative from southern whites—an un-likely event. Sumner thought the matter of means "an inferior question"; Chase, somewhat more attuned to constitutional issues, sought to overcome Johnson's reservations through his reports about conditions in the South. He believed that the president "does not now materially differ from me except as to the time of action. My time is *now*. All good men should try, by cordial support and friendly cheer, to make him feel that *now* is the safe time and best time." With that in mind he headed southward.[11]

In endeavoring to persuade Johnson that southern whites would accept whatever the president decided to do, Chase freely distorted or selectively interpreted his conversations with southern whites. They "would all like that restoration best which would give *them* most power and place, but they will just as clearly accommodate themselves to any mode of reorganization the national government may think best," including, Chase asserted, black suf-frage. "It is clear to me that the national Government must *take* or *suggest* the initiative." However, as reporter Whitelaw Reid, who accompanied Chase, noted, it was important to seize that initiative, for southern whites "stand ready to claim everything, if permitted, and to accept anything, if required." It was with this situation in mind that Chase advised the president to set forth recon-struction terms. Southern whites "would all welcome some simple recommen-dation from yourself, and would adopt readily any plan which you would suggest. They would receive, without resistance from any and with real joy in many hearts, an order for the enrollment of all loyal citizens without regard to complexion, with a view to reorganization."[12]

Chase was fooling himself. Johnson had adopted a policy of letting people think what they wanted to think; he would be most things to most people. In fact, for all of his rhetoric, he did not come to the presidency with any well-defined thoughts on postwar reconstruction policy. He had not been privy to Lincoln's meetings with the cabinet on the subject, and the two men had conversed but briefly on the subject. One needed only to compare Johnson's speech upon the fall of Richmond with Lincoln's final speech eight days later to measure the different concerns and temperaments of the two men. Johnson had spoken of punishing traitors; Lincoln had urged carving out a place for blacks in postwar America. Deprived of direct consultation, Johnson was left to derive what he thought Lincoln's policies would be from his wartime acts, interpreted in light of his own experiences in Tennessee. He had never heard Lincoln speak of black suffrage as anything but a state prerogative; if anything, Johnson had been more adamant on the subject of land confiscation and the need to revitalize widespread loyalty before moving forward with the restoration of civil government. Yet extrapolating from his own experiences in Tennessee proved problematic. There had always been a good number of unionists in Tennessee; much of the state came under Union occupation during the first eighteen months of the war, and the rest followed by the end of 1863. Those conditions did not obtain elsewhere, and in any case the war was drawing to a close. Johnson would struggle to find like-minded men with staunch Union credentials to manage provisional governments; in some cases the best he could find were reluctant Confederates who had initially opposed secession. Complicating the task still more was the existence of wartime unionist regimes in Tennessee, Virginia, Arkansas, and Louisiana. Although Johnson obviously looked with fond approval on the first of these governments, elsewhere he would have to work with what he found.

In large part because many of its main features remained ill-defined, the Lincoln legacy proved a rather malleable tool for Johnson to manipulate. He chose what best suited his own desires, invoking the name of the martyred president to deflect criticism. Once in a while he would either distort or simply fabricate Lincoln's words to justify his acts, as when he claimed that the only change Lincoln wanted in the Constitution was an amendment compelling states to send representatives to Congress, a perverse idea lacking supporting evidence. Johnson remade his predecessor in his own image and used Lincoln's name much as he used the Constitution—as a justification of his actions and nothing more.[13]

Although Lincoln's actions in establishing wartime regimes affected what Johnson could do in those four states, elsewhere he was free to impose his own vision of the course reconstruction should take. Much as Lincoln had appointed military governors and provided them with a few guidelines, Johnson would appoint provisional governors and outline his expectations. Like Lincoln, he would let white southerners shape their own governments, rather than mandate their form or content, by allowing them to convene a constitutional convention. In Tennessee, that convention had nullified secession, abolished slavery, and left the issue of black enfranchisement to the next legislature. Lincoln had approved the result; Johnson saw no reason not to repeat that pattern again. For the moment, he would have nothing to say about confiscation, although inevitably the need to offer new amnesty provisions (Johnson would muddle the concepts of amnesty and pardon throughout his presidency) inevitably involved questions about the restoration of property. Nor would he convene Congress in special session to frame appropriate legislation. Lincoln had not planned to do so; as military governor, Johnson had enjoyed wielding power unhindered by a pesky state legislature. Now it was his job to act again—alone. "It is the duty of the Chief Executive to inaugurate those measures which shall guarantee a republican form of government," he declared at Knoxville in 1864; soon afterward he applauded Lincoln's veto of the Wade-Davis Bill.[14]

The earliest concrete sign of Johnson's intentions reassured Republicans. Shortly after Lincoln's funeral train left Washington, Grant learned that Sherman had negotiated a peace agreement with Confederate commander Joseph E. Johnston in North Carolina. It allowed Confederate forces to march back to their state capitals to stack arms, recognized present civil governments as de facto administrative agencies, and offered amnesty to all Confederates, civilians as well as military personnel, along with restoration of all their property —neglecting to add whether slaves were to be included in this restoration. Sherman had dealt with issues far beyond his legitimate purview. Mistrustful of politicians, he had usurped their functions; yet, recognizing that he had exceeded his authority, he sent the agreement on to Washington in the hope that the very people he despised would approve of his handiwork. They did not: Grant had to defend his friend from charges that his actions constituted treason. The commanding general traveled to North Carolina to oversee the surrender of Johnston's forces on the basis of the Appomattox terms. Observers hailed the administration's actions as evidence that Johnson would punish the former Confederates.

All eyes turned to Johnson to see what would happen next. His mail contained suggestions from everyone on what to do; newspaper editorials and visitors to the White House also sought to impress the president with the proper course to pursue. Correspondents compared him to his hero Jackson and pledged their support to him. So long as Johnson said nothing, he would remain popular; as he defined his position, he was bound to disappoint some of his self-proclaimed supporters. Yet it was up to him to set reconstruction in motion. A Mississippi unionist spoke for many white southerners anxious to cooperate when he told the president, "I desire to harmonize our action, in all things, with the Executive policy"; with some anxiety, he added, "As yet, there has been no occasion for the development of your views."[15]

After three weeks in office Johnson began to act. On May 9, he reaffirmed the legality of the loyal government established in Virginia under Lincoln's supervision. In so doing, he did not call for black suffrage. Supporters of black enfranchisement responded quickly; on May 12, a group of congressional leaders convened a meeting at the National Hotel "to consider the necessity of taking decisive measures for saving the new Administration from the conservative control which now threatened it." Sumner and Wade advised caution, but Thaddeus Stevens smelled trouble. "Reconstruction is a very delicate question," he carefully wrote Johnson. "The last Congress, (I expect the present) looked upon it as a question for the Legislative power exclusively. While I think we shall agree with you almost unanimously as to the main objects you have in view I fear we may differ as to the manner of effecting them. . . . My only object now is to suggest the propriety of suspending further 'reconstruction' until the meeting of Congress. Better to call an extra Session, than to allow many to think that the executive was approaching usurpation. . . . Do not I pray you burden us further." To Sumner, Stevens was characteristically blunt: "I see the President is precipitating things. . . . I fear before Congress meets he will have so bedeviled matters as to render them incurable. It would be well if he would call an extra session of Congress."[16]

For all his effort to be tactful with Johnson—deep in his heart he doubted that the president and Republicans shared the same goals—Stevens was laying down the gauntlet. Who would control reconstruction: president, Congress, or both? Means would shape ends, especially when it came to issues such as black suffrage. But other Republicans were not ready to follow Stevens. Chase continued to operate under the assumption that he could bring the president around; Sumner discounted the example set by Virginia and looked instead to what Johnson would do in states lacking wartime unionist regimes. Here the example was North Carolina: the cabinet had already agreed to a plan drawn up by Stanton that called for the appointment of a provisional governor, the election of delegates to a state convention, and the revision of southern state constitutions. The only disagreement was over whether blacks would be allowed to participate in those elections; Stanton had included such a provision under pressure from Sumner. At the same time, Johnson was preparing a new amnesty proclamation. Attorney General James Speed had urged him to do so, pointing out that Lincoln's proclamation was framed in response to wartime priorities. Nevertheless, he observed, a generous policy would be best; wisely used, pardon and amnesty could "root out the spirit of rebellion" and bring peace to the land.[17] Only those who were pardoned, after all, could participate in postwar politics; Johnson could thus use his pardoning power to delineate the southern electorate.

On May 29, 1865, Andrew Johnson issued two proclamations. The first outlined his policy of amnesty and pardon. Like Lincoln, Johnson extended a blanket pardon to the vast majority of Confederates provided they first took an oath of future loyalty to the United States. Like his predecessor, he excluded former federal officials, officeholders, and U.S. military personnel as well as prominent Confederate leaders: they would have to secure individual presidential pardons. However, Johnson also excluded anyone who possessed over twenty thousand dollars in taxable property, a direct blow at landholders. Herein lay the potential for revolutionary change; herein also lay the basis for making deals, for with pardon came the restoration of all property (except slaves). And yet pardons were tricky means to make deals since there was no way to compel the person pardoned to comply with the terms of the deal after he received pardon—for example, one could not make them contingent on future behavior or revoke the pardon as a way to ensure compliance. Nevertheless, the way was now open for Johnson to reshape southern society and politics by excluding prominent secessionist leaders and the wealthy from the restoration process and perhaps confiscating their property.[18]

The second proclamation outlined how North Carolinians would rebuild their state government. It served as a model for subsequent proclamations for the other six ex-Confederate states that lacked wartime unionist regimes. In each case Johnson appointed a provisional governor (for North Carolina it would be William W. Holden) who would hold elections for delegates to a state constitutional convention. The president did not offer suggestions about what those constitutions should include; he defined the electorate for this initial contest as those people who would have been eligible to vote as of the day the state seceded and who had taken the oath of amnesty, thus excluding blacks from the process.[19]

A lenient peace and a rapid restoration of the rebellious states to the Union—these were Johnson's foremost desires. He continued to entertain the idea of punishing Confederate leaders, although even then he apparently intended to commute any promised executions, with the possible exception of Jefferson Davis. Only Grant's intervention prevented him from putting Robert E. Lee on trial for treason. But the reordering of southern society would be a rather limited one, and visions of social revolution were to be brought up short. Indeed, the very term "reconstruction" disturbed Johnson, for it implied a significant transformation in the relationship of the South to the rest of the Union. "General, there is no such thing as reconstruction," he informed War Democrat-turned-Republican John A. Logan. "These States have not gone out of the Union, therefore reconstruction is unnecessary." Adding that "it is the province of the Executive to see that the will of the people is carried out in the rehabilitation of these rebellious States," he "desired to have the seceded States return back to their former condition as quickly as possible."[20]

The administration's policy toward the freedmen remained undefined. "The general policy of the government is known to embrace emancipation," noted Georgia unionist Joshua Hill, "but the time and mode of retiring the institution are not so well understood." Former Confederate treasury secretary Christopher Memminger pointed out to Johnson that "neither the North or the South have yet defined what is included in that emancipation. The boundaries are widely apart which mark on the one side, political equality with the white races, and on the other hand, a simple recognition of their personal liberty."[21]

Johnson, despite public posturing that he cared for black people, at heart was a prisoner of his prejudices. One observer feared that the president "may hold almost unconquerable prejudices against the African races." Racist outbursts in private conversation betrayed his true sentiments. "This is a country for white men," he reportedly declared, "and by God, as long as I am President, it shall be a government for white men." Upon hearing that black soldiers were "committing depredations throughout the country, domineering over and in fact running the white people out" of his hometown of Greenville, Tennessee, Johnson angrily demanded an investigation, infuriated by reports that his own house had been turned into "a common negro brothel." These rumors proved false: army commanders denied other stories of misbehavior by black troops, although Johnson often gave them credence.[22]

Johnson believed that if anyone knew what was best for black people, it was neither northern whites, who supposedly did not know the "condition of colored men," nor the blacks themselves, but southern whites, including their former masters. Blacks had to learn that freedom meant work, not waiting for a handout from the government; they also had to conform to acceptable notions of family life. Under slavery, Johnson asserted, "four millions of people lived in open and notorious concubinage." That black efforts to maintain families had been disrupted by slaveholders' actions seems to have escaped the president's memory. In his mind blacks were lazy and promiscuous, certainly not models for the hard-working, family-minded (white) Americans that Johnson celebrated. He believed that most blacks would fail to meet the challenge offered by a free labor society. Assuring black listeners that he would "continue to do all that I can for the elevation and amelioration of your condition," he believed that "the time may soon come when you shall be gathered together, in a clime and country suited to you, should it be found that the two races cannot get along together." One political adviser came away from an interview with the president impressed by his skepticism about the future of blacks in America: "Of their ability to win a position that will enable them to be incorporated into our system of government as citizens he is not eminently hopeful, but feels that it must be fairly tried, with an open field for the negro. That failing, he looks upon colonization as the only alternative."[23]

Johnson insisted that the ex-slaves had to look to themselves for future advancement. As someone who had come from nowhere to somewhere, he believed that he was not asking impossibilities. But misunderstandings were understandable, especially in light of several of Johnson's wartime statements. In January 1864 he had called for the breaking up of large plantations into family farms—only later did careful listeners discover that such farms would be for whites.[24] This theme of condign punishment surfaced several more times, until it seemed a reasonable supposition that Johnson might well support the confiscation of Confederate estates and the distribution of the land to the freedmen. The president's pardon policy, with its promise of the restoration of all property except slaves, dimmed such hopes.

Before long Johnson dealt a death blow to confiscation and redistribution. In August he instructed Oliver O. Howard, the head of the Freedmen's Bureau, to restore all property claimed by recipients of executive pardon, then ended the confiscation of "the property of all men worth over $20,000." The following month he ended the practice of using proceeds from taxes and the use of abandoned lands to fund the Bureau. Whatever his promise to lead blacks to the promised land, the self-styled Moses from Tennessee did not intend to promise blacks their own land. "The President is clearly adverse to confiscation, and that question is practically settled," Alexander McClure reported in October.[25]

Johnson's refusal to mandate black suffrage sparked a lively debate. Many blacks reminded him of their contribution to Union victory. "It seems to us that men who are willing on the field of danger to carry the muskets of republics, in the days of peace ought to be permitted to carry its ballots," forcefully argued a group of North Carolina freedmen, "and certainly we cannot understand the justice of denying the elective franchise to men who have been fighting for the country, while it is freely given to men who have just returned from four years fighting against it."[26] Others argued that the freedmen needed the ballot to protect themselves. South Carolina blacks petitioned the president for the right to vote, for the ballot provided "the only means by which our class of the population of the State, will have the power of protecting ourselves and our interest, against oppression and unjust legislation." Moreover, advocates of black suffrage, echoing the pleas of Chief Justice Chase, pressed the president to act quickly before southern whites shook off the shock of defeat. "You know by *prompt* & vigorous action *now*, the question of negro sufferage can be *settled* & *accepted* by the people as an *accomplished fact*," offered a Tennessee unionist. It was "the *only* means effectual for their protection" against southern whites.[27]

Several northerners also expressed disappointment. "The enormity of your crime is that you put a ballot into the hands of Rebels stained with the blood of *loyal* men, & you deny it to loyal men who have fought for the *right* of *Suferage*," protested one New Yorker. "You . . . say you will make Treason odious. The way you do it is by giving Rebels votes & denying it to loyal men!" How, asked another New Yorker, could Johnson, so well aware of "the intense hatred, or at least prejudice," of whites toward blacks, place "the helpless Negro under the iron-heel of his oppressor—his late Master—with no redress for himself at the ballot box [?]" Carl Schurz offered a more pragmatic analysis. When "the old pro-slavery and disloyal element" came to reassert their influence, "the question of negro suffrage will then become the burning issue and is likely to have great influence upon the attitude of political parties and upon the relations between Congress and the Executive. It will depend upon events whether any difference of opinion will assume the character of direct opposition to the Administration, and events, if we may judge from present symptoms, bid fair to give sharpness to the controversy." As one northerner sadly concluded, "You have had a grand opportunity to settle the Negro question now and forever and we fear that you have missed it."[28]

Johnson preferred to listen to those arguments that confirmed his own decision. "And as you have very properly assumed the ground that *a State once in the Union cannot go out,* and that the rebellion has only been a gigantic *mob* that temporarily impeded the operations of the Federal government, I cannot see with what consistency you can now interpose Federal Executive authority to settle the right of suffrage in a state," seconded one self-appointed adviser. One Philadelphia Democrat celebrated the president's policy because it showed "that in working out the problem of their resuscitation and restoration to the Union the intelligent votes of white freemen are to be relied on and not the ignorant suffrages of emancipated slaves." From North Carolina, the president's close friend, Harvey Watterson, assured him that his refusal to impose black suffrage was building support for the administration. "Shield us, if possible against negro suffrage, negro equality or whatever tends to the rekindling of sectional animosities," begged one Georgian. "The people south are willing to give up slavery; but they are not yet willing to place themselves on terms of political and social equality with the African race."[29]

Johnson's decision to leave the question of enfranchising blacks to southern state conventions was consistent with previous policy, for Lincoln had done the same thing in Louisiana, Tennessee, and Arkansas. Much has been made of Lincoln's private advice to Louisiana governor Michael Hahn to urge the 1864 convention to extend the suffrage to a limited number of qualified blacks, but Lincoln accepted the resulting constitution despite its refusal to take the hint and never made black enfranchisement a prerequisite for readmission. Now Johnson looked to use his private influence to shape the debate over black suffrage in the South but in a spirit far different from that of his predecessor.

Many white Mississippians had anticipated Johnson's plans of restoration by holding meetings in April 1865 in which they expressed their desire to return to the Union; on June 13 Johnson appointed William L. Sharkey, a well-known (if not always active) unionist, as provisional governor. Under Sharkey's supervision, white Mississippians elected delegates to a constitutional convention, which met that August; Johnson then informed Sharkey of his wishes. Each state convention should abolish slavery in the state and ratify the Thirteenth Amendment. As to black suffrage, he was very explicit: "If you could extend the elective franchise to all persons of color who can read the constitution of the United States in English and write their names, and to all persons of color who own real estate valued at not less than two-hundred and fifty dollars and pay taxes on thereon, you would completely disarm the adversary and set an example the other States will follow. . . . you thus place the Southern States, in reference to free persons of color, upon the same basis with the Free States. . . . as a consequence the Radicals, who are wild upon negro franchise, will be completely foiled in their attempts to keep the Southern States from renewing their relations to the Union by not accepting their Senators and Representatives."[30]

It was a most revealing letter. Like Lincoln, Johnson preferred to suggest than to impose conditions (although in the end, like Lincoln, he eventually would impose some). Unlike Lincoln, who had come to believe that limited black suffrage would help "keep the jewel of liberty within the family of freedom," Johnson looked to counter more extreme measures and disarm his Republican critics. At a time when many Republicans were struggling to maintain common cause with the president, he presumed that there would be a confrontation with "the adversary."[31]

In months to come Johnson would cajole white southerners to comply with certain requirements. Not so with black suffrage. Sharkey replied that it would be better to leave the matter to be determined by the legislature, which would address several questions about the status of the freedpeople; he was much more interested in forming a state militia so that federal occupation forces could be transferred elsewhere. The president dropped his proposal and never raised it again in correspondence with the other provisional governors—perhaps because he thought it futile, perhaps because in the fall voters in several northern states defeated efforts to extend suffrage to blacks.[32]

The Mississippi convention was the first of seven such conventions called in accordance with Johnson's proclamations. The president asserted that it would "set an example that will be followed by all the states." Over the next several months everyone watched the proceedings in Mississippi and elsewhere for signs of the temper of white southerners. Everyone understood what was at stake. "The time is to come when each southern state is to take its own local affairs into its own hands," remarked one Republican journal, "and the only security we can have that it will then move on in a loyal orbit is to be found in the permanent forces we shall previously implanted in it."[33]

Johnson's pronouncements about being hamstrung by the Constitution fooled no one. "Strictly speaking," observed Schurz, "the appointment of a civil governor for a State by the Executive of the U.S. is an extraconstitutional act; nor has according to the accepted constitutional theory, the President the power to order a Governor of a State to call a convention of the people." Johnson's insistence that states determined suffrage qualifications did not stop him from defining who could vote for delegates to the constitutional conventions. That he possessed the ability to dictate terms was apparent to many in the North and South. "The President is really dictator," observed one Massachusetts paper; "that is, the southern people understand his strength, not only physical but moral and whatever he says must be done, they do." Even Johnson's military secretary reflected in October 1865 that "we had the opportunity when Lee surrendered and . . . when Lincoln was assassinated to make our own terms." Agreeing, Charles Sumner remarked, "Never was so great an opportunity lost, as our President has flung away."[34]

At first, Johnson, overlooking reports of continued intransigence, convinced himself that the process of "restoration" was well under way. The passage of a month made him optimistic enough to predict that it would be "nearly Complete" by the meeting of Congress in December. Doubtless one reason was that he was reading his mail, which revealed that there was indeed a growth in southern loyalty—to him. "Our *Southern* brothers are begining to know that you are their friend, their protector," wrote one woman, who added that "great misfortunes would be theirs if the rains of government should unfortunately fall into the hands of the radicals!" Others warned Johnson that secession sentiment had not been extinguished and that clemency was mistaken.[35]

The president proclaimed that he was simply following lifelong principles. "I stand where I did of old," he assured a delegation of white southerners, "battling for the constitution and the union of these United States." Reconciliation, not revolution, was his policy. "Why, then, cannot we come together, and around the common altar of our country heal the wounds that have been made?" Before long, however, for all his talk of the constitutional restrictions on his authority, Johnson felt compelled to inject himself more actively into the restoration process and outline his expectations more explicitly. His disappointment was evident as early as September, when he remarked, "There is no disposition on the part of the government to deal harshly with the Southern people. . . . Why cannot we all come up to the work in a proper spirit?"[36]

Part of the answer was that delegates to the various constitutional conventions showed little awareness of the world outside their state. "There is no doubt of their disposition to do what is proper," noted one South Carolina delegate, "but there is a remarkable ignorance or forgetfulness of our strange position." Northern newspapers rarely reached southerners, and mail facilities were woefully inadequate. It would be up to the president to provide cues about northern expectations and responses. Delegates had also forgotten that "they must do their full share to aid and strengthen" Johnson's hand. Certainly, as the South Carolinian pointed out, to restore to power "old politicians who have served with equal complacency in Rebel and in Loyal Congresses" would only "put additional embarrassments" on the president.[37] Yet this is what exactly happened, and it was due in part to Johnson's reluctance to make clear how such actions would be received in the North.

The struggle over the ratification of the Thirteenth Amendment provided a perfect example. Not all the conventions wanted to ratify it; others did so in ways that nullified the impact of the act. Johnson, aware that such heel-dragging would damage the prospects for acceptance of the results in the North, urged Benjamin Perry to advocate ratification in South Carolina, suggesting that "it will set an example which will no doubt be followed by the other states and place South Carolina in a most favorable attitude before the nation." Failing to hear a favorable response, Johnson prodded Perry again, warning, "This opportunity ought to be understood and appreciated by the people of the Southern States." The president encountered similar problems with Mississippi. Several state conventions did what they could to find wiggle room in meeting Johnson's directive to abolish slavery, often simply declaring it dead as a casualty of the conflict—and Georgians retained the right to seek compensation.[38]

Johnson also insisted that the state conventions repudiate the Confederate war debt. There was nothing unusual about this, and yet delegates in several states squirmed. Here explicit warnings bore fruit, for North Carolina's Holden reported that one presidential warning "had a most happy effect" in securing repudiation. A similar telegram went out to Georgia, and it worked there, too, revealing that white southerners would obey mandates when presented as mandates. However, neither South Carolina nor Mississippi complied. Perry argued that his state's war debt was "inconsiderable" and thus warranted no action, oblivious to the symbolic effect of failing to act. Finally, not every state convention nullified its act of secession: some repealed it, suggesting that the door remained ajar. Here, as elsewhere, Johnson failed to insist on the right response. As he later remarked, "The people of Mississippi may feel well assured that there is no disposition . . . to dictate what their action should be, but on the contrary, simply and kindly advise a policy" of reconciliation and restoration.[39]

Even more controversial was the effort of the southern state legislatures elected in the wake of the constitutional conventions to regulate the freedpeople. Drawing on prewar practices in both the North and South as well as local ordinances, several legislatures framed laws that would become known as the black codes. Over the protests of a minority of white southerners who saw such codes as indefensible and unnecessary, legislators sought to define exactly what black freedom meant in ways that maintained white supremacy and whites' sense of security. The codes varied in coverage and in nature from state to state; some of the worst were among the first, led by Mississippi and South Carolina. Not all the codes were adverse to blacks; some clauses actually sought to protect them. However, the restrictions on black rights were glaring, from forbidding blacks to own firearms to severe penalties for vagrancy and violating contracts as well as different punishments for convicted criminals according to their race. Other legislation prohibited blacks from serving on juries or testifying in court in many cases. Even Johnson understood the weaknesses in those proposals, although he was far less critical of the black codes as a whole. To a good number of northern whites, it looked as if southern whites were reinstating slavery in all but name, all the more reason to slow the pace of restoration.[40]

The president also failed to do a better job of sending clear signals to white southerners about the composition of the congressional delegations they would elect in the fall of 1865. Residents of Albemarle County, Virginia, confused about the choices before them, appealed to Johnson "for counsel and advice as to our proper course of action." Wanting to elect representatives to Congress "who will give the most efficient support to your administration," they queried whether the test oath would be required of representatives before they could take their seat in Washington. Here was an ideal chance for Johnson to inform southern whites of the temper of the northern electorate. He failed to seize it. Attorney General Speed replied that the president would not speculate about whether Congress would insist upon the ironclad oath (past as well as future loyalty) as a prerequisite.[41]

In adopting the position that he would offer advice rather than impose conditions, Johnson permitted southern whites to minimize the impact of defeat on their society. As a result, the tone and manner of political discussion changed throughout the South. At first white southerners had anxiously waited to see what would happen, recalling Johnson's vows of vengeance. "But the more lenient the government became, the more arrogant they became," recalled newspaper reporter John T. Trowbridge. The New York *Herald* noted the shift: "Now they do not plead for mercy, but demand their rights." The old Rebel spirit was reappearing. "In May and June last these rebellious spirits would not have dared to show their heads even for the office of constable; but leniency has emboldened them, and the copperhead now shows his fangs," remarked Holden. "I do not like the way in which the people are acting," observed General E. R. S. Canby, stationed in Louisiana. "They appear to think that all the concessions should be on the part of the Government." Other army officers agreed. "The public expression here becomes continually more hostile," one noted. "I doubt if it is so much the index of growing hostility of feeling, as a greater freedom of expression."[42]

The efficacy of Johnson's pardon policy also collapsed. The president grew less discriminating in granting pardons; he lacked the time to devote attention to more than a few petitions and often accepted the judgment of others about the applicant's fitness for forgiveness. One Georgian remarked, "The Truth is these men are no Better *now* then Before Although their *Present Status* Prevents them from Interfering as they would were they *Forgiven*." He was right. Unionists complained to Johnson that the secessionists' "only object in taking the oath is to qualify themselves to control elections, so as to keep themselves in power."[43]

Almost as disturbing was Johnson's willingness to allow his provisional governors to begin organizing state militia and local police forces. For southern whites, such organizations served to support their efforts to secure the removal of occupation forces; they also would prove quite helpful in keeping blacks in line. At times these motives were interrelated, for black regiments formed a large portion of the federal occupation force in the South, and local blacks flocked to them for protection. While some correspondents warned Johnson that the removal of federal troops would escalate violence against blacks, others protested that the reinstatement of local police forces and militia demonstrated the willingness of southern whites to behave in a lawful manner and would render unnecessary the provocative presence of black soldiers, removing the sense of shame and anger that many whites felt when they saw armed blacks exercise authority over them. The president agreed with the latter view, but for the moment he encouraged the formation of local forces while maintaining a federal military presence; meanwhile Grant did what he could to reassign or discharge black units. Johnson dismissed protests with ease. "The people must be trusted with their Government," he told Schurz; to General George H. Thomas he observed, "If the Southern States can be encouraged, I have no doubt in my own mind, that they will proceed and restore their Governments within the next six or seven months and renew their former relations with the Federal Gov't."[44]

Johnson knew that the failure of white southerners to follow his advice would spark more criticism of his policy, and he moved quickly to forestall it. In a widely circulated newspaper interview with abolitionist George Stearns, he hinted that he regarded his policy as experimental in nature. It was better, he thought, "to let them reconstruct themselves than to force them to it; for if they go wrong the power is in our hands, and we can check them in any stage, and oblige them to correct their errors; we must be patient with them." True restoration could only come with the passage of time: "We must give them time to understand their new position." He also left the impression that he was not opposed to enfranchising blacks in the abstract. Rather, it was an issue of preserving federalism that justified his refusal to require black suffrage as a prerequisite for full recognition. If he was in Tennessee, he told Stearns, "I should try to introduce negro suffrage gradually," limiting it first to Union veterans, literate blacks, and property owners. Immediate and total enfranchisement "would breed a war of races."[45]

Perhaps the Stearns interview stayed growing skepticism among some Republicans, but Democrats could have cared less. If Republicans sought assurance in Johnson's "private views which he steadfastly refuses to embody in official action we do not object," declared the New York *World*. "Give us his official acts, and you are welcome to his private sentiments." The president presented other explanations for his decision not to impose suffrage. Slaveholders, he claimed, would manipulate the votes of their former slaves "against the vote of this poor white man." Northerners found his constitutional arguments more convincing. Still, if the president could set forth concerns about the Confederate debt, ordinances of secession, abolition, and the Thirteenth Amendment, he also could have "advised" southern whites to adopt some form of black suffrage far more forcibly than he did.[46]

Johnson took his cue from the 1865 elections in the North. Although the Republicans swept to victory in state contests, they did not press to mandate black suffrage in the South; moreover, proposals to allow blacks to vote in Connecticut, Wisconsin, and Minnesota went down to defeat. From Connecticut, James Dixon assured Johnson that "the entire Democracy are with you" and "three fourths of the Republican party, here, most heartily approve your course." He was sure that "the day of radical fanaticism is over." The defeat of the black suffrage amendment in that state had convinced the senator that the enthusiasm for enfranchising southern blacks by federal action had subsided. If Congress refused to seat southern representatives in December, the people would vote out the Republicans, "so that in the end your policy is certain to be adopted whatever the next Congress may do."[47] But it was not the issue of black suffrage that proved crucial in 1865. Northerners were far more concerned with the recalcitrant behavior of white southerners. Had the war been fought in vain? And what was Andrew Johnson going to do about it? Or would it be left to Congress to act? Would Republicans work with or against the president?

By autumn 1865, the lines of division over reconstruction policy were becoming somewhat clearer. A coalition of white southerners, Democrats, and conservative Republicans rallied behind Johnson. "It is in your power, under your views of reconstruction, to make a grand, conservative national party that shall rule every thing, *and Save every thing*," advised one Pennsylvania Democrat. Moreover, "the work can all be done" before Congress met, avoiding the "whims & caprices" of that body. "All the conservative element of the country will enter actively upon an open support of the Government," concluded one Louisianan. "There is a magnetic attraction or affinity between Democrats, which though parted by circumstances for a time will reunite them again," commented an old associate, who added that Johnson's "truest and best friends in the future . . . will be found in the old Democratic party." Before long Montgomery Blair argued that "the Democracy if they are true to their own principles must sustain Andrew Johnson." Over the summer Blair wooed Democratic leaders to support Johnson, promising that an alliance of white southerners and northern Democrats would restore the Democracy to majority status. Invoking the magic name, the former postmaster general observed, "The President really is a democrat of the Jackson school." Ohio Democratic gubernatorial candidate George W. Morgan assured the president "that in the coming congress, your most earnest support will be from the democracy and the conservative element of the republican party."[48]

The exact outlines of this coalition remained in doubt. Although Johnson welcomed the support of Democrats, he was in no hurry to declare himself one. Some of his closest advisers, led by Seward, had always battled Democrats. Rather than revitalize his old party, Johnson hoped to forge a new conservative majority, pledged to the Union and the Constitution, excluding unrepentant secessionists and Copperheads (antiwar Democrats) as well as advocates of far-reaching changes in the South, including black suffrage and the confiscation and redistribution of planter property—which was a way of claiming that he stood with the centrist mainstream of white Americans. There was a real chance for this realignment to succeed—if Johnson could secure the readmission of the southern states on his terms. Once they "resume their proper place in the Union, . . . restoration is accomplished."[49]

Many observers looked to Johnson to instigate a "revolution of parties," as the New York *Herald* put it, by uniting moderates of both parties against extremists in the North and South. Others mocked the idea. "Johnson is trying to ride two horses and he probably means to join the party which finally keeps him uppermost," observed Democratic leader S. L. M. Barlow of New York, dismissing stories that the president intended to form his own organization. "Johnson is insane enough to suppose that he can build up a personal party in the South as well as in the North," he remarked, "which shall embrace the conservative elements of all the old factions and that thus he can rid himself of the necessity of an alliance with the democratic party proper."[50]

Several Radical Republicans were already bracing for a battle. Sumner asked Johnson to "suspend" his policy, for "it has failed to obtain any reasonable guarantees for that security in the future which is essential to peace & reconciliation." Others were also disappointed. A Pennsylvanian who had lost two sons in the war told the president that he was alarmed "by the tendency of your administration to fritter away much of what, by our blood and treasure, has been won." One Georgia freedman reminded the chief executive that "while southern people was carrying on an awful rebellion the colored people was bleeding and dying for the Union. While the southern people was trying to break the constitution the colored people was for the union. We have done all we can. We now look to you for help."[51]

Only the position of centrist Republicans remained in doubt. Many of them desired to support the president but not the results of his program. Johnson's claims that his policy was "experimental" rescued them from making a difficult choice. Nevertheless, they were concerned about what they heard about affairs in the South. "How shall we perpetuate our victory and make its fruits apparent?' queried one Wisconsin newspaper. "What changes shall be made in the political and social organization of the constituent parts of the government, so as to avoid future quarrels? What shall be done with the four millions of people who have been made free by the operation of the war?" Newspaper editor Joseph Medill warned Johnson of the costs of parting with the Republicans. "They Control 20 states and both branches of Congress. Four fifths of the soldiers sympathize with them. Can you afford to quarrel with these two millions of voters?" While Johnson might "inflict great injury on the union cause," he could not break up the party. "For God sake move cautiously and carefully. . . . Better stick close to old friends who carried you into the White House than to exchange them for Copperheads & rebels who will garrote you after using you."[52]

Johnson's efforts to justify his policy bought him time with northerners, especially those Republicans anxious to work with the new president. He presented himself as reasonable, flexible, and willing to adjust to circumstances. But success in the short term came at a high price in the long term. Once Johnson became more explicit he would lose support; his former allies, feeling betrayed, would attack him for misleading them, thus inhibiting efforts at future compromises. He was far less successful in communicating northern attitudes toward the South, failing to convey what northerners expected from southerners and their reactions to news about southern conditions and behavior. Perhaps he had deluded himself into believing that most northern whites supported his course. Yet the success of his policy depended upon white southerners' reaction to defeat and the minimalist terms of reunion imposed upon them and, in turn, on how northerners interpreted that reaction.

Realizing this, Johnson worried that northerners would find southern behavior unacceptable. Again and again he warned southerners that the rest of the nation was scrutinizing them carefully; he reportedly grumbled that "foolish Georgians were hindering him in the carrying out of his plans a good deal more than the worst of the northern radicals." His insistence on at least the appearance of voluntarism allowed southern whites to define the new order more narrowly than he would have liked. That the president shared many of the assumptions of this white supremacist order cannot be denied, but even he was bothered by some of its more extreme and violent manifestations, if for no other reason than because they jeopardized the acceptability of his plan in the North. As one observer told him, southern whites had "*cunningly*" thrown "the *odium* of every distasteful measure upon you" while "still not coming up to the requisitions." William W. Holden regretted "that in some instances your liberality and self-sacrificing disposition have not been responded to as they should have been."[53]

Johnson's actions suggested his displeasure. He maintained the provisional governors in office after governors had been elected in several states; federal soldiers remained on occupation duty. "The admission of members into the present Congress is a question to be determined by the respective houses," he told one South Carolina delegate. If the southern states elected "members who are unmistakably union in practice and sentiment and so amend their constitutions and pass laws in regard to emancipation and freedmen which will give them proper protection," he believed that "the basis for opposition will be substantially removed." But when Benjamin Perry pointed out that in South Carolina it would be nearly impossible to field a congressional slate if candidates had to take the ironclad oath, the president waffled.

Elsewhere Johnson was more explicit. He instructed Georgia's provisional governor, James Johnson, not to issue certificates of election to the congressmen-elect until it was clear whether they could take the ironclad oath. The election of former Confederate vice president Alexander H. Stephens to the Senate, he warned, would be "exceedingly impolitic. . . . There seems in many of the elections something like defiance, which is all out of place at this time." He told Perry that he hoped South Carolina would "adopt a code in reference to free persons of color that will be acceptable to the country at the same time doing justice to the white and colored population." Senator Jacob Howard of Michigan observed that the president's "dispatches & notes indicate his distrust of the experiment, & his resolution to be more rigid & exacting."[54] Yet these warnings proved insufficient to alert white southerners to northern impressions and expectations. Many southern whites believed Johnson would fight for them even as they cut from under him the ground on which he preferred to stand—that of a South willing to comply with certain expectations to rejoin the Union.

The clearest sign of such misunderstanding was the composition of the congressional delegations that white southerners chose to send to Washington in 1865. Several Confederate generals won election; so did Stephens in early 1866, despite Johnson's warning. That several of those elected were barred from serving because they could not take the ironclad oath made little impression on voters. Of the seven governors elected that fall, only one (J. Madison Wells of Louisiana, a state not covered by Johnson's proclamations) could have taken the ironclad oath—and Wells had been part of the state government set up in 1864 under Lincoln's watchful eye. Yet Johnson also sent mixed signals. When Mississippians elected General Benjamin Humphreys as their new governor, the president quickly pardoned him so that he could take office. One southern unionist warned that by restoring to power "a man whose hands are red with the blood of Union men," Johnson would "encourage all the late rebellious States to do the same thing, and the true Union men will every where be crushed and the rebel will be king of old."[55]

The president received enough letters insisting upon the persistence of southern disloyalty to make most readers doubt that conciliation had fostered true loyalty. One Georgian, complaining that not one of the state's delegation to the next Congress could take the oath of office, wondered how Johnson would respond. "Do you intend for men who are not citizens of the U.S.—and men who have declared that they will never take your amnesty oath, come forward to the polls & vote for members of Congress & elect them to seats in the National Congress, in defiance of your known restoration policy?" But most southern whites maintained that they had done what they could. Perry told Johnson that South Carolina's whites were "disposed to be faithful and loyal. . . . They have been disposed to do every thing required of them, and now they ask to be relieved of military rule."[56]

Johnson confronted a dangerous dilemma. He could admit that his "experiment," the product of hastiness and an eagerness to start the process of restoration as early as possible, had not succeeded in regenerating true loyalty and an acceptance of defeat and its consequences, and offer Congress an opportunity to propose new terms in cooperation with the chief executive. That, however, might fuel renewed support for black suffrage and confiscation and redistribution of land. Or he could decide to overlook or minimize southern behavior and portray his policy as a success and seek congressional acceptance if not approval of his course, abandoning the specious pretense that it was simply an "experiment." That risked conflict with Congress, for dissatisified Republicans might seek to impose new terms independently of the president. Either way, he would begin to whittle away at the ambiguity of his policy; as its parameters became clearer, support for it would erode. "President Johnson founds his practical policy upon the presumption that the South is fit to be trusted," observed the supportive New York *Times*. "His radical opponents found theirs upon the presumption that the South is unfit to be trusted." How southern whites behaved in the summer and fall of 1865 suggested who was justified in their presumption.[57]

Between April 15, 1865, and the meeting of Congress in December, Johnson's behavior and decisions gave rise to various interpretations of his intentions and goals. However, when Congress convened, he would have to share his views in his annual message. It looked as if he could no longer rely on ambiguity to retain support from different groups with different agendas. The New York *World* hoped the message would resolve "the present unnatural state of

things, in which men holding the most conflicting views on the most fundamental questions, are alike courting and claiming the President." Instead, it
merely prolonged the suspense.[58]

"It has been my steadfast object to escape from the sway of momentary
passions, and to derive a healing policy from the fundamental and unchang-
ing principles of the Constitution," Johnson declared, presenting his actions
as the product of a noble quest for peace and reunion. Secession was "null
and void"; the functions of the rebellious states were "suspended, but not
destroyed." He had worked toward restoring civil rule throughout the South.
"I know fully well that this policy is attended with some risk; that for its success it requires at least the acquiescence of the States which it concerns," he
admitted. "But it is a risk that must be taken," he added, and "in the choice of
difficulties, it is the smallest risk." Otherwise reconciliation would be a fraud.[59]

Johnson then turned to the questions raised by emancipation. Reiterating
his insistence that the question of suffrage was to be settled by the states, he
added that to have imposed it would have been unwarranted and unconstitutional. Eventually blacks might well "receive the kindliest usage from some of
those on whom they have heretofore most closely depended," but "good faith
requires the security of the freedmen in their liberty and their property, their
right to labor, and their right to claim the just return of their labor." Once
more he referred to a biracial society as an "experiment," urging people "to
avoid hasty assumptions of any natural impossibility for the two races to live
side by side, in a state of mutual benefit and good will." A careful reading of
this passage suggests that Johnson had no faith that the experiment would
succeed: he merely wished to make sure that its failure could not be "attribut-
able to any denial of justice." Having shorn the Freedmen's Bureau of the
power to redistribute confiscated property, he had no sympathy for its endeav-
ors to promote black aspirations, suggesting just how limited his commitment
to black freedom was.[60]

Johnson's message kept alive the ambiguity about his policy. So did some
of his actions. He had warned Mississippi's Humphreys that something would
have to be done to protect civil rights for blacks; he appeared to make ratification of the Thirteenth Amendment a requirement for readmission. If proponents of immediate and federally mandated black suffrage were disappointed,
they were not surprised. Other Republicans, still believing that Johnson deemed
his policy an "experiment" and convinced that he was willing to work with
Congress, thought the message promising.

Johnson's eagerness to place reports of antiblack violence and intimidation
in a wider context of social readjustment in the wake of war sought to mini-

mize the impact of these gruesome incidents. In fact, the nature of the violence suggested just how bitter southern whites were about emancipation and the threat of black equality. Reports of blacks attacked and sometime murdered by whites appeared in Republican papers throughout the summer and fall of 1865, forwarded by correspondents sent south to assess the temper of the defeated region. To be sure, here and there such accounts were exaggerated if not fictional, but on the whole the substratum of truth was hard to ignore. Yet Johnson was not moved to act—except in ways that allowed whites to unleash such violence. In working to remove black soldiers from the South, not only was he looking to honor notions of white hegemony by eliminating the disturbing sight of blacks armed and acting under authority, but also he would strip southern blacks of a major source of protection. In advocating the establishment of a southern militia, he knew that armed whites would keep blacks in line while overlooking a good number of white infractions. To the president, the restoration of order meant the restoration of white supremacy.

Johnson had ample opportunity to learn about antiblack violence, most notably from the letters of Carl Schurz, who toured the South at the president's behest during the summer of 1865. Time and again the presidential envoy offered graphic descriptions of murder and mutilation. He labored to document his charges, thus countering any accusations that his reports were little more than Radical propaganda. Yet that is exactly how Johnson chose to treat them. Writing from Alabama in late August, Schurz advised Johnson to ignore a petition seeking clemency for one James T. Andrew, who had been convicted in May for the murder of a black man. "I wish to state, that but recently two negroes were hung here for killing a white man, but that no white man has yet in this State been punished for killing a negro, except Dr. Andrew"; even now Andrew was walking the streets of Montgomery. "Unless the severest punishments known to the laws be visited upon white men killing negroes," Schurz argued, "the Southern States will soon be a vast slaughter pen for the black race. . . . If such things can happen in broad daylight under the very eyes of the State Government and of the military forces of the United States, what may happen where there is no such check upon the brutal instincts of the masses? It seems to me that in such matters lenity is out of place." Judge Advocate General Joseph Holt agreed, calling the incident "a brutal, worthless murder"; best to dismiss pleas for Andrew's release that claimed he was "infirm" and praised his "kind treatment of blacks." Within two months Johnson ordered Andrew's release.[61]

It was not that Andrew Johnson did not know what was going on; he simply did not deem it important or unexpected. That he was not particularly disturbed by the reports became evident when Charles Sumner visited the White House on the eve of the opening of the 39th Congress. After several hours of verbal sparring, Sumner exploded, charging that the president had sacrificed the fruits of Union victory by failing to stop the mistreatment of blacks. Johnson would not stand for that line of argument. After all, he reminded the senator, murders and assaults happened every day in Massachusetts; would Sumner thus recommend that Massachusetts be excluded from the Union? Whatever hope Sumner had of working with the president was gone; he discovered just how much regard the president had for him when, upon leaving, he reached for his top hat, only to discover that Johnson had used it for a spittoon.[62]

As Congress embarked on its own journey through the labyrinth of southern policy, it became evident that Republicans were not ready to accept Johnson's recommendations. They refused to seat any representatives from the former Confederate states, even if the state in question was not covered under Johnson's policy and the representative could take the ironclad oath, as in the case of Tennessee's Horace Maynard. They also formed a joint committee to take testimony on southern conditions and frame legislative proposals. What exactly constituted the state of affairs in the South was indeed a matter for debate. When Charles Sumner called upon the president to turn over Schurz's report, an account filled with documentation in support of Radical contentions about the unregenerate nature of white southern behavior, Johnson decided to pair it with a much shorter letter from General in Chief Ulysses S. Grant, who had just returned from a relatively brief excursion through the south Atlantic states. Although Grant's observations were clearly centrist—he believed that it was not yet time to restore civil government and noted that racial prejudices persisted—Johnson celebrated it as a vindication of his policy. In characteristic fashion Sumner lambasted the message, but to little purpose. The ratification of the Thirteenth Amendment almost went unnoticed.[63]

Through the first month of the 39th Congress, Johnson persisted in pursuing the politics of ambiguity and misdirection. Many Republicans and most Democrats still struggled to claim him as their own: both sides demanded patronage as the best sign that the president would reward them for their support while cutting off the opposition. But Republicans also alerted Johnson of the possible costs of breaking with the party. Iowa congressman James F. Wilson informed the president that several Republicans had concluded that the president's efforts "have not proved successful to the extent required to insure the future peace, safety and prosperity of the country." It was now Congress's turn to devise "some better plan," in part through the passage of proposed constitutional amendments designed to "furnish ample guarantees for the future." Wilson beseeched Johnson not "to interfere with and influence" congressional deliberations "by the distribution of patronage or in any other way," warning that "if you are disposed to interfere with Congress, by patronage or otherwise, and force your peculiar ideas and plans upon Congress and the country, you will meet with serious opposition by those that are now the friends of your administration, and desire sincerely to make it successful." Johnson replied that he did not desire a confrontation with Congress. Reiterating his belief in the wisdom of his policy, he "seemed to be fully persuaded of its present and future success."[64]

Congressional Republicans and General Grant were not so sure. In January 1866, reports of antiblack violence and intimidation and the black codes moved Illinois senator Lyman Trumbull to use the Judiciary Committee to frame bills to protect black civil rights and extend the life and expand the scope of the Freedmen's Bureau. At the same time Grant issued orders protecting blacks from being selectively prosecuted and punished by courts because of their race and told Johnson that it was not yet time to withdraw federal forces. None of these measures explicitly challenged the president's policy, nor did the president countermand Grant's directive. Trumbull looked to cooperate with the president. Surely, he thought, Johnson would have no problem extending the existence of the Bureau and clarifying some of its functions, including the distribution of public land to the freedpeople and jurisdiction over cases affected by the black codes. Meanwhile, the Joint Committee on Reconstruction struggled to frame another constitutional amendment to cover issues of representation in Congress, civil rights, and other matters. But by February it was clear that all was not well. Not everyone wanted to work with Johnson. "There are a few who are determined to have a quarrel with the President," Representative Henry Dawes, a Massachusetts Republican, noted, "and he is not disposed to disappoint them."[65]

Johnson warmed to the challenge. Meeting with black leaders, including Frederick Douglass, on February 7, he launched into a heated and lengthy discourse to prove that he knew what was best for black people, and that did not include the ballot. If anything, he insisted, he had been enslaved by his own slaves, who remained a burden on him; he claimed that poor whites' resentment towards slaves as well as masters promised violence. He would not favor former slaves over such people (actually, no one had asked him to do so); he would not ignite a war of races by imposing black suffrage on the South.

Any change would have to come from the "people"—by which he meant those who could already vote. Douglass tried to argue with him, to no avail. After the delegation departed, Johnson snapped, "Those d----d sons of b-----s thought they had me in a trap! I know that d----d Douglass; he's just like any other nigger, and he would sooner cut a white man's throat than not." The contrast with Lincoln's favorable impression of Douglass could not have been more marked. Henry J. Raymond, editor of the New York *Times* and one of Johnson's Republican supporters, tried to limit the damage by reporting that the president still considered himself a member of the Union party. Meanwhile, Johnson gathered information on the Freedmen's Bureau adverse to Trumbull's bill and began to suggest that "as we swing around the circle of the Union," one could find people in the North as well as the South who intended to destroy the government—an implied reference to his Republican foes. Ignoring a report from Grant that revealed the extent of interracial violence, he pressed the general to allow a Richmond newspaper editor who had criticized federal occupation forces to resume publishing after the editor promised to support the administration.[66]

On February 19, 1866, Andrew Johnson vetoed the Freedmen's Bureau Bill. Asserting that he possessed "the strongest desire to secure the freedmen the full enjoyment of their freedom and property," he claimed that until the present bureau expired there was no need for such legislation. Several of the propositions contained in the bill, including provisions to support refugees and freedmen and confiscate and redistribute land, transcended the powers of the government. One might disagree with these contentions, but Johnson couched his arguments in calm, reasonable language. Other claims were much more open to question. He believed that the freedmen could take care of themselves and that the present civil court system was sufficient to offer protection, in the face of evidence that blacks needed protection from violence and that the civil courts and state laws were stacked against them. Even less compelling was his assertion that the legislation was unwise because the ex-Confederate states were not yet represented in Congress, especially when one remembered the composition of the proposed delegations. The dispassionate tone of the veto was in marked contrast to some of Johnson's private ramblings, including one particularly bizarre notion that Congress would try to unseat him by proclaiming that Tennessee was not in the Union. He had forgone the opportunity to reject the bill on narrower grounds, instead treating Congress to a portrayal of conditions in the South that was at variance with what many Republicans believed.[67]

"Mr. Johnson, had he chosen, could have so vetoed that measure as to cause hardly a ripple on the surface of affairs," commented one newspaper. Instead, he provoked criticism. Trumbull, surprised and upset, pointed to instances of executive action that belied claims of a state of peace. If the war was truly over, then why were troops still stationed throughout the South, administering justice, censoring newspapers, and preserving order? Johnson had imposed conditions on the southern states, although he had no constitutional prerogative to do so; certainly Congress had at least as much right to do the same.[68]

Republican strength in the House was sufficient to override the veto. In the Senate, however, several Republicans had qualms about the constitutionality of the bill. Eight of them sustained the president, and the override fell short of the required two-thirds majority by a vote of 30–18. Far more explosive was a speech Johnson delivered to a crowd of supporters outside the White House three days later. Inspired by the moment—it was Washington's birthday—he launched into a long discourse on Washington and Jackson as great defenders of the Union, then placed himself alongside them. He pledged to battle the opponents of sectional reconciliation; prodded by the crowd, he identified Stevens, Sumner, and Wendell Phillips as committed to the destruction of the Union. He treated the audience to a recounting of his political rise and beliefs that contained faint echoes of his embarrassing exhibition when he became vice president nearly a year before. This time, however, he was sober.[69]

Johnson's veto disappointed moderate Republicans, who thought the president had betrayed them and thus forfeited an opportunity to work together; his intemperate remarks shocked them. They rejected his arguments denying Congress the right to impose conditions prior to readmission—after all, he had done so himself. "There need to have been no conflict between Congress and the President," commented Supreme Court associate justice David Davis. "But he cannot be driven and is naturally very combative and don't see clearly that as President he should not talk as he used to in a canvass in Tennessee. . . . If he had vetoed the Freedmen's Bureau bill and said nothing . . . and then quit making speeches, he would have been pretty strong—The great trouble at the present time is the *distrust* between the President and Congress." Still, many Republicans, reluctant to break with Johnson, urged their colleagues to give cooperation another chance. Senator John Sherman of Ohio reminded listeners that most northern states had yet to adopt black suffrage and that Johnson's plan resembled the measures outlined in the Wade-Davis Bill of 1864. Governor Jacob D. Cox of Ohio emerged from a White House meeting convinced that Johnson would support a measure to protect blacks' civil rights. So did the author of the Civil Rights Bill, Lyman Trumbull, who did all he could to ensure that the president would not object to the measure.[70]

In mid-March both houses passed Trumbull's bill as amended to narrow its scope in an effort to satisfy some constitutional concerns. Declaring that every person born in the United States (except for Native Americans, who were not taxed) was a citizen of the United States, it offered a definition of basic civil rights that came with that status, concerning primarily the ability to conduct economic transactions, commence litigation, and testify in court. Each citizen was entitled to "the full and equal benefit of the laws" and should "be subject to like punishment, pains, and penalties"—a statement aimed at overturning the black codes. Violation of this principle was judged a misdemeanor; the act authorized federal authorities to arrest, try, and punish violators when state courts failed to act. Other clauses shielded federal personnel from being sued for acts committed in compliance with federal legislation by removing those cases to federal courts and established the machinery of implementation. The bill said nothing about political rights or suffrage; although it was sparked by events in the South, it applied to the entire republic. So long as a state recognized the equal rights of all citizens in legislation and in prosecuting violators of civil rights, the federal government would remain on the sidelines. At best the bill offered a rather limited alteration in federal relations. As Trumbull argued, "It will have no operation in any State where the laws are equal, where all persons have the same civil rights without regard to color or race."[71]

Here was the president's chance to isolate the Radicals by forging an agreement with moderate Republicans. If Radicals—Sumner, Stevens, Schurz, and Chase—had dominated the correspondence the president received from Republicans in 1865, moderates filled his appointment book during these four critical months of the 39th Congress. Trumbull and William Pitt Fessenden, whose distaste for Sumner was well known, visited Johnson often. Fessenden believed that the majority of the members of the joint committee were committed to guaranteeing the security of blacks and white unionists but sought to avoid a conflict with Johnson "which would only result in unmixed evil." He and Trumbull were determined to forge a solution that would satisfy the president as well as a majority in Congress. Nor was the bill under discussion a particularly extreme measure; even Johnson's Senate supporters Doolittle and Dixon saw it as an unexceptional measure. Cox stressed the conservative nature of the bill to the president, arguing that if southern whites behaved, it would become "practically a dead letter."[72]

For several days it looked as if Johnson would sign the bill. A March 21 editorial in the administration's organ, the Washington *National Intelligencer,* suggested otherwise. "Until today I was satisfied the President intended to act within the Union party," Sherman grumbled. "In that view I have actively and earnestly at some risk of being misunderstood urged trust and confidence in him." Should the president veto the civil rights bill and fail to support Republican candidates, he would go too far. "The safety of our party & country consists in controlling the Executive authority until the Southern states agree to conditions. With the President and copperheads acting in concert with the Rebels I don't know what will become of the country."[73]

Johnson chose to pass up an opportunity to divide Republicans. Although he often lumped together most Republicans under the label of radical, he was well aware of divisions within Republican ranks. He counted upon the desire for reunion and the resentment of racism to carry his point. Once more he had misled Republicans willing to work with him; much of what was to follow reflected those Republicans' bitter sense of betrayal. Seward unsuccessfully urged him to tone down his message to leave room open for compromise and to build support for the administration; Johnson's message, issued March 27, 1866, cited broad constitutional concerns. The president objected to making blacks citizens; he opposed efforts to bar discriminatory legislation (specifically raising the specter of interracial marriage); he claimed that the bill violated the principles of federalism and would "resuscitate the spirit of rebellion." Race was never far from his mind. The bill "established for the security of the colored race safeguards which go infinitely beyond any that the General Government has ever provided for the white race. In fact, the distinction of race and color is, by the bill, made to operate in favor of the colored and against the white race." It was not simply black suffrage that Johnson saw as extreme—black equality in any form was a radical measure. To admit federal responsibility to protect black equality on any level opened the door to revolution and disorder.[74]

Johnson was well aware of the political consequences of his action. Many Republicans had warned him that a veto would destroy any real hope of cooperation. Angry moderates believed the president had deceived them. Radicals cheered, for Johnson's messages had helped unite Republicans against a common enemy. As Dawes ruefully observed, Johnson "is fool enough, or wicked enough . . . to furnish them with material fuel for the flame, depriving every friend he has of the least ground upon which to stand and defend him."[75] Johnson had become a bridge burner, not a bridge builder.

Cutting deals was not foreign to Johnson's nature, but he preferred to portray Reconstruction as a debate not over policy but principle. "My convictions in politics are things that I cannot change to suit the expediencies of this or any other moment," he once explained. "They have grown with my growth, they have strengthened with my strength, and they are to me only less sacred, and as much to be preserved, as my religious faith." His tendency to personalize conflict proved difficult to mitigate, while his inflammatory and at times sacrilegious rhetoric exacerbated existing tensions beyond the point of no return. Moreover, he chose rather poor terrain upon which to commence his battle for realignment. In vetoing the Freedmen's Bureau, he was able to exploit Republican divisions, garnering just enough defections to render an override impossible. In vetoing the Civil Rights Bill, however, he had assailed not merely the Radical faction of the Republican party but its main body on an issue that united, not divided, most Republicans.[76]

As Senate Republicans began counting noses to see if they could override the veto, Johnson pushed matters still further on April 2, 1866, by declaring the war virtually at an end throughout the South except for Texas. If that was the case, there could be no justification for the exercise of military authority in the occupied South. It was no accident that the declaration appeared as news of the Supreme Court's ruling in a case involving the jurisdiction of military commissions in Indiana during the war, *Ex parte Milligan,* leaked to the White House. Although the Court would not issue opinions until December, its decision to declare unconstitutional the military commission in Indiana on the grounds that a state of war did not exist there encouraged Johnson to believe that the same would hold true for the South. He was slow to act on this understanding and did not immediately withdraw what military forces remained in the South. But in unilaterally declaring the war at an end, he had provoked Congress yet again.[77]

Republicans had taken enough. On April 6, the Senate overrode the Civil Rights Bill veto; the House followed suit three days later, on the first anniversary of the surrender at Appomattox. It was the first time Congress had overturned a veto of significant legislation. But Johnson stood firm. After all, he told a newspaper reporter for the London *Times,* he knew the character and capabilities of blacks. The South, he believed, "would treat the negro with greater kindness than the North if it were let alone and not exasperated"; the Freedmen's Bureau was "little better than another form of slavery." He claimed that he supported civil rights for blacks, dissenting only in the way that the Civil Rights Act proposed to protect those rights.[78]

Johnson chose to confront Congress head-on. Vetoes might not keep Congress in check, but their ever-looming presence forced congressional Republicans to seek common ground and complicated the legislative process. In administering the laws, he could act in ways to defeat the purposes of their framers, all the while claiming that he was just doing his job. Rigid and static notions of constitutionalism, morality, and principle—all uttered in a rhetoric merging elements of populism, religious fervor, and stump speech combativeness—became his chief mode of expression. The growth of opposition to his administration only fueled his defiance. Cooperation with Congress was neither necessary nor desirable. Instead, the president began building up his own party of sober conservatives, men who rejected both extremes as dangerous to the preservation of constitutional liberty and government. He hoped to draw from former Whigs as well as Democrats, North and South, in forging this unionist movement: the price would be acquiescence in southern behavior. Wooing the northern electorate—essential if Johnson was to strike a blow at Republican power in Congress—provided its own challenges, for the president hoped to draw on the traditional Democratic appeals to limited federal power, constitutional liberty, and negrophobia without identifying himself with those Democrats who had pushed for a peaceful settlement of the sectional crisis or even a recognition of Confederate independence. As the New York *World* observed, Johnson sought to perform "the double work of a disintegrator and a reorganizer."[79]

Johnson's decisions during his first year in office fundamentally shaped the course of postwar reconstruction. His tolerance of southern intransigence fueled Republican rhetoric about an "unregenerate South," moving people toward the Radical position. His behavior gave Republicans a common enemy, enhancing party unity. But his use of the veto ensured that Republican reconstruction in the end would still follow fairly moderate contours, since such legislation, in order to withstand the expected veto, would have to please a large number of Republicans. Increasingly their concern to control the president outstripped their desire to establish a sound and lasting foundation for reconstruction in the South. Perhaps Johnson knew what he was doing after all.

4

"DAMN THEM!"

In vetoing the Civil Rights Bill of 1866, Andrew Johnson established the basis for his future dealings with the Republican-controlled Congress. He would rely not on forging alliances and crafting coalitions with mainsteam Republican members of that body but on the institutional prerogatives of his office. Thus the dynamic of reconstruction policy making for the remainder of the Johnson years was now well delineated. Republicans would strive to forge veto-proof supermajorities for legislative initiatives, while the Democratic minority and Johnson looked for opportunities to obstruct that process. When it became apparent that the president's willingness to block legislative intent extended beyond the veto process to the implementation of new laws, congressional Republicans found ways to handcuff executive powers. Eventually, this objective (and not that of establishing a sound foundation for a lasting reconstruction based upon Republican principles) came to dominate the legislative process.

Johnson's own duplicitous behavior had much to do with fostering this situation, as the case of Lyman Trumbull suggested. The senator from Illinois thought that he had done all he could to secure the president's approval of legislation. Misreading Johnson's sentiments, he persisted in believing that "there is really nothing" in the Republican agenda "which he hasn't approved one time or another." That the handiwork of moderate Republicans was too radical for Johnson to swallow—the president persisted in labeling all of his foes "Radicals"—was lost on Trumbull. However, he no longer sought to work with the chief executive. "I have no faith in his good intentions," he told his wife. "How could I after he so deceived me about the Civil Rights bill and the Freedmen's Bureau bill?" Mistrust made bargaining impossible for Republicans; Johnson had no desire to compromise.[1]

Each side looked for some way to end this deadlock. Johnson might strengthen his hand (and weaken his opposition) with a more systematic use of the patronage power, but in doing so he intensified political polarization without materially affecting the balance of power. Moreover, the Senate had to ratify many of his more important choices, limiting how far he could go. The president could look to the Supreme Court for decisions that would validate his claim that congressional initiatives trampled constitutional restraints on federal action, but that process could prove time-consuming and depended on the nature of the specific cases that contained challenges to Republican mandates. He deemed it best, therefore, to attack Congress head-on, looking to the elections of 1866 as a chance to erode Republican margins in both houses. It would not be easy. Although each member of the House of Representatives faced reelection, the Republicans enjoyed a rather comfortable majority. The extent of turnover in the Senate was inherently limited, with approximately a third of the seats up for reelection, but the nature of the Republican majority in the upper house and several special circumstances offered opportunities to make headway. That Johnson was not above striking bargains to shore up his position in the Senate became apparent in May when he vetoed a bill providing for Colorado's statehood only after failing to persuade its two senators-elect to support the administration on Reconstruction.[2]

Johnson's strategy had its own problems. It was unlikely that Congress would soon reseat congressional delegations from the former Confederate states, especially if claimants did not conform to the Republican notion of a rehabilitated southerner. This situation forced the president to concentrate on those states already represented in Congress. The border states offered promising ground for a Democratic resurgence, for Republicans had struggled long and hard to secure slim majorities in an environment shaped by wartime contingencies. Elsewhere, however, the Republican party remained strong, especially in New England, where only Connecticut offered prospects for Democratic success. Here and there Johnson might pick off a district or two, chipping away at Republican numbers, but it would take a great deal of work to win enough seats to create a minority large enough to sustain presidential vetoes. He might fare better in the Senate. Fifteen seats—ten held by Republicans, four held by Democrats or conservative Republicans, and a vacancy from New Jersey—were to be filled in the normal course of things, and Nebraska would elect its first senators. Of these seats, Democrats and their National Union allies had a reasonable chance to win in eight contests (New York, New Jersey, Maryland, Kentucky, California, Kansas, and both Nebraska seats) with some cause for hope in three more (Pennsylvania, Ohio, and Indiana). It might not be possible to eliminate the Republican majority, but a good showing at the polls could destroy Republican dreams of a veto-proof supermajority, leaving the president free to obstruct at will.

Republicans were well aware of the importance of the 1866 elections. Victory was not enough: an overwhelming triumph was essential. They sought to counter or to circumvent Johnson's authority and ability to block their initiatives. One way was through resorting to a constitutional amendment as a way to set forth certain reconstruction principles. Amendments were not subject to veto; at best the president could try to meddle in the ratification process by working to secure antiamendment majorities in state legislatures, again affirming the importance of the 1866 contests.

The process of framing the amendment offered another opportunity for Republicans to struggle with each other on what course to pursue. Radical notions of land redistribution and guarantees of black suffrage quickly faded in the face of moderate opposition. The result, as presented by the Joint Committee on Reconstruction and refined in debate, defined the meaning of national citizenship, placing in the Constitution the protections sought in the Civil Rights Law; set forth the allocation of seats in the House of Representatives in such a fashion as to reduce the number of seats for states who denied suffrage to any class of adult male citizens; disqualified for federal and state office anyone who had sided with the Confederacy after taking an oath committing him "to support the Constitution of the United States," subject to congressional action to remove such disability; and repudiating the Confederate war debt.

The amendment was clearly a moderate measure. No one could expect the United States to honor the Confederate war debt (Johnson's own program said as much); the number of white southerners disqualified from holding state or federal offices was small if select; and the adjustment in representation simply prohibited states from claiming an increased representation in Congress based on emancipation without enlarging the electorate with black votes. It did not mandate black suffrage, it recognized that states determined suffrage qualifications, and nothing in it could be interpreted as offering blacks preferential treatment. It simply looked to restore civil government on terms somewhat different from those offered by Johnson the previous year; however, it covered those states that had devised wartime regimes. Unable to do anything to thwart the passage of the amendment, the president offered some disparaging observations as he submitted it to the states for ratification.[3]

In deciding not to work with Congress, Johnson overlooked the extent to which the Fourteenth Amendment still honored notions of self-government in the South. It did not enfranchise blacks; it did not promise reforms beyond the definition of civil rights that would fall under federal protection if states failed to act. Southern whites could still do much to maintain racial supremacy. "The very great majority of these men who took part in the rebellion care but little about the representation of their State in Congress if they can but retain perfect control of all branches of the State government," observed one Florida Republican. To assume that courts "under the control of men who have perjured themselves and tried to kill men for loving their country for four years" would now deliver justice was naive. Perhaps they could not pass legislation that on its face was discriminatory: "Still you know they can in ten thousand ways so administer the laws as to make them very oppressive to union men and negroes."[4]

These clashes with Congress reminded the president of the importance of making inroads into Republican congressional strength. It would not do, he realized, simply to return to the Democratic party, for that would place him alongside the Copppperheads, whose unionism had been rendered suspect by their opposition to the war. Rather, he wanted to create a new party, positioned between those Democrats and those Republicans committed to congressional reconstruction. In terms relative to the political spectrum, he preferred a party of the center, although its views on race and federalism leaned toward Democratic principles. Borrowing from the Union party nomenclature employed by Republicans in 1864 to attract support for the Lincoln administration, Johnson and his confidants decided to christen it "the National Union movement." On June 25 a call went out for delegates to attend a gathering in Philadelphia on August 14. Among the signers were conservative Republican senators Doolittle and Cowan; two more conservative Republicans, Norton and Dixon, endorsed it, as did their Democratic colleagues, Thomas Hendricks of Indiana and James Nesmith of Oregon. Reading the announcement for what it was, congressional Republicans denounced the movement as nothing more than a stalking-horse for the revival of Democratic prospects and promised to read out of the party any Republicans who dallied with it.[5]

Realizing Johnson's vision of a party of the center proved problematic. Conservative Republicans still mistrusted Democrats; Democrats saw no reason to abandon their party, considering the movement primarily as a way to erode Republican strength. Nor was it clear what sort of clout conservative Republicans exercised with the electorate. Welles, who harbored great suspicions about Seward and his longtime adviser, Thurlow Weed, admitted, "The proposed convention has no basis in principles. It will be denounced as a mere union with Rebels."[6]

The fate of legislative initiatives throughout the remainder of the first session of the 39th Congress gave observers and participants alike a glimpse of what was ahead. No sooner had the Civil Rights Act become law than Republicans revived efforts to pass a new Freedmen's Bureau bill. Stripped of several provisions concerning land redistribution (an issue supposedly addressed by a Southern Homestead bill, an act not vetoed by Johnson), the bill still sought to resolve questions arising from previous federal policies concerning land in South Carolina and Georgia; however, it concentrated on providing protection and educational opportunities for the freedpeople, the former through the use of military commissions to act in place of civil courts. On July 16, Johnson vetoed the bill, arguing that the present bureau would remain in operation into 1867, giving Congress plenty of time to frame additional measures if necessary. Congress immediately overrode the veto.

Within a week Congress and the president clashed again. Tennessee moved quickly to ratify the Fourteenth Amendment. No qualms about federal interference in state affairs had prevented Johnson from attempting to prevent a quorum in the state legislature, although these efforts went for naught. Straightaway Republicans, despite some Radical reservations, pressed for the immediate and full restoration of the state's representation in Congress. Johnson decided not to veto the resulting joint resolution, although he disavowed portions of the preamble that set forth Republicans' understanding of Congress's role in the reconstruction process. He questioned the constitutionality of compelling ratification of a constitutional amendment as a prerequisite for the restoration of congressional representation (although he had made ratification of the Thirteenth Amendment a precondition for readmission in his plan, thus exposing the contradictory and self-serving nature of his constitutional logic) and went so far as to doubt whether Tennessee had in fact ratified the amendment. Republicans buried the response by referring it to committee.[7]

Undeterred, the president pressed ahead with the National Union movement and decided to put it to good use in reconstituting his cabinet. He had good reason to doubt the loyalty of four of its members: Stanton, James Speed (attorney general), William Dennison (postmaster general), and James Harlan (secretary of the interior). In May he had asked them to declare whether they preferred his plan or that outlined by the Joint Committee on Reconstruction's report. Stanton and Harlan had expressed reservations about administration policy, but in such an indirect fashion that Johnson did not confront them. As June drew to a close, he prodded Doolittle to write to each cabinet member to secure endorsements for the upcoming National Union convention. Seward, Welles, and Secretary of the Treasury Hugh McCulloch complied immediately. Dennison resigned his post on July 11, specifically citing differences over the Fourteenth Amendment and the National Union movement; Speed made public his resignation on July 15; Harlan followed suit on July 27. In their places Johnson appointed Alexander Randall of Wisconsin, a supporter of the National Union movement; Henry Stanbery of Ohio; and Illinois's Orville H. Browning, another booster of the conservative coalition. None of these appointments did much to strengthen the president politically, although Stanbery would prove an able adviser.

Stanton proved far more troublesome. Better, he thought, to remain in the cabinet than to surrender his critical post. Johnson waffled. He distrusted Stanton, yet he failed to shove him out of the way, much to the astonishment of his supporters, who highlighted it as an example of the president's unwillingness to exert himself. The schism between the two men widened as the administration responded to the escalation of political violence in the South. In May a riot in Memphis targeted blacks who had just left military service and their families. Forty-six blacks (and two whites) perished in the ensuing violence, and a number of black homes, churches, and schools were pillaged or destroyed. Several civil officials were among the rioters. That they justified their action by pointing to the blacks' earlier unruly behavior satisfied Johnson, who had long held that such clashes were a natural outgrowth of social readjustments to the postemancipation order. He appeared oblivious to the outrage that northerners expressed over this manifestation of "the demoniac spirit of the southern whites toward the freedmen." Nor was the president alarmed by other outbreaks over the next several months. That violence was motivated by politics as well as race became evident when on July 30 a major riot took place in New Orleans.[8]

What happened in New Orleans was a product of the collapse of Lincoln's efforts to construct a loyal state government willing to extend some measure of equality toward blacks. White conservatives took charge of the state government and New Orleans in 1865, with Johnson supporting their efforts to shore up the foundations of white supremacy. Dissatisfied Louisiana Republicans sought recourse by invoking a resolution passed by the 1864 constitutional convention that allowed its members to reconvene—a rather broad interpretation of a provision to reconvene the convention had Louisiana voters failed to ratify the 1864 constitution. With that constitution ratified, there was no need to perpetuate the existence of the convention. But politics in Louisiana during Reconstruction always partook of the strange and unsavory; as Congress had yet to recognize the new government by seating its representatives, the status of the state government was uncertain. An effort by conservatives to call a new constitutional convention in 1866 fell short when a delegation returned from a visit with Johnson convinced that it might damage the president's policy. Republicans hit upon the reconvening plan as the best way to secure a government friendly to their interests.

Johnson left it to his local supporters to handle the matter. They proposed to break up the meeting; the local military commander, Absalom Baird, advised against it, pointing out that there was nothing wrong with people assembling to discuss political questions. Whether the meeting had the authority it claimed as a constitutional convention could be settled later. Conservative leaders, including the mayor of New Orleans, disagreed. Both they and Baird wired Washington for instructions. Johnson replied that the federal military would support the actions of state authorities in dispersing the meeting through judicial action, demonstrating that he had no problem in using federal authority to bolster his supporters. Stanton failed to reply to Baird's telegram; Baird's superior, Philip H. Sheridan, chose to visit Texas.

On July 30, whites and blacks clashed outside the hall where the members of the 1864 convention were to meet. Police joined the riot, firing into the building. Baird, misinformed about the time that the meeting would start, quickly dispatched troops to the scene. By the time they arrived, 34 blacks and 4 whites had been killed; another 119 blacks and 27 whites were wounded. The ratio of blacks to whites suggested who had come looking for a fight.[9]

Johnson's reaction demonstrated that he was willing to do whatever it took to promote his policy. He deleted a crucial passage from Sheridan's initial report of the riot that characterized the whites' actions as "so unnecessary and atrocious as to compel me to say that it was murder" before releasing it to a newspaper reporter, thus distorting the thrust of the general's dispatch by making it appear that Sheridan blamed the convention supporters for what happened. Johnson agreed with Welles that the Radicals were to blame for what happened; Welles thought it was part of a deliberate conspiracy to promote black suffrage. That these supposed conspirators found ready, even eager, allies among Johnson's conservative white allies appears to have eluded the secretary's fine mind. Yet Stanton's inaction led to charges that he had deliberately suppressed the dispatch in order to facilitate the riot. One does not have to accept such dire interpretations to conclude that in this matter he was asleep at the switch.[10]

A dispassionate examination of the Memphis and New Orleans riots suggests that local authorities seized upon somewhat provocative behavior to deal brutal blows to their enemies on behalf of white supremacy. "Justice," such as it was, was not color-blind; retribution was color-specific. However, Johnson could have limited the impact of these incidents—and foiled the aims of the supposed conspirators—had he denounced the responses of local authorities as inappropriate and excessive. Instead, he revealed that his real aim was not to preserve constitutional order but a white supremacist one; his willingness to distort reports in a quest for political advantage demonstrated the true measure of the man. Republicans had a field day in arguing that Memphis and New Orleans demonstrated that the South was not peaceful, that the war spirit still lingered, and that Johnson's pronouncements about the restoration of civil rule, law, and order rang hollow.

Just over two weeks after the New Orleans riot, delegates gathered in Philadelphia to attend the first meeting of the National Union movement. During the next several days they passed resolutions critical of congressional initiatives and supportive of the president. When the meeting adjourned, a delegation traveled to Washington to present the convention's handiwork to Johnson. In typical self-deprecating fashion, the president declared that he stood before them as a fearless man, "sounding the tocsin of alarm when I deemed the citadel of liberty in danger; . . . neither the taunts nor jeers of Congress, nor of a subsidized, calumniating press, can drive me from my purpose."[11]

This was the first in a series of attacks against his foes. Just as Lincoln had taken advantage of the dedication of a cemetery at Gettysburg to set forth his principles, Johnson decided to use the opportunity of an invitation to be present at the dedication of a statue to Stephen A. Douglas in Chicago to share his sentiments with anyone who would listen. The result was a whistle-stop campaign tour throughout several northern states that came to be known as "The Swing Around the Circle," a term grounded in Johnson's own words. Along for the ride were Grant and Admiral David G. Farragut. Johnson wanted the military heroes present as silent endorsements of his plan, while Seward also thought that they would serve as excellent hostages against any efforts at sabotage by political opponents. Little did the secretary know that the president would prove most effective in sabotaging himself.

Johnson's decision to make his case to the public seemed a rather dramatic and perhaps effective way of building support. However, it was not in keeping with how Americans thought presidents should behave. They might like stump speeches, but they were not used to a president taking to the campaign trail; previous presidential tours were explicitly ceremonial and only implicitly political. Moreover, Johnson forgot that he was not in Tennessee and that he was president. Used to giving the same basic speech with suitable variations and flourishes, he forgot that newspaper accounts of his remarks would render them familiar, predictable, and stale to audiences down the line—and offer hecklers wonderful opportunities to interrupt at the appropriate moment. That Johnson, used to the give-and-take of the stump, would reply to such remarks was to be expected; that a president would exchange taunts with the people was not. Johnson had never watched his tongue; if anything, cheering crowds inspired him to explore the treacherous terrain of rhetorical excess, as his Washington's Birthday speech revealed. Just before Johnson embarked on his journey, Browning "begged" him for assurances "that no speeches should be made, except in acknowledgment of honors paid and kindnesses shown." Doolittle warned him to "say nothing which has not been carefully prepared. . . . *Our enemies, your enemies,* have never been able to get any advantage from anything *you ever wrote.* But what you have said extemporaneously, in answer to some question or interruption, has given them a handle to use against you."[12]

As the caravan made its way north to New York City at the end of August, it looked as if the president was on his good behavior. However, as the train chugged through upstate New York, observers saw the first signs of the catastrophe to come; when it pulled into Cleveland on September 3, the president and his hecklers engaged in the first of what was to become a rather predictable pattern of give-and-take. The train would stop; Johnson would emerge and commence his sermon, complete with familiar phrases; hecklers would interrupt; the president, sometimes flustered, sometimes anxious, would reply. It did not help that he invoked comparisons to Judas Iscariot and Jesus Christ; it did not help that he asked listeners why he should not hang Wendell Phillips and Thaddeus Stevens or accused the Republicans of causing the riot at New Orleans. As he once put it, "I care not for dignity."[13]

Some people wondered if the president was drunk; others speculated that perhaps he was losing his sanity. Grant, embarrassed by the whole business, privately termed the president's speeches "a national disgrace," adding, "I am disgusted at hearing a man make speeches on the way to his own funeral." Sometimes the exchanges became so heated that the train began to move before the president concluded his remarks. In all probability, the speeches changed few votes either way, but the trip raised questions about Johnson's understanding of circumstances and equipped his foes with new ammunition. It also subjected him to much ridicule, badly tarnishing the image he had of himself as the shining defender of the Constitution. It was mortifying and humiliating—except, it seems, to Johnson, who never expressed regrets about his performance.[14]

Election results in September and early October presaged a Republican land-slide. In response, Johnson contemplated removing Stanton: his supporters claimed that would energize voters. However, the president fumbled when he also conspired to send away Grant on a trip to Mexico, hoping that his replacement, William T. Sherman, would support administration policy. Realizing what was up, Grant refused to go; signs that Johnson planned to use federal military force to sustain Maryland conservatives suggested what would happen in his absence. Sherman, reluctant to become embroiled in controversy and anxious not to cross Grant, volunteered to go to Mexico in Grant's place. Eventually Johnson gave way, even retaining Stanton, although there was no good reason to do so. Nor did he make mass removals of Republican officeholders, although here and there he made changes, thus opening himself to the very attacks he had sought to avoid by refraining from a more extensive use of the patronage power to reward and punish. Patronage proved to be a rather limited weapon. Turning people out of office tended to make martyrs of them; after a while Republicans who still held office had to reassure their friends that they had not betrayed their principles for position. Moreover, patronage was most useful in influencing those who were in a position to help, including members of Congress. To distribute jobs to out-of-office Democrats or marginal Republicans had virtually no impact on his contest with Congress.[15]

It soon became apparent that Republicans would emerge victorious from the 1866 elections. The behavior of white southerners enabled Republican candidates to argue that the fruits of victory would be jeopardized if Johnson and his supporters gained enough power to block the Republicans in Congress. One needed only to look at what had happened in Memphis and New Orleans to conclude that waving the bloody shirt was no mere exercise in exaggeration. White southerners must not be allowed to gain in peace what they had been unable to secure through war. There was no need to raise the question of black suffrage; it was enough to tell voters that the fruits of military victory were at risk.

Nevertheless, the results were an overwhelming triumph for Republicans, who secured veto-proof majorities in both houses of Congress. Of the Senate seats up for election, Democrats held their own in one case (Kentucky) and even succeeded in gaining a seat in Maryland, but Republicans took away three seats from Johnson supporters (Pennsylvania, California, and Oregon), captured a vacancy previously held by another Johnson supporter (New Jersey), elected both senators from Nebraska, and otherwise held their own, strengthening their hold on the upper house. Johnson's efforts to block the seating of the Nebraska senators by vetoing the bill declaring it a state did not withstand a successful override. Republicans also built upon their majority in the House. The National Union movement collapsed. As Wendell Phillips declared at a victory rally, "Let us pray to God that the president may continue to make mistakes."[16]

In the aftermath of the elections, speculation mounted that Johnson would retreat from his opposition to the Fourteenth Amendment. A good number of Republicans were willing to readmit southern states upon their ratification of the amendment. Instead, the president urged southern legislatures to reject it. With little hesitation, they followed his lead, sacrificing the chance for southern whites to shape their own future, despite warnings by moderate Republicans, Grant, and others that rejection of the amendment would lead to more demanding terms. The president's behavior foreclosed any opportunity for compromise. "He is obstinate without being firm, self-opinionated without being capable of systematic thinking, combative and pugnacious without being courageous," observed Governor Jacob D. Cox of Ohio, who had once sought to cooperate with the president. "He is always *worse* than you expect."[17]

In light of the election results, Johnson's behavior might appear obtuse if not suicidal. But he calculated that the Fourteenth Amendment would fall short of ratification unless Republicans took measures to secure supportive state legislatures in the South—or excluded the ten remaining states from the ratification process altogether. The former would require legislation that would reshape the southern electorate either by disfranchising large numbers of whites or by enfranchising large numbers of blacks. The latter would compel Congress to provide for long-term federal supervision of affairs in the South. Johnson believed that northern voters would reject black suffrage or the punitive punishment of large numbers of former Confederates, and that they would grow impatient with the prolonging of reconstruction. Many Democrats agreed and with Johnson hoped that in framing more radical responses the Republicans would destroy themselves.[18]

These calculations, based as they were upon reasonable assumptions, were nevertheless flawed. A large number of northerners wished for some resolution to matters in the South so that they could move on to other topics on the political agenda. Nor was there much support for punishing the mass of southern whites (as opposed to southern leaders): that would render hopeless any notion of sectional reconciliation. But white northerners were not nearly as bothered by the prospect of blacks voting in the South as they were by the idea that perhaps they should be allowed to vote in all the northern states as well. They blamed Johnson and white southerners for prolonging political controversy by rejecting what seemed to be a reasonable measure, the Fourteenth Amendment. After all, had white southerners been willing to accept a reduction in political clout in terms of representation in the House of Representatives and Electoral College votes, they could have denied blacks the right to vote—for that was the deal offered by the terms of the very amendment they refused to ratify. Thus northerners could argue that they were driven to support black suffrage in the South not by choice but by necessity. Grant, who believed that it was hypocrisy to urge the enfranchisement of blacks in the South while opposing it in the North, observed, "I never could have believed that I should favor giving negroes the right to vote, but that seems to me the only solution of our difficulties."[19]

The president seized other opportunities to obstruct reconstruction. On December 17, the Supreme Court finally issued its opinion in *Ex parte Milligan*. Speaking for the majority, Justice David Davis declared, "Martial law can never exist when the courts are open, and in the proper and unobstructed exercise of their jurisdiction." This statement was enough for Johnson, who immediately started dissolving the military commissions on which Grant and the Freedmen's Bureau had relied as an alternative to civil courts that did not afford blacks justice. Nor did he neglect to exercise the veto power. He rejected a bill enfranchising blacks in the District of Columbia, despite the fact that Congress possessed the authority to determine suffrage requirements there. He opposed bills granting statehood to Nebraska and Colorado, highlighting clauses that made the ballot box color-blind. Here he enjoyed one of his few victories: the Senate failed to override the Colorado veto. Elsewhere, however, his resistance proved futile, as Congress overrode the D.C. suffrage and Nebraska statehood vetoes. Alert to the possibility of presidential obstruction down the line, Congress also revised the calendar for its successor, which would convene on the heels of the end of this Congress in March instead of the traditional December date—just so they could keep an eye on the chief executive. Johnson did not even waste a veto on the measure.[20]

Behind the scenes there were hints that the president might yet prove flexible. When several southern leaders proposed an amendment that would limit the franchise to citizens who were literate or who owned $250 worth of property (with a grandfather clause exempting current voters), Johnson endorsed it. In adopting the representation, citizenship, and war debt clauses of the Fourteenth Amendment, this proposal embodied certain critical concessions. But to moderate Republicans it did not go far enough. It was unclear exactly how many blacks would thus become eligible to vote. Republicans, who might have accepted such a proposal had it been presented a year earlier, now insisted on a broader definition of eligibility for suffrage. Nor did they concur in the proposal's elimination of the disqualification clauses in the Fourteenth Amendment. Finally, they no longer trusted Johnson. Another proposition, which involved ratification of the Fourteenth Amendment and black suffrage in exchange for the preservation of the Johnson state governments, also fell through.[21]

Most congressional Republicans were no longer willing to work with Johnson. They had been burned before. Now, with the majorities in both houses afforded them by the voters, they were determined to strike out on their own. "The people expect a bold and independent course with regard to the President," Ben Wade declared. Voters wanted Congress to limit executive power: "To this end they have armed Congress with full power to carry out the mandates of the people independent of the President and now if we fail to do it, the fault is our own."[22] This statement betrayed a shift in Republican concerns. Debates on how best to shape the postwar South in accordance with Republican principles were giving way to efforts to devise ways to handcuff the chief executive. Means were supplanting ends as the major focus of discussion. Yet the very proposals Congress considered, especially those including military supervision, provided a wedge for presidential obstruction. The best Congress could do was to restrict the president's freedom of action. In this the legislation proved only partly effective, one sign of its poorly framed provisions that left loopholes for obstruction by both the president and recalcitrant southern whites. Legislative initiatives sought to secure self-government for southern blacks as well as whites and nothing more; it would be primarily up to southerners to decide what the postwar South would look like.

The clearest example of Republican desires to control Johnson was the Tenure of Office Act. Aware that the president was at last learning to use his patronage powers to punish opponents, reward supporters, and influence the implementation of legislation, Republicans framed a bill that would require the Senate to concur in the removal of officers it had confirmed. The scope of the legislation proved problematic: what was its impact on cabinet members? Many Republicans wanted to shield Edwin M. Stanton from removal, while others backed away from such an aggressive assumption of power. Compromise wording waffled, providing that cabinet members held office "during the term of the President by whom they may have been appointed, and for one month thereafter, subject to removal by and with the advice and consent of the Senate." This confusing construction did not clarify Stanton's status. Was Johnson simply serving out Lincoln's term? Was he to be hamstrung by Lincoln's appointments? It would be just one of several instances in which congressional Republicans failed as legislative draftsmen. As Wade had opined, the fault would be their own.

Yet Johnson also botched his handling of the proposed legislation. When he discussed it in cabinet, everybody—including Stanton—doubted the bill's constitutionality. Why Stanton spoke so about an effort to protect him from Johnson remains a puzzle, although perhaps he realized that the act was deeply flawed. However, when the president seized the opportunity and asked Stanton to draft the veto message, the war secretary, pleading ill health, backed away. At that point Johnson should have removed Stanton. He had nothing to gain and much to lose by retaining him in office. Perhaps Stanton's very support of the bill was designed to prevent removal by appeasing Johnson, especially as the bill was destined to become a law in any case. Although Stanton had made clear that he did not advocate impeachment, the Tenure of Office Act, or other extreme measures, he deeply disagreed with Johnson over reconstruction. Johnson's hesitation had fateful consequences.[23]

Congress also limited the president's powers as commander in chief. Alerted by Stanton and Grant as to Johnson's efforts to displace or circumvent the general in chief, Republicans inserted clauses in the Army Appropriations Act of 1867 requiring the president to issue orders through the general in chief, who could not be transferred from headquarters at Washington without his consent. Nor could the president remove, suspend, or relieve the general in chief without the consent of the commanding general or the Senate. Violation of the legislation constituted a misdemeanor and thus an impeachable offense. Such provisions clearly narrowed Johnson's powers, but after consultation with his cabinet the president decided to forgo a veto and merely signify his dissatisfaction.[24]

The Tenure of Office Act and the clauses in the Army Appropriations Act were efforts by congressional Republicans to buttress what they thought would be the crowning achievement of the second session of the 39th Congress—a new reconstruction bill. Efforts to cultivate the consent of white southerners in some form of semivoluntary reconstruction had failed. Republicans chose to start again in an effort to establish a new foundation for the erection of southern state governments. The ten ex-Confederate states that had failed to ratify the Fourteenth Amendment were organized into five military districts, each headed by a general. The civil governments erected under presidential supervision (including the Lincoln governments) were declared provisional and placed under military supervision. Voters in each state would elect delegates to a new constitutional convention—and this time blacks would be eligible to cast ballots and be elected. However, those whites excluded from holding office under the provisions of the Fourteenth Amendment could not participate in the process. The constitutional conventions had to eliminate race as a barrier to voting; only when a state had ratified its new constitution and the Fourteenth Amendment would Congress consider admitting its representatives to their seats.

As Republicans debated, Johnson waited, impatient for the chance to strike back at what he deemed clearly unconstitutional legislation. In an interview with Charles Nordhoff, managing editor of the New York *Evening Post,* he could hardly contain himself as he "expressed the most bitter hatred of the measure in all its parts, declaring that it was nothing but anarchy and chaos, that the people of the South, poor, quiet, unoffending, harmless, were to be trodden under foot 'to protect niggers.'" Nordhoff came away convinced that Johnson was "a pig headed man, with only one idea . . . a bitter opposition to universal suffrage and a determination to secure the political ascendancy of the old Southern leaders, who, he emphasized, must in the nature of things rule the South." There was no question that he would veto the Reconstruction Act; there was also no question that congressional Republicans would override the veto. Both occurred on March 2.[25]

That a veto would prove useless in stopping the enactment of the Reconstruction Act raises the question of whether it might not have been shrewder for the president to have signed it. Several moderate Republicans made it known to Johnson through intermediaries that he could thus disarm the Radicals. But it was not in Johnson to agree to the measure. He honestly believed that it went too far; he hoped that voters, once alerted to its revolutionary nature, would reject its authors at the polls. Still, had he chosen simply to pocket the bill and let the 39th Congress expire, as several of his advisers urged, he would have forced Republicans to undergo the painful process of framing legislation all over again. That might have promoted Republican divisiveness and played upon frayed nerves; however, angry Republicans might well have used to advantage their increased majorities in the 40th Congress to pass even more demanding and rigorous requirements for reconstructing southern state governments in line with Radicals' preferences. All this was rendered moot by the president's tactless veto message, which breathed defiance instead of offering arguments on which he could persuade enough Republicans to sustain his veto. Nevertheless, his arguments were not without some merit: he scored a telling point when he pointed out that Republicans had accepted the votes of state legislatures elected under his plan when it came to the ratification of the Thirteenth Amendment. Now to declare those same state legislatures provisional was sharp practice indeed.[26]

Here and there remained loopholes for Johnson to exploit. He was empowered to name and to remove the five military district commanders, although the decision to limit commanders to the rank of major general and above limited his options. Nor had Congress provided for the initiation of the process it had outlined: the 40th Congress, which convened on March 4, quickly passed legislation providing for the registration of voters, the convening of conventions, and the ratification of the proposed state constitutions. Observers noted that the new legislation seriously reduced the role of the existing state governments in overseeing the process. The now familiar routine of veto and override followed.

The Reconstruction Act suggested much about the way many Republicans' thinking about southern policy had changed over the previous two years. Gone were notions about federally mandated confiscation and redistribution or prolonged military supervision of the defeated South. When Stevens or Sumner raised such issues, their colleagues ignored them. Instead, most Republicans embraced the paradox of using federal power to resurrect self-government though state institutions, although in a way that did much to determine the initial shape of the polity that would construct and govern those institutions. They were just as intent on determining which branch of the federal government would supervise the process as that the federal government oversee the process in the first place. They worked to minimize Johnson's ability to obstruct even as they backed away from eliminating him entirely from the process—a decision fraught with serious consequences. Such concern for process came at the cost of pondering the substance and outcome of policy. Once Radical Republicans had sought to reshape the South through direct federal action: now they had to settle for establishing the process and preconditions within which southerners would devise their new order. In their haste to construct a policy based upon the restoration of civil government in a timely fashion, moderate Republicans overlooked the possibility that without a prolonged period during which everyone in the South would come to accept the new order of things, it was not clear that any change would prove enduring.[27]

Some Republicans had wanted to go further. Rather than tie Johnson's hands, they urged his removal through the impeachment process. Attempts to do so during the second session of the 39th Congress failed. There was little basis for sustaining a charge, and the majority of Republicans believed that impeachment was unwise, unwarranted, and unnecessary. The impeachment proponents embarrassed themselves in attempting to link Johnson to the conspiracy to assassinate Lincoln or to implicate him in negotiations with Jefferson Davis. "We have very successfully and thoroughly tied [Johnson's] hands, and if we had not, we had better submit to two years of misrule . . . than subject the country, its institutions, and its credit, to the shock of an impeachment," Senator James Grimes of Iowa noted. Better, most Republicans believed, to keep an eye on the president. With that in mind, the 40th Congress adjourned at the end of March after it passed a second Reconstruction Act on March 23 detailing how military authorities would supervise southern elections. It made provisions to convene again in July.[28]

Some Radicals opined that regardless of the checks Congress had placed on presidential powers the initial Reconstruction Act was fundamentally flawed precisely because its use of military commanders meant that the president would administer the law. "As well commission a lunatic to superintend a lunatic asylum, or a thief to govern a penitentiary!" argued one newspaper. At first Johnson moved slowly, adjusting to the new political environment, aware that Congress was still in session. He followed Grant's recommendations for district commanders, with the result that of the five generals named, one (Philip Sheridan) was in clear sympathy with congressional Republicans, with two more (Daniel Sickles and John Pope) only somewhat less so. The remaining two, John M. Schofield and Edward O. C. Ord, tended to ally themselves with moderates and conservatives regarding the South. He also supported Attorney General Stanbery's decision to contest an effort by Mississippians to secure a Supreme Court injunction forbidding him from executing the Reconstruction Acts.

When it came to implementing the legislation, however, the president, aided by Stanbery, counterattacked. Vaguely worded and ambiguous clauses concerning the registrars' authority to exclude voters offered rich ground for this endeavor. What exactly was covered by the term "office"? Did it include minor administrative posts or postmasterships? Could registrars determine whether someone was committing perjury and thus refuse to register that person? Could military authorities punish uncooperative state officials, and how? When military commanders sought answers to these questions, Johnson and Stanbery went to work, aware that sometimes the best way to thwart intent is through interpretation. On May 27 the attorney general issued an opinion that severely circumscribed the powers of registrars; a second opinion concerning the removal power of military authorities followed several weeks later. However, the president then faltered, refusing to embody these opinions in the form of orders to the district commanders. As a result, those commanders, supported by Grant, followed the general in chief's advice to continue interpreting the laws as best they saw fit.[29]

When Congress reconvened in July, Republicans looked to close the loopholes exposed by Stanbery's opinions. A third Reconstruction Act explicitly defined the provisionary status of the Johnson state governments and made them subject to congressional control through its agents, the district commanders, who could suspend or remove recalcitrant officials and appoint replacements as they saw fit. It also gave registrars rather broad discretion in disqualifying prospective voters and offered more precise definitions of who could not vote or serve as a convention delegate. District commanders and registrars would not be subject to "any opinion of any civil officer of the United States," thus silencing Stanbery. So far, so good—but not good enough. Obsessed with the need to curtail the attorney general's impact, congressional Republicans failed to consider other means of obstruction open to the president, including the dismissal of district commanders and their military subordinates. In so doing they disregarded Grant's advice to shield his generals from removal. Supposedly ignorant of politics, in this case the general's insight into potential presidential responses proved far superior to that of congressional Republicans, whose skills in drafting legislation remained flawed. They compounded this error by adjourning for the summer, ignoring Grant's suggestion to keep an eye on Johnson by staying in session. As Zachariah Chandler growled, instead of eliminating Johnson congressional Republicans "undertook to surround him with nets, to hem him in." Now, he added, "this Congress seems to hope that the same animal that thrust his paw through the net when it was new will not thrust it through again when it is merely a patched net."[30]

In the almost obligatory (and futile) veto message, Johnson pointed out that the provisions of the Third Reconstruction Act, like its predecessors, "attempted to strip the executive department of the Government of some of its essential powers." The legislation certainly did impair presidential authority, as it was intended to do, although perhaps not as completely as some wanted—much to Republicans' later chagrin. Once again constitutional concerns checked proposals for more far-reaching provisions that would have gone further to limit the autonomy of the executive. The president could also take some satisfaction in the failure of yet another effort to define grounds on which to impeach him, although, as one moderate Republican observed, Johnson persisted in doing "the most provoking things. If he isn't impeached it wont be his fault."[31]

No sooner had the senators and representatives left the sweltering heat and humidity of summertime Washington than Johnson sprang into action. Still holding the power to remove district commanders, he decided to strike at Sheridan, who had been all too eager to remove civil officials in Louisiana and Texas. At the same time, he finally decided to depose Stanton. Acting in accordance with the Tenure of Office Act, he suspended the fractious cabinet minister and persuaded Grant to serve as secretary of war ad interim. He hoped to deflect criticism and perhaps earn applause by making good use of the general's popularity. If Grant accepted, Republicans might well grow suspicious of him, bringing an end to a ripening relationship; if he declined, he risked seeing Johnson turn to someone much less to his liking. Finally, Johnson shared Gideon Welles's assessment that Grant was little more than a simpleton susceptible to manipulation by others. Nor did it hurt that Grant had not always worked well with Stanton and questioned some of his actions against Johnson.

The plan worked at first. Stanton grumbled but gave way gracelessly; Radical Republicans criticized Grant, while moderates wondered why the general had allowed himself to become the president's pawn. However, when Johnson persisted in his determination to remove Sheridan, Grant protested, observing that it would "only be interpreted as an effort to defeat the laws of Congress" and would "embolden" the "unreconstructed element" of the South. The president brushed aside the general's objections, then decided to oust Daniel Sickles as well. Grant was powerless to resist, although he made public his opposition to Johnson's course, thus reassuring most Republicans of his trustworthiness.[32]

Johnson's behavior revived support for impeachment. Fessenden, who opposed the idea, shook his head in amazement: "It does seem as if Johnson was resolved upon destruction."[33] Even some supporters who approved Stanton's removal were taken aback. Johnson "has a strong sense of right, and a stubborn determination to do it, but his action, when he acts, is never in the right time," observed Thomas Ewing Sr. "It is spasmodic." Better to have long since removed Stanton than to raise questions about the Tenure of Office Act. It was left to the French newspaper correspondent Georges Clemenceau to observe that the effort to restrain Johnson had failed once again. "At each session they add a shackle to his bonds, tighten the bit in a different place, file a claw or draw a tooth, and then when he is well bound up, fastened, and caught in an inextricable net of laws and degrees, more or less contradicting each other, they tie him to the stake of the Constitution and take a good look at him feeling quite sure he cannot move this time," he reported. Each time Johnson "burst his cords and bonds," repeatedly causing Republicans to "flee in disorder to the Capitol to set to work making new laws stronger than the old, which will break in their turn at the first test."[34]

The flurry over Stanton's displacement died down as both parties geared up for the fall elections. Northern Republicans were intent on taking the case for black suffrage to their constituents through a series of referenda and state constitutional amendments. In so doing they made a major miscalculation. Their overwhelming victory in 1866 was due to their ability to play up white southern recalcitrance, punctuated with the examples offered at Memphis and New Orleans. A majority of voters were willing to protect southern blacks against violence; they were not quite as willing to allow northern blacks to vote. Nor was it clear that enfranchising blacks would strengthen Republicans at election time, for some white Republicans would defect or stay at home. Democratic voters, of course, stood firm against the idea; aided by some Republican defections and the emergence of other issues, the Democrats scored several victories. The results clearly marked how far the Republicans could go in promoting black rights; party interests were far better served by waving the bloody shirt and reviving wartime concerns and associations than by pressing for justice to blacks.[35]

Johnson did what he could to foster this turn of events by keeping his mouth shut. There was no sequel to "The Swing Around the Circle"; instead, he remained in Washington. Delighted by the results, he argued that they vindicated his administration. In truth, Democrats had avoided mentioning him, and their triumph suggested that he was a liability to their electoral prospects, even if it might be worthwhile to encourage him to attack the Republicans. That such outbursts were in the offing surprised no one. As one of Grant's staff officers put it, "No doubt now the Elections have gone as they have Mr. J. will be on the *rampage* again."[36]

In 1866, Johnson had observed to a delegation of Washington blacks, "I know how easy it is to cater to prejudices, and how easy it is to excite feelings of prejudice and unkindness." He now decided to demonstrate what he meant. Reassured of the persistence of racism in the North, he increasingly emphasized the theme in his remarks, decrying "the subjugation of the States to negro domination." In his annual message he declared that "negroes have shown less capacity for government than any other race or people. . . . [W]herever they have been left to their own devices they have shown a constant tendency to relapse into barbarism." The 1867 results suggested that it was time to play the race card at every opportunity. Before long, however, it became apparent that appeals to racial prejudice were of limited utility when an election was not in the offing. Many Republicans, aware of the election results, dropped black suffrage in the North. The participation of southern blacks in the political process in the South proved far less disturbing to a majority of northern white voters.[37]

Just as alarming was another portion of the message, in which Johnson hinted that he had considered extraconstitutional means to resist congressional encroachments. He noted that such resistance "would be likely to produce violent collision between the respective adherents of the two branches of government"; such a conflict "must be resorted to only as the last remedy for the worst of evils." Such comments revived concerns about the damage he might inflict on reconstruction. Convinced now that nothing short of removal would stay the president's course, several Republicans pressed once more for impeachment. Speaker of the House Schuyler Colfax observed that "the election returns & his wicked advisers have so excited 'the humble individual' that he is decidedly on the war path." More moderate Republicans, whatever their sentiments about Johnson, worried that impeachment would hurt the party; in December their arguments helped turn back a formal effort to secure a vote for impeachment.[38]

The result pleased Johnson, increasing his sense of invulnerability. Although he welcomed the sort of confrontation promised by an impeachment crisis, he had long expressed concern that Congress might try to displace him from office during the trial itself. Now he could dismiss his worries as needless. Still lingering, however, was the fate of Edwin M. Stanton. In removing him, Johnson had complied with the procedures set forth in the Tenure of Office Act. Now it was up to the Senate to decide whether Stanton was indeed covered by the act and, if he was, whether he should be reinstated. As the Senate deliberated, Johnson continued to press forward, asking Congress to commend the conservative course pursued by Winfield Scott Hancock, Sheridan's successor as head of the Fifth Military District, while replacing Republican favorite John Pope with George G. Meade as commander of the Third Military District. Southern Republicans believed that such changes rendered their efforts to construct state governments far more difficult. "Cannot Congress devise some means of checkmating the villainous conspiracy of Johnson & Co. to defeat the restoration . . . of the Southern states?" wailed the Chicago *Tribune*. One way was to reinstate Stanton.[39]

Johnson endeavored to prevent his opponent's return to office. He sought Grant's cooperation. Perhaps the general would withdraw from the department and allow Johnson to select a replacement. Perhaps Grant would remain as secretary, thus forcing a court test of the legislation. When the general pointed out that such a course of action would subject him to fines and imprisonment, the president volunteered to pay the fine and serve the time himself—a rather remarkable offer by a man who could hold forth for hours on his knowledge of law. Grant refused to be a party to such a transaction, but in other ways he proved willing to help Johnson, especially by suggesting possible replacements. However, he made it clear that he would vacate the office if the Senate reinstated Stanton. The president refused to act upon the general's suggestions. He was not looking for a resolution of this conflict. He knew Grant was no longer reliable: according to the Tenure of Office Act, Stanton's reinstatement automatically terminated Grant's tenure. Perhaps he was procrastinating again; in light of what happened, however, it appears that he was now eager to confront Grant in an effort to discredit the leading candidate for the Republican presidential nomination in the eyes of the American people.

On the evening of January 13, the Senate by a vote of 36–6 refused to concur in Stanton's removal. News of the vote made its way to a White House reception, although neither Johnson nor Grant alluded to it when they met. The next morning Grant entered the War Department, locked the door to the secretary's office, handed the keys to a department administrator, and walked over to army headquarters, where he penned a letter notifying Johnson that he was no longer secretary of war. Apparently Grant thought this sufficient warning (after all, the letter only confirmed what the Senate had already decided). However, he was unprepared for what happened next. Not long after Grant left the War Department, Stanton arrived, took the keys, entered his old office, and then summoned Grant, who had naively assumed that the secretary would take his time to claim his office, allowing Johnson some time in which to name another replacement.

Worse was to come the general's way. In response to Grant's note, Johnson invited him to a cabinet meeting, then turned to the general and asked for the report from the War Department. Grant reminded Johnson that he was no longer secretary of war; Johnson, evidently aware of Stanton's return, charged that Grant had promised to hold on to the office to provoke a court test or to return it to Johnson before the Senate acted. Neither of these statements was true, but Johnson, catching Grant off balance, made the general look bad as he fumbled in attempting to respond to his interrogator the president. Johnson duped several of his cabinet officers and a good number of historians into believing that Grant had betrayed the president. In truth, Johnson was out to destroy Grant, for the general, who had labored to find Johnson a suitable substitute, had made it clear that he would not be a party to a court test and would vacate the office upon learning of the Senate's action. Nor had he delivered the office to Stanton; it was far more accurate to say that Stanton had seized the vacated office—as if occupation of a room was all that was necessary to be recognized as secretary of war.[40]

Johnson's actions over the next several days reflected his determination to discredit Grant regardless of events. The general, flustered by Johnson and annoyed by Stanton, unsuccessfully tried to persuade the secretary to resign; meanwhile, Johnson leaked an account of the cabinet confrontation to a local newspaper that suggested there had been collusion between Grant and Stanton, Johnson's personal knowledge to the contrary notwithstanding. When Grant asked Johnson to issue an order directing army personnel not to heed Stanton's orders, thus casting doubt upon Stanton's authority, the president assented; however, when Grant learned that other cabinet members were transacting business with Stanton as secretary, he concluded that there was no reason to pretend otherwise in the absence of specific orders "limiting or impairing" Stanton's authority. The two men then took their dispute to the press, a process facilitated by a congressional call upon Stanton for correspondence. Advised by his chief of staff, John A. Rawlins, to abandon efforts to explain what had happened or to accept that Johnson might have misunderstood him, Grant agreed with Rawlins's decision to explicitly reject the president's insinuations about Grant's character and remind readers that the president had tried to involve him in illegal activities.[41]

Johnson's plan backfired badly. Grant's actions reassured Republicans that the general was indeed suitable presidential material, and Stanton was back in office. What made the dispute all the more ridiculous was that it was totally unnecessary. Grant and others had offered Johnson a way out. Even after Stanton returned to the War Department, Johnson could have won the general over, an act that would have done far more to taint his prospects to become the Republican nominee by playing on preexisting hostilities between the general and the secretary. Instead, he made an implacable enemy of the most popular man in America.

Despite this result, Johnson otherwise lost very little. Another impeachment effort proved abortive, giving him new confidence—perhaps too much. Previously he had prevaricated on the issue of whether he would observe the terms of the Tenure of Office Act, for at first he had honored the letter of the procedures spelled out by the legislation and failed to push the argument that Stanton was not covered by it. Now he decided to defy the act itself by removing Stanton outright. It was difficult to find a willing replacement.

Sherman, who had seen enough while at Grant's side in January, once more rejected an offer. Finally the president settled upon Adjutant General Lorenzo Thomas, who had returned to obscurity after his wartime activities on behalf of the freedmen. Thomas proved amenable; on February 21, Johnson finally acted, removing Stanton and naming Thomas secretary ad interim. "He had, he said, perhaps delayed the step too long," Welles noted. "At all events, it was time the difficulty was settled."[42]

The news jolted Republicans. "Didn't I tell you so?" Thaddeus Stevens gloated. "What good did our moderation do you? If you don't kill the beast, it will kill you." The Senate voted 28–6 that Stanton was covered by the Tenure of Office Act; in the House, Republicans commenced the impeachment process once more. Johnson was not surprised. "If I cannot be President in fact," he told his private secretary, "I will not be President in name alone."[43]

This time, however, impeachment proved more than a nearly idle threat. As Stanton made plans to hole up in his office, turning it into a small fort, the House moved forward with a motion to impeach the president. Between the weekend and Washington's Birthday, it was not until Monday, February 24, that the House finally voted to impeach Johnson, 128–47. Stanton nearly misstepped when he ordered Thomas's arrest, thus providing Johnson with the court test he claimed he desired; the war secretary hurriedly dropped the charges. Meanwhile, a special House committee framed articles of impeachment. By early March, House Republicans had agreed upon eleven articles. Eight covered matters connected with Stanton's removal and the Tenure of Office Act; one concerned a possible violation of the clauses outlining the chain of command in the Army Appropriations Act; another, drafted by Benjamin Butler, charged that the president's speech making had made Congress a subject of ridicule (not exactly an impeachable offense, and the article itself justified some ridicule); and a final article claimed rather broadly that Johnson's violations of the Tenure of Office Act, the Army Appropriations Act, and the Reconstruction Acts made him guilty "of a high misdemeanor in office." Within days the Senate commenced preliminary proceedings. At last the ultimate confrontation would take place.[44]

In January and February 1868, Johnson frittered away his advantages gained during the last five months of 1867. His public feud with Grant proved counterproductive, serving only to reconcile most Radicals to the general as the Republican nominee for president. Undeterred, the president brought his confrontation with Congress to a climax in attempting to remove Stanton outright, finally convincing Republicans that impeachment was in fact a proper response. The president bungled his way into the impeachment crisis. His actions were unnecessary, counterproductive, and nearly destructive. He would have been better off to have done nothing whatsoever: his actions had virtually no impact either on the course of events in the South or on the presidential contest, except insofar as he strengthened Grant with the Republicans.

The president's primary task now was to survive in office. In the past he had come alive when confronted with dire circumstances. This time, however, he could not lash back at his critics, lest he contribute to their case against his reckless use of presidential power. The strategy he chose was shaped by the realization that shrewd tactics could drive a wedge between the Republicans temporarily united in opposition to his actions. While his lawyers worked to exploit the loopholes and loose ends in the articles of impeachment, the president assumed a low profile and contemplated ways to quell the concerns of moderate Republicans. At last it seemed that he was willing to cut some deals, if only to escape conviction. In so doing he demonstrated that he indeed possessed the political skill to compromise and reach settlements.

On the advice of his lawyers, Johnson kept his mouth shut. There would be no responses to serenades at the White House or ill-tempered stump speeches; he would not give Republicans any more ammunition. When supporters offered to maintain him in office by force if necessary, he remained silent. It proved one of the most trying parts of the entire ordeal. Johnson fantasized about defending himself on the Senate floor; once in a while he let slip a sharp comment to the press. Nevertheless, on the whole the strategy of silence persisted, lending the president an aura of dignity that he might dispel if he started to talk.

Republican legislative successes also reduced the threat Johnson posed to congressional reconstruction. Yet another Reconstruction Act, declaring that a majority of the votes cast (not a majority of registered voters) was sufficient to ratify proposed state constitutions, thwarted white southerners' attempt to defeat them by boycotting elections. Facing yet another override, Johnson wisely allowed the measure to become law without his signature, thus forgoing an opportunity to issue yet another of his veto messages. When Republicans feared that the Supreme Court would take advantage of a case involving the arrest by army officers of a Mississippi newspaper editor, William McCardle, to declare the Reconstruction Acts unconstitutional, they hurried through an act stripping the Supreme Court of jurisdiction to hear McCardle's appeal. Johnson was disappointed. He had anticipated that if the Court ruled against Republican interests, the Tenure of Office Act would suffer the same fate, the grounds for impeachment would collapse, and he would complete the withdrawal of occupation forces from the South. By sharing these thoughts with a reporter for the Democratic New York *World,* he alerted Republicans to what was going on, prompting them to curtail the Court's jurisdiction. A veto proved useless; a majority of the Court declined to challenge Congress. Ironically, by protecting their legislative enactments from the possibility of a Court decision, Republicans had also safeguarded themselves from the president, thus reducing the need to remove him.[45]

In preparing to defend the president, Johnson's lawyers probably anticipated that congressional Republicans would be careless in their drafting of specific articles of impeachment, much as they had been sloppy in framing reconstruction legislation. They were not to be disappointed. That the president had acted to obstruct the intent of legislation was clear. However, the articles rested instead on alleged violations of the Tenure of Office Act, the procedures concerning the issuing of orders to military personnel outlined in the Army Appropriations Act, and a catchall article that basically concluded that he did not like Congress. These were frail reeds indeed on which to base a vote of conviction, especially since it remained a matter of some dispute as to whether the Tenure of Office Act protected Stanton.

There was something faintly humorous in the course adopted by defense counsel in responding to the charges involving the Tenure of Office Act. It was unconstitutional, the defense maintained; even if it was constitutional, (a) it did not cover Stanton, (b) Stanton was still in office, (c) Johnson had merely intended to test the law's constitutionality by violating it, and (d) Johnson had not committed an impeachable offense. This defense was ingenious but not persuasive, although the multiple responses reflected Johnson's own contradictory justifications. Indeed, to accept the premise that presidents could break the law in order to seek judicial rulings would be to open a Pandora's box brimming with potential abuses of power. Elsewhere the defense found it easier to erect reasonable explanations that deflected the force of the prosecution's charges.[46]

Nevertheless, both sides knew that the impeachment trial would be settled as much on political as on judicial grounds. Had conviction brought something other than permanent removal from office—say, had it provided for a new presidential contest—Johnson would have lost his battle. But expulsion would indeed be extreme, especially in light of the nature of the articles of impeachment. Moderate Republicans pondered the political and institutional costs of removing Johnson. After all, a presidential contest was pending. Republican chances for victory looked good so long as the party did not go too far in a Radical direction. Yet the possible elevation of Radical Benjamin Wade to the presidency (as president pro tem of the Senate, he was next in the line of succession) might dampen these prospects. At a time when Republicans remained divided over economic policy, Wade's advocacy of inflation and protective tariffs might prove divisive. Voters had repudiated Radicalism in the elections of 1867; it might prove difficult to present Grant as the epitome of Republican moderation with Wade in the White House. Opposition to Johnson and the Democrats, not harmony on policy, was the foundation of Republican unity. Perhaps there were better ways of nullifying the president's impact on reconstruction without taking the extreme step of conviction, a step that might well run roughshod over moderate concerns about process in the haste to achieve Radical ends.

Johnson facilitated the process whereby moderate Republicans could accept his acquittal by demonstrating that he was willing to cater to their concerns. He declined to interfere when Grant reversed several of Hancock's decisions in Louisiana, resulting in Hancock's transfer elsewhere. He abandoned whatever notion remained of installing Lorenzo Thomas or Thomas Ewing Sr. as secretary of war and instead sent forward the nomination of John M. Schofield to replace Stanton. The move placated moderates; although Schofield had shown conservative leanings in his administration of affairs in Virginia, he was acceptable. In response to a contact established by Senator Edmund G. Ross of Kansas, Johnson forwarded the South Carolina and Arkansas constitutions to Congress for approval, thus suggesting that he would not stand in the way of the Reconstruction Acts. Such measures were nothing more than politics as usual; Johnson rejected less savory ways of securing acquittal, including striking a deal with Ross's fellow Kansan, Samuel C. Pomeroy, whereby the senator would vote to acquit in exchange for patronage.[47] Perhaps he suspected that the wily Pomeroy was baiting a trap.

Republicans commented on the effectiveness of the president's tactics. As the first impeachment vote drew near, the Chicago *Tribune* grumbled: "Andrew Johnson has been a changed man. The country has been at peace. The great obstruction to the law has been virtually suspended." Thus assuaged, several moderate Republican senators openly expressed their reservations about the merit of the articles. It soon became apparent to the prosecution that it was in trouble. Enough questions had been raised in the minds of certain senators about the Tenure of Office Act to render those articles ineffective as a basis for conviction. In an attempt to muster the two-thirds majority necessary to remove Johnson, the impeachment forces decided to call for a vote on the all-encompassing eleventh article. They lost. On May 16, by a vote of 35–19, Andrew Johnson held onto the presidency by a single vote. Subsequent attempts to obtain conviction on other articles also fell short by the same slim margin, and on May 26 the Senate ended the trial.

Andrew Johnson may well have committed impeachable offenses, but they were not among the articles of impeachment. Since it was at best unclear as to whether the Tenure of Office Act covered Stanton (although surely Johnson at times acted as if it did), the articles addressing that issue could not muster a sufficient majority to secure conviction. The prosecution failed to demonstrate that the president had violated the Army Appropriations Act. Nor did the offenses alleged in Stevens's broad article merit impeachment or conviction. Congressional Republicans were once again the victims of their own failure to draft precisely worded legislation to effect their ends. When Johnson moderated his behavior, enough Senate Republicans were able to suppress their uneasiness about the president to acquit him.

Acquittal, however, did not mark a triumph for the independence of the executive, although it clearly demonstrated the difficulty of removing a president through impeachment. Far from protecting the independence of the executive, Johnson's behavior had come quite close to endangering it by sparking impeachment in the first place. He owed his survival to seven Republicans whose concern for preserving the balance between executive and legislature, while mentioned by some, was not the overriding factor in their decision for acquittal: political considerations prevailed. Many Republicans were skeptical of Wade as president; in less than a year they hoped to regain control of the White House through the normal procedure of election. Nor did Johnson's impeachment or acquittal have a significant impact on Reconstruction. He had already done his damage several years earlier, especially in the first twenty months of his presidency. Much of the inherent weakness in the Republican program was due to the increasing attention Republicans paid to tying Johnson's hands. Acquittal meant very little in itself, although the news depressed southern Republicans.

Johnson survived, but at the cost of his ability to influence the course of events in the South. By tempering his obstructionist behavior (although he never abandoned it), he obviated the need to remove him from office. Thus, in its way, impeachment achieved its real goal of controlling Johnson. At best he had once again diverted Republicans' energy from addressing policy issues to debating how best to handcuff the chief executive. Conviction might have created more problems than it would have solved for Republicans and might have imperiled their chances in 1868. Thus moderate Republicans were pleased with the result. In contrast, although publicly the Democrats celebrated Johnson's acquittal, privately several of them groused about the lost opportunity that conviction might have offered them in damaging Republican prospects.[48]

Besides, by the end of the impeachment trial Republicans had settled on pursuing more traditional ways of recapturing the presidency. The nomination of Ulysses S. Grant on May 21 proved a welcome relief from the tensions of the trial: when, in accepting the nomination, Grant intoned, "Let us have peace," many Americans embraced what they saw as a promise to put an end to political strife. The outcome of Democratic deliberations over their standard-bearer served only to enhance Republican prospects. Passing over Johnson (much to the president's chagrin) as well as Chief Justice Salmon P. Chase and several other contestants, the delegates took twenty-one ballots to choose New York's Horatio Seymour to head the fall ticket, with former general and congressman Frank P. Blair Jr. as his running mate. Both choices proved unfortunate. As governor, Seymour had addressed New York City draft rioters as "my friends"; Blair, in a fiery public letter, had promised that a Democratic president would dismantle Republican achievements in reconstructing civil governments in the South. The contrast to the peaceful general could not have been more marked. As one observer noted, "Seymour and his men rarely open their mouths that they do not strengthen Grant's hand."[49]

Thus marginalized, Johnson became irrelevant. Republicans ignored his arguments as they overrode his veto of a bill readmitting Arkansas; they did so again when he objected to the readmission of other states and again when he rejected legislation prolonging the life of the Freedmen's Bureau. Nevertheless, he persisted. He did what he could to enhance Democratic prospects, turning a blind eye to evidence of white supremacist terrorism against southern Republicans while charging that Republicans deliberately provoked such incidents. It was perhaps closer to the truth to acknowledge that news of Johnson's acquittal had infused southern conservatives with renewed determination to thwart the rise of southern Republicans. With the appointment of Alvan Gillem to supervise affairs in Mississippi, Johnson was able to thwart the ratification of that state's constitution, thus keeping it out of the November election. In Louisiana another one of Johnson's supporters, Lovell Rousseau, declared that if Republican voters were afraid of violence, they should stay home. Resistance was especially evident in Georgia, where Democrats did all they could to nullify the results of a Republican victory in the state elections in April. They displaced black state legislators and embarked on a campaign of violence against Republicans. Ironically, the very success of the Republican program in constructing new state regimes also terminated the operation of the Reconstruction Acts in those states, so that the military could intervene only at Johnson's behest.[50]

Grant's victory depressed Johnson. With the general in the White House, the Republicans would be free to impose their will. Or so it seemed. By the time of Grant's election only three former Confederate states (Virginia, Mississippi, and Texas) had failed to comply with the procedures set forth in the Reconstruction Acts; the other seven states once covered by the acts were no longer so, diminishing Republican power to shape the boundaries of reconstruction from Washington. Moreover, much of Grant's support came from the belief that with his election Reconstruction, far from continuing, would come to an end. Many Americans, especially northern whites, were impatient to move on.

As Johnson's term dwindled down to its final days, he remained defiant. He assailed Republican reconstruction policy in his last annual message; on Christmas Day he issued one last amnesty proclamation covering all former Confederates. On inauguration day, he refused to attend Grant's swearing in (which was just fine with Grant, who had made known that he would not share a carriage with his predecessor). Rather, in an effort to squeeze out every last second of executive authority, Johnson remained at the White House, signing bills and conversing with cabinet members until noon. Then he left.

Andrew Johnson could have handled himself far better in his struggles with Congress while conceding little if any of his position. His desire to seek confrontation and his explosive rhetoric offered his opponents opportunities they exploited to great advantage. He need not have courted the possibility of impeachment, then conviction; he could have stood his ground far more calmly and effectively. Had he reprimanded white southerners for their more outrageous acts, he would have defused Republican charges that he was shielding the forces of white supremacy. Provocative behavior and an eagerness for confrontation damaged his own cause. As Clemenceau observed in the summer of 1867, if the president "consents to keep a little quieter, he will get out of this with a fright"; however, his "systematic hostility is extremely useful to the Republican party by preventing it from splitting."[51]

Johnson should have demonstrated more faith in his fellow southern whites. By deciding to pursue a policy of reconstituting civil governments in the South under a loose umbrella of federal supervision, congressional Republicans eschewed the far more fundamental revolution that would have been wrought by prolonged federal supervision and far-reaching economic reform. Indeed, had Johnson been shrewder, he could have curtailed what change did happen by pressing for ratification of the Fourteenth Amendment, for once civil government was restored, white southerners would have the opportunity to act. However, like a good number of his fellow southern whites, issues of race touched Johnson at his core, inspiring reactions that were inevitably passionate, even irrational; like them, he sought legitimacy in posing as a defender of constitutional liberty, although, also like them, all too often his practice of constitutional interpretation was transparently self-serving. The fruits of his obstructionist policy were not immediately apparent: that in their struggles with him congressional Republicans spent much energy and time that could have been invested otherwise was overlooked by people who chose to assess his accomplishments as of noon on March 4, 1869. Time would tell.

PART THREE
ULYSSES S. GRANT

5

"LET US HAVE PEACE"

"To bind up the wounds left by the war, to restore concord to the still distracted Union, to ensure real freedom to the Southern negro, and full justice to the Southern white; these are indeed tasks which might tax the powers of Washington himself or a greater than Washington, if such a man is to be found." So observed the *Edinburgh Review* at the beginning of Ulysses S. Grant's administration. The new president faced difficult challenges as he took office. Would the new Republican regimes in the South be able to survive and prosper? Could Grant push for additional reconstruction legislation in the face of an emerging consensus that enough had been done already and that it was time to move on? Would the Republican party that elected him be able to retain its identity and majority status as the political agenda shifted? Could he—or anyone—successfully forge a southern policy that would both make blacks part of the American polity and heal sectional strife?[1]

Grant was committed to trying. He had accepted the presidency in large part because he distrusted the ability of politicians to preserve in peace what had been won in war. "I have been forced into it in spite of myself," he explained to William T. Sherman. "I could not back down without . . . leaving the contest for power for the next four years between mere trading politicians, the elevation of whom, no matter which party won, would lose to us, largely, the results of the costly war which we have gone through." A majority of American voters in 1868 wanted someone above politics who would restore order. Grant was that man. "Let us have peace," he had declared upon accepting the nomination. Those four words were susceptible to many meanings, a key to their wide appeal. Peace between North and South; peace between black and white; peace after years of war and political conflict—in each case, not a clarion call to rally the troops for a new beginning but an expressed desire for a cease-fire. In the fall campaign Republicans emphasized that the general sought only to serve the people. They suggested that his experience in the military with filling offices based on merit and efficiency and his administrative skills ideally suited him for the job. Those people who attack Grant for not being enough of a politician forget that Americans found his apolitical image appealing.

Grant was no political innocent. During the Civil War and the early years of Reconstruction he had displayed an awareness of the larger political issues connected with the war and its resolution; he had usually played politics skillfully in his relationships with his civil superiors and fellow officers. Whether these were sufficient to guarantee success as president was another matter entirely. The political skills that served him well in uniform would not be the same ones he would have to exercise in the White House. He had to learn how to influence others and build coalitions, how to distribute patronage and bargain for support. "To go into the Presidency opens altogether a new field to me, in which there is to be a new strife to which I am not trained," he admitted. He thought politicians led "a most slavish life"; his experiences during the Johnson administration left him disillusioned about the selflessness of public service. "All the romance of feeling that men in high places are above personal considerations and act only from motives of pure patriotism, and for the general good of the public, has been destroyed," he once grumbled to Sherman.[2]

Grant did not hunger for the presidency. During the war he had made clear that he did not want the position, once deflecting inquiries by joking that all he wanted was to become mayor of his hometown of Galena, Illinois, to make sure that the city would complete the sidewalk to his house. (When Grant returned in triumph to Galena in 1865, a banner across Main Street proclaimed, "General, The Sidewalk Is Finished." Obviously, Galena's leaders knew how to contain a threat when they saw one.) He enjoyed frustrating politicians' attempts to pump him, responding to their leading inquiries with a puff on his cigar, a comment about horses, or simple silence. After years of seeking economic security for himself and his family, he had finally found a job he could keep—that of general in chief. To take the presidency for four or eight years would eventually leave him without employment long before he was prepared to retire. And he was well aware of how partisan controversy could mar his hard-won reputation.[3]

Grant entered office at a time when Congress had become experienced in a politics of confrontation with the chief executive, featuring efforts to curtail executive power. Veto overrides, the 1867 Army Appropriations Act, the Tenure of Office Act, impeachment—all reflected a desire to strike back at executive independence first expressed in the Wade-Davis Manifesto. It was naive to think that congressional Republicans would simply abandon their concerns about strong executive leadership. Grant reassured Americans that he would not follow in his predecessor's footsteps, asserting that the president was "a purely Administrative officer" who "should always be left free to execute the will of the people." This statement deceived listeners at the time and historians ever since, who emphasize the phrase "purely Administrative officer" to denote a rather limited, almost clerkist conception of the presidency, whereas what followed—"free to execute the will of the people"—sounded Jacksonian (and almost Johnsonian) in its statement of independence. The same theme appeared in his inaugural address. Announcing that "all laws will be faithfully executed, whether they meet my approval or not," he reminded Americans that he was not another Johnson. "I shall on all subjects have a policy to recommend, but none to enforce against the will of the people." Listeners failed to heed statements preceding that declaration which revealed his willingness to initiate legislation and veto bills not in accordance with his understanding of the Constitution.[4]

The new president struggled to reconcile several goals in his quest to frame a southern policy. He simultaneously sought to protect black civil and political rights and conciliate white southerners in aiming to establish a stable postwar political order resting on the consent of all of the governed, white and black. That the protection of blacks and the conciliation of whites often seemed irreconcilable objectives complicated the already demanding task of framing a policy that would be just to everyone and accepted by all involved. Moreover, he was enough of a politician to understand that he had to maintain Republican political power. Given declining northern concern about southern affairs and a growing reluctance to endorse federal intervention in the South, persistent efforts to protect southern Republicans might erode the party's voter base in the North. To sacrifice the party nationally as a result of its southern policy would be suicidal, and if one characteristic marked Republican regulars in the 1870s, it was their tenacious commitment to survival. Thus Grant's actions concerning the South would be tempered by the limits of what was possible politically, reflecting a sense of the pragmatic and a healthy (and, as it turned out, warranted) skepticism about the willingness of northern whites to do what was right.

If the ends of policy were hard to reconcile, the means of policy were limited due in large part to the contracting boundaries of reconstruction. Johnson had dashed whatever hope there may have been for reconstituting the structure of the South socially, economically, and politically through confiscation and redistribution. Grant still might push for programs to promote southern development, but otherwise he could do little to recast many aspects of the southern social and economic order in light of prevailing notions of federalism and the proper scope of government. In readmitting all but three former Confederate states by the end of 1868, congressional Republicans further narrowed the federal government's ability to act. Only under the guarantee clause of the Constitution might Grant intervene in southern affairs, and that could be invoked only in extreme circumstances of widespread violence that overwhelmed state resources—and in response to a request from state authorities.

Grant's options were inherently problematic. A conciliatory policy had to be based on more than goodwill. At best, the president could promise that he would not intervene in southern affairs unless circumstances warranted. Other policies would be limited as well in scope and impact: states remained the primary shapers of economic policy. Intervention was at least equally troublesome. Not to intervene left southern Republicans to defend themselves against acts of intimidation and violence; to intervene left the impression that southern Republicanism could not survive on its own and was dependent on outside support, rendering difficult its search for legitimacy and acceptance as part of the postwar political order. In such circumstances, intervention, far from restoring order and stability, led to the need for more intervention.[5]

Just as terrorism was designed to serve the political interests of white supremacists, intervention to protect Republicans against terrorism also bolstered Republican chances in southern states. Critics thus charged that it was politically motivated, giving credence to claims that Grant aspired to military dictatorship. Constitutional concerns and the rudimentary means of enforcement raised questions about its long-term effectiveness. Finally, the patience of the northern public was finite, and its interest in the fate of the freedpeople was limited. People wanted to put Reconstruction behind them and get on with their own lives.

Most northerners thought that Reconstruction was over. "The election of Grant settles the Southern question," the New England industrialist Edward Atkinson declared.[6] With the Republicans in charge of both Congress and the presidency, all would go well now—an indication of how Johnson's fight with congressional Republicans, and not the substance of policy, had come to dominate discussions of southern policy. Aside from a final constitutional amendment to secure black suffrage, the majority of white northerners did not see what else should or could be done in the South by the federal government. Under such circumstances it would be difficult to mobilize public support for measures to protect blacks. In later years historians would deplore the Republican practice of waving the bloody shirt as a cynical attempt to manipulate northern voters by reviving wartime sentiments. However, white supremacists in the South, both during and after Reconstruction, also waved the bloody shirt with at least equal effectiveness, judging by the persistence of a fondness for the Confederate cause. And the bloody shirt was often still wet with the blood of blacks and their white allies in the South, as even a cursory look at Reconstruction violence will suggest. Republicans understood that by recalling wartime antagonisms they gained popular support for some of their measures to bring law, order, and justice to the South, measures the northern electorate would be more reluctant to endorse if they were presented simply on their merits.

Although Republicans appeared to be in control in 1869, it was easy to exaggerate their power. Grant's majority was a tribute to his own vote-getting ability: he outpolled the party ticket in most northern states. In nominating Grant and in equivocating on black suffrage in the party platform, Republicans recognized that a moderate stance was essential to attract support. In nominating Seymour and Blair and pledging to undo Republican reconstruction policy, Democrats threw away their chance of swaying swing voters. Even so, a majority of white voters had voted Democratic. With Reconstruction supposedly "settled," Democrats might broaden their appeal and reinvigorate the allegiance of old supporters by adopting new issues.

Republicans argued that Grant's election would secure the fruits of Union victory and bring an end to political controversy. Yet southern policy had defined party identity for fifteen years: Andrew Johnson's obstinacy had forced the party to unify. Johnson, as Charles Francis Adams Jr. had observed, served as a hoop holding together the staves of the Republican coalition. Now with Johnson gone and the reestablishment of civil government in the South just about completed, one could ask—and many did—if the Republican party had served its purpose. What, if anything, could hold together this diverse coalition now that its mission had been achieved? Republicans were divided on issues of economic policy—tariffs, monetary policy, and the like. Would the party's triumph prove its undoing? Certainly the times seemed ripe for realignment.[7]

Southern Republicans faced their own problems. Political strategies were dictated in part by party demographics. In states where a large black electorate existed, Republicans struggled to protect black voters and to retain a small white vote. Where Republicans needed white support to ensure a majority, they sought a different course designed to attract white voters by stressing issues of economic development while deemphasizing matters of concern to blacks. These variations held important implications for federal policy. In states where the black electorate approached a majority of a state's entire eligible voters—Mississippi, South Carolina, and Louisiana—intervention enhanced Republican chances, but such actions might hurt party fortunes in other states where Republican survival depended on wooing whites. These variations contributed to what some have seen as the incoherence of Grant's policy. A uniform policy toward the South would not have served all southern Republicans equally well and would have had differing impacts on states according to party demographics.

Nor was this all. Contrary to the implicit assumptions of most historians, Republicans did not constitute a natural majority in most southern states, especially where native white southern support was critical. The party had been forged in unique circumstances; would it endure once those circumstances no longer operated? Moreover, the terrorist tactics of conservative counterrevolutionaries conflated war and politics and replaced partisan competition with a struggle for survival. Every election season became a pitched battle to retain control of government against the repeated assaults of Conservatives and Democrats, with Republicans fearing that defeat would extinguish the party forever.

Faced with these challenges, southern Republicans needed to stick together if they were to stick around. Unfortunately, factionalism was endemic to southern Republicans. The interests of carpetbaggers, scalawags, and blacks often diverged. Many whites wanted black votes but were reluctant to respond to black interests or black participation in framing the political agenda. Many of the issues in which blacks took an active interest—public education, for example—required state appropriations, and the money for such appropriations came in large part from the taxes paid by whites, fueling feelings that whites were being asked to pay for programs that benefited blacks disproportionately. Southern white Republicans, seeking to broaden the base of the party, which in reality meant attracting more whites to the party, played down issues of importance to blacks. Personal rivalries and battles for patronage also contributed to damaging party fortunes.

The dilemmas Grant and his fellow Republicans faced posed serious problems. At a time when one might presume that at last the party could implement its policy, it was easy to forget that the actions of the previous four years had done much to compromise the opportunities of 1865. Whether Grant and his allies could reforge the Republican majority to meet the political agenda of the 1870s and remain the majority party nationally was enough of a challenge; whether they could do so while bringing reconstruction to a successful conclusion suggested the difficulties that would have confronted any Republican chief executive assuming office that year.

In his inaugural address, Grant called upon Americans to approach reconstruction "calmly, without prejudice, hate, or sectional pride, remembering that the greatest good to the greatest number is the object to be attained." That statement reassured those southern whites who welcomed his rise to power. Augustus Garland of Arkansas believed that Grant could "rescue us from destruction, and lay broad, deep, and permanent, the foundation for our own future well being." Possibly the new president "might surround himself with decent, moderate and able men of the republican party" whose moderate principles would guide policy. Grant, after all, had never been identified with the Radical wing of the Republican party, and many Radicals had grudgingly accepted his nomination. "It is our true policy, it seems to me, to extend to Gen'l Grant a 'generous confidence' as the best mode of winning his favor," conservative Herschel V. Johnson told Alexander H. Stephens. If Grant was "just and generous, . . . the great Southern heart, warm, magnanimous and brave, will leap for joy and throb with gratitude," he declared. Others agreed. Virginians, reported one resident of the Old Dominion, "are favorably disposed toward Genl. Grant," believing that the incoming president "is free from rancorous feelings toward the South." Grant's "independent course is calculated to inspire the South with hope and confidence," one Texan remarked. There was political wisdom in winning white support, for, as the editor of the Springfield (Mass.) *Republican,* Samuel Bowles, observed, "The Republican party cannot long maintain its supremacy in the South by negro votes alone."[8]

At the same time, Grant advocated the "security of person, property, and free religious and political opinion in every part of our common country, without regard to local prejudice." Behind such platitudes he pledged to press for black rights. North Carolina governor William Holden told blacks that Grant's election "has given you practical assurance of your freedom." White terrorists no longer posed a threat. Grant's victory grounded the nation "so securely on the principles of Freedom and Justice that hereafter we may fear nothing." Once again the fundamental ambiguity present in "Let us have peace" appeared—although Grant did not see it. Others might portray him as either a supporter of conciliation with whites or as a supporter of black rights. Grant thought he could be both. His initial cabinet veered toward moderate assumptions about reconstruction, even after he had to name early replacements for the State and Treasury Departments. Hamilton Fish (secretary of state) was a conservative Republican, while George Boutwell (treasury secretary) had long been identified with the Radicals; if Interior Secretary Jacob D. Cox and Attorney General Ebenezer R. Hoar were not deeply committed to reconstruction, Maryland's John Creswell (postmaster general) was. "The Southern Radicals are delighted with Creswell's nomination," enthused the abolitionist New York *Independent*. "He was their choice, and is to the last drop of blood in his veins a through Radical Republican."[9]

Grant first moved to the center when he addressed the status of the three states still under military supervision: Mississippi, Virginia, and Texas. In each state, Republicans worked to bar former Confederates from participation in the new regimes, but a majority of voters proved unwilling to support that position. If Grant placated centrist whites, he might lay the groundwork for broadening the Republican base of support. The first concrete move toward realignment took place when a delegation of white Virginians approached Grant. They would accept black suffrage and equality before the law but rejected the proscriptive measures on voting and officeholding included in the proposed state constitution. Grant acceded to a proposal whereby such clauses would be voted on separately, and forwarded the idea to Congress. "It is desirable to restore the States which were engaged in the rebellion to their proper relations to the Government and the country at as early a period as the people of those States should be found willing [both] to become peaceful and orderly [and] adopt and maintain such constitutions and laws as will effectually secure the civil and political rights of all persons within their borders," he argued. When white southerners proved willing to do so, then it was important "that all causes of irritation be removed as promptly as possible."[10] He urged that Mississippians be allowed the same option in a second ratification vote. Three days later Congress complied, adding Texas to the list of states where Grant could call for the separate submission of these proscriptive clauses. However, it added one new requirement: each state would have to ratify the Fifteenth Amendment before its representatives would be seated.

Virginians would vote first under the terms of Grant's proposal. State Republicans were divided over whether to push for the proscriptive clauses, exposing a division in that party's ranks that would reappear elsewhere in the years to come. Radical Republicans held firm to the idea of exclusion; moderates and conservatives, looking to attract native white voters, opposed it. Grant favored the moderate position, having been reassured by no less an authority than Robert E. Lee that white Virginians would accept black suffrage and the results of the war. In July, the Radicals suffered defeat. The proscriptive clauses were voted down; Gilbert C. Walker, a native Virginian who stood as the Conservative Republican candidate, won over his Radical opponent; Conservative Republicans and Democrats secured a majority in the state legislature, although 29 of the 183 legislators were black. Some northern Republicans protested the result; others either praised or acquiesced in the result. "We can't back out of the results of a fair submission, under authority of Congress and the Administration, of the constitution of Virginia," observed Cox. Better to secure Virginia's vote for the Fifteenth Amendment, "so that we may take a last affectionate farewell of the Reconstruction."[11]

Grant was not so pleased. In wanting moderate Republicans to win the day, he did not look to hand the state over to the Democrats. And yet he could not protest too much, for the elections had been peaceful and fair. The restoration of civil government did not necessarily mean the continuation of Republican rule. The following month, Grant permitted the state legislature to convene without requiring its members to take the test oath, thus allowing legislators to avoid disqualification. However, in Tennessee, Republican chances to retain power crumbled because of party factionalism. Conservative Republican DeWitt Senter, who had assumed the governorship when incumbent William G. Brownlow won election to the U.S. Senate at the beginning of the year, sought to retain the office; state Radicals supported the candidacy of William B. Stokes. Senter bolstered his majorities by helping ex-Confederates dodge disfranchisement, most notably by appointing new registrars who chose not to ask too many questions. Democrats supported Senter and concentrated their efforts on securing control of the legislature. In August they claimed victory and prepared to undo the policies of their predecessors.[12]

What happened in Tennessee illustrated for Republians the risks of wooing conservative support. A similar result in Mississippi and Texas would damage the Republican party in both the South and the nation. Grant publicly shifted his support to regular Republicans when he spurned the efforts of a Mississippi fusion movement to secure his support by nominating as their gubernatorial candidate Lewis Dent, the president's brother-in-law. Mississippi Republicans triumphed in the fall elections, although the proscriptive clauses fell, and moderates controlled the party. Texas proved more challenging. Although proscription was not an issue, Republican factionalism was especially intense. Grant relied on an old West Point classmate, district commander Joseph J. Reynolds, to advise him on what to do; Reynolds eventually sided with the Radicals. For several months the president wavered between Radicals and moderates, hoping that the two factions would work out their differences.

When Democrats decided to support the moderates in an effort to repeat what had happened in Virginia, Grant threw the administration whole-heartedly behind the candidacy of Radical Edmund J. Davis, who won in a close contest.[13]

These attempts to define a vital center in southern politics conducive to Republicanism had produced mixed results. Conciliation in Virginia had delivered the Old Dominion to a coalition of conservative Republicans and Democrats; in Texas, the failure of party factions to find common ground had led to a Radical triumph. Only in Mississippi had Grant seen both moderation and Republicanism triumph. Different circumstances in each state suggested that it would be difficult for the president to take a uniform approach. However, if he tailored policy to fit individual circumstances, the result would contain contradictions and tensions, leading unwary observers to conclude that he had no policy at all.

When Congress convened in December 1869, Grant urged it to recognize the new state governments of Virginia, Texas, and Mississippi "and thus close the work of reconstruction." But Republicans in Congress divided over whether they could or should impose requirements on Virginia before readmitting the state, with Radicals pushing for the taking of the test oath of the Fourteenth Amendment by Virginia officeholders and a promise not to alter the state constitution in ways adverse to black suffrage, civil rights, and education. Perhaps some Radicals wanted to block Virginia's readmission by raising the reservations; the Virginians shrewdly gave way, confident that once the state was readmitted, Congress would be unable to check subsequent developments. The readmission of Mississippi and Texas proved less troublesome because Republicans were unquestionably in power.[14]

Elsewhere Grant demonstrated his concern with the fate of black Americans, having assured a delegation of black Tennesseans that he "would do all in his power to protect them." First was the problem of political violence in Georgia. Republicans there had started off well—so well, in fact, that Georgia's Democrats decided to put a stop to it after the Republicans secured victory in the April 1868 state contests. Democrats had successfully purged the state legislature of black representatives; Republican factionalism further damaged the party's fortunes. That fall, Democratic-supported political terrorism targeted Republican voters, black and white. The Johnson administration winked, guaranteeing the state for Seymour and Blair.[15]

Grant remained silent about Georgia throughout the first several months of his administration because it served his interests in encouraging moderate approaches in Virginia, Texas, and Mississippi. In December, he called upon

Congress to enable Georgia's governor, Rufus Bullock, to convene the original legislature and disqualify those members who were not eligible to hold office under the terms of the Fourteenth Amendment. Congress agreed, mandating ratification of the Fifteenth Amendment as a prerequisite to readmission. Grant went further and remanded the state to military supervision, arguing that congressional action revived the supervisory structure outlined in the Reconstruction Acts. However, he became restive when Bullock sought to use the opportunity of reorganizing the state government to push forward several initiatives. If Republicanism was to survive in Georgia, it would have to demonstrate that it could do so without the protection of federal bayonets. Radicals lost their bid to postpone elections for the state legislature from 1870 to 1872, which would have given Bullock and his followers increased leverage. Grant himself urged Congress to reach some accord on Georgia, for, as one newspaper noted, he was "very solicitous that the whole reconstruction business shall be ended immediately." Vice President Colfax revealed the administration's increasing skepticism about Georgia, wishing a delegation of black Georgians good luck in their struggle to maintain Republican rule even as he openly wondered whether the legislature could sustain itself.[16]

To enable blacks to shape their own future at the ballot box, Grant pushed for the ratification of the Fifteenth Amendment. Immediately after the war he questioned whether it was time to enfranchise blacks until the persistence of white southern recalcitrance convinced him that blacks had to be given the means to defend themselves at the polls. Unhappy with the hypocrisy inherent in Republican efforts to mandate black suffrage in the South while leaving it up to each northern state to accept it, Grant saw in the Fifteenth Amendment a way to erase the color line at the ballot box. Its adoption would secure black voting rights in the South and end the mostly futile process attending efforts to bring about the enfranchisement of blacks in the North. It was not clear whether the amendment would increase narrow Republican majorities in several key states, since white backlash might more than nullify the augmentation of Republican strength. Grant believed that with the passage of the amendment debate over southern policy would fade into the background, and before long parties and voters would turn to new issues. With that in mind, he urged ratification in his inaugural.[17]

Grant closely followed the course of the ratification struggle. He urged Nebraska's governor to call a special session to secure ratification there, "in order that it may no longer remain an open issue, and a subject of agitation before the people"; he twisted arms to gain Nevada's assent. He even contemplated rushing through the readmission of Georgia and Texas, complete with their ratification of the amendment, in time to enfranchise blacks for spring elections in Connecticut. In March he took the unusual step of commemorating the amendment's ratification by issuing a proclamation that characterized it as a complete repudiation of the Dred Scott decision that blacks had no rights that whites were bound to respect. The amendment was "a measure of grander importance than any other one act of the kind from the foundation of our free government to the present day." He reminded blacks of "the importance of their striving in every honorable manner to make themselves worthy of their new privilege" while advising whites, "the race more favored heretofore by our laws," to "withhold no privilege of advancement to the new citizen." The president called upon Congress to assist the emancipated in their quest for advancement through support for public education. Failing to act on this suggestion, Congress even considered terminating the Bureau of Education but backed down when Grant pointed out, "With millions of exslaves to be educated, now is not the time to suppress an office for facilitating education."[18]

"The issues of the rebellion and the war pass away," proclaimed the Washington (D.C.) *National Republican* on the eve of ratification. The past five years had witnessed a veritable revolution in the republic's constitutional framework. It was time to rest and take stock. "The present generation must rest content with knowing that so far as legal principles are involved, the process of reconstruction has reached its limits in the legislation of 1869," that political pundit of distinguished pedigree, Henry Adams, remarked. Republicans far more committed to social justice than Adams agreed. "It is not the theory of [our] government that any able-bodied citizen shall be carried, but that none shall be impeded in the fair and equal race of life," declared Congressman James A. Garfield. To the Ohio Republican, the Fifteenth Amendment "confers upon the African Race the care of its own destiny. It places their fortunes in their own hands." This achievement, he thought, was enough. "The South ought now to be dropped by Congress," declared the *Nation,* a journal with Radical roots that was having second thoughts. "All that paper and words can do for it have been done." Others echoed that sentiment. "It is the general feeling that we have done enough, gone far enough in governmental reconstruction, and that it is best for all that the southern communities should be left to manage themselves," concluded one Ohioan. The New York *Times* asserted that "now that reconstruction is at the very point of completion, there ought to be no need of additional laws." It warned that "the utmost caution should be observed in the exercise of the Executive prerogative," for any misstep would provide Grant's opponents with "ground for cavil and complaint."[19]

Grant initially believed that the ratification of the Fifteenth Amendment went a long way to completing reconstruction. He had even considered issuing a general amnesty in his proclamation celebrating ratification but continuing antiblack violence caused him to withhold it.[20] There were other things he could do to enhance black opportunity. One was to protect blacks from violence, so that bullets could not stifle ballots. Another was to arm black Americans with yet another tool, economic clout. With confiscation and redistribution now eliminated as possible means of such empowerment, he turned to foreign policy, embarking on one of the most controversial initiatives ever embraced by a president.

Many Americans had coveted the island republic of San Domingo for many years. William H. Seward had negotiated to annex the republic during the Johnson administration. Newspaper editors, including Joseph Medill, Horace Greeley, and Charles Dana, approved the idea, as did Henry Adams. They were joined by congressional leaders Nathaniel P. Banks, Benjamin F. Butler, and John Logan. Grant also warmed to the idea. He believed that the island offered a wealth of natural resources and an ideal location for a naval base and a coaling station to enable the U.S. Navy to protect American interests in the Caribbean and Central America, including a possible canal across Nicaragua. No doubt the republic's inhabitants would flourish under the stability offered by American control.

These were the justifications offered by many an imperialist, but Grant saw something else. He observed that the republic could support "the entire colored population of the United States, should it choose to emigrate." Americans must overcome the obstacle to race relations caused by "the prejudice of color. The prejudice is a senseless one," he added, "but it does exist." So far he seemed to be repeating Lincoln's thoughts on the matter, although in calling prejudice "senseless" at least he ventured where Lincoln hesitated. But Grant did not believe that blacks and whites required separation because they were innately incompatible. Instead, he hoped to offer blacks in the South a bargaining tool. Black labor was essential to the economic reconstruction of the South. Should the black worker be empowered to go elsewhere, "his worth here would soon be discovered and he would soon receive such recognition as to induce him to stay." In short, annexation would provide blacks with economic leverage that they had lost with the collapse of confiscation and redistribution of southern lands. "What I desired above all was to secure a retreat for that portion of the laboring classes of our former slave States, who might find themselves under unbelievable pressure," Grant later explained. "And I believed that the mere knowledge of that fact on the part not only of the freedmen but of their former masters, would serve to prevent anything like widespread injustice."[21]

Although other observers believed that San Domingo "would not only be made a State of great importance, but an asylum for our negro population & the solution of the Negro Problem," the idea was problematic. Blacks had shown little willingness to relocate in the past, and it was not clear how black families would fund the journey to the Caribbean island. Nevertheless, the idea comported with current notions of laissez-faire; San Domingo would be part of the American republic. Grant was reluctant to offer these arguments concerning blacks in public, with the result that he sounded like an everyday imperialist promoting his next target.[22]

Circumstances surrounding the negotiations for a treaty of annexation and the politics of race doomed Grant's dream. The president's private secretary, Orville E. Babcock, visited the republic in 1869 on a fact-finding mission. Befriending several men of questionable morals and motives who sought to manipulate the process to their own advantage, Babcock became so zealous an advocate of annexation that he returned with a draft treaty. Grant chose to overlook these irregularities and improprieties in his eagerness to achieve his goal. Others did not, and before long the entire enterprise was surrounded by rumors of dark dealings and evidence of unsavory behavior. Several of Grant's own cabinet members were less than enthusiastic about the plan, but those who opposed it largely kept their sentiments to themselves. Undeterred, Grant sought and thought he secured the support of Charles Sumner, head of the Committee on Foreign Affairs, only to discover later that the Massachusetts senator opposed the plan.

Sumner had good reason to be suspicious. He was extremely uncomfortable with the circumstances surrounding the negotiations and was appalled by the document itself, with its characterization of Babcock as the president's "aide-de-camp" and its pledge that Grant would "use all his influence" to secure ratification. Sumner also feared that annexation might threaten the sovereignty of the black republic of Haiti. But he erred mightily in not discussing the matter with the president, who felt betrayed. Disagreement became opposition and then enmity, driving apart two men who believed more than most in black equality and opportunity. Other opponents of annexation used less admirable arguments, making race an issue. Democrats, who before the war would have welcomed annexation as a means to expand the domain of slavery, now stood solidly against it and spoke darkly of the mongrelization of the American population. So did that erstwhile friend of the freedmen, Carl

Schurz, who argued that the tropics were not a suitable environment for the growth of representative institutions.

Grant was so enamored with the prospect of annexation that he failed to prepare for a fight over it, convinced that once senators saw things the way he did, it would sail through. Only when it became apparent that substantial opposition existed did Grant start lobbying to win votes. Southern Republicans indicated that they were willing to support the president but at a price: the replacement of Attorney General Hoar with a southern Republican. Apparently Hoar did not appear to be vigorous enough in battling southern terrorism, although no one had raised that point before; Postmaster General Creswell's Maryland credentials were not sufficiently southern. Perhaps better was the complaint that the attorney general did not cooperate with Senate patronage requests. Grant had other reasons to be uneasy with Hoar, but they concerned his inability to get along with Senate Republicans, who had turned back his nomination to the Supreme Court. Nevertheless, politics was politics. Grant abruptly requested Hoar's resignation, nominated Amos T. Akerman of Georgia as the new attorney general, and informed cabinet members that he would henceforth demand loyalty from senators (and others) as the price for heeding their patronage requests. When the Senate failed by a vote of 28–28 to ratify the annexation treaty on June 30, 1870, he directed Hamilton Fish to request the resignation of John Lothrop Motley, the minister to England, who had been Sumner's choice for the position.[23]

During the next ten months the debate over annexation escalated: the break between Grant and Sumner widened beyond possibility of repair. The Massachusetts senator blasted the president, implying that he was personally profiting from annexation, a statement as wrongheaded as it was unworthy. His wild rhetoric comparing the debate over annexation to the Kansas-Nebraska Act and his assertion that Grant was committing the republic to "a dance of blood" caused colleagues to roll their eyes. However, so long as Senate Democrats remained united against annexation, dissident Republicans could block ratification. Although Grant toyed with the idea of a joint resolution, he grew so infuriated with Sumner's insinuations about his integrity that he eventually abandoned annexation in favor of personal vindication. In December 1870, his congressional supporters called for the appointment of a committee to visit the republic and gather information about its people and resources, an inoffensive proposal designed to separate critics of hasty annexation from diehard administration opponents. Despite Sumner's long-winded efforts, it passed easily, as many Republicans contemplated the costs of opposition to Grant.

The political motives behind the project were clearly revealed in Grant's se-
lections of commissioners and staff. Andrew D. White, the president of Cornell
University, countered the objections of intellectuals; Benjamin F. Wade rallied his fellow Radicals; Samuel G. Howe fulfilled the need for a New England
antislavery reformer; Franz Sigel served to rebuke Sumner's ally, Carl Schurz,
by appealing to German-Americans; and Frederick Douglass gained a long-
sought-after federal post. That Douglass, who had passionately rejected colonization in the past, endorsed annexation suggested that he accepted the
president's reasoning. All the appointees but White had been openly identified with the welfare of American blacks. The committee fulfilled its mission
of vindicating Grant and documenting the resources of the Caribbean republic, but it did not save annexation (nor does it seem that Grant hoped it
would).[24]

Thus, Grant's plan to annex San Domingo did shape reconstruction policy,
albeit not as he had intended. His dreams of offering blacks an opportunity to
amass leverage vanished when he was unable to convince enough Republicans to support him; the resulting struggle exposed fissures in party ranks, none
more lasting than that between Grant and Sumner. Along with other issues,
the debate over annexation ignited the process of party realignment. Grant
played an active role in that process, forging alliances with party leaders. If he
failed in securing annexation, at least he began learning how to wield the tools
of presidential power, although sometimes he did so quite clumsily. Those
Republicans uncomfortable with the result cast about for alternatives for 1872.

"There is no doubt that a feeling prevails that the work of the Republican party
. . . ends with the adoption of the Fifteenth Amendment," observed the New
York *Times*. Emerging divisions in party ranks suggested that realignment was
likely; there were new issues on the political agenda, issues on which there
was no unified Republican position. Some observers attributed the resulting
political disruption in Republican ranks to "the removal of the strong cohe-
sive power of the Reconstruction issues." Yet reconstruction concerns were
central to shaping the course of realignment in both parties. Democrats called
for a "New Departure" in which party spokesmen pushed for dropping the
politics of race in favor of a new agenda. "We must accept the inevitable and
move onward to new fields," declared one Mississippi newspaper. "The real
question for sensible men to address themselves to, is not whether the negro
will vote, but *how* he will vote." Accepting the verdict of the war and resulting
legislation would muffle reconstruction as an issue. "It is reconstruction and

the issues growing out of it which preserve the Republican party," observed Georgia's Democratic chairman. "Strip them of the support which this question gives them and their dissolution will speedily follow."[25]

For Republicans, the challenge of realignment was complicated by the fact that at the same time that northern Republicans wrestled with new issues, southern Republicans debated over whether to consolidate their electoral base, grounded in black votes, or to reach out to attract more whites to the party by emphasizing issues of economic development. The two struggles were related, for unless southern Republicans succeeded in their quest to be accepted as a legitimate force in southern politics, thus ending the use of violence as a tool of party competition, the party would have to continue to rely upon federal protection just as northern Republicans were seeking new issues and wondering if they in fact had already done as much as they could for the South. A similar problem daunted the efforts of northern and southern Democrats, for those southern Democrats who persisted in advocating color-line politics feared that the triumph of the New Departure among northern Democrats would mean the end of party efforts to check legislation to protect blacks and their white allies from intimidation and violence.

In the South, both parties competed for white voters who were willing to leave behind the politics of race. Southern Republicans sought to attract white votes to reduce Democrats to minority status; New Departure Democrats sought to win over many of the same voters that Republicans pursued as well as possibly some blacks, believing that without reconstruction the Republican coalition would crumble. Centrists on both sides were primarily in quest of a new majority for their party, not new parties, muting the cries for realignment. Moreover, for southern Republicans, the debate over whether to expand the party's electoral base and how to go about it was a risky proposition. All too often, debates over the future direction of the party promoted factionalism, thus reducing the party's chances to maintain its sometimes tenuous hold on power, discrediting the party in the eyes of many northerners, and allowing Democrats to maneuver to advantage. Republicans were known to train their weapons on each other; Democrats always kept their eyes on the same target.

In their efforts to gain white support, some southern Republicans were willing to restore many former Confederates to full political participation. Should the party fail to gain as a result, its measures of magnanimity would serve only to enlarge the ranks of their opponents, which is exactly what happened in Missouri, thanks in large part to Carl Schurz. Radical Republicans, led by Senator Charles Drake, held fast to constitutional provisions that provided for a test oath and disfranchisement of leading ex-Confederates. Schurz, his influence waning with Grant, came out in opposition to these positions in time for the fall campaign.[26]

Grant might not possess the cultural flair or flamboyant dramatic sense of Schurz, but he knew far more about the basics of politics than did the Missouri senator. He was willing to tolerate Schurz's opposition to the annexation of San Domingo, but this situation was different. In combating Drake, Schurz served only to strengthen Missouri's Democrats. Once Drake was out of the picture, they would turn on Schurz and assume control of the state's politics. As the president predicted, Missouri Republicans went down to defeat that fall. The new state legislature, revealing the true sympathies of the Democrats who Schurz had so naively wooed, filled the Senate seat vacated by Drake with Frank Blair, the 1868 Democratic vice-presidential candidate and a bitter opponent of Republican reconstruction. Schurz rushed to the White House to explain himself to Grant, but the president coolly rebuffed him.[27]

Grant was not blind to the need to broaden the Republican party's appeal in the South. "Sooner or later the President must look to the South for a party," observed the New York *Standard*. "He can only have a sound party when he accepts and welcomes every loyal and peaceful influence." Yet he also had to secure southern Republicanism's base. Not all southern Democrats embraced the tenets of the New Departure, relying instead upon violence and intimidation to beat back Republican regimes. Unless something was done to curb political violence against Republican voters and officeholders, black and white, the newest constitutional amendment would be little more than a dead letter. On May 31, 1870, Congress responded to continued terrorism by passing what would become the first in a series of laws collectively known as the Enforcement Acts. The initial legislation banned the use of force, bribery, or intimidation to interfere with the right to vote and prohibited state officials from discriminating among voters on the basis of race. Those accused of violating the act were to be tried in federal courts, thus circumventing uncooperative state courts. The president could employ federal marshals to investigate violations and arrest violators of the law and dispatch federal soldiers to keep order at the polls.[28]

This first effort at mandating peaceful elections in the South proved insufficient. Most newsworthy was the triumph of counterrevolution in North Carolina. The fall of Governor William W. Holden should have troubled many

Republicans, North and South. A reluctant convert to black enfranchisement, Holden reasoned that the party would not long survive unless it attracted more whites through a program of economic development. Railroad investors presented a golden vision of economic prosperity spearheaded by railroad construction funded by state bonds. However, the lines collapsed in the wake of manipulations by speculators, financial setbacks, bankruptcy, and default, leaving the state saddled with a large debt. Charges of incompetence and corruption resounded throughout the state, and Democratic Conservatives seized the initiative. Republican officeholders and black supporters were assassinated; before long political violence spread across the state, although most incidents took place in several closely competitive piedmont counties. Holden first sought to conciliate his opponents. When terrorist activity mounted, he pushed for new militia legislation, although he still worked for a peaceful solution. Finally, in March 1870, he asked Grant to send federal soldiers to the state to preserve order while he mobilized the militia, adding that if Grant gained the ability to suspend the writ of habeas corpus, the vigorous exercise of military authority would soon guarantee "peace and order throughout all this country." The president dispatched a regiment to the Tarheel State and authorized federal forces to assist Holden, pledging "the moral, and if necessary, physical support of the Government to maintain law and order in North Carolina."[29]

In June 1870 Grant augmented federal forces in North Carolina and armed the state militia. The following month, in response to rumors and reports of increasing violence, he ordered additional forces to North Carolina to keep the peace but added that federal intervention would be forthcoming only after Holden had exhausted all means at his disposal to quell terrorism. It would be up to North Carolina's Republicans to defend themselves. Holden assumed the responsibility, albeit reluctantly. "If Congress would authorize the suspension, by the President, of the writ of habeas corpus in certain localities, and if criminals could be arrested and tried before military tribunals, and shot, we would soon have peace and order throughout all the country," he told Grant. "The remedy would be a sharp and a bloody one, but it is as indispensable as was the suppression of the rebellion." The preservation of law and order, the protection of life and liberty, and the survival of the Republican party were all at stake in the fall elections. Perhaps this was so, but Grant insisted that Holden had to look first to mobilizing his own resources to prevail, which proved counterproductive. Every action that Holden took to preserve the peace, especially his mobilization of the state militia and his call for federal assistance, became parts of a conspiracy to assure Republican victory—or so charged the opposition. The Republicans could not win unless they suppressed the violence, and the Democrats could not win unless their campaign of intimidation triumphed.[30]

Grant's support of Holden, however lukewarm, drew severe criticism for going too far. Predictably, Democratic papers decried intervention; much more significant, however, was the reaction of several traditionally Republican journals, who also took a dim view of the administration's decision to back the Holden regime. Many northerners were reluctant to expand the boundaries of federal supervision over Reconstruction governments in the South, even when it came to shielding them from violence; press accounts blamed Holden for the condition of the state. Democrats swept to victory in early August. Some North Carolina Republicans held Holden responsible for the setback; so did the New York *Times,* which argued that "the high-handed doings of the Governor" had recoiled against him.[31]

In the aftermath of the election Holden ordered the arrest of several political enemies, most notably newspaper editor Josiah Turner Jr., on charges that they had encouraged insurrection against the state government. He planned to hold them for military trial. Democrats immediately sought the release of Turner and his cohorts. Failing to secure the immediate cooperation of state judges, they appealed to U.S. District Court judge George W. Brooks to issue a writ of habeas corpus to force Holden to bring the incarcerated insurgents before him. Brooks, a Johnson appointee, complied on the basis that the Fourteenth Amendment and the Habeas Corpus Act of 1867—both Reconstruction measures—prohibited Holden's use of a military tribunal to try Turner. In response, Holden told Grant that since murder and assault were not under federal jurisdiction, Brooks had no authority to issue a writ binding on state officials. Attorney General Akerman, well aware of the problems facing a scalawag in southern politics, nevertheless conceded Brooks's point and advised Grant that Holden should give way and try the accused under state law. Grant agreed and forwarded Akerman's opinion. When the state attorney general failed to present evidence against Turner and his associates, Brooks understandably ordered their release from confinement. Prosecutions commenced in state courts, but they did not go far.[32]

Grant's decision did not contribute to the disaster in North Carolina, for the election took place prior to Turner's arrest. Holden's vigorous response to the mounting evidence of terrorist activity, however justified, added to his reputation as a divisive figure in Tarheel politics. Turner's arrest reinforced charges that Holden had exceeded the legal limits of his power and led to his impeachment. Although a congressional investigation uncovered much evidence of white supremacist violence in North Carolina, it also revealed that the governor transcended the legitimate exercise of his authority. Holden lobbied Republicans in Washington for some form of legislation, arguing that "if Congress does not do its duty there will be no safety for loyal people in the South." He observed that northern Republicans "hate the Southern Democrats and distrust the Southern Republicans." North Carolina Democrats triumphed in the impeachment trial, removing Holden from office in March 1871.[33]

Events in North Carolina reminded many Republicans that work remained to be done; so did the overwhelming Democratic triumph in Georgia and lesser gains elsewhere throughout the South. "We must have equal laws and equal protection for all men in all sections of the country. . . . If not, the war was a failure and republican government is a sham," declared the Washington (D.C.) *National Republican*. "Is the whole fabric of reconstruction to be pulled down, and a state of chronic rebellion to be inaugurated from henceforth?" The party faithful were sure this would not happen. "Grant is not Buchanan, and the present Congress is not one to put up with rebellion and outrage because a few of its members spout about the horrors of war and the rights of states," proclaimed the *Army and Navy Journal*. Reports of terrorism did not move all Republicans. Senator J. R. West of Louisiana reported that many party leaders "agreed in the opinion that our colored brethren are asking too much, and that the strong hand must be used to bring them to their senses in time for 1872." Others cited constitutional concerns. James A. Garfield asserted that while the war "has vindicated the centripedal power of the nation, and has exploded . . . the disorganizing theory of state sovereignty, . . . we should never forget that there is danger in the opposite direction. The destruction or serious crippling of the theory of local government would be as fatal to liberty as secession would have been to the Union." More than a few people were simply worn out. "Reconstruction has been under consideration for five years," snapped Senator William Stewart of Nevada. "The country wants it terminated if it can be done with safely. . . . We want an end to Reconstruction."[34]

At first Grant did not move vigorously to protect blacks by asking for additional legislation. His annual message in 1870 concentrated on other matters, notably annexation, foreign policy, and civil service reform. Congress passed measures to repair loopholes and offer details missing in earlier legislation— shades of the Reconstruction Acts—but Grant was not satisfied. He waited for the meeting of a new session of Congress in March 1871 to act. The "deplorable state of affairs in some parts of the South" demanded "the immediate attention of Congress," he told House Speaker James G. Blaine. He requested legislation to empower him to use federal force to stop political terrorism. But substantial opposition by some Republicans led to deadlock within weeks. "Public affairs here are hastening from bad to worse very rapidly," observed Garfield on March 23. "We have now been in session three weeks and have received not a word from the President in regard to public affairs and yet the South is crying out for protection against murder and outrage. . . . There are many ugly signs of disintegration in our party." On the very day Garfield wrote, Grant went to the Capitol to confer with congressional leaders and again impress upon them the need for legislation. He was otherwise reluctant to sanction continued federal intervention in the South, lest he confirm charges that he was exercising dictatorial powers. Several leaders balked, compelling Grant to compose a message calling for Congress to pass the needed legislation.[35]

Congress wrangled for another month. Garfield, who had waxed eloquent on the need to stop political violence in criticizing Grant's inaction, seemed less inclined to do something about it once Grant acted (which indicated why so many thought he was a typical congressman). He grumbled that "we are working on the very verge of the Constitution." Jacob D. Cox, who had left the cabinet in October 1870 after repeatedly clashing with Grant, moaned "that we are getting further and further away from any hope or chance of making a Union with . . . the thinking and influential native Southerners," whom he defined as "the intelligent, well-to-do, and controlling class of whites in the South." Conservative Republicans agreed with the New York *Evening Post* when it charged that the bill was "plainly contrary to the spirit and letter of the Constitution," adding, "Freedom cannot exist under a centralized government." Finally, as one Illinois congressman complained, "We have reconstructed, and reconstructed, and we are asked to reconstruct again. . . . we are governing the South too much."[36]

Other issues threatened to complicate the struggle for new enforcement legislation. In March, Grant's supporters in the Senate had dumped Sumner from his chairmanship of the Foreign Relations Committee, despite protests against party tyranny and presidential despotism. Hardly had these complaints died down when the members of the San Domingo commission returned, reviving talk of annexation. The Baltimore *American* advocated annexation "as the only mode of restoring peace and order to the South," for "the freedmen of the South will have a safe and sure haven to fly to from their persecutors." Like Grant, it saw annexation as empowering the black man. "Once give him the means of escape, and it will become the interest of the Southern people to keep him at home, and to put down and suppress the ruffians who are disgracing them and their section." Others still opposed the measure for racial reasons. "Our people don't want Southern territory & are afraid of the addition of any more ignorant negroes in our body politic" was how one observer bluntly put it. Sensing that he lacked support for the measure, Grant decided to use the committee's report to rebuke Sumner's wild charges. Wisely, he remarked, "I do not wish to make annexation a party question"; he let the matter die.[37]

Freed from distractions, Republican supporters of additional enforcement legislation pushed onward. Congressman John A. Bingham declared that Grant "had never rested nor wearied in his pledge to secure to every citizen of the Republic, white and black, the full enjoyment of the rights guaranteed to him by the late amendments to the Constitution." Speakers revived memories of the war. As Rutherford B. Hayes told John Sherman, "Nothing unites and harmonizes the Republican party like the conviction that Democratic victories strengthen the reactionary and brutal tendencies of the late rebel states." Finally Grant's allies worked through a bill, fittingly called the Ku Klux Act after the most renowned terrorist group, which authorized the president to call out military force and suspend the writ of habeas corpus (limiting the power to do the latter to the end of the next session in 1872). Federal marshals could form posses, federal soldiers could enforce court orders, and federal courts exercised original jurisdiction in suffrage cases.[38]

On April 20 Grant signed the Ku Klux Act into law. Democrats charged that "Kaiser Ulysses" was eager to exercise despotic power, but the president hoped that the passage of legislation alone might quell some outbreaks. Calling upon white southerners to cease such activities, he warned that he would exercise his new power if necessary. Akerman dismissed previous efforts at conciliation as fruitless. "It is my individual opinion that nothing is more idle than to attempt to conciliate by kindness that portion of the southern people who are still malcontent," he observed. "They take all kindness on the part of the Government as evidence of timidity, and hence are emboldened to lawlessness by it." Such disaffection "will only disappear before an energetic, but at the same time, strictly just and lawful exercise of power."[39]

South Carolina presented the president with the first opportunity to use his new powers. Republican governor Robert K. Scott had attempted to protect his regime by forming state militia forces, but the fact that many of the militiamen were black simply heightened racial tensions. In February 1871, he had called on Grant for assistance, adding the next month that "an actual state of war exists in York and Chester counties." Grant cited the guarantee clause of the Constitution as authorizing him to use force if terrorism did not cease.

However, it was not until violent incidents increased in number with the approach of the fall elections that he acted, invoking the Ku Klux Act for the first time. On October 12 he issued the obligatory warning, and five days later he authorized intervention in nine piedmont counties. South Carolina Republicans welcomed the proclamation "as a thunder clap from a clear sky." The use of force revealed to terrorists that the federal government "means business . . . and it is the only kind of business that they respect." Yet Grant acted only when all other efforts short of intervention had failed. "We know that the President was anxious to avoid the exercise of power which he has just put forth," commented the Washington (D.C.) *National Republican*. "He had hoped to conciliate these people, and to win them back to their allegiance by kindness and loyalty."[40]

Much has been made of Grant's actions as breaking the Ku Klux Klan in South Carolina, although more careful research suggests that terrorism may have started to decline before the fall of 1871. At least as important, however, was that the federal government lacked adequate resources to engage in more than selective arrests and even more selective prosecutions of violators. This intervention was more than a police action. Attorney General Akerman argued that "these combinations amount to war, and cannot be effectively crushed on any other theory." However, the newly created Justice Department was still too small to handle the resulting caseload, and federal courts were swamped. Nor did extending the olive branch to those implicated in terrorist acts achieve much. "Clemency is mistaken for cowardice," noted Major Lewis Merrill, commanding the detachment of the Seventh Cavalry sent to South Carolina.[41]

Even avid supporters of enforcement came to admit that public support for prolonged intervention was frail. "We can keep their attention upon the South in such striking matters as the Ku Klux and the rebellious utterances of some of the prominent leaders," Akerman maintained at first. He believed that "all that is necessary to hold the majority of the northern voters to the Republican cause, is to show then how active and cruel the Confederate temper still is in the South." Within weeks he changed his mind. "The feeling here is very strong that the Southern Republicans must cease to look for especial support from Congressional action," he remarked as Congress met. "Such atrocities as Ku Kluxery fire up Congress and the North, and there is much more of a disposition to aid in proceeding against that monster, than to render help in a matter that is directly political." Before long he added that "the real difficulty is that very many of the Northern Republicans shrink from any further legislation in regard to the South. Even such atrocities as Ku Kluxery do not hold their attention, as long and as earnestly, as we should expect. The Northern mind, being active and full of what is called progress, runs away from the past."[42]

Grant featured southern policy in his 1871 annual message, the last before the presidential contest of 1872. The "condition of the Southern States is, unhappily, not such as all true patriotic citizens would like to see," he remarked. "Social ostracism for opinion's sake, personal violence or threats toward persons entertaining political views opposed by the majority of the old citizens, prevents immigration and the flow of much-needed capital into the states lately in rebellion." Disorder, in short, disrupted the return of prosperity—a prosperity achieved by the injection of northern money. "It will be a happy condition of the country when the old citizens of these states will take an interest in public affairs, promulgate ideas honestly entertained, . . . and tolerate the same freedom of expression and ballot in those entertaining different political convictions." Yet these words followed Grant's request to Congress to consider removing prohibitions on officeholding for most former Confederates imposed by the Fourteenth Amendment.[43]

This was not the only sign that the administration was willing to embrace conciliation once more. Grant refused to intervene in Georgia, where Republicans, desperate to do anything to forestall the Democrats' return to power, hit upon the idea of allowing Bullock to resign the governorship to escape impeachment. Democrats, not to be deterred, passed legislation providing for a special election for governor in order to displace Bullock's successor, Benjamin Conley. He looked to Washington for help, telling Grant, "It rests with you to determine whether the enemies of the administration and of the government in this State shall be allowed by the illegal exercise of a power fraudulently obtained, to crush the last vestige of republican government in Georgia." To others, however, there was no good reason for Grant to act. Akerman thought it better if Georgia's Republicans learned to "stand on their own feet. They must not depend always on propping from Washington, and might as well learn the lesson now." As a result, the Democrats triumphed. It was one of the last pieces of advice Akerman offered as a member of Grant's cabinet, for the president replaced him with George H. Williams of Oregon.[44]

Grant also acted with restraint in Louisiana, although there he and others were confounded by Republican factionalism. In wooing whites, Republican governor Henry Clay Warmoth offended many black Republicans, who were particularly put off by his veto of a civil rights bill in the first year of his administration and his hostility to similar subsequent measures. Carpetbaggers growled at the governor's decision to appoint several Democrats to office. Before long, dissatisfied Republicans united under the leadership of James F. Casey, collector of customs in New Orleans and married to one of Julia Dent Grant's sisters, and drew on federal patronage to counter Warmoth's dispensing of state offices. By the summer of 1871, the party had divided into Warmoth and anti-Warmoth wings, the latter denoted as the Custom House party, and wrestled with each other as Democrats looked on, eager to exploit the contest for their own ends. "The muddle down there is almost beyond my fathoming," Grant confessed, a sentiment he would have cause to recall in the years to come. The intraparty fracas nearly exploded into violence at the beginning of 1872, as Warmoth fought off efforts to impeach him. Casey and his allies may have been disappointed with Grant's failure to use federal force to support their movement, but the president wisely refused to do more than preserve the peace, lest a more vigorous response provoke charges of military dictatorship (which would have had the ring of truth to them). In light of what was to come, perhaps he should have washed his hands of the whole mess. In seeking to protect Louisiana blacks, he eroded support for such efforts elsewhere, as critics latched on to the corrupt morass that passed for Louisiana politics to discredit Reconstruction across the board.[45]

In 1872, Republican support for a vigorous policy of intervention subsided, in part because many party leaders thought it might damage the party's prospects in the North. Congress failed to extend the time limits for Grant to suspend the writ of habeas corpus under the Ku Klux Act owing to the eagerness of Grant's supporters to deprive dissident Republicans as well as Democrats of grounds for complaint with the administration as a centralized tyranny; that sentiment also doomed proposed additional enforcement proposals. A vocal minority of Republicans, including some of the party's elder statesmen, were unhappy with the incumbent. Reformers and office seekers (some were one and the same) found fault with Grant for not serving their interests. So did Sumner, Schurz, and several other senators and congressmen. Many dissidents deplored the administration's course on reconstruction as destructive of federalism. Others claimed that a continuing emphasis on reconstruction took attention away from other concerns. James Rood Doolittle asserted that a new party was necessary "to preserve constitutional civil liberty, and the substance of republican government" from Grant's military "despotism." Lyman Trumbull complained of "the frequent assumption of unwarranted powers by the Federal Administration." Anti-Grant campaign literature spoke of the president's "overweening fondness for military rule" and claimed that he "has held the civil powers in subjection to the military."[46] There were other reasons for disgruntlement, including annexation, patronage distribution, and charges that the administration paid insufficient attention to reform, but such charges were primarily aimed at Grant's reconstruction policy. However half-hearted and halting the president's behavior might seem today, these critics faulted Grant for an all too vigorous exercise of presidential power, much as others had assailed Lincoln and Johnson. The sort of legislation necessary to buttress a more assertive policy of intervention would have sparked even more impassioned opposition.

By the spring of 1872 many of these dissident Republicans, satisfied that Grant would capture renomination, decided it was time to form their own party, known as the Liberal Republicans. The resulting coalition lacked ideological coherence when it came to economic policy or reform, lending credence to the charge that its rallying cry was "Anything to beat Grant!" However, the vast majority favored a policy of reconciliation with white southerners and rejected continued federal intervention to protect blacks: Sumner stood nearly alone in his continued advocacy of federal protection for civil rights. Whether the bolters could overcome the fact that the movement's origins lacked grass-roots support remained unanswered for the moment.

Some degree of political realignment was inevitable in the 1870s. The founding generation of the Republican party was giving way to a new cadre of leaders, most of whom were not part of the original antislavery crusade. Some party veterans found common cause with Grant, but many of the leaders of the 1850s—Sumner, Trumbull, Greeley, and Schurz—migrated elsewhere. Nor was the political agenda of the 1870s the same as it had been in the 1850s. With slavery dead and the Union preserved, the early goals of the party had been achieved. Issues of economic policy and reform never united the party faithful and did not stir them to the depths of their souls. The new generation of Republican leaders, led by New York's Roscoe Conkling and Maine's James G. Blaine, intended to build upon the estate left them by their predecessors, reforging a Republican majority that would thrive in the changed environment of postwar America. Overwhelming majorities in Congress, especially in the Senate, had led to a slackening of party discipline and an increase in intraparty divisiveness, and this time there was no common foe in the White House to compel compromise. Although Grant's actions as president helped shape how Republican divisions came to the fore, any Republican in the White House would have had to face eroding party unity.

The Liberal Republicans were not alone in retreating from Reconstruction. Party regulars also believed that its importance was declining. "Little is thought of or cared for on the civil rights question—in this section," noted one Ohioan, "and we regard the amnesty matter as virtually settled by the Fourteenth Amendment." The tariff, he believed, was now the most important issue.[47] Yet among Republican regulars, reconstruction issues provided the best source of party unity among available issues. They also remained the primary concern of the party's black spokesmen, led by Frederick Douglass. Thus Republicans adopted much the same position as they had in 1868, portraying Grant as the candidate of conciliation with whites and justice for blacks. In speech after speech and pamphlet after pamphlet, Republican speakers argued both that the president would see reconstruction through and that he would bring it to an end. Once more they brought out the bloody shirt and reminded listeners of what might happen if former Confederates came to power in the republic they had just tried to destroy, while they pointed to the support offered to Grant by former Confederates such as John S. Mosby as proof of the president's ability to heal sectional wounds.

Perhaps the best evidence of Grant's willingness to welcome back former Confederates was his call for amnesty legislation in 1871, which would remove the Fourteenth Amendment's prohibition on holding office from all but a handful of former Confederates. Coming as it did at the same time that he was celebrating the use of federal power to suppress terrorism in South Carolina, the proposal highlighted his willingness to extend the olive branch to the truly repentant. It would help him search for new allies among prominent former Confederates, while countering Democrats' demands for amnesty. Sumner complicated matters by affixing a civil rights bill, long a passion of his, to the proposed legislation. This ambitious proposal would have barred discrimination in jury selection and desegregated schools, public transportation, public places such as hotels and theaters, and churches and cemeteries. Although its aim was laudable, it lacked effective means of enforcement and grated upon many whites' racial prejudices, welcome news to Democrats, who overlooked their own talk about a "New Departure" in opposing the measure. So did Liberal Republicans. Grant noted that by acting as he did, Sumner made it less likely that his measure would pass, for the amnesty bill required a two-thirds vote as outlined in the Fourteenth Amendment. His supporters preferred to support a bill far narrower in scope; they allowed Sumner to attach the bill, then watched as the result went down to defeat. It would not be until May that the amnesty measure passed, shorn of Sumner's bill.[48]

By that time the presidential contest was under way. Dissident Republicans had traveled to Cincinnati, where after a confusing convention delegates nominated New York *Tribune* newspaper editor Horace Greeley as their candidate.

Shocked by the nomination, several prospective bolters made their way back into Republican ranks, but many Democrats, pleased with Greeley's support for reconciliation with the South (and doubtful that they could successfully mount an independent challenge to Grant's reelection), endorsed Greeley's candidacy. The Republican convention's choice was a foregone conclusion. In accepting renomination, Grant expressed his desire "to see a speedy healing of all bitterness of feeling between sections, parties or races of citizens" and looked forward to "the time when the title of citizen carries with it all the protection and privilege to the humblest that it does to the most exalted."[49]

In the election that followed, Republicans ruthlessly assailed Greeley, and none more so than cartoonist Thomas Nast of *Harper's Weekly*. In cartoon after cartoon Nast linked Greeley to the Confederacy and once showed him extending his hand in friendship to John Wilkes Booth over Lincoln's grave. Democratic cartoonist Matt Morgan of *Leslie's Illustrated* in turn attempted to portray the president as a drunkard and a dictator, but on the whole he lacked Nast's skill. Grant's own mission was a little more complex. He had to reassure blacks and abolitionists, many of whom counted Sumner as an ally, that he would continue to protect black rights, while at the same time he presented himself as willing to welcome southern whites back into full fellowship in the Union. Occasionally he sounded both themes simultaneously. "My oft-expressed desire is that all citizens, white or black, native or foreign born, may be left free, in all parts of our common country, to vote, speak and act, in obedience to law, without intimidation on account of his views, color, or nativity," he assured abolitionist Gerrit Smith. "With these privileges secured there is no political offense that I would not advocate forgiveness and forgetfulness of, so far as the South is concerned."[50]

Both themes surfaced as campaigning got under way. John M. Langston declared that Grant "has showed himself an active, honest advocate of the negro and their friend"; Frederick Douglass added that "at all times he gave every aid to the development of the industry and of the improvement of the colored race." Other administration spokesmen emphasized their chief's moderation. Amos Akerman remarked, "It is charged that he has advised and enforced exceptional legislation. This was done in order to suppress exceptional wickedness." George Boutwell spoke of Grant's "indisposition . . . to use the national power as a substitute for, or even as an aide to local law." One Republican journal commented that "no one in the country has done more toward reconciliation than he."[51]

Such comments, intended to praise the president, highlighted that during his first term he had failed to formulate a policy that could achieve both sectional reconciliation and real equality and freedom for blacks. Motivated by good intentions, he failed to translate them into a consistent and coherent approach, veering back and forth in response to circumstances. Perhaps this result was inevitable, for other politicians achieved consistency and coherence by establishing priorities (or dismissing either reconciliation or equality altogether). It remained an open question whether there was a better way. Could any Republican stop factionalism among party adherents in the South? Was there any way to devise adequate safeguards for blacks in light of notions of federalism and limited governance? Would northern Republican voters continue to support the party's southern policy, or were they more eager to address new issues closer to home? Even though Republicans had persevered in working against or around racism before, was racism so intractable that no policy could completely overcome it?

Grant's reelection by an overwhelming margin offered no answers. Nor did his 1872 annual message. "Reckless and lawless men, I regret to say, have . . . committed deeds of blood and violence," he observed, adding that "the prosecution and punishment of many of these persons have tended greatly to the repression of such disorders." Although he was willing to consider extending clemency to those convicted of such acts if that would "tranquilize the public mind," he warned that any such act should not be interpreted as an unwillingness to persist in prosecuting offenders—although that was exactly how it would be interpreted. More important was the fact that the statement was buried in a message that emphasized foreign policy and other matters. Little more was to be found in his second inaugural address, delivered on a particularly cold March day. Blacks, he observed, were not "possessed of the civil rights which citizenship should carry with it. This is wrong, and should be corrected. To this correction I stand committed, so far as Executive influence can avail." He clarified what he meant by civil rights: "Social equality is not a subject to be legislated upon, nor shall I ask that anything be done to advance the social status of the colored man, except to give him a fair chance to develop what is good in him, give him access to schools, and when he travels let him feel assured that his conduct will regulate the treatment and fare he will receive." He pledged that during his second term he would work for "the restoration of good feelings between the different sections of our common country." Admirable as such principles might be, they were no substitute for a policy.[52]

6

"UNWHIPPED OF JUSTICE"

Although during his first term Ulysses S. Grant had failed to craft a southern policy to secure both reconciliation with former Confederates and equality for blacks, he had succeeded in conducting a fairly able holding action, reacting to circumstances as they unfolded. Each state had presented its own challenges, severely complicating efforts to formulate an overall policy. Democrats had regained power in several states, but it was unrealistic to expect a solidly Republican South. Indeed, it might have been better had Grant from the beginning accepted a divided South as inevitable and worked to consolidate Republican control in several states while conceding the rest. In laboring to preserve party fortunes in each state, he acted in ways that appeared vacillating and inconsistent, undercutting Republican prospects elsewhere.

Whether Grant could continue to juggle reconciliation and justice was another matter entirely, and not one completely in his hands. However warranted intervention might be, that alone could not provide the base for a lasting Republican presence in the South, especially in those states where white voters were in the majority. Yet Grant was unable to offer much in the way of incentives for white southerners to join the party unless he was first willing to soft-pedal issues of interest to blacks. It would be left to southern Republicans to find ways to broaden their base and render themselves acceptable as legitimate participants in the region's politics instead of relying on support from Washington. Whether they could do so was open to question, especially in light of factional rifts that threatened to destroy the party from within, increasing its vulnerability to violence and exasperating northerners, including Grant.

Nor could Grant continue to rely upon federal intervention to protect southern Republicans. Congress and the northern public alternated between sporadic demands for action, expressions of concern that the federal government was doing too much, and a growing desire to move on to other issues. Despite the establishment of the Justice Department and the passage of enforcement legislation, the federal government lacked sufficient means to put down violence and keep the peace for long. Each act of intervention propped up Republican regimes in the short run while damaging their long-term quest for legitimacy and acceptance. Prolonged efforts to coerce southern whites ran counter to the desire of most people to restore civil government, raising charges that Grant was bent on creating a centralized despotism on behalf of Republican fortunes.

So long as the president reacted to circumstances as they unfolded, he could not play a controlling role in southern affairs. Southern whites held the upper hand. The success of reconciliation depends on one's willingness to be reconciled; the intense determination of many southern whites to strip blacks and their white allies of political power by any means promised a struggle in which they, and not a majority of white northerners, had the will to persist. With the Union preserved and slavery destroyed, a majority of white northerners (virtually all Democrats and a minority of Republicans) were willing to let southern whites manage their own affairs, having always expressed reservations (and worse) about the capabilities of blacks to become full and equal members of the American polity. All that remained open to question was whether southern Democrats would be skillful enough to take advantage of their opponents' errors and conduct their affairs to minimize the chances of provoking federal intervention.

Grant and the Republicans did not long enjoy the glow of electoral triumph. As Congress assembled in December 1872, several prominent members faced charges that they had accepted stock in Credit Mobilier, a front used by stockholders of the Union Pacific Railroad to rake in profits from the construction of the transcontinental railroad. Although the shady transactions took place during the Johnson administration, their revelations during Grant's presidency tainted his administration. Although Grant was blameless in this instance, a second congressional snafu came closer to home when Congress voted itself a retroactive pay raise and doubled Grant's salary (the former salary of $25,000 had been in place since Washington's presidency). This so-called salary grab further tarnished the image of the victorious party in the eyes of the electorate.

By year's end, events overshadowed this less than auspicious beginning. Throughout the spring and summer, investors and businessmen were critical of the government's financial policy as inflationary, and people grew suspicious of the security of their stocks, bonds, and savings. A sharp downturn in the price of gold in September triggered a panic, forcing several banks and brokerage houses, notably Jay Cooke and Company, to close. The Panic of 1873 and the ensuing depression proved disastrous for the fortunes of southern Republicans by severely damaging the effectiveness of both conciliation and federal protection in promoting party fortunes in Dixie. The collapse of Cooke's firm crippled efforts to broaden the party's base through the promise of economic development spearheaded by railroad construction—the so-called gospel of prosperity. Railroad construction ground to a halt; state governments found themselves in financial trouble. As the depression deepened, southern whites became increasingly more resentful of the taxes they had to pay for public services that helped blacks, and they blamed both the freedmen and the Republican party for tough financial times. Grant contributed to these woes in April 1874 when he vetoed a measure that promised some relief in the form of mild inflation. Northern workers, struggling to make ends meet or searching for employment, asked why the federal government would use funds to help southern blacks and not northern whites. Democrats, capitalizing on such discontent, argued that it was time for the government to let go of the South and address the needs of the northern workingman—although party spokesmen were rather vague as to what exactly they proposed to do.

Enough confusion already existed in southern politics without such complications as depression and a Democratic resurgence in the North. To be sure, in 1872 Republicans had regained ground in North Carolina, and Grant had carried Virginia as well as the Republican states of South Carolina, Florida, Alabama, Mississippi, and Arkansas. But the results in Louisiana were under dispute, and there were rival claimants for the state government there as well as in Arkansas and Alabama. In all three states, Republican factionalism proved costly, perhaps fatal. It was not clear what Grant could have done to salvage these situations. If anything, his intervention proved counterproductive, not only to the preservation of Republican rule there but elsewhere, and disrupted his efforts to foster reconciliation with southern whites.

Louisiana proved the most troublesome. Schisms in Republican ranks offered Democrats an opportunity to regain power. With the assistance of outgoing governor Warmoth and the usual mix of intimidation, violence, and fraud, they claimed victory for gubernatorial candidate John McEnery. Republican regulars, led by their candidate for governor, William Pitt Kellogg, and James F. Casey, fought back and got a federal judge to uphold their claim. They quickly organized a legislature, impeached Warmoth, and began revamping the state judicial system; Democrats responded by setting up a rival legislature. Both sides sought relief from Washington. Although Grant expressed his disgust with the wrangle, he sided with Kellogg, Casey, and company. Congress, unable to decipher the returns, threw out the state's electoral vote. Some Republicans, unhappy that Grant had recognized Kellogg, pressed for a new election—a measure that in itself marked federal intervention in state politics of an even more far-reaching import—while Grant supporters, led by Oliver P. Morton, backed the president for making the best of a bad situation. Grant finally forced the issue by stating that if Congress failed to act, he would sustain Kellogg; congressional Republicans, fleeing from taking responsibility, did nothing. Thus Grant got his way, although the president was not exactly enthused about the kind of people he had endorsed. If he had preserved Republican rule for the moment, he had not gained Democrats' acceptance of the result. They would continue to contest Kellogg's claim to office by all available means, and Grant would find himself allied to a regime worthy of the same contempt earned by its opponents.[1]

Alabama and Arkansas offered variations on these themes. In Alabama, Republicans regained the governorship, but who controlled the legislature was disputed. Grant looked at first to stay aloof but eventually threatened to intervene if both parties could not settle matters, which led to the seating of a Republican-controlled legislature. Disputed election returns in Arkansas caused Congress not to count its electoral votes, while Republican Elisha Baxter made good his claim to victory in the governor's race over Joseph Brooks, the Democratic–Liberal Republican nominee. It remains a mystery as to which party was entitled to victory in either state; the resolutions of these controversies left the winners with scant claims to legitimacy.[2]

In sustaining Republican claimants, Grant opened himself to charges of serving partisan ends; maintaining those regimes, as he found out, might not have been worth the cost. Had he conceded victory to the Democrats, however, he would have sanctioned their efforts to win by whatever means possible. If southern Republicans in these three states failed to take advantage of their new leases on life to repair internal divisions and become self-sustaining, they would remain dependent upon federal intervention to survive. There were no easy answers, then or now: the underlying problem was the assumption that it was time for matters to return to normal in the face of abundant evidence that politics as usual in the Reconstruction South were anything but normal.

Ironically, even as Grant intervened in these three states, he was contemplating a revival of conciliation and moderation as the guiding notions of his southern policy. Perhaps he thought this approach was the best way to bring an end to such acrimony; there had to be a better way to restore order and legitimacy to the southern political scene. Among those who agreed with that policy was none other than one of Grant's old battlefield opponents, Tennessee's Gideon Pillow. "To win back the *hearts* of the southern people— so as to bring them again into the great National Family, in true *allegiance* and *love* to the Government, all *patriots must feel* is the *wisest,* and only *true* policy," Pillow told the president. "Kindness and confidence in them, on your part—and manifestation of sympathy and respect for them, will bring to your support the great body of the intelligent southern white population." Grant had hoped to promote such loyalty by touring the South, but the fear of assassination ended such plans, in itself a rather telling sign.[3]

Grant received feelers that southern whites would respond positively to a renewed effort at sectional conciliation. One way for him to cultivate that sentiment was by carrying out his promise to pardon many of those convicted under the Ku Klux Act. The administration acted, explained Attorney General Williams, "in the hope that the effect will be to produce obedience to the law and quiet among the people." Williams also narrowed the scope of prosecution, directing subordinates to restrict arrests to "flagrant cases of murder &c." Althouth these guidelines reflected the limited resources with which Williams had to work—resources strained to the limit by the prosecutions in South Carolina—it also meant that far fewer white southerners would be subject to prosecution.[4]

Some southern whites sincerely desired reconciliation. They had failed to join the Republican party, argued Georgian Henry Wayne, because "the public confidence and influence is bestowed on men foreign to the community, not respectable in their education, manners, habits and associations, who openly represent the lowest political sentiments, and who to further the extreme radical purposes use the confidence and influence they have to stir up the animosities of the Negro against the white race." There were native-born southern whites "ready and able to protect the negro in his newly acquired rights with dignity and character, and whose social standing deserves respect." To render Republicanism acceptable, "you must secure the intelligence, honor, and integrity of the leading minds of the South. Otherwise you seek to make bricks without straw." Running for Congress from South Carolina, William H. Trescot sought to reach common ground with the administration. "I believe that no reason exists why there should not be a cordial understanding between the Administration and the real representatives of the character and intelligence of this State," he told Hamilton Fish, "and that once reached, there would be a rapid improvement in public affairs."[5]

Grant's decision to woo southern moderates and recast the image of Republicanism in the South reflected his increasing frustration with southern Republican behavior. "I begin to think it time for the Republican party to unload," he declared in January 1874. "There has been too much dead weight carried by it. . . . I am tired of this nonsense. . . . This nursing of monstrosities has nearly exhausted the life of the party. I am done with them, and they will have to take care of themselves." If southern Republicans became dependent on intervention to survive, that would confirm characterizations of Republican regimes as illegitimate entities imposed on the states by the federal government. Meanwhile, party factionalism continued to take its toll. Grant understandably looked for alternatives, in the process alienating some party regulars.[6]

The conciliationist strategy even sparked rumors of a political realignment in which some southern Democrats contemplated pushing for a third term for Grant and an acceptance of black political participation, albeit under the umbrella of white supremacy, in exchange for an end to federal support for Republican regimes. This movement was most evident in Virginia, where at the end of 1873 incoming governor James L. Kemper looked to forge an alliance with the president; John S. Mosby did what he could to facilitate an understanding. In the negotiations that followed, Grant made it clear that black civil and political rights must be respected; once that was achieved, he would be glad to work with southern whites. "The point on which they hang is our sincerity," one Virginian reported to Kemper. "When convinced on that point all will go well. When they have got the whites of Virginia as allies they can let the negro go and will do it." Virginia Republicans complained that "capable, honest, influential and hard-working Republicans are ignored," while "the relentless enemies of loyalty and Republicanism" were rewarded with patronage.[7]

Grant's decision to let Republicans in Texas fend for themselves signaled his willingness to explore new approaches. Democrats had carried the state in 1872; the following year it appeared that they had also triumphed in state elections. Republicans sought refuge in claiming that the election violated the state constitution as a way to discard the results, and Governor Edmund J. Davis called on Grant to send federal soldiers to sustain the party. The president declined, noting that Texas Republicans had approved the very law they now deemed unconstitutional. Doubtless the Democrats had used violence to reduce black turnout, but their large margin of victory suggested that it was not decisive. Grant thought it would be "prudent, as well as right, to yield to the verdict of the people as expressed by their ballots." Faced with no alternative, Davis stepped down.[8]

Grant also moved to appease southern whites when it came to additional civil rights legislation. He was sympathetic to black wishes for equal treatment, telling one delegation of blacks that he understood their "desire to obtain all the rights of citizens," adding that "a ticket on a railroad or other conveyance should entitle you to all that it does other men." But it was not clear whether legislation would so much help blacks as it would increase racial friction. There were some things beyond the reach of government, including the immediate eradication of racial prejudice. Grant believed that it was unwise to push for desegregated public schools, since white southerners would close down public education altogether rather than have their children share classrooms with blacks.[9]

Equally troubling was the tepid response of most northern whites to proposals for more civil rights legislation, in part because it would apply to the entire nation. Most Democrats still adamantly embraced the tenets of white supremacy and minimal government interference in shaping social norms of behavior. Calls for additional civil rights legislation allowed them to revive charges that the Republicans were the party of meddlesome centralization, with the added argument that Republicans seemed more interested in promoting black equality than in remedying white economic distress. Nor were Republicans united in support of the idea. A growing number of them saw such measures as politically counterproductive and requiring enforcement machinery beyond anything they were willing to pass; even civil rights advocates wanted blacks to take the initiative in remedying violations by filing suit. In the end, Congress could not agree on appropriate legislation, although the framing of proposals provided sufficient ammunition for the arsenals of Democratic spokesmen who welcomed a return to playing upon white prejudices to win votes.

Grant's efforts at working out new alliances with white southerners in the interests of order and acquiescence in black civil and political equality proved a flat failure and did little to help southern Republicans in their struggle for survival and acceptance. Indeed, his efforts left many of them feeling abandoned, even if one thought that it was time in certain cases to abandon them. Those white southerners who welcomed conciliation, like Kemper, had no desire to desert their own party but instead had looked to create a more harmonious relationship between their state governments and the Grant administration to minimize federal interference. Elsewhere, southern Democrats saw in the politics of terror a better chance to gain control of their own states. Nor did conciliation help Republicans retain support in the North. At a time of economic distress, most northern voters were interested in other issues of more immediate importance to their welfare. Moreover, some voters were unhappy with proposals for more civil rights legislation, for the result would apply to the North as well as the South. It was the lesson of 1867 all over again: Republicans could not mobilize sufficient popular support for measures to help black people. Southern blacks, even those who were increasingly unhappy with the Republican party, questioned whether white southern conservatives would respect blacks' new political and civil status.

In short, conciliation was tantamount to abandonment. Unless Grant was willing to foreswear intervention regardless of the merits of the case, southern conservatives would not become full partners in any rapprochement. His decision to send federal forces to Petersburg, Virginia, in 1874 ended his dalliance with Kemper; his response to the escalation of political violence in Louisiana that September marked his full return to intervention in those states where it might prove decisive, namely those with large black electorates. He continued to look for ways to promote more acceptable Republican regimes, hoping that they might still come to terms with enough white southerners to become self-sustaining.

South Carolina offered an ideal opportunity to test this approach. Grant well remembered the state's record of political violence. Once he lost his composure when he met with a delegation of South Carolinians seeking relief from the tax burdens imposed by the Republican state government, reminding them that it had been the recalcitrant behavior of white southerners that had pushed a North disposed toward leniency toward legislation that authorized federal interference. He was also fed up with the state's Republicans, characterizing Governor Franklin J. Moses and his supporters as "that corrupt crew." Reports of their misbehavior, exaggerated by journalists, damaged the image of the party across the South, as critics accepted the writings of James S. Pike and others as not only accurate but also representative of southern Republicans everywhere. As the elections of 1874 approached, Grant endorsed a movement for reform within the party. "You must stop the robbery!" he warned one party leader. Other northern Republicans passed along the same message.[10]

South Carolina Republicans feared that if the party failed to purge itself of corruption, the Democrats would regain power. Yet, as one reminded Grant, blacks remained subject to violence and intimidation: "It will yet require *force* to secure their rights to them." Politics in the Palmetto State had become quite a mess. "These people have much to complain of at the hands of republican administrations in several of the states," a Republican observed, "but all their corruption and fraudulent legislation does not justify violence and [Democrats'] extremism as a party." The reformers offered Daniel H. Chamberlain, a Massachusetts carpetbagger, as their candidate, and Chamberlain secured victory in the fall elections. He pushed to cut spending, a move that won white support but angered many black Republicans who opposed corresponding cuts in services. Before long the governor found himself in the same position that had daunted previous moderate southern Republicans, battling party factionalism and the refusal of many Democrats to abandon color-line politics. Once more centrist politics did not pay off.[11]

Meanwhile, old trouble spots reappeared. Affairs in Arkansas proved perfectly confounding, offering a particularly rich example of Republican factionalism at its worst. Governor Baxter looked to broaden his support by wooing Democrats, whereupon disillusioned Republicans swung behind Brooks, who renewed his claim to office, triumphantly waving a court decision that declared him the winner. Brooks's armed supporters ousted Baxter and his followers from the statehouse, in effect staging a coup d'etat. Grant instructed the commander of federal military forces at Little Rock not to intervene in the dispute unless violence threatened, thus refusing to force a confrontation as he sought a peaceful solution to the problem. He appeared to have succeeded when he got the two candidates to agree to let the state legislature decide the legitimate governor, but Baxter violated the agreement and claimed that he was installed as governor. Grant grudgingly accepted the result. To have done otherwise would have been to sanction in Arkansas nearly the same behavior he had opposed in Louisiana, making it clear that he was for the maintenance of Republican regimes, not civil government, by any means possible.[12]

Democrats seized upon Baxter's triumph to eliminate Republican influence. They ousted judges and officeholders and framed a new state constitution, curtailing the governor's power in several areas, including appointment, while reducing the governor's term from four to two years to get an election in 1874. It provided a model for future Democratic efforts to retain power once they regained it by stripping the Reconstruction constitutions of their progressive elements. That fall, Democrat Augustus Garland won election as governor; Republicans turned to the White House for relief. They claimed that the Republican lieutenant governor had been elected for four years and had succeeded to the governorship when Baxter stepped down; the constitutional convention, by shortening that term to two years, had acted illegally. For the moment Grant again hesitated, ostensibly on the grounds that he was awaiting a congressional report on affairs in the troubled state, but in reality because he simply did not know what to do.[13]

As Arkansas affairs heated up in 1874, so did the continuing conflict in Louisiana. Democratic terrorist activity continued: some one hundred blacks were slaughtered at Colfax in April 1873. Over the next fifteen months Kellogg informed administration officials that he had matters well in hand. With such assurances Grant believed that the Republicans were solidifying their hold on power in Louisiana and did not need federal assistance. Still, there was a growing sense that Louisiana's Republicans were not worth the cost of supporting them. "That Louisiana business is very unfortunate," Elihu Washburne observed from Paris. "The sooner the whole gang is thrown overboard the better it will be." Violence escalated in 1874 as Democrats formed a paramilitary group known as the White League to wage an organized campaign of terrorism. Making its presence felt at Coushatta that August, White Leaguers decided to subdue what they called a black "insurrection" by assassinating Republican officeholders. Several weeks later they carried their campaign into New Orleans itself and, working alongside a self-styled militia regiment, battled the city police on September 14. Kellogg wired Grant for help.[14]

Grant weighed his distaste for state Republicans against his determination to punish overt and widespread terrorism too blatant to ignore. On September 15 he issued the all too familiar proclamation threatening military intervention if peace did not return to Louisiana. At a cabinet meeting the next day, Grant and others denounced "Kellogg's weakness and imbecility," but, as Hamilton Fish realized, to recognize McEnery would throw the state into turmoil and encourage additional overthrows in other states. Other Republicans agreed. Grant "grew black in the face" discussing the riots; Postmaster General Marshall Jewell thought Kellogg "a first-class cuss, but there's no way of getting rid of him." Grant was chagrined to find out that Kellogg's previous boasts of strength were hollow; Jewell mourned that there was no way to help Louisiana Republicans "without backing those worthless reprobates." Within days, federal forces restored order in New Orleans. Whatever peace had been achieved was fragile and short-lived, and Grant's decision to intervene terminated chances to reach an understanding with southern conservatives. Henceforth the continued survival of the Kellogg government depended upon federal force. There was no alternative basis upon which to found a Republican party, and there was also no doubt that something had to be done to stop the White League's reign of terror and murder. Yet the sight of a Republican president using federal force to sustain a Republican governor lent credence to Democratic charges of military despotism. No choice was a particularly good one, and Grant would be criticized no matter what he did.[15]

The implications of Grant's action for other southern Republicans were apparent. "The government must suppress the Revolution in Louisiana in order to prevent similar movements and general disturbances in all the Southern

States," warned one federal marshal in South Carolina. Another Republican warned that if Grant failed to support Kellogg, Mississippi Democrats would overthrow the administration of Republican Adelbert Ames "inside of four weeks," adding, "Just now it looks as if though we would have war all over the South." For these people Grant's action was cause for celebration. "If the Government had hesitated a moment and not shown a determination to use its whole power to put down those scoundrels, we would have been lost," Elihu Washburne observed. "The knife of the assassin would have been put to the throat of every loyal man in the South, white as well as black. The Govt. must give the fullest protection to *all* its citizens, everywhere. . . . Failing in that it fails in the first duty of a government. But it won't fail, so long as Genl Grant is at its head."[16]

Republican political prospects dimmed in 1874. Economic depression, the continued unpopularity of reconstruction and civil rights, and the accounts of corruption in Congress all damaged party fortunes. It goes too far to say that the congressional contests represented a referendum on Reconstruction, but the party's southern policy offered no advantages with voters. In the South rumors that Congress might pass yet another civil rights bill prohibiting various forms of discrimination contributed to summertime Republican defeats in Tennessee, Kentucky, and North Carolina, with more to follow. Southern Republicans sought to rally their forces when they met in Chattanooga, but the low attendance and inability to agree on positions symbolized the party's weakness. Some northern Republicans, sensing a Democratic resurgence, played down reconstruction issues and at times criticized their southern allies. The attempted overthrow of the Kellogg government did little to reverse this trend, for many voters were far more concerned with troubles at home than with violence in the South. Democrats scored an overwhelming triumph, capturing control of the House of Representatives and a number of northern states. More impressive was the crushing of southern Republicans in congressional contests, where the party garnered only seventeen seats while the Democrats captured eighty-nine.[17]

Many factors contributed to Republican defeat. A party in power invariably suffers losses in times of economic depression, since voters hold it responsible for the economic downturn. They also recalled Credit Mobilier and the salary grab, two signs of Republican malfeasance in Congress. Talk that Grant was interested in seeking a third term also hurt. Although the president did not desire reelection, he refused to issue a public statement that he would step down after his second term, because he thought such an announcement presumptuous and he doubted that a denial would be sufficient to end speculation. Moreover, the notion of the third term had been useful in his efforts to forge links with southern conservatives, although that was no longer a viable consideration.

Yet affairs in the South hurt Republican prospects, especially in a midterm election where the presidency was not at stake. An increasing number of northern voters were skeptical about southern Republicans, who appeared to be bumbling idiots who fought with each other or corrupt operators busily lining their own pockets; federal intervention in hapless Louisiana suggested that there was no end in sight. A good number of northern voters (and not just Democrats) were put off by the revival of proposed civil rights legislation. Some observers complained of "undue efforts to force civil rights at the expense of *all* rights," but others pointed out that critics "signally fail to point out what should be done." The bill probably damaged southern Republicans most; even there, however, hard times and anger with Republican rule contributed to the result. "We have got a hard lot from the South," grumbled Postmaster General Jewell, "and the people will not stand it any longer, nor do I blame them."[18]

The election result was decisive for reconstruction policy. A Democratic House of Representatives would never pass additional enforcement legislation. Congressional Republicans, worried about retaining and recovering the support of northern voters, would place their needs first and in no case would they appear willing to devote more national resources to the South while denying them to the North. In the South, Republicans still held on to Louisiana, Mississippi, Florida, and South Carolina, but it was obvious that the party would need help to preserve their largely black majorities against terrorism.

In his annual message that December, Grant treated Congress and the country to a rather lengthy discussion of reconstruction. He reminded Americans that the elections of 1874 in the South were characterized by violence and intimidation against Republican voters. Such acts threatened to overturn the Fifteenth Amendment; the purpose of the Enforcement Acts were to stop such behavior. Yet when Grant enforced these laws, he came under criticism for exercising federal power. The president snapped back, pointing out that "if said amendment and act do not provide for such interference under the circumstances as above stated, then they are without meaning, force, or effect, and the whole scheme of colored enfranchisement is worse than mockery and little better than a crime."

Clearly bothered by the critics who charged him with exercising the powers of a military despot, Grant shared his understanding of why it remained necessary. "The whole subject of Executive interference with the affairs of a state is repugnant to public opinion, to the feelings of those who, from their official capacity, must be used in such interposition, and to him or those who must direct," he explained. "Unless most clearly on the side of the law, such interference becomes a crime; with the law to support it, it is condemned without a hearing. I desire, therefore, that all necessity for Executive direction in local affairs may become unnecessary and obsolete." Most southern whites, he believed, were law-abiding citizens. "But do they do right in ignoring the existence of violence and bloodshed in resistance to constituted authority?" Some Republican governments were less than ideal, but southern whites were far from innocent bystanders: "Violence has been rampant in some localities, and has either been justified or denied by those who could have prevented it." Grant pledged to enforce the law "with rigor, but with regret that they should have added one jot or tittle to Executive duties or powers"— a statement calculated to refute charges that he was set upon establishing himself as an American Caesar. For people who were tired of racial politics and continuing strife, the president had a suggestion: "Treat the negro as a citizen and a voter, as he is and must remain, and soon parities will be divided, not on the color line, but on principle. Then we shall have no complaint of sectional interference."[19]

Frustrated by his failure to reach an accommodation with southern conservatives, it appeared that at last Grant was willing to accept intervention as the price he would have to pay if he was to protect black rights. Present circumstances reinforced the wisdom of this view. A conciliationist strategy had always made the greatest sense when applied to those southern states where it was essential to appeal to white voters because a party based on black votes alone was condemned to minority status. However, all but one of those states were now controlled by Democrats or some coalition of white conservatives. Grant's effort to work with several of these governments in 1873–1874 proved a dismal failure. Of the four southern states where Republicans remained in power—Mississippi, Louisiana, South Carolina, and Florida—in all but the last blacks constituted approximately half of the electorate (and the majority of Republican support). Intervention remained necessary to preserve Republican regimes in these states against a resurgence of white supremacist violence. To succeed, however, Grant would need new powers. Forwarding to Congress a petition from black Alabamians seeking protection for their rights served as a reminder that new legislation was needed. Marshall Jewell noted that Grant "is hopeful and plucky and serene, and proposes to protect the colored voter in his rights to the extent of his power under the law, and if we cannot protect them we shall lose most of the fruits of this tremendous war."[20]

Before long, events tested his resolve. Violence in Vicksburg, Mississippi, proved too difficult for state authorities to contain, and on December 21, Grant issued the traditional proclamation and waited for things to settle down.[21] But this development proved only a prelude to another crisis in Louisiana. Both parties claimed victory in the 1874 state legislative elections. Typically such disputes were characteristic of the state's politics; so was the way in which both sides sought to gain the upper hand. On January 4, 1875, Democrats disrupted the organization of the state legislature to secure a majority, actually requesting the aid of federal troops to preserve the peace in the aftermath of their attempted coup d'etat. Kellogg rallied his supporters and with the assistance of those very soldiers reasserted Republican control. Grant, anticipating some sort of incident, had dispatched Phil Sheridan to New Orleans; the general bluntly declared that the only way to deal with white supremacist terrorists was to declare them "banditti" and execute them.[22]

Accounts of what happened shocked northerners. Overlooking the past history of the White League and the actions of the Democrats in attempting to seize control, most observers expressed horror at the use of federal force to organize a state legislature. Sheridan's "banditti" dispatch, critics charged, signified the military's willingness to circumvent civil procedure in pursuit of arbitrary rule. One Louisiana paper claimed that in authorizing intervention Grant "seems to have thrown off even the flimsy pretense of being the chief Civil Magistrate of the country, and grasping the sword essays to play the role of Caesar." Even staunch Republicans quivered with fear. "This is the darkest day for the future of the Republican party I have ever seen," reflected James A. Garfield. "The Louisiana question now appears to be the mill stone that threatens to sink our party out of sight. That question is difficult when handled with the utmost wisdom, but it has been so terribly botched by the President and General Sheridan during the last four days as to place the great burden of the trouble upon us. . . . If I do not mistake the temper of the times, there will be a general howl of indignation throughout the country. Wise and careful management would have put the odium upon the rebels where it justly belongs."[23]

Although the Ohio congressman refrained from assailing the administration after he discovered additional details, others showed no such hesitation. Democratic senator Thomas Bayard complained of Grant's "jack-boot domination" of affairs. Speakers at New York's Cooper Union denounced "this act of military despotism," concluding that the people of Louisiana "must be left to work out the problem among themselves." Carl Schurz launched one last attack at Grant before he gave his up his Senate seat—to the Democrats he had once helped—in a speech that verged on hysterical paranoia: "If this can be done in Louisiana, and if such things be sustained by Congress, how long will it be before it can be done in Massachusetts and in Ohio? How long before the Constitutional rights of all the states and the self-government of all the people may be trampled under foot? How long before a general of that Army may sit in the chair you occupy, sir, to decide contested-election cases for the purpose of manufacturing a majority on the Senate? How long before a soldier may stalk into the National House of Representatives, and, pointing to the Speaker's mace, say, 'Take away that bauble'?"[24]

"Noisy clamours of 'despotism' widespread by the enemies of the President seemed to have stunned & stupefied some of his old friends," one Republican remarked. "Sensible people were frightened, believing that the President had by military authority disposed a legally constituted legislature." Grant's policy, noted the New York *Times,* "has been characterized by a curious mixture of boldness and moderation, the latter being so conspicuous and so commendable in the cases where it has been shown—as in Arkansas and Mississippi—that it renders the former the more noticeable, as in the case of Louisiana." Nevertheless, in this case his policy "is ruinous, not only to his party, but to the fundamental provisions of the Government." Another Republican asked why "our party should be ruined and have to go to the wall through the careless labor of such cattle as Kellogg, Casey & Co.? I believe Genl Sheridan told the simple truth—but the truth is our people are tired out with this worn out cry of 'Southern outrages'!!! Hard times & heavy taxes make them wish the 'nigger,' 'everlasting nigger,' were in ____ or Africa."[25]

Even Grant's cabinet divided over how the administration should respond. Secretary of State Fish, whose commitment to the administration's reconstruction policy had always been lukewarm, advised Grant to disavow Sheridan's acts. Secretary of the Treasury Benjamin Bristow also was displeased by Sheridan's behavior, although he had no illusions about Louisiana's Democrats. "I have no faith whatever in Kellogg's ability to maintain himself," he commented, "and have, if possible, less faith in the patriotism or peaceful purposes of the people who are fighting him." Although the treasury secretary "would wash the hands of the Administration entirely of the whole business," he understood what was at stake. "I am all out of patience with the idea that this Government, after having manumitted four millions of slaves cannot

by law protect them from murder and outrage. If this be true we have per-
petuated a cruel outrage in making them free." He was for "the most vigorous measures for the suppression of [the White League]. . . . In doing this I
would go to the very verge of Constitutional power, upon the most liberal
construction of Constitutional provisions, but this is as far as I can consent to
go." Although Fish, Bristow, and Marshall Jewell advised Grant to distance
himself from Sheridan, Secretary of War William Belknap, Secretary of the Navy
George Robeson, and Attorney General Williams pressed him to support the
general.[26]

Only after conferring with cabinet members and Senate leaders did Grant
decide to explain matters in a message to the Senate on January 13. "To say
that lawlessness, turbulence, and bloodshed have characterized the political
affairs of that State since its reorganization . . . is only to repeat what has become well known as a part of its unhappy history," he observed, yet it was
important to remind all Americans that violence and fraud had characterized
politics in Louisiana for nearly a decade. Admitting that neither side was free
from blame, he nevertheless found that Democrats were at least as equally
implicated in the carnival of fraud and corruption that passed for an election
in the state: to resort to terrorism to achieve their ends was inexcusable. He
recalled the Colfax massacre, that "butchery of citizens . . . which in blood-
thirstiness and barbarity is hardly surpassed by any acts of savage warfare."
Nevertheless, Louisiana Democrats had done their best to justify the massacre as they obstructed federal efforts to apprehend and try those accused of
murder and characterized the ensuing trial as another example of "Federal
tyranny and despotism"—much as Schurz and others had denounced the
actions of the army in New Orleans. Such charges angered Grant. "Fierce
denunciations ring through the country about office holding and election
matters in Louisiana, while every one of the Colfax miscreants goes unwhipped
of justice, and no way can be found in this boasted land of civilization and
Christianity to punish the perpetuators of this bloody and monstrous crime."[27]

Grant then recalled Coushatta's victims. "Some of them were Republicans
and officeholders under Kellogg. They were therefore doomed to death. Six
of them were seized and carried away from their homes and murdered in cold
blood. No one has been punished, and the conservative press of the State
denounced all efforts to that end and boldly justified the crime." Other Republicans, white and black, faced death nearly every day. "To say that the murder
of a negro or a white Republican is not considered a crime in Louisiana would
probably be unjust to a great part of the people," Grant grimly remarked, "but
it is true that a great number of such murders have been committed and no

one has been punished therefor; and manifestly, as to them, the spirit of hatred and violence is stronger than law." And he was not finished. He recited the events of September 1874, when the withdrawal of federal soldiers, deemed by white conservatives a step essential to peace, instead offered them an opportunity to overthrow the state government by force. Failing in this measure, Democrats did what they could to intimidate black voters through coercion and intimidation. Military intervention was not prearranged; it was the Democrats who first called on the bluecoats to preserve order (a fact often overlooked by administration critics). Had the Democrats not planned to disrupt the organization of the legislature, there would have been no federal intervention. Perhaps Sheridan spoke out of turn in advising summary measures to punish White Leaguers, Grant admitted, but the circumstances were rather peculiar and extreme.[28]

"It is a deplorable fact that political crimes and murders have been committed in Louisiana which have gone unpunished, and which have been justified or apologized for, which must rest as a reproach upon the State and country long after the present generation has passed away," Grant declared. He did not welcome either this ugly reality or the need to exercise his power to change it. "I have deplored the necessity which seemed to make it my duty under the Constitution and laws to direct such interference," he reminded Americans, and he would be quite happy to see "reconciliation and tranquility everywhere prevail." However, "neither Kuklux Klans, White Leagues, nor any other association using arms and violence to execute their unlawful purposes can be permitted in that way to govern any part of this country," and he could not "see with indifference Union men or Republicans ostracized, persecuted, and murdered on account of their opinions, as they now are in some localities."[29]

So there it was, a forthright statement of conditions in the South, in some of the most impassioned language used by any president. Most southern whites, for all of their talk about liberty and freedom, justice, law, and Christian virtue, refused to apply those principles to their black neighbors. At best, they chose to sit by and watch as such acts took place; at worst they participated in such atrocities—and then attacked as a tyrant and despot anyone who sought to punish those guilty of committing such acts. And many northern whites were little if any better. Northern Democrats dismissed stories of atrocities as claptrap, while Republicans wrestled with their consciences—at least some of them did.

It is a mark of how Republicans were coming to view reconstruction as a political albatross that they welcomed Grant's message not as a forthright statement of southern conditions but as an adroitly worded effort to limit the political damage Republicans had incurred over the last week. "The President's message has greatly changed the public tone," noted New Yorker Edwards Pierrepont. "Party lines in both Houses have straightened up wonderfully since this Louisiana fight, and both parties have resolved to stand or die in the old attitude toward the South," reported Republican representative Henry Dawes. "We shall recover our lost ground—by bringing up the Southern question again . . . and giving [the party] new life and vigor," predicted another Republican. However, this enthusiasm was not matched by a revived commitment to support their southern cousins. As newspaper editor and Republican veteran Joseph Medill told Blaine, "Our party can not carry that load of inequity and corruption."[30]

That the moral message of Grant's statement fell on deaf ears became apparent nearly a month later when the president offered his revised assessment of events in Arkansas. Realizing that to adhere to his former decision to recognize Baxter would prove disastrous to Republican chances in the state, Grant now claimed that Brooks was rightfully governor, and "that in 1874 the constitution of the state was by violence, intimidation, and revolutionary proceedings overthrown. . . . These proceedings, if permitted to stand, practically ignore all rights of minorities in all the States." Still, Grant realized that while he might outline consequences, it was up to Congress to act. Republicans cut their losses by crafting a solution to the Louisiana imbroglio that split control of the state's legislature, with Republicans retaining a majority in the state senate while Democrats took over the lower chamber—thus giving the Democrats much of what they had sought. They failed to act on Grant's recommendations for Arkansas, encouraging Democrats in southern states to initiate massive constitutional revisions. "That Arkansas message of Grant's ought to be met by the Republicans in Congress by adverse action before it adjourns," John Harlan told his fellow Kentuckian Bristow. "By so doing they will strengthen the party before the country."[31]

The failure to pass a new enforcement act proved more damaging. Grant wanted a new law to provide a broad legal basis for federal intervention, including the power to suspend the writ of habeas corpus. But congressional Republicans decided against enhancing Grant's ability to intervene in southern affairs to protect voters. "There is a social, and educational, and moral reconstruction of the South needed that will never come from any legislative halls, State or national; it must be the growth of time, of education, and of Christianity," Republican representative Joseph Hawley declared. "We cannot perfect that reconstruction through statutes. . . . We cannot put justice, liberty, and equality into the hearts of a people by statutes alone."[32] Political reality also suggested that such a measure would lose more Republican votes in the North than it would gain in the South. Medill complained that it would "do our party infinite mischief and arm the Democrats with a club to knock out our brains."[33] Speaker of the House James G. Blaine, who was busily calculating his own chances for the White House in 1876, agreed. By adroit maneuver he helped ensure that the Force Bill passed the House too late to be acted upon in the Senate. "In my judgment, if that bill had become a law the defeat of the Republican party throughout the country would have been a foregone conclusion," he reportedly remarked to a black congressman. "We could not have saved the South even if the bill had passed, but its passage would have lost us the North. . . . In my opinion, it was better to lose the South and save the North, than to try through such legislation to save the South, and thus lose both North and South."[34]

Even the one act that Congress took on behalf of black rights was misleading. Grant attributed the midterm election setback largely to the controversy over civil rights legislation. But pressure for such legislation, shorn of its public school provisions, persisted during the ensuing session of Congress, for many Republicans realized that it was either now or never. The Civil Rights Act of 1875 prohibited racial discrimination in various public areas; noticeably absent were public schools. Lacking any meaningful provisions for enforcement, the bill was an empty declaration of virtue, and not much of one at that. One Philadelphia paper pointed out that "a measure which offends equally the colored people of the North and the White Leaguers of the South, which satisfied neither the Conservative Republican element North nor the Radical Republican element South, is surely not statesmanship." The New York *Tribune* added that the measure destroyed whatever chance remained of attracting southern whites to the party: "The passage of the bill, therefore, can at best only retain strength, which will not prevent defeat, and cut off strength that is essential to victory." With Republicans unwilling to do more and northern voters unwilling to support doing more, Grant could do little. He told Benjamin F. Wade that he could not understand why southern atrocities were overlooked and excused while federal policy received so much criticism. Should white southerners continue to test him, he pledged that "they will find him a very different customer than Buchanan or Lincoln was to deal with, but he cannot get Congress to help him."[35]

Nor could Grant look to the federal judiciary for much assistance. Everyone knew that whatever legislation Congress passed would be subject to challenge in the courts. It was thus critical to get right-minded people on the bench. "What we want just now is two or three sincere and obstinate radicals on the

Supreme Bench," the abolitionist *Independent* declared in 1870, just as Grant prepared to name two men to the Supreme Court. After all, enforcement was already difficult enough—when the administration sought to pursue it with vigor. The Justice Department did not possess sufficient personnel or budgetary resources to prosecute the law effectively, and many military officers cared little to serve as federal police. Federal courts were not prepared to handle the caseload resulting from vigorous prosecution, and not all judges were supportive of the legislation. The Democratic victory in 1874 meant that the House of Representatives would curtail the already paltry appropriations.[36]

Thus, it came as a devastating blow when federal court decisions rendered questionable the constitutionality of key clauses of enforcement legislation. In the fall of 1873, federal judges in Kentucky declared portions of the First Enforcement Act unconstitutional in *United States v. Reese et al.*, in which prosecutors charged that the tax collector in Lexington, Kentucky, effectively disenfranchised black voters by refusing to collect the poll tax that one had to pay in order to be entitled to vote. The case made its way on division to the Supreme Court, where on January 13, 1875—the same day Grant sent his powerful Louisiana message to Congress—none other than Attorney General Williams opened on behalf of the government. More work was ahead, for enforcement was already under attack in a second case involving the prosecution of Louisiana whites arrested for involvement in the Colfax massacre. A first trial in New Orleans in February 1874 resulted in a hung jury on seven defendants (an eighth was acquitted); the second trial, in May, proved even more ominous, for defense counsel had requested Associate Supreme Court Justice Joseph P. Bradley, in his capacity as a circuit judge, to join the presiding judge. In so doing they hoped that Bradley would employ the Supreme Court's year-old decision in the so-called *Slaughterhouse Cases,* which by crafting a rather narrow definition of federal citizenship under the Fourteenth Amendment endangered the grounds for key components of enforcement legislation. It proved a wise move, for Bradley argued that it was the responsibility of the state government, not the federal government, to suppress crimes such as murder, which meant that key clauses of the Enforcement Act of 1870 were unconstitutional. Having declared thus, Bradley found against the federal government in *United States v. Cruikshank et al.* in June 1874, assuring that the case would make its way to the Supreme Court. In March 1875 both sides presented their arguments.[37]

Although the Court did not deliver its decisions until March 1876, Republicans were not optimistic about the results. Doubtful of the federal government's ability to secure convictions under the Enforcement Act, Williams advised district attorneys to suspend prosecutions, complicating an already difficult endeavor. Many southern whites defied the law as unconstitutional, and grand juries were hard-pressed to indict under such circumstances. Witnesses feared for their lives if they testified, while juries pondered their own fate as well as that of the accused.[38]

"If we believe in our principles we should see to it that they are sustained by the courts rather than the principles of our enemies," George S. Boutwell had advised in 1873. "We ought not to expect the people to be satisfied with courts that overrule or avoid every provision of the constitution designed to secure equality of rights." Yet Grant had helped to determine who would be members of those courts: he had nominated Bradley. And in fumbling to find Salmon P. Chase's successor as chief justice when Chase died in 1873, he demonstrated little in the way of an overall approach to finding judges who would endorse congressional legislation. Roscoe Conkling, whose heart was not in southern policy, turned down Grant, who then turned to Attorney General Williams, a second-rate lawyer whose support for black rights ebbed and flowed according to circumstances. When it became apparent in the wake of several damaging revelations that the Senate would have trouble confirming Williams, Grant hit upon Caleb Cushing. In light of his previous record and conservative views, the New York *Tribune* noted that the Massachusetts jurist was "an unsafe man to whom to intrust the decision of numberless important questions arising out of the war and the constitutional guarantees resulting from it."[39] Cushing withdrew when it was revealed that he had recommended someone for a position in the Confederate bureaucracy. When Grant finally named Morrison R. Waite, the Senate confirmed him more out of a sense of relief than a belief that he was equal to the office—and no one seems to have explored his sentiments on civil rights and federal policy toward the South.

Under such circumstances intervention's future effectiveness was problematic. Lacking increased powers, and with a Justice Department and an attorney general skeptical about whether the Supreme Court would sustain key components of existing enforcement legislation, Grant could only do so much. Moreover, the president had good reason to wonder whether he would enjoy continued support when he did act. The failure of congressional Republicans to buttress his authority and their willingness to devise compromise solutions to settle southern disputes suggested that they would no longer give him their enthusiastic backing. Finally compelled in May 1875 to declare that he had no interest in a third term, he watched as Republican leaders scrambled to position themselves as his likely successor, a process that often involved distancing themselves from the incumbent. Finally, he had to consider how northern voters might respond to intervention. His January message may have salvaged things for the moment in Louisiana, but the public outcry served as a warning that patience was running thin. At a time when Republicans had to rebuild their majority in the North in the wake of defeat, it would be best if he did not give party foes more ammunition. Good intentions might not survive the test of political pragmatism.

By the beginning of 1875 only four southern states—Mississippi, Louisiana, Florida, and South Carolina—remained Republican. In three of these states—Mississippi, Louisiana, and South Carolina—blacks formed the vast majority of the party's electorate, and politics was becoming increasingly polarized along racial lines. In the aftermath of events in Louisiana and Arkansas, the image of southern Republicanism was none too good in the eyes of northerners. "I'm not a bad Republican," reporter Charles Nordhoff claimed, "but I've been South, & think & see that the country cannot afford to support the gang of thieves in office who call themselves Republicans down there." He shared his perceptions with northern readers in a series of columns that eventually were republished as a book. Even more vicious was James S. Pike's *The Prostrate State,* which told a story of Republican corruption and black incompetence and ignorance in South Carolina. These attacks proved effective in reinforcing negative images of southern Republicans, complicating the task of Grant and his supporters. "Public sentiment is indeed likely to force them to give up their Southern policy," Schurz observed.[40]

Grant confronted a serious dilemma. If he continued to press for federal intervention in the South—and such intervention was important, perhaps essential, to preserving Republican regimes in states with large black electorates—he risked damaging party prospects in the North at a time when Republicans were already reeling from the disaster of 1874. That, in turn, could help Democrats to reclaim the White House in 1876, effectively ending Reconstruction. However, if he refrained from intervening in the South, it was unclear whether the remaining Republican state governments would survive, especially in the face of southern Democrats determined to regain control of their states by whatever means were necessary. Either way, Reconstruction's future was dim at best; Grant knew that the right political move was to shore up party strength in the North.

The first test of the continued viability of intervention came in Mississippi. The radical wing of the state's Republicans, led by Adelbert Ames, felt confident enough in the aftermath of electoral triumphs in 1871 and 1872 to dismiss the efforts of James L. Alcorn and others to broaden the party's appeal. Grant endorsed this policy, in part because of the influence of Ames's father-in-law, Benjamin F. Butler, a stalwart Grant supporter, and in part because of Alcorn's increasing criticism of the administration. Ames claimed victory with his election as governor in 1873. However, his hold on power proved precarious, despite efforts toward political reform and reducing government spending. Economic depression, complaints about tax burdens, continuing intraparty friction, and Ames's increasing apathy about his job frittered away the party's position. Democrats, who once wondered if their party would survive, returned to politics with a commitment to win that transcended peaceful forms of campaigning. Events in Vicksburg in December 1874 provided a forecast of what was to come. When Grant sent troops to quell violence against county officials, those Democrats who had endorsed the New Departure gave way to their more militant colleagues.[41]

State legislative elections in 1875 proved critical to Republicanism's chances of survival in Mississippi. Democrats adopted a new approach, soon dubbed the Mississippi Plan. Most accounts quaintly summarize the plan's credo as a campaign to achieve victory "peaceably if we can, forcibly if we must," but Democrats realized that to secure victory they must act in such a way as not to provoke federal intervention. Democratic leader Lucius Q. C. Lamar pledged that Mississippians were prepared to govern themselves without federal interference and would guarantee the civil and political rights of all, white and black. He looked forward to the day when "brains, intelligence, and moral strength will ultimately rule," for that would result in "obliterating the color line and ranging men in parties without regard to race," something impossible under present circumstances. But there was no doubt that Democrats had decided to practice the politics of racial polarization. "A white man in a white man's place," proclaimed one hard-line paper. "A black man in a black man's place. Each according to the eternal fitness of things."[42]

Democratic hopes that their campaign would not spark federal intervention were jeopardized by news of a riot at Clinton on September 4. Ames moved, somewhat halfheartedly, to organize a largely black militia to counter intimidation and violence. He was aware that to do so promised a bloody race war; he preferred the prospect of federal intervention. Assured by Butler that assistance would be forthcoming should trouble arise, Ames finally called upon

Grant for help. The president instructed military commanders to prepare to move to Mississippi, but told Ames that the attorney general would review the governor's request to ensure that it complied with the law. Unfortunately for Ames, George Williams was no longer attorney general, having left office in the wake of revelations about his use of funds. In his place was Edwards Pierrepont, a close friend of Hamilton Fish and no proponent of intervention, making him a poor choice to implement the president's policy (if Grant indeed still embraced intervention).[43]

The political implications of intervention were ominous. In October voters in Ohio would elect a governor and state legislature. Democrats named as their candidate inflationist William Allen, who talked of relief from tough times; Republicans countered by persuading former governor Rutherford B. Hayes to seek the office for a third term. It would be a close race. More federal intervention might tip the scales in favor of the Democrats. "As soon as you possibly can, go to Long Branch. See the President at once. Give him your full view on Ohio matters," Pierrepont urged one Ohio Republican. Party leaders argued that "the loss of Ohio this fall would insure a Democratic victory next year and lead to inflation of the currency, repudiation, the undoing of all that has been accomplished by the War and Republican Administrations in the way of reconstruction, and national disgrace," Grant observed. He disagreed, believing that the election's consequences were more apparent than real. Ames, "fully alive to the fact" that his request for troops "will be like an exploding shell to the political canvass at the North," told Pierrepont: "Permit me to express the hope that the odium of such interference shall not attach to President Grant or the Republican party. . . . Let the odium, in all its magnitude, descend upon me."[44]

Ames's plea lacked persuasiveness, because voters would hold Grant accountable for what happened. However, when Ames argued that without the presence of federal troops he would have to concede defeat, the president reconsidered his position. "I am somewhat perplexed to know what direction to give in the matter," he admitted to Pierrepont. "The whole public are tired out with these annual, autumnal outbreaks in the South, and there is so much unwholesome lying done by the press and people in regard to the cause and extent of these breaches of the peace that the great majority are ready now to condemn any interference on the part of the Government." He hoped a proclamation was not necessary to restore order, but if it was, "I shall instruct the commander of the forces to have no child's play." Grant directed Pierrepont to prepare a proclamation but not to issue it before learning whether Ames was using all the resources at his command to preserve order.[45]

Pierrepont, convinced that intervention was unnecessary, made use of Grant's letter to compose one of his own with a significantly different message. Taking advantage of the president's evident ambivalence, the attorney general reminded Ames that most Americans, "tired out with these annual autumnal outbreaks," were "ready now to condemn any interference on the part of the government." He thus asked Ames once more to prove that he had exhausted his own resources to maintain order. The governor threw up his hands. "I have endeavored time and again to organize militia and have utterly failed," he complained to his wife. "I have been heretofore disgusted at the condition of affairs, but Pierrepont's telegram has quite exasperated me." There was no question that Democrats used violence and intimidation to gain ground, but Republicans were not so much unable as they were unwilling to respond, as Ames himself testified: "Call on the President, call on the President, is the constant cry—and the more delinquent the individuals in efforts on their own behalf—the louder and more persistent is this appeal to me." For the moment, however, Ames's failure to first exhaust all means at his disposal meant that Grant would not sanction intervention. Pierrepont might take credit for that result, but the president was responsible for it. He had appointed Pierrepont; he was aware that the attorney general had selectively quoted his letter; he could have overruled Pierrepont.[46]

On October 13 Ohioans went to the polls. Republicans narrowly triumphed, with Rutherford B. Hayes claiming victory by a mere 5,000 votes. Mississippi Democrats, realizing that Grant was now free to intervene, moved quickly to head off such action. That very day party leaders met with Ames and pledged not to intimidate Republican voters or candidates, preparing the way for a free election; in response, Ames took steps to disband his militia. The governor celebrated the agreement in a letter to Pierrepont. "The opposition was to do all in its power to preserve the peace. I have faith in their honor and implicit confidence that they can accomplish all they undertake. Consequently I believe we will have peace, order, and a fair election." Pierrepont relayed back that Grant approved of Ames's action. But intervention was not yet dead, as the attorney general indicated. "You will be advised of the preparations made to aid you, in case the opposition violate their honor and break their faith." Instead, Democrats waited until it was too late to intervene to renew their campaign of intimidation. On October 27, Pierrepont's man on the scene reported, "It is impossible to have a fair election on November 2nd without the aid of U.S. troops."[47]

Orders went out to use federal forces to preserve order, but the damage had been done. Democrats swept to victory; Ames avoided impeachment by re-

signing the following March. Grant pondered the costs of his political pragmatism in a conversation with Representative John R. Lynch, a black Mississippi Republican. "I should not have yielded," he admitted. "I believed at the
time that I was making a grave mistake. But as presented, it was duty on one
side, and party obligation on the other. . . . If a mistake was made, it was one
of the head and not of the heart." If he had believed "that any effort on my
part would have saved Mississippi I would have made it, even if I had been
convinced that it would have resulted in the loss of Ohio to the Republicans,"
he explained. "But I was satisfied then, as I am now, that Mississippi could
not have been saved to the party in any event and I wanted to avoid the responsibility of the loss of Ohio, in addition. This was the turning-point in the
case." Such an explanation is rendered less compelling by the fact that Grant
failed to intervene even after the Ohio contest, but it contained some truth.
Ames's constant requests for assistance convinced Grant that before long
Mississippi would turn into another Louisiana; he had lost interest in helping
southern Republicans who did not help themselves, especially when to do so
might cost the party votes in the North.[48]

That Grant himself was casting about for new issues on which to unite the
party was evident when he traveled to Des Moines, Iowa, in September 1875
to attend the reunion of the Army of the Tennessee. Several weeks before, he
had waffled on whether to intervene in Mississippi. Now, as the election in
Ohio approached, he decided to reinforce the efforts of Republicans in that
state to emphasize enthnocultural and religious issues by charging that the
Catholic Church's effort to secure public money for sectarian schools was a
threat to American values. Overcoming his natural reluctance to speak in public,
he pressed for the importance of public education, adding: "If we are to have
another contest in the near future of our national existence, I predict that the
dividing line will not be Mason and Dixon's, but between patriotism and intelligence on the one side, and superstition, ambition, and ignorance on the other"
("superstition" was a favorite term used by opponents of the Catholic Church).
But he also took the opportunity to state his position on reconstruction: "We
will not deny to any of those who fought against us any privilege under the
government which we claim for ourselves. On the contrary we welcome all
such who come forward in good faith to help build up the waste places, and
perpetuate our institutions against all enemies, as brothers in full interest with
us in a common heritage." Irritated at the tenor of recent debate, he reminded
the veterans that "we are not prepared to apologize for the part we took in
the great struggle." Perhaps not, but as Republican reconstruction crumbled,
it was only right to wonder what four years of bloody war had achieved.[49]

It was telling that Grant said nothing about reconstruction in his annual message as 1875 drew to a close. In choosing to highlight public education and the separation of church and state, he was looking for new issues upon which Republicans would seek to retain the White House in 1876. Before long, however, he was overwhelmed by revelations of corrupt behavior by cabinet members and close associates, most notably private secretary Orville E. Babcock. As he struggled with such problems, other Republicans distanced themselves from the lame-duck chief executive, worried only about how such scandals would affect party prospects. The Supreme Court added to Grant's burdens at the end of March when it struck down key components of enforcement legislation in *U.S. v. Cruikshank* (the Colfax case) and *U.S. v. Reese*. Justice Bradley insisted that the way remained clear "for Congress to pass laws to enforce rights and privileges granted by the Constitution, and to prevent people from being oppressed on account of their race and color." This observation was nothing more than idle speculation. Democrats controlled the House of Representatives, and many Republicans wanted nothing more to do with intervention in the South. "We must get rid of the Southern question," the Springfield *Republican* argued. "There is no chance or hope of healthy politics until *we do* get rid of it."[50]

However, many Republican leaders began to realize that certain aspects of Reconstruction were useful to emphasize in order to bolster the party's chances for victory in 1876. James G. Blaine, a leading contender for the presidential nomination, hit upon excluding Jefferson Davis from a proposed general amnesty as the best way to revive wartime loyalties. In a clear concession to the wisdom of the bloody shirt strategy, he offered voters a vivid and disturbing image of former Confederates and their traitorous Democratic allies back in control, eager to subvert the legacy of Union victory. Outrages in the South were to be deplored, not in themselves but as a sign of the real character of these cutthroats, for Blaine and others said not a word about reviving attempts to empower the federal government to protect blacks and preserve justice.

Blaine's shrewd political strategy fell short of securing the nomination for him, in large part because allegations of corrupt behavior detracted from his appeal at a time when Republicans were already reeling from the revelations of wrongdoing in the Grant administration. Other leading contenders could not surmount their own shortcomings, personal or political, and in the end the Republicans nominated Governor Rutherford B. Hayes of Ohio as their presidential candidate. Grant was not a factor in the process. Democrats decided upon another governor, New York's Samuel J. Tilden, to lead them in the fall contest. The ensuing campaign focused on southern affairs because it was hard to define distinct party stands on other issues. Both candidates preached the gospel of reform; neither spoke clearly on economic issues.[51] Republicans did not defend continued intervention but warned northern voters of the impending disaster facing the republic should the Democrats win the election and thus hand the nation over to the very people who had tried to destroy it years before. Democrats, aware of the still potent appeal of the bloody shirt, advised southern whites not to engage in overt acts of violence, lest such outbreaks verify Republican charges of a resurgent Confederate spirit.

Not all white southerners heeded such cautionary warnings. On July 4, 1876, in Hamburg, South Carolina, whites protested a parading column of black militia. When the marchers hesitated before allowing a buggy driven by two white men to pass through their ranks, the whites charged them with obstructing a public highway. Four days later, as the case was to go to trial, hundreds of whites gathered at Hamburg, surrounded the blacks, and demanded that they surrender their weapons. A series of firefights ensued; after the blacks surrendered, several of their leaders were released, only to be killed.

The Hamburg affair, horrendous as it was, was a godsend to some Republicans. As Benjamin F. Butler declared, "I cannot help waving the bloody shirt when men are being murdered." Here was evidence that white southerners were not repentant; here was another reason to keep the Republicans in power. Several weeks later, in response to a letter from Chamberlain, Grant noted that the massacre, "as cruel, blood-thirsty, wanton, unprovoked, and uncalled for, as it was, is only a repetition of the course which has been pursued in other Southern states within the last few years, notably in Mississippi and Louisiana. Mississippi is governed to-day by officials chosen through fraud and violence, such as would scarcely be accredited to savages, much less to a civilized and Christian people." Strong words, these, especially if one overlooked Grant's refusal to intervene to stop such incidents in 1875. What followed suggested why. "How long these things are to continue, or what is to be the final remedy, the Great Ruler of the universe only knows"—a flat confession that he no longer knew how to answer that question. Sarcastically he added that what white southerners really wanted when they talked about their rights was "the right to kill negroes and Republicans without fear of punishment and without loss of caste or reputation," which was not acceptable. "A government that cannot give protection to life, property, and all guaranteed civil rights (in this country the greatest is an untrammeled ballot) to the citizen is, in so far, a failure, and every energy of the oppressed should be exerted, always within the law and by constitutional means, to regain lost privileges and protection. Too long denial of guaranteed rights is sure to lead to revolution—

bloody revolution, where suffering must fall upon the innocent as well as the guilty."[52]

Once more the president had waxed passionately about the horrors of southern terrorism. A more careful reading, however, revealed that despite his pledge to "give every aid for which I can find law or constitutional power," Grant was directing Chamberlain to rally his supporters and fight back through the courts and the use of state militia. Only if Chamberlain followed the procedures outlined by the guarantee clause would Grant consider a more vigorous response. Meanwhile, the president readily complied with a request by the Republican-controlled Senate to provide copies of correspondence concerning the incident, stretching his reply to include material gleaned from Mississippi. What happened at Hamburg, he declared, was a "disgraceful and brutal slaughter of unoffending men"; he added that in Louisiana, "murders and massacres of innocent men for opinion's sake or on account of color have been of too recent date and of too frequent occurrence to require recapitulation or testimony here. All are familiar with their horrible details, the only wonder being that so many justify them or apologize for them." He awaited the results of a Senate investigation of the 1875 Mississippi election, confident "that it will fully sustain all that I have stated relating to fraud and violence" there.[53]

For all their sound and fury, Grant's words signified very little. It was one thing to denounce southern outrages, another to stop them—especially when to do so would revive charges that a military despot was doing all he could to secure his party's triumph. It was not until October that he was finally willing to act. On October 17—five years to the day since he had suspended the writ of habeas corpus in South Carolina—he issued a proclamation calling on local "rifle clubs" and other terrorist groups to disperse. Otherwise, citing the guarantee clause as authority, he would direct federal soldiers to intervene. The timing was critical. On October 10 the Democrats claimed victory in the pivotal state of Indiana; Republicans squeaked through in neighboring Ohio, Hayes's home state. Although Republican leaders still held forth hopes of winning without carrying a single southern state, most calculations depended on winning New York. Grant, who recalled losing New York to another Democratic governor in 1868, thought it best to look elsewhere. Many Republicans feared that intervention in South Carolina would injure Republican prospects elsewhere. Charles Nordhoff noticed "a perceptible and general alarm" in New York, adding that additional intervention would cost the party "a great many votes, and secure it none which it would not get under any circumstances." He predicted that "armed interference in the South will lose the Republicans New York and some other Eastern States, by carrying a widespread alarm and indignation." Grant accepted the risk of alienating more voters with yet another example of federal interference, for if he failed to act, Tilden looked like a winner.[54]

On the evening of the election, Tilden still looked like a winner. But first appearances proved deceiving, and before long it became clear that the returns would be disputed. Initially Grant thought that Tilden had triumphed, but eventually he came to believe that Hayes was entitled not only to the disputed states of South Carolina, Louisiana, and Florida—which together would secure Republican victory by a single electoral vote—but also would have won easily had a fair election been held in several other southern states. He dispatched prominent Republicans to the three states and arranged for military protection of the returning boards. "No man worthy of the office of President should be willing to hold it if 'counted in' or placed there by fraud," he declared. "Either party can afford to be disappointed in the result, but the country cannot afford to have the result tainted by the suspicion of illegal or false returns."[55]

Grant protected Republican governors from violent overthrow but refused to use military force to recognize either side's claims of victory in state elections. "To be plain," he explained to General Thomas Ruger, commanding U.S. troops in Columbia, "I want to avoid anything like an unlawful use of the military." Partisans from both sides threatened violence to secure the presidency. Grant would take no chances: he would not repeat James Buchanan's "temporizing, vacillating, and undecided policy of '60–'61." What was needed to prevent trouble "was firmness, promptness, and decision, as well as having force enough at command to nip it in the bud." Several companies of infantry, batteries of artillery, and the warship *Wyoming* were soon posted around Washington. These precautionary measures spurred additional rumors that Grant himself would use force to secure Hayes's election. A few extremists went so far as to predict that Grant would simply declare himself dictator, revealing at last the Caesarism lurking under his republican toga.[56]

Grant reassured Democratic national committee chairman Abram Hewitt of his intent to resolve the crisis peacefully, claiming no man "could afford to take the place of President, unless the general judgment concurred in the belief that he was fairly elected." He believed that both South Carolina and Florida had gone for Hayes; reported Democratic majorities there were the result of violence and fraud. There was so much confusion surrounding the situation in Louisiana that he was willing to throw out the results altogether, a sign of his disgust with that state's Republicans and his concern that members of the returning board were for sale to the highest bidder. Congress should devise a solution equitable to both parties, and if as a result of such deliberations Tilden won the presidency, Grant pledged to make sure that he took office so that he could "retire from office with the country at peace."[57]

"A good deal depends upon the President, in reference to his action upon the rival governments," noted Garfield. Recognition of either claimant might well affect the electoral vote of the state. Grant posed as an honest broker to retain his political influence; it was also the only way that Hayes could survive, for if Democrats sensed that Grant was out to secure Hayes's election, they would cry fraud. He quieted fears about the possible employment of military force to secure Hayes's election but added that force would be met with force. Before long it became obvious that Florida was lost to the Democrats, although a set of electoral votes for Hayes would be sent to Washington; this achieved, Grant withdrew the soldiers sent there.[58]

South Carolina and Louisiana presented more difficult problems. Grant wanted to protect the incumbent Republican governors (Chamberlain in South Carolina and Kellogg in Louisiana) to ensure that both states forwarded a Republican set of electoral votes to Washington. Although he refused to recognize Chamberlain as the winner of the 1876 gubernatorial contest in South Carolina, he scoffed when Wade Hampton, the Democratic gubernatorial claimant, promised peace, observing that "if the Federal troops should be withdrawn there would be peace, but it would be the rest of death." In Louisiana, he refused to recognize Republican gubernatorial candidate Stephen B. Packard's claim to victory and rejected Kellogg's attempt to get the army to enforce Packard's directives. But the efforts of Democratic candidate Francis T. Nicholls's supporters to usurp control moved Grant to warn that if he was forced to act, he would have to recognize the choice of the returning board, Packard. The president merely hoped to hold Nicholls in check; for the moment he preferred not to recognize either candidate. To recognize Packard might help defeat Tilden, but it would harm Hayes, for it would contribute to the impression of an election stolen by fraud. To recognize Nicholls would be to give the whole game away in advance by depriving Grant of bargaining power.[59]

Privately Grant hoped for a Hayes victory, although he added that his "political feelings" would not dictate his actions. He sincerely believed that the Democrats were trying to do on the national level what they had successfully accomplished in several southern states—subvert the electoral process through terrorism. A Tilden presidency would mean an end to the federal protection of southern blacks. For all of Hayes's talk about a new southern policy, he had pledged to protect the freedmen. Grant, unhappy as he was with the quality of the Republican regimes in the South, still desired to do the same, although his willingness to do so was tempered by a realization of its political cost. He was so depressed by events that he confided to Fish that the Fifteenth Amendment "had done the negro no good, and had been a hindrance to the South, and by no means a political advantage to the North." A Hayes victory offered freedmen the only hope they had left, allowing Republicans to strike a deal whereby the Democrats would be allowed to assume power in South Carolina and Louisiana on the condition that they respect black civil and political rights. The Republican regimes in those states were untenable; to recognize them would simply confirm Democratic charges of election stealing at both the state and national level. The backlash might result in a Tilden victory, allowing Hampton and Nicholls to take their seats unfettered by promises to protect the freedmen.[60]

Grant realized that how Hayes won was just as important as the fact of winning itself. Unless his victory was accepted as legitimate by all concerned, the Union would be thrust into another crisis akin to that of 1860–1861. Thus Grant had to find some means of resolving the disputed election fairly. He wanted Hayes to win, but by a process in which both sides would acquiesce. He would accept the possibility that such a process might well result in the elevation of Tilden to the presidency; indeed, he had to, for otherwise Democrats would challenge the entire process and Grant would lose the leverage gained by his pose of impartiality. Neutrality was the only way to preserve Hayes's chances. To recognize Republicans would lead to charges of fraud, while to recognize Democrats would be to lose leverage and possibly electoral votes. Thus Grant advocated the creation of an electoral commission, composed of members of both houses of Congress and justices of the Supreme Court, to resolve disputes over the electoral count. When Congress finally framed a bill, he lobbied for its passage.[61]

After much debate, leaders of both parties settled upon a commission composed of five members of the House (three Democrats and two Republicans), five members of the Senate (three Republicans and two Democrats), and five Supreme Court associate justices (two Republicans and two Democrats who would choose a fifth justice). Implicit in this arrangement was the belief that each member of the commission would favor their partisan affiliation; thus, attention focused on the fifth justice. Democratic hopes that Justice David Davis, supposedly an independent despite his ill-concealed Democratic leanings, would hold the balance in his hands were dashed when he refused to join in the aftermath of his election to the U.S. Senate from Illinois, although Davis, who later claimed that he would not have served on the commission in any case, thought that Hayes was entitled to the presidency. Instead, Joseph P. Bradley, a Grant appointee, became the commission's fifteenth member. Everyone knew that the result was a commission that tilted ever so slightly in favor of the Republican party, although Bradley's ambivalent record on reconstruction legislation held out hope for a Democratic triumph.[62]

The counting of the electoral votes evolved into a story alternating between the deliberations of the electoral commission and the attempts of Democrats in the House of Representatives to delay the completion of the count by filibuster. Grant's action safeguarding the returning boards in South Carolina, Louisiana, and Florida ensured the presentation of at least one set of Hayes electors in each of the three disputed southern states. In each case, the electoral commission decided in Hayes's favor. Most observers, including Grant, believed that Tilden's best chance lay in Louisiana. After his defeat there, the choice became not Hayes or Tilden but Hayes or anarchy brought on by the filibuster in the House of Representatives. To recognize either Packard or Chamberlain would fuel support for the filibuster, while to maintain a policy of neutrality between rival factions would help complete the count. The price of southern acquiescence in Hayes's election would be the withdrawal of federal support from Packard and Chamberlain; other incentives for compromise, though important to some, were distinctly secondary. Louisiana Democrats informed the president that they would abandon Tilden if they could secure home rule under Nicholls, promising that Nicholls would protect black civil and political rights. Although Grant remained skeptical about that pledge, he kept the door open by refusing to recognize Packard. "I think the entire people are tired of the military being employed to sustain a State Government," he told reporters. In private he told Garfield that Packard and his supporters "will be driven from the state as soon as the electoral count is decided."[63]

Grant had lost faith in southern Republicanism's ability to sustain itself. He informed Packard that "public opinion will no longer support the maintenance of the State government in Louisiana by the use of the military," and drafted an order announcing that he would not use federal soldiers "to establish or pull down either claimant for control of the State." The same reasoning applied to South Carolina, for Grant believed that "the whole army of the United States would be inadequate to enforce the authority of Governor Chamberlain. . . . If a Republican government cannot sustain itself, then it will have to give way." Yet Packard and Chamberlain would remain to compel southern Democrats to end the filibuster. The strategy worked. On March 2, the day the count was completed and Hayes certified the winner, he arrived in Washington. Late the next evening he took the oath of office. Although Grant had directed Sherman to withdraw military support for Packard, orders were never issued (nor did Grant seem overly upset that they were not). It would be up to the incoming president to decide matters in Louisiana and South Carolina.[64]

With Hayes installed as his successor, Grant could leave office satisfied that at least he had made sure that the determination of the election of 1876 had not followed the course of events over the past years in several southern states. In so doing, he had headed off the threat of a second civil war that would have torn the nation apart, regardless of the outcome. He had acted skillfully, blending a commitment to principle with due attention to Republican interests—an accomplishment overlooked by critics of his southern policy. But he remained aware that much had been sacrificed over his eight years in office. Uneasy at the result, he pondered whether he could have prevented it, but hindsight offered little help. In years to come, historians would assail his approach to southern policy, first for being too harsh on southern whites, then for neglecting black interests, and finally for being inconsistent and vacillating. But none were able to suggest how he could have forged a policy that would have achieved both sectional reconciliation and justice for black Americans. Perhaps it was not his failure after all.

PART FOUR
RUTHERFORD B. HAYES

7

"THE GREAT PACIFICATOR"

Most accounts of Reconstruction conclude with the first months of Rutherford B. Hayes's administration. Hayes came to office, so goes the story, willing to terminate federal intervention in the South. That promise formed part of the heralded Compromise of 1877, in which Hayes was declared president in the aftermath of a disputed election that tested yet again the viability of American political institutions. Once in office, he proved a man of his word: the withdrawal of federal support from Republican regimes in Louisiana and South Carolina marked the end of Reconstruction.

But Hayes did not view his presidency so much as an end to Reconstruction as an opportunity to implement a new southern policy. Unlike Grant, who had vacillated between conciliation and coercion, Hayes, convinced that intervention had proved counterproductive, committed himself to conciliating white southerners to entice them to join the Republican party. The vast majority of accounts claim that in pursuing this policy, he abandoned the freedpeople to the tender mercies of their former masters; Hayes, on the other hand, insisted that his aim was to protect the freedmen by removing race as the primary dividing line in southern politics, compelling white southerners to bid for black votes to win elections.

In the end, Hayes's policy proved misguided. Although there were signs of a potential realignment in some southern states, the Republican party did not regain majority status. White southerners took what they could get without reciprocating. The erosion of black rights continued, although in some states blacks were able to exercise some control over their own lives at the local level. Hayes was unwilling to admit that his policy had failed, but by 1880, Republicans realized that they need not worry about the South as they assembled an electoral majority at the national level. If some Republicans persisted in attempting to revive the southern wing of their party, most realized that success was unlikely and would cost more than it was worth.

As a Republican congressman during the first years of Andrew Johnson's administration, Rutherford B. Hayes loyally supported congressional reconstruction. He believed that emancipation had made blacks citizens, although not necessarily voters, and that they should be protected in the exercise of their civil rights. He refused to consider the readmission of southern representatives prior to the adoption of an amendment that would base representation on suffrage, thus forcing the southern states either to enfranchise blacks or lose seats in the House of Representatives. "The Rebel States will always be represented (during our day, at least) by repudiators—by men willing to assume every sort of claim payable South," he observed. "Rebel influences are now ruling the White House," he concluded in February 1866, and "the sooner Johnson is clear over the better for us." But Hayes expressed skepticism about some policies. Although he agreed that blacks as citizens had the right to vote in territories, he still believed that states should decide who should exercise the suffrage. Personally he preferred an educational qualification for both blacks and whites. Still, he rejected claims of black inferiority and denounced Democratic race baiting. Blacks deserved to enjoy opportunities to move up in American society; education would create and enhance such opportunities. There were limits to Hayes's vision of black freedom, but it was a far broader vision than that possessed by many of his fellow white Americans.[1]

In 1867 Hayes ran for governor of Ohio. In the fall contest he claimed that reconstruction remained the primary issue facing the country and advocated amending the state constitution to enfranchise black males. Although he managed to win the governorship by a slim majority, the black suffrage amendment went down to defeat and the Democrats secured a majority in the state legislature, reminding him of the costs of supporting black rights in the North. Enthusiastically supporting Grant's candidacy in 1868, he argued that Grant's opponent, Horatio Seymour, "is for a reconstruction of the South which will be agreeable to the Rebels, and opposes the reconstruction which gives safety and power to the loyal." He worked hard to put the Fifteenth Amendment through the Ohio state legislature, a remarkable achievement in light of Ohio's earlier hostility to black suffrage. But the success of that amendment, Hayes reflected, marked the end of federal activity. It was time to move on. "An era of good feeling prevails here to a degree not seen before in fifty years," he told Guy M. Bryan, a friend from Texas. "The old sectional bitterness is dying out rapidly never to revive. New parties and new divisions in which I shall take no prominent part are in plain view ahead." Although he supported Grant's reelection, Hayes expressed some reservations about several aspects of that administration. Before long these reservations ripened into open doubts, and he began to criticize intervention. "I doubt the ultra measures relating to the South," he confided to his diary. The Civil Rights Bill of 1875 ran contrary to his own beliefs about race relations. "I, of course, don't believe in forcing whites and blacks together," he disclosed to Bryan. He judged that "'the let-alone policy' seems now to be the true course."[2]

Hayes's lack of enthusiasm for Republican reconstruction was evident when he ran again for governor in 1875. Unlike 1867, when he insisted that it was of prime importance, he now shied away from it and focused on other issues, including Catholicism in the schools and proposals to inflate the currency or to coin silver, to attract votes. Hayes once more secured victory by a narrow margin, this time with a Republican legislature; some people observed that Grant's refusal to intervene in Mississippi contributed to the result. The lesson seemed clear: support for black ballots cost Republicans more support than they stood to gain. The party needed to turn elsewhere to win elections.

No sooner had Hayes been elected governor than people began to speak of him as a possible candidate for president. The man who could carry Ohio in such dire times might well carry the nation for the Republican party. At first Hayes rested content with listing those papers who urged his nomination, but as winter came he took a more active interest. Although few Republicans outside of Ohio spoke of Hayes as their first choice, supporters of other candidates remained favorably disposed to him. "I think his chief excellence is in his intuitive perception of what at the moment is practically attainable," noted one Ohio supporter as he pushed forward Hayes's name. By the time the delegates gathered at Cincinnati, each of the major contenders carried serious liabilities, not the least of which was that next to securing victory for their favorite, delegates seemed determined to deny the nomination to rival aspirants. Such a situation was tailor-made for Hayes. He had no enemies, inspired no enmity, and both reformers and party regulars found him an appealing second choice—certainly preferable to any of the other contenders. On the seventh ballot he secured the Republican nomination for president.[3]

The Republican platform reaffirmed the party's commitment to reconstruction, although its pledge to protect the rights of all men was more rhetorical than realistic. Hayes's letter of acceptance was adroitly phrased to appeal to a wide spectrum of sentiment. "What the South most needs is peace, and peace depends upon the supremacy of the law," he declared, pledging to support the Reconstruction amendments and "a hearty and generous recognition of the rights of all," a phrase that meant different things to different people. The same ambiguity was also evident when he promised to pursue "a civil policy which will wipe out forever the distinction between North and South in our common country" and secure to southerners "the blessings of honest and capable local government." Hayes did not see any contradiction or ambiguity in his statements, but he had consciously tailored them for maximum political effect, noting that such pledges allowed him to remind voters of his support for "the rights of the colored man and at the same time to say what I could for the interests and feeling of the well disposed white man." Privately he assured Carl Schurz that he favored "a policy of reconciliation" and successfully wooed the former insurgent by making clear his commitment to make civil service reform "the issue of the canvass."[4] By identifying reform as a cardinal principle Hayes sought to remove the burden of "Grantism," with its taint of corruption, from his shoulders.

Hayes initially planned to make civil service, sound money, and nonsectarian education the prime issues of the fall campaign, repeating the formula that had led to success in Ohio in 1875. But such issues proved to have limited appeal, especially after the Democrats nominated Samuel J. Tilden of New York in June. Tilden possessed a reputation as a reformer; he did not advocate inflation; he downplayed church/state issues involving education. Thus on the very issues that Hayes intended to emphasize, Tilden either adopted or refused to contest Hayes's position. The Democrats preferred to indict Republicans as the party of bad economic times and a mistaken southern policy. Much to Hayes's surprise, another issue energized Republican voters. "I wonder if you see what I am discovering beyond all question in Ohio," he wrote Schurz. "A vast majority of 'the plain people' think of this as the main interest in the canvass: *A Democratic victory will bring the Rebellion into power.*" The war retained its ability to stir voters' memories: "The true issue in the minds of the masses is simply, Shall the late Rebels have the Government?"[5]

It did not take Hayes long to become an enthusiastic advocate of waving the bloody shirt. "Are you for the Rebel South, or are you for the loyal North?" he jotted down in his diary one day as he tried to fashion campaign slogans. "Are you for the Nation, or are you for the Rebels? . . . Should we give the Government to the men who tried to destroy it? . . . Are you for the men who wore the gray, or are you for the men who wore the blue?" For all the talk of new issues, it was the old issue of the war that revived Republican spirits. "The people *do dread* a victory for the United South," he observed on the eve of the October elections. "Our strong ground is the dread of a solid South, rebel rule, etc., etc.," he told Blaine. It would lead voters "away from hard times which is our deadliest foe."

Hayes distinguished between the restoration of "home rule," as supporters of nonintervention euphemistically called the abandonment of Republican regimes in the South, and the return of the Democrat party to power on the national level. By the mid-1870s, the Republican version of the bloody shirt was designed to retain majorities in the North and in the nation, not to justify a policy of intervention. Blaine, who had done his share to stir up old emotions, told Hayes that by "conciliating Southern whites, on the basis of obedience to law and equal rights," Republicans could "divide the Southern whites and so protect the colored people." Newspaper correspondent Charles Nordhoff advised him to contact "quietly a few of the prominent old Whig leaders of the Southern States, & confer with them. . . . I think you might without much trouble & with no embarrassing engagements make sure of carrying Louisiana, North Carolina, Virginia, & Arkansas."[6] Hayes was less sure, especially so long as he had to carry enough northern states to offset sure Democratic triumphs in most of the South. Reconciliation and realignment would have to wait until he was in office.

Most observers predicted a close contest. Democrats hit hard on the issues of bad times and failed policies; Republicans were not sure that their response of waving the bloody shirt was enough. Such shaky prospects forced them to look to Louisiana, South Carolina, and Florida for electoral votes. In these three states Democrats did what they could to intimidate Republican voters without committing acts of open violence, although there were plenty of incidents, headed by the clash at Hamburg. Southern Republicans prepared to respond in the time-honored manner of using the machinery of vote counting by their returning boards to even the score. Early returns on election night indicated a Democratic victory. It seemed as if Reconstruction was over, repudiated by the electorate. Hayes lamented that Tilden's triumph would prove disastrous for "the poor colored men of the South," for southern whites would trample the Reconstruction amendments "and then the colored man's fate will be worse than when he was in slavery."[7]

By now the story of the resolution of the disputed presidential election of 1876 is well known. Both Republicans and Democrats claimed victory in Louisiana, South Carolina, and Florida. Republican-controlled returning boards did their job of reversing Democratic returns, using deception to counter intimidation and fraud. Neither Hayes nor Tilden held clear claim to the presidency, and neither possessed an electoral majority. Republicans had to capture all the disputed votes to lay claim to the presidency.

At first, Hayes thought he had lost; then he came to believe that the Democratic party had tried to cheat him out of victory. He realized that the electoral dispute was rooted in the continuing debate over southern affairs. Visitors and correspondents from the South made clear their eagerness for reconciliation if Hayes abandoned intervention. "It is so desirable to restore peace and prosperity to the South that I have given a good deal of thought to it," he declared. "The two things I would be exceptionally liberal about are education and internal improvements of a national character"—issues that appealed to old Whigs. But when others waxed enthusiastic over the possibly of using the promise of change to woo southern support during the electoral crisis, Hayes expressed skepticism. "I am not a believer in the trustworthiness of the forces you hope to rally," he told his friend and adviser William Henry Smith, manager of the Western Associated Press. "After we are in, I believe a wise and liberal policy can accomplish a great deal. But we must rely on our own strength to secure our rights."[8]

The alternative was far less compelling. If he sustained Republican regimes in Louisiana and South Carolina, he would have to use federal force to protect them, eroding Republican strength in the North and subjecting him to criticism from reform-minded Republicans. That Democrats in the House would cut funding for an army already understrength and overcommitted if Hayes revived intervention rendered that response problematic at best. Moreover, the success of a realignment of parties in the South that would divide whites depended upon the willingness of southern whites to abolish color-line politics. The attempt would decouple his administration from the legacy of intervention under Grant; if successful, Republicans in the North could concentrate on other issues. It seemed worth the risk. "It is evident that the Republican party can no longer be maintained on past issues," warned one southern white, "and that a new line of policy must be adopted."[9]

Thus, like Lincoln, Johnson, and Grant, Hayes considered forging a bisectional alliance with southern whites—specifically the old Whigs who supposedly were reluctant secessionists. Nor was he alone in entertaining such hopes. "The old Whig or Union party of the South should have been invigorated as it could have been," argued Pennsylvania congressman William D. Kelley, "and it and the colored people would have given us clear majorities composed almost exclusively of Southern people in the States south of Kentucky and Virginia." Jacob D. Cox claimed that "we ought not to have great difficulty in finding means to rally to the support of a Republican administration a strong body of the best men representing the capital, the intelligence, the virtue and the revived patriotism of the old population of the South." Chicago *Tribune* editor Joseph Medill believed that "the old Whig feeling in the South is beginning to crop out in spots, and if carpetbaggery can be got rid of, and 'home rule' in state affairs be substituted, a Southern white Republican party can be organized down there which, with the aid of the blacks, will give us control of half of the South." Several southerners agreed. "With Gov. Hayes as President," asserted James Longstreet, "the party can be so organized, as to divide the white and colored vote, not only in Louisiana but throughout the South, and make the party strong." Nordhoff predicted that Hayes "will find it very easy to form a real and honest Republican party in the South."[10]

If Hayes let it be known that he shared these sentiments, perhaps he could help his electoral prospects. James A. Garfield told him that several "thoughtful Republicans . . . believed it possible to make an inroad into the Democratic camp," dividing southern Democrats and some northern businessmen from the remainder of their party. "Just what sort of assurances the South wants, is not quite so clear," he added, but he recommended that Hayes find some way to say "that the South is going to be treated with kind consideration by you. Several Southern men have said, within a week, that in the matter of internal improvements they had been much better treated by Republicans than they were likely to be by the Democrats—and they talk a good deal about the old Whigs having been forced, unwillingly, into the Democratic party."[11]

In reaching out to these old Whigs, northern Republicans could unload the albatross of carpetbaggers and scalawags that had proved an overwhelming burden. "We as Republicans cannot escape a share of the responsibility for the deplorable condition of things in the South," opined Cox. Blacks had fallen under the spell of "mere adventurers and demagogues." Other observers argued that the reconciliation/realignment strategy would protect blacks. William Henry Smith advised Hayes to foster the formation of "a conservative Republican party in the South that shall effectively destroy the color line & save the colored people." Cox believed that blacks' support of one party "is no longer essential to their safety. On the contrary, it is now the cause of their greatest danger." One North Carolinian assured Hayes: "With each party bidding against the other, the negro's rights are assured. In a contest between parties based on distinctions of race the negro must eventually go down."[12]

Hayes accepted such arguments. At no time did he believe that he was abandoning blacks. He assured Frederick Douglass that he believed in "a firm assertion and maintenance of the rights of the colored people of the South according to the 13th, 14th and 15th amendments—coupled with a readiness to recognize all Southern people, without regard to past political conduct, will now go with me heartily and in good faith in support of these principles." But his enthusiasm for reconciliation proved controlling. "My anxiety to *do* something to promote the pacification of the South is perhaps in danger of leading me too far," he admitted. Still, he agreed that Republicans "must do all we can to promote prosperity there. Education, emigration and immigration, improvements occur to me. . . . The South is more on my mind than anything else."[13]

Hayes also heard from those who believed that under no circumstances should he abandon southern Republicans. "You cannot dismiss those gentlemen with a wave of the hand," William Henry Smith, himself an advocate of realignment, warned him. Their fate "must be determined by considerations other than those of mere party expediency. Unless the decision shall be based upon justice and truth it cannot stand." Other Republicans reminded Hayes how southern Democrats had resorted to violence and intimidation, and expressed doubt that they would willingly abandon their quest to establish white political supremacy. But Hayes remained committed to his policy of reconciliation and realignment. As the counting of the electoral vote moved into its final stages, he reaffirmed his position. "Assure any of our Southern friends that I am impressed with the necessity of a complete change of men and policy." He was making a virtue of necessity. Little enthusiasm remained for sustaining present Republican regimes. "We have tried for eight years to uphold negro rule in the South officered by carpetbaggers, but without exception it has resulted in failure and almost ruin to [the] party," observed Medill. "Statesmanship consists of making the best use of the means at command, and of producing popular contentment."[14]

On March 1, Hayes departed Columbus for Washington. His parting remarks reinforced his commitment to reconciliation as essential to achieving a true reunion. The Union must be "a union of hearts"; obedience to the Constitution had to be grounded in respect and reverence for the principles it embodied, "not merely because of force that compels obedience."[15] As he traveled east, the electoral controversy was resolved, but not before some last-minute negotiating cleared the way for an end to filibustering tactics. Southern Democrats, assured by Grant and other prominent Republicans that Hayes would not uphold the claims of Chamberlain and Packard, dropped their support of the filibuster, as did northern Democrats who feared the label of disunionist. Much was made of agreements between Republicans and southern Democrats

meeting at the Wormley House, but these agreements served merely to reaffirm previously existing understandings.

If white southerners believed that they had extracted from Hayes a promise
to pursue a policy of conciliation in the give-and-take of negotiations, he would
not disabuse them. If they were willing to allow the Republicans to organize
the House of Representatives with Garfield as speaker, so much the better. Of
far less importance, at least from Hayes's point of view, was an extensive series of negotiations carried out between newspaper correspondents, railroad
builders, and southern Democrats looking for federal support for internal improvements. Whatever high hopes the participants in these discussions had for
recasting the contours of American politics, in the euphoria of believing that
they were actually striking binding agreements they took themselves a bit too
seriously and made promises they could not fulfill. From Hayes's point of view,
his attitude toward reconstruction facilitated a settlement of the dispute; the
dispute did not determine his policy.

Grant presented Hayes with the opportunity to do whatever he wanted to
do, leaving the fate of the Chamberlain and Packard regimes to his successor.
Yet that decision seemed foreordained. As one bystander cried out to a South
Carolina Republican who was leaving a meeting with Hayes, "You can't expect us in the North to allow our party to be torn into shreds in an attempt to
uphold and defend the sort of government you have in South Carolina." He
was not alone. One Republican, who had left South Carolina, advised Hayes
"to accept things as they are not as you would have them, and build up a new
party south—you can't fight the hopeless battles of minorities."[16]

On March 5, 1877, Hayes was publicly sworn in as the nineteenth president
of the United States, although he had already taken the oath of office privately
on the evening of March 3. His inaugural address outlined the principles that
would shape his policy toward the South. He sought "the permanent pacification of the country upon such principles and by such measures as will secure
the complete protection of all its citizens in the free enjoyment of all their
constitutional rights." Southerners deserved the right of self-government, but
he added that "only a local government which recognizes and maintains invio-
late the rights of all is a true self-government." Those governments must protect "the interests of both races carefully and equally"; it must submit "loyally
and heartily to the Constitution and the laws." The federal government had
"a moral obligation" to protect the freedmen's rights, but it was state and local
government that served "as the true resource . . . for the contentment and
prosperity" of citizens. Hayes pledged "to put forth my best efforts in behalf
of a civil policy which will forever wipe out in our political affairs the color

line, and the distinction between North and South, to the end that we have not merely a united North or a united South, but a united country." Such sentiments were noble ones—and they had been shared by Hayes's predecessors. Grant had grown to distrust the sincerity of most southern whites; Hayes still took them at their word and hoped to cultivate reconciliation by abandoning coercion.[17]

Aware of the need to use his cabinet to build support for his policies, he constructed a slate that reflected his independence and his desire to reconcile conservative Republicans, former members of the Liberal Republican movement, and potential southern allies in an effort to build a Hayes coalition in Washington. Several appointments suggested the direction he intended to take on reconstruction. William M. Evarts, his choice for secretary of state, had served in Andrew Johnson's cabinet after successfully defending him in the impeachment trial; he had organized a New York meeting to protest against Grant's use of troops in Louisiana in 1875. Treasury secretary–designate John Sherman's commitment to Republican reconstruction was suspect in the eyes of many Republicans. Most abrasive was the naming of Carl Schurz, a passionate opponent of the Grant administration and its southern policy, to head Interior. All three cabinet officers could be counted upon to support Hayes's promise of a new policy toward the South.

Perhaps the clearest indication of Hayes's approach to the South was his desire to appoint a white southerner to the cabinet. Appointing a southern Republican would not create a realignment in the same way that a southern Democrat might. Hayes entertained the idea of naming former Confederate general Joseph E. Johnston to head the War Department until William T. Sherman, doubtless nettled by the prospect of reporting to a man who had once surrendered to him, and others warned Hayes that such a nomination would enrage many of the old boys in blue. Finally Hayes settled upon Tennessee's David M. Key for postmaster general. Key would have plenty of patronage at his disposal, which if used wisely could help to build up the southern wing of the Republican party along the reconciliationist lines promised by Hayes.[18]

For several days the Republican-controlled Senate refrained from confirming most of Hayes's cabinet slate, and even John Sherman saw the usual courtesy senators extended to one of their own neglected when his nomination was confirmed only after being referred to committee. Evarts, Key, and Schurz drew most of the Republicans' wrath. Support for Hayes's cabinet appointments came from several southern Democrats, adding new hope to the promise of realignment. Eventually the entire slate was confirmed, in part due to public pressure. Hayes cited it as a victory; other observers offered that it was merely a prelude to future disputes.[19]

With his cabinet in place, Hayes went to work to implement his policy "of peace and home rule—of local self-government." "My policy is trust—peace, and to put aside the bayonet," he remarked. But the question of what to do in Louisiana and South Carolina proved more troublesome than he anticipated. Although he did not want to decide contested elections in the South through the use of federal troops, refusing to employ troops would also decide the elections. "I incline to think that the people will not now sustain the policy of upholding a State Gov't agst a rival Gov't by the use of the forces of the U.S.," he confided to his diary. "If this leads to the overthrow of the de jure Govt in a State, the de facto Gov't must be recognized." It was "not the duty of the President of the United States to use the military power of the Nation to decide contested elections in the states." After all, local self-government meant "the determination by each State for itself of all questions as to its own local affairs," a banal truism that overlooked recent events. He wanted "to restore harmony and good feeling between Sections and races." How to reconcile these two principles was the crux of the matter, and on that crucial issue he remained silent.[20]

Hayes's noble-sounding declarations overlooked reality. As one abolitionist observed, however hard it might be to abandon Chamberlain and Packard, for Hayes to persist in upholding their regimes through federal intervention would "doom his administration to disastrous failure." The question was not whether to withdraw federal support, but how. New elections could be ordered in both states; the state legislatures could be entrusted to resolve the dispute; Packard and Chamberlain could be recognized, then left to fend for themselves; or Hayes could "withdraw troops and leave events to take care of themselves." These options sought to obscure the end result of Hayes's policy by establishing means that on the surface smacked of fair play. To abandon them too quickly to the fate of dispossession by their Democratic counterparts would increase the criticism of hostile Republicans anxious to grapple with Hayes. Better to wait for Congress to adjourn before acting. Delay would also allow the president to decide how best to justify his decision to recognize the Democratic claimants in these states. Never did he seriously contemplate doing otherwise. It was not what to do but how to do it that occupied his attention. As one Ohio adviser reminded him, the "bayonet policy . . . *no longer protects.*" Such a policy "must be maintained with a high hand. . . . The country will not *now* sustain that."[21]

The first test came in Louisiana. On March 20, Hayes met with his cabinet to discuss the situation. Except for Secretary of War Charles Devens, no one favored using force to sustain Packard's ramshackle government, and even Devens was not certain about what to do. Together they decided to send a commission to Louisiana to construct a compromise. Hayes accepted that self-determination might not turn out as he wished: "If this leads to the overthrow of the de jure Govt in a State, the de facto Gov't must be recognized." With these words he sealed the fate of the Packard regime. Ostensibly he instructed the members of the Louisiana Commission to report to him on conditions in the state; in reality it served to sanction his decision to withdraw federal support from Packard and allow Democrat Francis T. Nicholls to take over. Evarts made clear to the commissioners Hayes's intention to end intervention; the president simply desired assurances that such an act would not signal an outbreak of violence or the repression of blacks.[22]

Hayes took a somewhat different approach in South Carolina, summoning both Chamberlain and Hampton to the White House. Although Chamberlain refused to give way, he acknowledged that he could not hope to maintain his position without federal support. He realized that the "North is tired of the Southern Question and wants a settlement, no matter what." Hampton promised to protect black rights and preserve the peace, and pledged to do what he could to assist the Republicans to organize the House of Representatives, although clearly his power to do so was rather limited. Nevertheless, Hayes was satisfied. The troops departed their stations around the statehouse in Columbia on April 10. Left defenseless, Chamberlain gave in, and Hampton assumed the governorship.[23]

Two days after Congress adjourned, and just over a week after Chamberlain had given way to Hampton in South Carolina, the Louisiana imbroglio was settled when enough Republican legislators defected to the Democratic house to form a quorum. Nicholls pledged to grant equal protection of the laws to blacks and whites alike. The next day Hayes directed that the federal soldiers protecting the Packard government return to quarters on April 24. Packard had no alternative but to submit, remarking that "one by one, the Republican State Governments of the South have been forced to succumb to force, fraud, or policy."[24]

Hayes insisted that abandoning Packard and Chamberlain did not necessarily mean the abandonment of the freedmen. He secured pledges from the southern Democrats in Louisiana and South Carolina to observe the Civil War amendments and promise "that the colored people shall have equal rights to labor, to education, and to the privileges of citizenship." Hayes was prepared for criticism, however. "I know how sore a trial this business is to staunch antislavery veterans like you," he told Ohio Republican William D. Bickham. "I expect many to condemn. I shall not worry or scold if they do. I know they mean well."[25]

Many prominent Republicans criticized Hayes's policy, believing that it betrayed southern Republicans. Designed to split the southern Democracy in twain, the policy threatened to split the Republicans as well. To court one's enemies, these critics declared, meant deserting one's friends. It was one thing to accept the failure of intervention but quite another to embrace it. Garfield observed, "It is clear that below the surface of approval there is much hostile criticism and a strong tendency to believe that Hayes's policy will be a failure." Blaine wondered out loud how Hayes could refuse to recognize Packard and Chamberlain while claiming that he had carried those states. Hayes had dropped the bloody shirt in his rush to clasp hands across the bloody chasm; the foes of the Grant regime, led by Schurz and the equivocating Evarts, were now in control of administration policy. "No doubt he meditates the destruction of the party that elected him," groused the aging Benjamin Wade.[26]

There was reason to question some dissenters' sincerity. To Blaine, waving the bloody shirt promised political advantage; to do anything about it promised political damage. Hayes even asserted that Blaine's failure to secure a cabinet post for one of his supporters sparked his newfound concern for southern Republicanism—overlooking Blaine's 1876 speeches warning of the revival of Confederate spirit (speeches Hayes had then heartily endorsed). To see the administration abandon party warhorses in an effort to woo old enemies, whether southern Democrats or Liberal Republicans, was too much for many party regulars. It was naive for Hayes not to expect opposition and unfair for him to characterize it as a mere squabble for office. Patronage was the lifeblood of political parties: Hayes himself used it to draw in party dissenters and woo southern Democrats.[27]

Other Republicans sighed in relief. Newspapers weary of Grant's policy of intervention applauded Hayes's decision to abandon Packard and Chamberlain. "Gen. Grant held up the Southern Republican administrations by main force for more than four years, and they got no stronger on their legs, but rather weaker and weaker," observed the New York *Tribune. Harper's Weekly* declared that "a policy which had lost the Republicans every Southern State, which has not effectually protected the Negro, and which has embittered the jealousies of classes and race . . . is not a wise permanent policy." Editor George W. Curtis, a strong Hayes man, argued that to continue federal protection of southern Republican regimes "would have wholly overthrown the party within two more years. . . . Viewed partywise, the only hope lay in a bold and vigorous change of policy. Not to have made it would have been to destroy the party."[28]

Hayes's decision to withdraw the troops combined political pragmatism with hope. Many people would no longer tolerate the policy of intervention. To have continued to support Republican governments in the South would have subjected him to far greater criticism than to abandon them. Yet Hayes also believed that blacks might actually prosper under the new order. No longer the targets of political controversy (or so Hayes believed), perhaps blacks would now be allowed to assume their rightful places in southern society as equal under law. Hayes "is full of the idea of being a great Pacificator," remarked Senator L. Q. C. Lamar of Mississippi, although he added that while the new president was "well-meaning, but is very ignorant of the South." But even Hayes realized that it was too soon to celebrate. It still had to be seen whether a new Republican coalition would emerge and whether blacks' civil and political rights would be respected. As he admitted, "Time will tell."[29]

The withdrawal of federal support for the Packard and Chamberlain regimes was but a first step in inducing a realignment of parties. "The President believes we can organize the next House and is willing to favor internal improvements in the South, including the Southern Pacific Railroad if that will bring Southern support to the Administration to make it worthwhile," Garfield noted. "The pacification policy still gains," Hayes observed at the beginning of May. "I am confident it will secure North Carolina, with a fair chance in Maryland, Virginia, Tennessee, and Arkansas, and I am not without hopes of Louisiana, South Carolina, and Florida." The president believed "that his policy would blend men of all political opinions into one belief," noted Thomas Donaldson, a longtime associate. "I wonder if he really dreams of such a thing."[30]

Hayes chose to take his case to the people. In May he visited Tennessee, where he laid wreaths on the graves of both Union and Confederate soldiers. He journeyed to Boston and New England, pledging his adherence to both reunion and equality. "I tried to impress the people with the importance of harmony between different sections, States, classes and races," he commented, "and to discourage sectionalism and class prejudice." But he also countered charges that he was deserting southern blacks. In several newspaper interviews he made it clear that he believed that reconciliation was the best guarantee of racial justice. Critics, unpersuaded, denounced the president as a traitor to the party. Chamberlain and Packard, carpetbagger casualties of Hayes's policy, spoke at several gatherings. State party conventions battled over planks voicing support of the administration. But many northerners were more worried about signs of labor unrest than about southern affairs.[31]

In September Hayes embarked on a tour through the South. He planned to speak of reconciliation and "the reign of peace and good will over the whole of our recently agitated (disturbed) and afflicted land" to Union veterans and southerners alike. His remarks stressed peace and fraternity between the sections. To whites he urged tolerance and a new politics: "Let us wipe out in our parties the color line forever." He repeatedly reminded them of their promise to observe the Reconstruction amendments and treat blacks as civil and political equals. At Nashville he asserted that most southern whites had "no desire to invade the rights of the colored people." He also reiterated his belief that his policy of conciliation would in the end help southern blacks. "I believe that your rights and interests would be safer if this great mass of intelligent white men were left alone by the general government," he told Atlanta blacks. At Chattanooga he left a similar message: "Our confidence . . . was perfect that with the bayonets removed from the South, the people of all colors would be safer in every right, in every interest, than they ever were when protected merely by the bayonet." Whites were less pleased when Hayes reaffirmed his intent to enforce the Reconstruction amendments. Wade Hampton accompanied Hayes during part of the president's journey. Although the South Carolina governor pledged his support of the president's policy, careful listeners noted that it was conditional and omitted mention of realignment: "While he performs his constitutional duty, I think it is our duty to say to him that we will sustain his policy, whether he be Democratic or Republican."[32]

An enthused Hayes returned to Washington convinced that the cheering crowds marked the smashing success of his policy. "Received everywhere heartily," he scribbled in his diary. "The country is again one and united! I am very happy to be able to feel that the course taken has turned out so well." He remained convinced that "there are thousands of intelligent people who are not Democrats, & who would like to unite with the Conservative Republicans of the North." Some Republicans believed that the president was distancing himself from his party. "It would have been more just and more politic to have associated his party with his proffers of good will," Garfield observed, as he went to the White House to talk things over with Hayes. But the president did not rely solely on his speech making to gain his point. He extended patronage to select southern senators in return for the prospect of their support in organizing the House under Republican control—although it would seem that the patronage would have been better directed toward southern representatives, who would actually elect the Speaker, for that purpose.[33]

But the understandings and promises worked out in February and March disintegrated in the fall. Southern congressmen did not support Garfield for Speaker; Hayes opposed the long anticipated subsidy for the Texas and Pacific Railroad. Garfield noted "great differences of opinion" within Republican ranks and thought "the prospects of a division in our party were very strong." Most Republicans denounced Hayes "as a traitor and a man who was going to Johnsonize the party," while "his defenders were comparatively few." Reminding voters of Hayes's endorsement of bloody shirt tactics in 1876, party leader William E. Chandler charged that he had turned his back on Republicans North and South.[34]

Democrats were not willing to grant Hayes much credit. One congressman growled that had Hayes been able to draw upon a Republican Congress and the army, "he would have followed Grant's course and his Southern policy would have been vigorous Republicanism." The gratitude of southern whites also had its limits. Senator Zebulon Vance of North Carolina noted that while southern Democrats were "grateful to him for withdrawing the army," the idea that Democrats would vote the Republican ticket "is all simple bosh." Hayes "is certainly being deceived by men who claimed to know the South about Democrats going to support him . . . for the purpose of building themselves up in his good graces." Several other southern congressmen pointed out that only the Democrats of South Carolina and Louisiana felt under any obligation to Hayes, for home rule had already been achieved elsewhere.[35]

Hayes was unmoved by these attacks. When Thomas Donaldson told him bluntly that the South would go as a unit into the Democratic column, Hayes questioned such dire predictions. He favorably compared his approach to that of his two immediate predecessors. Johnson's efforts had failed "because the times were not ripe for it" (in rather sharp contrast to his comments at the time); Grant "was finally compelled to let go" after two terms of intervention. Now was the time to try reconciliation. But in the same conversation he struck a far different pose. He had no choice, for "the House was against me and I had no army, and public sentiment demanded a change of policy." Hayes was trying to have it both ways. "Besides, if my plan fails, our party will be aided by it and the Independents stopped from further talk."[36] Republican critics would have chortled at that rationalization, one absent from Hayes's previous musings.

Since there had been no federal elections in the South during 1877, a deceptive calm prevailed, adding credence to Hayes's claims of success. Appearances were indeed deceiving. There was no sign of a realignment. As postmaster general, Key had turned scores of Republicans out of office; their replacements (Democrats in many cases) failed to reciprocate by forging a cadre of support for the president. This result mirrored a larger failing of Hayes's ability to wield patronage to weld together a southern following. In wooing former enemies, he forgot old friends. Southern Republicans, many of whom were dependent upon their offices for a livelihood, complained that they were being killed off by Hayes's policy. The president was losing their support without gaining anything in return.[37] True, Hayes did protect those Louisiana Republicans who as members of the returning board had counted him in, and Daniel Chamberlain chose not to accept office, but other southern Republicans bemoaned their fate. Hayes's decision not to support internal improvements removed yet another incentive for cooperation. To believe that a realignment would be effected simply on the basis of goodwill and conservative leanings was foolhardy and naive. The fall elections were quiet because many southern Republicans had given up the fight.

Hayes's policy had scant chance of success. The potential for a Republican revival in North Carolina and Tennessee was real, but only if Hayes appealed to poor whites, not the stolid conservatives. These states had been under Democratic control for some time, and the old Republican organizations included a good number of whites. But reports of realignment in Louisiana, South Carolina, Georgia, Alabama, or Mississippi lacked substance. The indigenous roots of white Republican support in those states were rather shallow. At the same time, Hayes's policy was sure to cut into the Republican black electorate. Bereft of patronage or protection, blacks became far less politically active in many areas. Thus, a policy designed to build support for the Republican party served instead to erode it.[38]

Certainly Hayes had a point that policy considerations alone did not dictate Republican opposition. It seemed entirely irresponsible and hypocritical for congressional Republicans to attack Hayes for deciding to abandon the very policy they had failed to sustain under Grant. Intervention had proved a political liability, and Hayes sought to salvage something from the less than favorable circumstances. Blaine had always waved the bloody shirt most vigorously when it was least likely that a policy of intervention would be supported by legislation. Yet Hayes, eager to appear that he was not subject to congressional dictation, also contributed to the chasm by failing to communicate with party leaders. Donaldson told Hayes it was time to repair that breach. "If you had called them in on the start and talked over your position and your difficulties," he told Hayes, "they would have aided you, would have agreed with you, if not in fact, would appear to, for the party's sake. After this they would have followed you like a troop of school boys."[39]

As the administration completed its first year, Hayes reflected upon his accomplishments. He realized that party regulars were dissatisfied but accepted that as the cost of nonpartisanship, although in rewarding friends and distributing patronage Hayes had indeed pursued partisan and personal ends. Yet this pose of nonpartisanship had partisan advantages, as he was quick to point out: "We are in a period when old questions are settled and the new are not yet brought forward. Extreme party action, if continued in such a time, would ruin the party." He believed that his approach to reconstruction had brought "peace, safety, [and] order in the South, to an extent not known for half a century."[40] That conclusion was debatable. But his approach had not brought about a realignment: Hayes could have achieved the same end simply by abandoning southern Republicanism without feting its enemies and dividing northern Republicans. He had removed the burden of intervention, but it was unclear whether he had any choice.

If the benefits of Hayes's policy were not clear, their costs were. "The policy of the President," snapped Garfield, "has turned out to be a give-away from the beginning. He had nolled suits, discontinued prosecutions, offered conciliation everywhere in the South while they have spent their time in whetting their knives for any Republican they could find." Conkling ridiculed Hayes, noting that "in spite of the fact that he can command no votes at the South," the president "seems possessed of the delusion that he is able to create a party of his own there." Other Republicans complained that Hayes's course was destroying the party. "Day by day the party is dropping away from him," Garfield noted, "and the present state of things cannot continue much longer without a total loss of his influence with the Republicans." Unless something happened, he concluded, the administration would collapse. "He is losing friends every hour, and unless some favorable turn in the current occurs, he will be left almost without a supporter among the Republican Congressmen."[41]

Hayes seemed undisturbed by such reports, believing that "he and his party differed because there was nothing essential to agree upon." He preferred to prepare to battle Conkling for control of New York's patronage. The New York senator's relentless criticism of his policies after his ambivalence during the electoral crisis irked Hayes; he chose to bolster the efforts of William Evarts and his allies to take control of the state party organization. Such tactics would simply add to the complaints about the president's southern policy. Far from being concerned about the resulting disunity, he reminded himself that John Quincy Adams had once found himself in a similar position. Hayes came close to claiming that his unpopularity was the best sign of the wisdom of his policy.[42] However comforting he might find such logic, it left him with little else.

Hayes seemed determined to foment further party divisions through his actions in 1878. Ignoring the signs of hard times, the president renewed efforts to halt efforts to inflate the currency, an issue on which Republicans struggled to find common ground. Some Republicans wanted the government to reissue greenbacks to inflate the currency; a greater number, including some of Hayes's fellow Ohioans, supported coining silver to provide a more modest inflation, while eastern Republicans remained fiscally conservative. Hayes's veto of Congress's answer—the Bland-Allison Act, which provided for the limited coinage of silver—was overridden. But the president was not discouraged. He decided to strike again at Conkling by nominating anti-Conkling Republicans for several key posts in the Empire State. In the battle that followed, both Hayes and Conkling framed their political dispute in institutional terms, as the New Yorker spoke of senatorial privilege while the president held forth on the independence of the executive. But most observers viewed it for the political dispute it was. Even some of Hayes's supporters thought he had gone too far. James A. Garfield believed that in resisting congressional dictation of appointments Hayes had veered to the other extreme of ignoring Congress altogether. Furthermore, the president's desire to prohibit any sort of political activity on the part of officeholders struck Garfield as suicidal: "I am inclined to think that his election has been an almost fatal blow to the party."[43]

In May 1878, House Democrats called for an investigation of the disputed presidential contest of 1876. Hayes objected, believing that it would disturb the nation's economic recovery, weaken faith in the nation's political institutions, and interrupt "the course of pacification between the Sections, and races." The House inquiry, he believed, was a Democratic conspiracy to overturn the decision of the electoral commission. But the Democrats were not alone in supporting the establishment of a committee of investigation headed by Clarkson Potter of New York. Roscoe Conkling and Benjamin Butler, angry with the administration's patronage and Reconstruction policies, were willing to weaken Hayes's hold on power. When Hayes heard that the Democrats hoped to replace him with Tilden, he defiantly declared: "Such schemes cannot be carried out without war. . . . I should defend my office and the independence of the Executive against any intruder."[44]

The fall contests provided the first true test of the sincerity of southern whites' promises to honor black rights. Before long it became evident that little had changed. Riots in Sumter and Williamsburg, South Carolina, reminded observers of the Hamburg incident in 1876. Displeased by such outbreaks, Hayes nevertheless counseled patience, claiming that election day would be the true test of his policy. As additional reports of violence arrived, however, he grew more concerned: "What good people demand is exact justice, equality before the law, perfect freedom of political speech and action, and no denial of rights to any citizen on account of color or race—the same to colored as to whites." He planned to discuss the matter in his annual message, although it would appear a month after the election, depriving it of any impact on the 1878 elections.[45]

The collapse of southern Republicanism in the elections of 1878 exploded whatever was left of Hayes's policy. Fraud, violence, and intimidation left their mark, but just as significant was southern Republicans' loss of faith in the administration. Hayes had left them to fend for themselves; they returned the favor by not voting. Republicans carried only one-half of the black belt counties they had carried in 1876; Republican support also eroded in primarily white counties.[46] Realignment to produce a southern wing of the Republican party had failed. Hayes's strategy had served to strengthen southern Democrats by eroding much of what was left of Republican strength. White southerners would move away from color-line politics after crushing black political influence as a prerequisite to discussing issues upon which whites might differ without depending on the black vote to decide the outcome.

Hayes assessed the midterm election results with mixed feelings. Although he observed that the party had done well for a midterm contest, he could not ignore the fact that because of the emergence of a Democratic South, the Democratic party had seized control of both houses of Congress for the first time since the Civil War. "The South is substantially against us," he concluded. "The whites must divide before we can hope for good results there. The blacks, poor, ignorant, and timid, can't stand alone against the whites." Before long more details of election day in the South reached him and darkened the picture still more. "By State legislation, by frauds, by intimidation and by violence of the most atrocious character colored citizens have been deprived of the right of suffrage," Hayes remarked, even though southern whites in 1877 had "solemnly pledged" to protect those rights. At last the truth dawned on him. "I tried an experiment in Southern matters," he confessed to a reporter. "It was a piece of policy, but it failed. The conciliation matters came to a bad end but I did it to bring all our people together. From this time on I intend to be Radical enough to suit our people." He now accepted that "fair elections with free suffrage for every voter in the South are an impossibility under the existing condition of things." It was uncertain what alternatives existed since Republicans had no intention of renewing the policy of intervention. "The man who attempts to get up a political excitement in this country on the old sectional issues," Garfield declared, "will find himself without a party and without support."[47]

In his annual message in the aftermath of the election, Hayes turned first to the South. He attacked southern whites for failing to let blacks exercise their political rights freely and without fear. "It is the right of every citizen, possessing the qualifications prescribed by law, to cast one unintimidated ballot, and to have his ballot honestly counted." Those who infringed upon such rights deserved punishment. "No means within my power will be spared to obtain a full and fair investigation of the alleged crimes, and to secure the conviction and just punishment of the guilty." But Hayes's message was no call to arms. "People are weary of sectional controversy," he mused. "It will gradually drop out of sight." Change could only be achieved gradually. "Let the rights of the colored people be secured and the laws enforced . . . and wait for the healing influences of time and reflection to solve and remove the remaining difficulties," he told Guy Bryan. Financial issues "will aid in putting out of sight sectional and color controversies and will be a healthy change." The president even contemplated appointing another southern Whig, Virginia's A. H. H. Stuart, to his cabinet, although he added that "the attacks on such a course by the bitter brethren would damage the good cause of pacification." Quick to overcome his disappointment about the election results, it looked before long as if he had forgotten it completely. On Christmas Day, 1878, Hayes enthused, "The Southern policy safely vindicated."[48] How was not clear.

Reconstruction was far from Hayes's mind as Congress met during the winter of 1878–1879. Instead of confronting old Confederates, he chose to renew his clash with Conkling over the appointive powers of the president versus the power of confirmation by the Senate. Hayes's characterization of this conflict as a battle over reform obscured the fact that it was really a contest for power, and a rather costly one, for such actions proved far more successful in dividing his own party than in promoting realignment in the South. Democratic leaders came to the rescue. By winning control of both houses in 1878, the Democrats had changed the dynamics of Hayes's feud with Senate Republicans, for now both would have to contend with the opposition in the majority. Moreover, Democrats in their newfound confidence reached beyond their grasp in an effort to destroy Republican chances in 1880. Their missteps revived their opponents and gave new life to one of their most potent appeals—the bloody shirt.

Democrats had to deal first with the embarrassing legacy of the Potter committee. Its investigation of the disputed election of 1876 failed to call into question Hayes's title to the presidency. Instead, the most embarrassing revelations concerned Democratic activities in the aftermath of the 1876 election. Investigation uncovered a series of telegraphic dispatches in cipher that, when decoded, unmasked efforts by some of Tilden's advisers and other party leaders to bribe Florida, South Carolina, and Louisiana officials in charge of counting the ballots. These charges, which first appeared in Republican papers on the eve of the 1878 elections, received fuller attention the following winter. It soon became clear that advisers close to Tilden had offered bribes to members of the returning boards during the electoral controversy. The findings crippled chances of a successful Tilden candidacy in 1880.[49]

Even more damaging to Democrats was their attempt to repeal several key clauses of the Enforcement Acts and other legislation governing the conduct of federal elections. Hoping to seize upon public distaste for bayonet rule, they moved to eliminate legislation that authorized the posting of federal troops at polling places to preserve peace. Lacking the votes in the Senate for a successful frontal attack on the legislation, Democrats chose to tack their measure onto the Army Appropriations Bill. Angered by the continued existence of provisions for test oaths for members of federal juries, they attached a provision calling for an end to the oaths on another appropriations bill, this one covering the operations of the government at large. This second bill also contained another rider repealing previous legislation that authorized the use of federal marshals to supervise the polls. If these riders were not accepted, Democrats pledged not to pass an appropriations bill. They planned to present Hayes and the Republicans with the difficult choice of accepting the evisceration of the Enforcement Acts or allowing government operations to grind to a halt. Faced with this dilemma, Hayes and the Republicans, Democrats believed, would bow.

Hayes had no intention of reviving the intervention policy of the Grant administration, but he did not mind reminding voters of the link between the Democratic party and the state supremacist attitudes often associated with the Confederate cause. He also sought to forge thematic links between his rejection of riders and his struggle for civil service reform and the appointing powers of the chief executive, for in each case he was battling to preserve the independence of the executive from the efforts of Congress to transcend the separation of powers and assume a position of dominance. Republicans held a different perspective. They still saw the political potency of the bloody shirt. One waved it not in hopes of regaining the South but because one wanted to retain control of the North and the federal government. One also waved it to demonstrate, once and for all, the failure of Hayes's policy. In the contest to follow, the Democrats played right into the hands of both Hayes and the congressional Republicans, allowing these uneasy allies to wax eloquently on their favorite subjects.

Senate Republicans refused to surrender to House Democrats, so Congress adjourned on March 4, 1879, without having passed either appropriations bill. Hayes immediately called for a special session of the new Congress—this time with Democrats in control of both houses—to meet two weeks later. He looked forward to the confrontation. As with executive appointments, Hayes saw the riders controversy primarily in terms of institutional prerogatives. To him it was an effort "to place the Executive 'under the coercive dictation' of a bare majority" of Congress, an attempt to evade "the constitutional provision as to the President's participation in legislation." He was determined to stop this "unconstitutional and revolutionary attempt to deprive the Executive of one of his most important prerogatives" by forcing him "to approve a measure which he in fact does not approve."[50]

The riders controversy was first and foremost intended "to break down the functions of the Executive by coercion," Hayes declared. Only later did he acknowledge that other matters were at stake: "Experience has shown that the protection and conduct of national elections cannot safely be left to the States." Efforts to repeal such legislation would strip the federal government of its rightful power to regulate congressional elections. He would not allow states' rights to reign triumphant over national power. Partisan considerations also entered his calculations: "If there had been free and fair elections in the States during the last few years there would now be Republican majorities in both Houses of Congress." Referring to Wade Hampton's Red Shirts, a quasi-military organization that had proved crucial in securing Democratic majorities in South Carolina by force and intimidation, Hayes asked, "If the red shirts can be present at the polls in South Carolina why can not the blue coats be called in also?"[51]

Hayes's primary concern, however, remained the issues of national and executive power. He saw the riders controversy primarily in institutional terms and sought to avoid their implications for matters of racial justice. "The present controversy is in no sense partisan and it is not a question of race or color," he insisted. "The old question [of] States Rights always seems closely related to Sectional and race conflicts, but this is chiefly as a reminiscence. No present interest of a Sectional character is involved." Others warmed to the conflict for different reasons. "If this is not revolution, which if persisted in will destroy the government, I am wholly wrong in my conception of both the word and the thing," Garfield declared as he prepared to battle the Democrats. Back in Ohio, Burke Hinsdale observed that it looked as if Hayes and his supporters were reviving an old tactic: "The coming of Hayes saw the shirt folded and laid away; and then the question was, what rag shall we now brandish before the eyes of the North to excite the necessary fury? As far as I can see, the new 'rag' is 'conspiracy,' 'revolution'; 'the South capturing the Capitol,' etc."[52]

On April 26, Congress passed the Army Appropriations Bill and sent it on to the White House. It contained a rider forbidding the use of federal troops or federal marshals to keep peace at the polls. Hayes prepared for a confrontation, having commenced drafting a veto prior to the bill's passage. He reminded Democrats that the purpose for such intervention was for each American citizen "to cast one unintimidated ballot and to have his ballot honestly counted." The House sustained the veto. Just as important, Hayes had rediscovered the value of working with the leaders of his party in Congress. The president had shared his veto message with Garfield to enable him to prepare a speech in support of the veto.[53]

Undeterred, Democrats framed another army appropriations bill forbidding use of federal troops at polls unless state officials requested their presence. "This thing of States Rights has gone far enough," Hayes exploded. "What a preposterous idea that the United States cannot enforce its own laws, can't protect its own citizens in their rights; or control for good in the interest of peace or in the election of its own officers. The Democrats insist that the polls, places sacred to peace and quiet, shall be the only places in the country where crime is to be permitted and the laws are not to be enforced." When Democrats justified their actions by characterizing the election legislation as a set of "war measures," Hayes reacted sharply. "We are ready to muster out the soldiers, but we don't muster out the flag nor the powers of the law and of the Constitution which enabled us to gain the victory," he confided to his diary. "We don't muster in again the evils that caused the war. Besides it is for the victors to say what shall remain—not for the vanquished." Another veto followed. Garfield pronounced it "by far the ablest paper which President Hayes has ever produced." House Republicans cheered as the clerk read it.[54] They sustained it the next day.

By now Republicans were alert to the political benefits of such a contest. "The Republicans are solid with President Hayes now and the lines are formed for 1880," one enthusiast reported. "The Democrats are utterly hopeless and totally defeated and routed. . . . The veto is praised by everybody. It is undoubtedly one of the ablest political vetoes sent to Congress in many years." Among the celebrators was Garfield: "I have no doubt that the President's position has been productive of good; for it has demonstrated, more clearly, the real character of the Southern people than the old policy could have done."[55]

Democrats stubbornly plugged away, passing a general appropriations bill with riders repealing election laws. Hayes struck it down with a third veto on May 29, insisting on the necessity to preserve federal supervision over federal elections. The first veto, explained Hayes, argued for the necessity of legislation to protect elections; the second declared the right of the federal government to legislate about congressional elections; the third maintained the independence of the executive. Once again the veto was sustained. Democrats then decided to exclude "certain judicial expenses" from a general appropriations bill, without riders; a new army appropriations bill contained clauses prohibiting the use of the army to police the polls. Hayes, satisfied that he was giving up nothing, signed these bills, since the army did not serve as a "police force" and had already been prohibited from such action by prior legislation. But when Democrats sent up for signature their appropriations for those "certain judicial expenses" excluded from the general bill, they failed to appropriate funds to implement the election laws. "Having failed to secure the direct repeal of the election laws," Hayes observed, "it is now proposed to prevent their enforcement." Again came the veto; again it was sustained. "Hayes understands politics better than I imagined," commented Republican congressman Joseph R. Hawley.[56]

Finally the Democrats sought to terminate the dispute while saving face. Aware that Hayes had no objection to efforts to repeal the test oath and was amenable to adjusting the role of the marshals, they decided to frame yet another bill providing for the expenses of the judiciary that repealed the test oath and failed to provide for the payment of marshals. Hayes accepted the measure but then vetoed another bill that would have restricted the employment of marshals. Once more it was sustained. With that the contest ended. The Democrats had to rest satisfied with their sole achievement of refusing to pay the fees of federal marshals.[57]

Some observers in the press celebrated the outcome of the struggle as a triumph for the president. "The Administration had become in the last three months the head of the party. . . . Mr. Hayes has the great body of Republican Representatives behind him," celebrated one journal, adding that Hayes had proved "a shrewd and long-headed politician, and a far wiser and safer party leader than the irate Senators who have vainly battled against him so often." Others viewed the significance of the struggle in party terms. Garfield, who had ably directed the Republican resistance in the House, cheered that the debate "has united the Republicans more than anything since 1868—and it bids fair to give us 1880."[58]

Although Hayes was aware of the political impact of the vetoes, he had not issued them to unite Republicans. He recognized that he had not placated his old opponents in the Senate. Blaine, he thought, should have been an ally; Conkling, however, was "so naturally mean a man" that it was "useless to attempt to conciliate such a person." Those Republicans who had opposed him were "the implacables" and "the patronage brokers." Indeed, some Senate Republicans, led by Conkling, went further in advocating that the president veto all appropriation bills containing riders. But their motives were suspect: Garfield believed, not without cause, that Conkling was determined to embarrass Hayes by making him appear to give in to the Democrats.[59]

Republicans returned home from the special session more convinced than ever of the political efficacy of reviving wartime sentiments. Even the president engaged in a little waving of the bloody shirt—although, one might add, the blood was real, the red blood of southern blacks. At Youngstown, Ohio, Hayes told veterans of his old regiment, "No one can overstate the evils which the country must suffer if lawlessness and violent opposition to the enjoyment of constitutional rights is allowed to be permanently successful." The protection of black civil and political rights was among the fruits of victory, he claimed. "The settlements of the war in favor of equal rights and the supremacy of the laws of the Nation are just and wise, and necessary. Let them not be surrendered." But this stirring call to arms did not commit him to reviving federal intervention to protect black rights. Hayes had declared his sentiments, not a policy.[60]

In the fall elections Republicans made decided gains in the North. In Ohio they secured the governorship by a margin of 17,000 votes and won majorities in both houses of the state legislature. By November it was clear that the Republicans had achieved victories throughout the North. Prospects looked good for the 1880 election. It was unclear what if anything affairs in the South had to do with the result, although its fading importance was reflected in Hayes's decision to devote a single paragraph to the region in his annual message for 1879.[61]

But if the riders controversy gave Republicans new opportunities to wave the bloody shirt and presented Hayes with a chance to uphold the power of the nation and the executive, it had no impact at all upon the life of southern blacks. Nor did it promote the long awaited realignment: indeed, it ended what chance remained for one. "Not much is said now about the independent political organization which was to be developed at the South under the invigorating influence of the new departure," commented one northern newspaper. "The old Whigs failed to come to time, and the Democrats had no idea of wandering off into strange paths."[62]

Determined to forge alliances with southern gentlemen of property, education, and standing, Hayes chose not to exploit the emerging divisions between southern whites over economic issues. Poor whites, angry at the debts left by state governments, Democratic as well as Republican, and the tax systems that made them pay a disproportionate amount of that debt, carried their protest into politics. The classic case occurred in Virginia, where former Confederate general William Mahone led the Readjusters, so named because of their desire to readjust the terms of the state debt. To Hayes and others, this position smacked of the twin devils of inflation and repudiation, a threat to stability and the sanctity of capital. The president showed no interest in wooing Mahone or the leaders of similar movements in other states; to do so would have been to betray Republican positions on economic issues.[63]

Hayes maintained an interest in the welfare of black Americans, displaying particular interested in education as a means to provide uplift and opportunity. Education, he believed, extended beyond the classroom. Blacks needed to inculcate the values of "industry, self-reliance, self control, economy, [and] thrift." Hayes was not so encouraging when it came to the matter of black migration to the Midwest. "Stay where you are," he told one Florida black educator. "It is not best for you to go to the climate of Ohio or Indiana. You are natives of the South and you are entitled to remain there. I know you are assaulted and bulldozed, but stick. Time and the North will set you right."[64]

But Hayes saw possible advantage in the threat of migration. "The exodus of colored people from the South still attracts some attention," he observed at the height of the riders controversy. "Its effect is altogether favorable. The tendency will be to force the better class of Southern people to suppress the violence of the ruffian class, and to protect colored people in their rights." This reasoning, reminiscent of Grant's advocacy of annexing San Domingo, proved more hopeful than realistic. Moreover, at a time when Hayes was battling Congress over the riders controversy, his failure to link it with the black migration suggested that whatever his disposition toward blacks, he did not intend to exercise vigorously the very powers he was fighting to preserve on behalf of those who needed protection—especially when there seemed little chance of support or success. As one Hayes supporter told the president, Democrats "want to kill with impunity so many negroes as may be necessary to frighten the survivors from the polls, in the South."[65] It was unclear how Hayes's stand on the riders issue had done anything to halt the erosion of black rights or of southern Republicanism, but at least he had resisted efforts to wipe off the books laws intended to protect black rights.

Hayes's declaration that he would serve only one term meant that the politics of the last years of his term were shaped by Republicans making a bid to succeed him in 1881. Ulysses S. Grant and James G. Blaine emerged as the top contenders for the nomination. Neither, however, could command a majority at the convention, and on the thirty-sixth ballot James A. Garfield, Hayes's floor leader during the riders controversy, emerged as the winner. Hayes, pleased, believed it was an endorsement of his administration, for he believed that Garfield "has uniformly been friendly," which was stretching a point. Hayes entertained the notion that the Republicans would carry several southern states. Nor was he averse to raising as a campaign issue Democratic efforts to nullify the Fifteenth Amendment in the South.[66] In the fall contest Garfield edged Democratic nominee Winfield Scott Hancock. The election result demonstrated two truths. The dismal performance of the Republican ticket in the South confirmed the Grand Old Party's minority status in the former states of the Confederacy. Garfield's triumph nationally, along with Republican gains in Congress, revealed that the party could thrive without southern votes.

For Hayes, the result constituted a vindication of his southern policy. "My judgment was that the time had come to put an end to bayonet rule," he reflected in the spring of 1880. "I saw things done in the South which could only be accounted for on the theory that the war was not yet ended." Thus he withdrew the troops. "My task was to wipe out the color line, to abolish sectionalism, to end the war and bring peace," he added. "To do this, I was ready to resort to unusual measures, and to risk my own standing and reputation with my party and the country." But he denied that he had abandoned southern Republicans, adding that "the practical destruction of the Republican organization in the South was accomplished before my Southern policy was announced."[67] From this position he never wavered for the rest of his life.

One must evaluate separately the several components of Hayes's southern policy before assessing it as a whole. Although he is often criticized for abandoning federal intervention in the South, his decision was prudent politically. As Hayes himself pointed out, by the time he entered office only two states, Louisiana and South Carolina, had Republican regimes protected by federal force. Other southern Democrats, having regained control of their states prior to Hayes's inauguration, were under no obligation to him, depriving him of leverage. But Hayes did not abandon intervention to gain the support of white southerners. He did so because it was politically unpopular, counterproductive for the party's future, and difficult to sustain with any assurance of ultimate success. Had northern Republicans supported their southern allies, the party would have lost its majority in the North and thus the nation, and a Democratic rather than a Republican administration would have overseen the end of Reconstruction. A majority of northern voters, including a sizable minority of Republicans, were either hostile or apathetic toward black aspirations for equal rights and opportunity. Only those aspects of southern policy that revived wartime antagonisms electrified the northern electorate, as Republicans saw when they waved the bloody shirt. It is simply unfair to blame Hayes for abandoning southern Republicans, for in truth he had no politically feasible choice.

But if an end to intervention was inevitable, the realignment of southern politics in ways beneficial to Republican prospects was improbable. Hayes's efforts, misconceived from the start, were based on a series of false assumptions. In the aftermath of the election of 1876, southern Democrats expressed their displeasure with northern Democrats, especially over the latter's frugal attitude toward internal improvements; it did not necessarily follow that southern Democrats were divided among themselves. Only if such divisions existed was there potential for realignment *within* the South. When both southern Democrats and Hayes backed away from carrying out understandings about organizing the House of Representatives under Republican leadership in return for Republican support of federal internal improvements for the South, there was no reason for southern Democrats to desert their northern counterparts.

Hayes's policy also failed to stimulate party divisions within southern states. The end of intervention did not provide positive incentives for realignment, and in any case only the Democrats of Louisiana and South Carolina were under any obligation to Hayes on that score. In pushing for an end to color-line politics in a way that would divide whites as well as blacks, Hayes simply misunderstood the imperatives of white supremacy. He believed that if whites divided over new issues, they would seek black votes to secure victory at the polls; in turn blacks, possessing political leverage, could secure white acquiescence in their exercise of equal rights in return for their support. What Hayes failed to see was that southern whites in the 1870s had no desire to reempower blacks as the decisive factor in their politics. Whites could divide over the future of the South only after blacks were removed as a deciding factor. The chief principle of white supremacist governance was that it was politics of white people, for white people, by white people. Blacks could participate (as they did to some extent) only when they accepted these ground rules. They could even govern in areas where blacks were in the overwhelming majority and where black political activity did not threaten white supremacy. When it did (as it would in years to come), southern white conservatives moved to excise blacks from the body politic. What potential remained for a two-party South rested with whites pushing to alter the economic and political contours of the polity in ways that Republicans abhorred.

Hayes's southern policy, born of necessity, had no chance to change the face of southern politics. For Hayes in the face of such failure to proclaim repeatedly that it had been a success suggests his ability for self-delusion and his reluctance to admit that he had erred in entertaining hopes that things could have been different. In accepting that the passage of time and education would reshape the South, Hayes may have been far more realistic than those who sought change both sudden and lasting. But in reiterating his belief that all would be well for blacks some day, he chose to avert his eyes from the painful sights around him.

CONCLUSION

An overview of how four presidents pursued reconstruction reminds us of how difficult it is both to govern and to evaluate the performance of those who govern. It also suggests how difficult it is to try to understand why and how people acted as they did in a narrative that heeds context and circumstance without leaving the impression that the process and outcome were somehow inevitable and preordained. And yet one of the greatest challenges of Reconstruction historiography is to decide whether, in the end, what happened was about as good as one could have hoped for, given circumstances, contexts, and human frailties and shortcomings. Could they—or we—have done better? Really?

Although war augmented Abraham Lincoln's executive powers, Union war aims and the need to retain political support for the administration placed constraints on what he could do. When it became clear that in order to achieve reunion it would be necessary to strike at slavery, Lincoln did so, but institutional and political considerations shaped the particulars of his response in different circumstances. Nor could he give full attention to defining what black freedom meant: winning the war and ending Confederate resistance remained paramount. His personal desire to destroy slavery in accordance with institutional procedures led him to explore several alternatives, from compensation to colonization, before the course of the war opened new opportunities for action. In acting as he did, he had to consider the reaction of congressional Republicans: partisan, institutional, and policy concerns interacted in the relationship between president and Congress. Lincoln had to balance his desire for black freedom with his determination to construct loyal governments in the South and retain (and perhaps expand) his party's base. All were essential to a successful reconstruction of the nation on Republican terms; to emphasize one of these priorities at the expense of others distorts our understanding of what Lincoln sought to achieve and the extent of his achievement.

April 1865 wrought fundamental shifts in the context of reconstruction policy and in the character of the president who would oversee it. With the end of wartime imperatives and priorities, the question of how best to reconstruct southern society and politics took center stage. How and when would civil government be reestablished? Who would set the terms? What did emancipation mean? What role would the federal government play in defining freedom? The president who offered his own answers to these and other questions was markedly different from his predecessor. Whatever Lincoln's racial prejudices, they paled in comparison to those of Andrew Johnson, whose virulent racism was an essential component of his view of the world. So were his traditional Jacksonian principles of white democracy and the vigorous exercise of executive power, even when it meant confrontation with Congress. Lincoln looked to Johnson to broaden the Republican party's base of support across the South and with War Democrats. As president, Johnson preferred to build his own conservative centrist coalition, which would have divided Republicans and left his opponents in the minority—or so he thought. The success of Johnson's plan rested upon the rapid restoration of the former Confederate states to equality in the Union while preserving essential aspects of the southern political and social order. His tolerance and even justification of white antagonism toward blacks enabled Republicans to charge that the result placed in jeopardy what had been won in war.

Had Johnson possessed different attitudes toward blacks, he would not have taken the course he did. But his racial attitudes were not the sole determinant of his policy: he embraced a political style that featured confrontation and defiance, and his embrace of Jacksonian principles, however informed by his prejudices, also transcended them. However, he clearly fumbled away an opportunity to gain much of what he sought. Had Johnson held white southerners to the terms he had outlined in 1865, had he acted vigorously to suppress violence and held white southerners accountable for their actions, had he sought common ground with Republican moderates whose initial agenda did not far outstrip his own, he might have established the foundation for a fundamental political realignment. It was possible to strike a deal whereby the southern states would have returned to Congress fairly soon after the war; once seated, these delegations, even if reduced in size somewhat by the impact of changes in determining representation, would have enabled Johnson to resist any more attempts to inject the federal government into the process of reshaping southern society. Meanwhile, with "home rule" reestablished, white southerners could have shaped their society in accordance with their preferences and prejudices.

Instead, Johnson sought a confrontation with congressional Republicans, relying upon his institutional powers to get what he wanted. In the contest that followed he did not choose his ground wisely, allowing Republicans to make antisouthernism and the revival of wartime concerns the core of their appeal. His extreme exercise of executive prerogatives sparked responses that threatened a fundamental shift in executive-legislative relations. It is simply foolish to contend that Johnson's actions sought to preserve the independence of the executive, for it was his behavior that imperiled presidential power: he did much to erode the position of the presidency in the constitutional and political order for some time to come. That he survived impeachment was due to the concerns of moderate Republicans, his belated decision to temper his own actions, and the chance for Republicans to capture the presidency through traditional means. Johnson's real achievement was in diverting Republican energies from reconstructing the South to restraining his use of presidential power to obstruct legislative intent. In the end, Republicans decided that it was best to allow black and white southerners to shape their own future through drafting new state constitutions and crafting new governments. Whether one wants to take pride in that achievement and its consequences is another question altogether.

Throughout his eight years in office, Ulysses S. Grant struggled with perhaps the most daunting challenges reconstruction posed to any of the four chief executives under discussion. Valuing both the restoration of harmony between former foes and the need to protect black citizenship, he could never fashion a policy that embodied both principles. Present-day critics charge that he was weak and did too little; in his time opponents claimed he verged toward despotism. The task he selected for himself was beyond his powers of office to achieve; in light of popular attitudes about the proper scope and extent of federal power, neither he nor congressional Republicans could have created the means necessary to sustain an effective policy of protecting southern Republicans from violence. He explored alternatives, from forging new alliances to offering blacks economic leverage consistent with laissez-faire beliefs, but none worked. Some of this lack of success was due to circumstances beyond his control, reminding us of the limits of presidential power. The power to persuade does not amount to much if someone is unwilling to be persuaded. Moreover, his expressions of outrage at violence against blacks rebuke claims that he was indifferent to their fate.

Although Grant was not a master at the art of politics, harsh assessments of his acumen and skill fall wide of the mark. He understood that politics was the art of the possible, displaying a fairly good sense of what the northern public would tolerate even when he tried its patience. Faced with difficult choices that embodied moral dilemmas, he realized that it was not always easy to do the right thing, because it was not always clear what the right thing was. Unlike Johnson, he believed in giving blacks a chance and in protecting their rights, but he could not impose his preferences on others. Proponents of a more vigorous and assertive federal policy toward southern terrorism forget the limits imposed upon Grant by legislation and public opinion or the ways in which intervention undermined the very legitimacy of the regimes it was designed to save. Perhaps he would have done better to accept that Republicanism would not thrive throughout the South and instead concentrated on saving some states to the party without impairing the party's fortunes in the North, but there is no evidence that had he persisted in pursuing any one approach, the result would have been markedly different. At a time when the practice of self-government sometimes mocked its values, he realized that his actions might threaten those values; in turn, most scholars severely underestimate his contribution to preserving the peace during the electoral dispute of 1876–1877, in which he served both his country and his party very well.

The circumstances in which Grant took office did much to shape his options as he sought to frame and implement a southern policy. He was frustrated by factionalism among southern Republicans, angered by the unwillingness of white conservatives to protest violence, disappointed with the eroding interest of many northern voters in southern affairs, and impatient with accusations that he was some sort of tyrant. He became president at a time when most Republicans, claiming Reconstruction was at an end, were eager to pursue new agendas that would result in some sort of realignment. Unlike Lincoln and Johnson, he had to wrestle with civil governments in the South without the extraordinary resources afforded by presidential war powers; it proved more challenging than keeping a dozen corks under water with just one's hands. Other political issues demanded attention; economic depression and Democratic resurgence put him on the defensive. Who else could have done a better job, and how? Was there some way to reconcile his principles with each other and with political circumstances? Why is it that scholars, imbued with hindsight, have failed to develop any sort of satisfactory alternative, resting content to criticize what he did do? What is needed is not necessarily sympathy but perhaps a little empathy.

Rutherford B. Hayes's approach to reconstruction has been praised as an exercise in healing statesmanship or damned as a betrayal of black aspirations. It was neither. In truth, Hayes played the hand that was dealt him, although he often pretended to make a virtue out of necessity. Had he done nothing

after acceding to the Democrats' return to power in Louisiana and South
Carolina, the course of events during his administration would have been much
the same. He had no other choice but to abandon intervention in the South,
and, for the most part, Grant had already abandoned it for him. His attempts
to forge coalitions with southern whites seemed admirable but were naive; they
were not even original with him, for Grant had taken tentative steps in that
direction during his presidency. At least he was spared tangling with southern
Republican regimes. Much is made of his reassertion of presidential prerogatives, probably too much. Like his predecessors, he used the veto to ward off
congressional intrusions; like Johnson, he tended to render political disputes
in terms of crusades over principle, regardless of the consequences.

Battling members of one's own party is not necessarily a sign of presidential ability or achievement, and Hayes proved less effective than Lincoln or
Grant in dealing with foes. Arguments that he revived respect for the presidency rely on embracing partisan attacks on his predecessor as objective descriptions; by foreswearing a second term, he further limited his effectiveness. And,
despite his sincere interest in the future of black Americans, he sometimes
minimized the consequences of Reconstruction's collapse on them. Ever hopeful that things would improve, he failed to grasp the depths of southern racism.
And at times, especially when he expressed pleasure at the success of his policy,
he was either countering self-doubts or fooling himself; here and there his diary
entries have fooled others, too. Like Grant, he was a well-intended man, but
he lacked Grant's skepticism about the willingness of others to share those
intentions or Grant's disappointment that they did not.

By looking at how these four presidents approached reconstruction, we gain
some idea of what was possible to achieve; only then can we even pretend to
engage in debating whether it was a "success" or "failure." What exactly constitutes success or failure? According to whom? Historians, like politicians, have
to distinguish between what is desirable and what is possible; they must weigh
the consequences of alternatives before evaluating the policy pursued. They
cannot simply impose their personal values and priorities on the past, unless
they believe that their primary task is to judge rather than to understand it.
To some extent, to describe events is to explain how and why they unfolded
as they did.

For example, had Lincoln pushed more vigorously for black rights, including suffrage, would he have secured them and at what cost? Was it better for
him to encourage Louisiana whites to consider some limited form of black
suffrage or to impose it outright as a condition for recognition? Could Andrew Johnson have compelled southern whites to comply with his admittedly

minimal requirements in 1865 and gained Congress's approval of the result? What would have been the consequences had Grant decided to intervene in Mississippi in 1875, regardless of the impact of his actions on the contest in Ohio? If Hayes had decided to sustain Packard and Chamberlain, would he simply have committed himself to a long-term intervention for which there was little support? To some extent, these exercises in counterfactual inquiry highlight the fact that historians, implicitly or explicitly, weigh these alternative scenarios in assessing what happened. In turn, the best assessments take into consideration matters of context and the interplay of other variables. What were the limits of northern support for federal intervention to protect blacks during the Grant administration? If, as one suspects, such support was rather fragile and sporadic, then it is easy to understand why that policy was not vigorously pursued for extended periods in the South. One reason Republicans resorted to the bloody shirt in the early 1870s was to garner support for a policy that would not receive it on its merits alone. Eventually, it became a tool to keep Democrats out of power nationally and in the North but had little to do with building support for policies to help southern blacks.

Despite the significant differences in the circumstances, challenges, and opportunities that each president confronted, there were also some common themes. One is the importance of the northern electorate. Most obvious to some observers is northern racism. A solid minority of white northerners, the vast majority of whom voted the Democratic ticket, had little to no interest in helping black people. Another significant portion of the electorate had less well-defined racial prejudices of varying impact on their views toward federal policies concerning blacks. The failure of black suffrage referenda in several northern states after the war reminded Republicans that they could only go so far in pushing certain issues, rendering it all the more remarkable that as many of them persisted as long as they did in advocating at least some steps to help blacks. In examining Republican racism, it is to easy to overlook Democratic racial attitudes, just as those historians who delight in pointing out the flaws in Republican reconstruction policy often forget the sort of horrible behavior by white southerners that demanded a response in the first place. Nevertheless, one must heed the spectrum of racial attitudes among Republicans to understand how the party acted as it did.

Racism does not explain everything, however. Northern voters displayed two other interrelated characteristics that affected presidential reconstruction policy. First, even among those northern whites who favored firm measures to protect southern blacks and to compel obedience by southern whites, there was a recurring sense of impatience, a hope that before long southern affairs would be out of the way. If change was to happen, let it happen so we can be done with it and move on. There was little in the way of the sort of patience and commitment needed to sustain an extended effort to transform the South. One reason Republicans supported enfranchising southern blacks, after all, was to enable them to protect themselves, thus freeing the federal government for other tasks. Most northerners, in fact, wanted to address other needs. Reconstruction was only one of many issues that concerned them, and it was rarely the most important one. Voters understandably wanted politicians to share their own priorities and address those issues of immediate concern to them, especially after depression struck in 1873. In declaring Reconstruction over as early as 1868, many northerners revealed that they were anxious to turn to new issues.

Another common theme is the role that white southerners played in the minds of the four Reconstruction presidents. Each sought to build some sort of alliance with southern whites; Lincoln, Grant, and Hayes even targeted similar groups. These alliances were short-lived, especially on matters involving race relations, in large part because most southern whites were unwilling to live up to their end of the bargain. Some white southerners even defied Andrew Johnson in 1865, which would have forced him into a difficult position had he not chosen to give way. However well-intended presidential proffers of conciliation coupled with a desire for voluntary compliance might be, one senses that had it been possible, it would have been better if presidents had been empowered to coerce compliance for prolonged periods of time. Lacking either the means or the political capital to do so left them with little alternative but to try to find a basis of understanding.

This conclusion then highlights another theme: Americans' commitment to civil government and federalism. For many people, "reconstruction" was primarily the restoration of loyal civil governments, pure and simple. However much one wants to debate the extent to which congressional proposals were conservative or revolutionary, they all looked to this end, one way or another. In turn, that objective restricted what one could do to protect black rights. Even in the 1870s, when it should have been obvious that the process of self-government in the South verged on collapse in several states, people still spoke of those governments in ways that bore a tenuous relation to reality, and never more so than when they referred to self-government. A prolonged federal occupation to supervise extensive changes or to buy time for things to settle was out of the question for most people. Grant later remarked that "the wisest thing would have been to continue for some time the military rule. . . . Military rule would have been just to all, to the negro who wanted freedom, the white man who wanted protection, the Northern man who wanted Union. . . . The trouble about military rule was that our people did not like it. It was not in accordance with our institutions. I am clear now that it would have been better for the North to have postponed suffrage, reconstruction, State governments, for ten years, and held the South in a territorial condition."[1] His very remarks betrayed his realization that however wise the idea might be, it would have been impossible to implement because of the commitment to restore self-government.

The final theme, closely related to the previous one, was the importance of preserving the American union. It is well to remember that whatever the shortcomings of Reconstruction, the American republic did reunify after a fashion. Flawed as that process might have been, nevertheless the polity showed relatively few scars for having been torn apart by civil war. Lincoln constantly reminded people of the importance of preserving the republic; Grant acted on that belief in his response to the electoral crisis of 1876–1877, which under less able leadership would have visited the ills of Louisiana on the nation. Current scholarship, interested in the effort to establish a biracial democracy, often takes reunion for granted; contemporaries did not.

Only when historians consider context and the interplay of variables can they return to the impact of personal style and beliefs on presidential leadership. Never is this clearer than in considering racial attitudes and reconstruction policy. Lincoln often distinguished between what he could do and what he wanted to do, especially concerning slavery. Andrew Johnson came closest to pursuing a policy in accordance with his racial attitudes, thus leaving a troubling legacy. Neither Grant nor Hayes could transform good intentions into meaningful policy. It would be an extreme distortion to reduce how each of these four men approached reconstruction to a simple expression of their attitudes on race. Nor, in light of the seemingly intractable racial problems that continue to challenge us, does it do any good to demand of past Americans what we find so difficult to ask of ourselves. Hindsight is not foresight. Historians need not forswear passing judgment when assessing people in the contexts and circumstances in which they acted, so long as it is understood that it is important first to understand what happened and why. Historians owe it to their subjects as well as their audiences to do at least that.

NOTES

ABBREVIATIONS

CHS   Chicago Historical Society

CWAL   Roy Basler et al., eds., *The Collected Works of Abraham Lincoln.* New Brunswick, N.J.: Rutgers University Press, 1953–1955.

HL   Henry E. Huntington Library, San Marino, California.

HPC   Rutherford B. Hayes Presidential Center, Fremont, Ohio.

LC   Library of Congress

NA   National Archives

PAJ   LeRoy P. Graf, Ralph Haskins, and Paul H. Bergeron, eds., *The Papers of Andrew Johnson.* Knoxville: University of Tennessee Press, 1967–.

PUSG   John Y. Simon et al., eds., *The Papers of Ulysses S. Grant.* Carbondale: Southern Illinois University Press, 1967–.

UVa   University of Virginia

INTRODUCTION

1. Compare C. Vann Woodward, "The Lowest Ebb: Grant's Story Administration," in Allan Nevins, ed., *Times of Trial* (New York, 1958), 157, with his remarks in *New York Review of Books,* March 19, 1981, 3–4, 6.

CHAPTER 1. "BROKEN EGGS CANNOT BE MENDED"

1. Mark E. Neely Jr., *The Fate of Liberty: Abraham Lincoln and Civil Liberties* (New York, 1991), 211.

2. Ibid., 215–22.

3. Allen Thorndike Rice, ed., *Reminiscences of Abraham Lincoln by Distinguished Men of His Time* (New York, 1886), 336.

4. Lincoln to Isaac M. Schermerhorn, September 12, 1864, *CWAL,* 8:1.

5. Lincoln to James T. Hale, January 11, 1861, ibid., 4:172; Lincoln to William S. Speer, October 23, 1860, ibid., 4:130; Lincoln to Nathaniel P. Paschall, November 16, 1860, ibid., 4:139–40; Lincoln to Lyman Trumbull, December 10, 1860, ibid., 4:149–50.

6. James G. Randall, *Lincoln the President* (New York, 1945–1955), 1:247; Lincoln to John A. Gilmer, December 15, 1860, *CWAL*, 4:152; see the more often quoted Lincoln to Alexander Stephens, December 22, 1860, ibid., 4:160.

7. Lincoln to John A. Gilmer, December 15, 1860, *CWAL*, 4:152; James A. Garfield to Burke Hinsdale, February 17, 1861, in Mary L. Hinsdale, *Garfield-Hinsdale Letters* (Ann Arbor, Mich., 1949), 56.

8. Daniel W. Crofts, *Reluctant Confederates: Upper South Unionists in the Secession Crisis* (Chapel Hill, N.C., 1989), 221; Michael F. Holt, "Abraham Lincoln and the Politics of Union," in John L. Thomas, ed., *Abraham Lincoln and the American Political Tradition* (Amherst, Mass., 1986), 122. See *CWAL*, 4:150 (December 12, 1860) for the planted editorial.

9. Lincoln to Gilmer, December 15, 1860, *CWAL*, 4:151–52; Crofts, *Reluctant Confederates*, 246. For Lincoln's reaction to such distortions, see his letter to Henry J. Raymond, December 18, 1860, *CWAL*, 4:156.

10. Holt, "Abraham Lincoln and the Politics of Union," 122; Crofts, *Reluctant Confederates*, 241.

11. Lincoln to Seward, February 1, 1861, *CWAL*, 4:183; Crofts, *Reluctant Confederates*, 247–55; Richard N. Current, *Lincoln and the First Shot* (Philadelphia, 1963), 37.

12. Lincoln, First Inaugural Address, March 4, 1861, *CWAL*, 4:271.

13. Lincoln to Elihu B. Washburne, December 21, 1860, and to David Hunter, December 22, 1860, both in *CWAL*, 4:159; Randall, *Lincoln*, 1:208.

14. Current, *Lincoln and the First Shot*, 28, 66; Montgomery Blair to Lincoln, March 15, 1861, *CWAL*, 4:285; Memorandum on Fort Sumter, [March 18, 1861], ibid., 4:28–90.

15. William H. Seward to Lincoln, April 1, 1861, *CWAL*, 4:317–18; Holt, "Abraham Lincoln and the Politics of Union," 125; Current, *Lincoln and the First Shot*, 31, 34; Stephen Oates, *With Malice Toward None: The Life of Abraham Lincoln* (New York, 1977), 223.

16. Holt, "Abraham Lincoln and the Politics of Union," 117.

17. Lincoln to Orville Browning, September 22, 1861, *CWAL*, 4:532.

18. Lincoln, Message to Congress, July 4, 1861, *CWAL*, 4:437, 439; Edward McPherson, *The Political History of the United States of America During the Great Rebellion, 1860–1865* (New York, 1972 [1865]), 286. Herman Belz, *Reconstructing the Union: Theory and Policy During the Civil War* (Ithaca, N.Y., 1969), 25, suggests that antislavery Republicans who supported the resolutions did so because they did not specifically mention slavery. However, everybody understood the resolutions to exclude abolition as a war aim, so this interpretation seems strained.

19. Richard H. Sewell, *A House Divided: Sectionalism and Civil War* (Baltimore, 1988), 161.

20. Tyler Dennett, ed., *Lincoln and the Civil War in the Letters and Diaries of John Hay* (New York, 1939), 19 (May 7, 1861).

21. Lincoln to Beriah Magoffin, August 24, 1861, *CWAL*, 4:497; Dennett, *Lincoln and the Civil War*, 25 (August 22, 1861).

22. Armstead L. Robinson, "Lincoln and the Politics of Emancipation: Commentary on 'Lincoln and Black Freedom,'" in Gabor S. Boritt, *The Historian's Lincoln: Pseudohistory, Psychohistory, and History* (Urbana, Ill., 1988), 207; Lincoln to John C. Frémont, September 2, 1861, *CWAL*, 4:506; Sumner to Francis Lieber, September 17, 1861, in Beverly Palmer, ed., *The Selected Letters of Charles Sumner* (Boston, 1990), 2:79.

23. Sumner to Martin F. Tupper, November 11, 1861, in Palmer, *Letters of Sumner,* 2:83; Sumner to John Jay, August 11, 1861, ibid., 2:76.

24. Lincoln to George Bancroft, November 18, 1861, *CWAL,* 5:26; James G. Randall and Theodore C. Pease, eds., *The Diary of Orville Hickman Browning* (Springfield, Ill., 1933), 1:512 (December 1, 1861); see also ibid., 1:478 (July 8, 1861), in which Lincoln expresses a preference for colonization.

25. Drafts of Bill, [November 26(?), 1861], *CWAL,* 5:29–31; Lincoln, First Annual Message, December 3, 1861, ibid., 5:48–49.

26. See Phillip Shaw Paludan, *The Presidency of Abraham Lincoln* (Lawrence, Kans., 1994), 130–33; Eric Foner, *Free Soil, Free Labor, Free Men: The Ideology of the Republican Party Before the Civil War* (New York, 1970), 267–80.

27. Lincoln, Message to Congress, March 6, 1862, *CWAL,* 5:145–46; Lincoln to Henry J. Raymond, March 9, 1862, ibid., 5:152–53; J. W. Crisfield, "Memorandum," March 10, 1862, in E. McPherson, *Political History,* 210–11.

28. Lincoln to Horace Greeley, March 24, 1862, *CWAL,* 5:169; Lincoln, Message to Congress, April 16, 1862, ibid., 5:192.

29. Lincoln, Proclamation, May 19, 1862, ibid., 5:222–23.

30. Sumner to John Bright, August 5, 1862, in Palmer, *Letters of Sumner,* 2:122.

31. Lincoln to Pierpoint, March 20, 1862, *CWAL,* 5:166.

32. Johnson, Appeal to the People of Tennessee, March 18, 1862, *PAJ,* 5:209–12; Lincoln to Johnson, July 3, 1862, *CWAL,* 5:303; James E. Sefton, *Andrew Johnson and the Uses of Constitutional Power* (Boston, 1980), 90; David W. Bowen, *Andrew Johnson and the Negro* (Knoxville, Tenn., 1989), 92–100.

33. On Stanly and North Carolina, see Norman D. Brown, *Edward Stanly: Whiggery's Tarheel "Conqueror"* (University, Ala., 1974); Wayne Durrill, *War of Another Kind: A Southern Community in the Great Rebellion* (New York, 1990), 105–7, 121; and William C. Harris, "Lincoln and Wartime Reconstruction in North Carolina, 1861–1863," *North Carolina Historical Review* 63 (April 1986): 149–68.

34. The leading studies of wartime Reconstruction in Louisiana are Peyton McCrary, *Abraham Lincoln and Reconstruction: The Louisiana Experiment* (Princeton, N.J., 1978), and LaWanda Cox, *Lincoln and Black Freedom: A Study in Presidential Leadership* (Columbia, S.C., 1981). Also of use is Ted Tunnell, *Crucible of Reconstruction: War, Radicalism, and Race in Louisiana, 1862–1877* (Baton Rouge, La., 1984).

35. Belz, *Reconstructing the Union,* 88, 97–98; Sumner to Edward Atkinson, March 5, 1862, in Palmer, *Letters of Sumner,* 2:104; Sumner to Orestes A. Brownson, October 5, 1863, ibid., 2:196.

36. Belz, *Reconstructing the Union,* 85.

37. Lincoln, Remarks, July 12, 1862, *CWAL,* 5:317–19.

38. Lincoln, Message to Congress, July 14, 1862, ibid., 5:324–25.

39. Second Confiscation Act, July 17, 1862, in E. McPherson, *Political History,* 196–97; Randall and Pease, *Diary of Browning,* 1:558 (July 14, 1862); Lincoln, Message to Congress, July 17, 1862, *CWAL,* 5:328–31.

40. James M. McPherson, *Battle Cry of Freedom: The Civil War Era* (New York, 1988), 504; Lincoln, Emancipation Proclamation—First Draft, [July 22, 1862], *CWAL,* 5:336–37.

41. Lincoln to Reverdy Johnson, July 26, 1862, *CWAL,* 5:342–43.

42. Lincoln to Cuthbert Bullitt, July 28, 1862, ibid., 5:344–46; Lincoln to August Belmont, July 31, 1862, ibid., 5:350–51.

43. J. McPherson, *Battle Cry of Freedom,* 508–9.

44. Lincoln, Remarks, August 4, 1862, *CWAL,* 5:356–57; Lincoln to Horace Greeley, August 22, 1862, ibid., 5:388–89; Rice, *Reminiscences of Abraham Lincoln,* 526.

45. Lincoln, Reply to Emancipation Memorial, September 13, 1862, *CWAL,* 5:419–25.

46. Lincoln, Preliminary Emancipation Proclamation, September 22, 1862, *CWAL,* 5:433–36.

47. William B. Hesseltine, *Lincoln and the War Governors* (New York, 1948), 249–62; Rice, *Reminiscences of Abraham Lincoln,* 532–33.

48. Lincoln to Edward Stanly, September 29, 1862, *CWAL,* 5:445; Lincoln to Benjamin F. Butler and George F. Shepley, October 14, 1862, ibid., 5:462–63; Lincoln to Ulysses S. Grant and Andrew Johnson, October 21, 1862, ibid., 5:470–71; Lincoln to Frederick Steele and John S. Phelps, November 18, 1862, ibid., 5:500.

49. J. McPherson, *Battle Cry of Freedom,* 561–62.

50. Lincoln, Second Annual Message, December 1, 1862, *CWAL,* 5:527–37.

51. Lincoln to John A. Dix, December 31, 1862, *CWAL,* 6:26.

52. Randall and Pease, *Diary of Browning,* 1:596 (December 15, 1862); Lincoln to Members of the Cabinet, December 23, 1862, *CWAL,* 6:17; John Hay and John Nicolay, *Abraham Lincoln: A History* (New York, 1890), 6:300 (the position of secretary of the interior was not filled at the time of this discussion); Lincoln, Opinion on the Admission of West Virginia into the Union, *CWAL,* 6:26–28.

53. Lincoln, Emancipation Proclamation, January 1, 1863, *CWAL,* 6:28–30; on Johnson, see Bowen, *Andrew Johnson and the Negro,* 99.

54. Lincoln to Salmon P. Chase, September 2, 1863, *CWAL,* 6:428–29.

55. Lincoln to John A. McClernand, January 8, 1863, *CWAL,* 6:48–49; Randall and Pease, *Diary of Browning,* 1:611–12 (January 9, 1863).

56. Lincoln to Stephen A. Hurlbut, July 31, 1863, *CWAL,* 6:358; Lincoln to Nathaniel P. Banks, August 5, 1863, ibid., 6:364–65.

57. Lincoln to James C. Conkling, August 26, 1863, ibid., 6:406–10.

58. Dennett, *Lincoln and the Civil War,* 106 (October 23, 1863). That Jesus brought Lazarus back from the dead is a point Hay never seems to have considered.

CHAPTER 2. "MUCH GOOD WORK IS ALREADY DONE"

1. Lincoln to Zachariah Chandler, November 20, 1863, *CWAL,* 7:24.

2. Lincoln to Stanton, April 25, 1863, ibid., 6:187 and note; Lincoln to Johnson, September 19, 1863, ibid., 469.

3. Lincoln to E. E. Malhiot, Bradish Johnson, and Thomas Cottman, June 19, 1863, ibid., 6:287–88; Lincoln to Nathaniel Banks, August 5, 1863, ibid., 6:364–65; Herman Belz, *Reconstructing the Union: Theory and Policy During the Civil War* (Ithaca, N.Y., 1969), 145.

4. Lincoln to Stephen Hurlbut, July 31, 1863, *CWAL,* 6:358; Lincoln to Edwin M. Stanton, July 29, 1863, ibid., 6:354–55; Lincoln to Nathaniel P. Banks, August 5 and September 19, 1863, ibid., 6:364–65, 465–66; Lincoln to Johnson, September 11, 1863, ibid., 6:440; Lincoln to Banks, November 5, 1863, ibid., 7:1–2; William C. Harris, *With Charity for All: Lincoln and the Restoration of the Union* (Lexington, Ky., 1997), 86–96.

5. See Lawrence N. Powell and Michael S. Wayne, "Self-Interest and the Decline of Confederate Nationalism," in Harry P. Owens and James J. Cooke, eds., *The Old South in the Crucible of War* (Jackson, Miss., 1983), 29–46; Ludwell Johnson,

Red River Campaign: Politics and Cotton in the Civil War (Kent, Ohio, 1994 [1958]); Gabor S. Boritt, *Lincoln and the Economics of the American Dream* (Memphis, Tenn., 1978), 242–49; Harris, *With Charity for All*, 90–91, 147–49.

6. Lincoln, "Fragment," n.d. [1863–1864], *CWAL*, 6:410–11.

7. Lincoln, Proclamation, December 8, 1863, ibid., 7:53–56. Lincoln merged together the different concepts of amnesty and pardon.

8. Lincoln, Third Annual Message, December 8, 1863, ibid., 7:51–52.

9. Tyler Dennett, ed., *Lincoln and the Civil War in the Letters and Diaries of John Hay* (New York, 1939), 135 (December 10, 1863); Lincoln to Thomas Cottman, December 15, 1863, *CWAL*, 7:66–67; Banks to Lincoln, December 30, 1863, ibid., 7:124; Harris, *With Charity for All*, 135.

10. William B. Hesseltine, *Lincoln's Plan of Reconstruction* (Tuscaloosa, Ala., 1960), 96–97; David Herbert Donald, *Lincoln* (New York, 1995), 487–88; Harris, *With Charity for All*, 176–79.

11. Belz, *Reconstructing the Union*, 169–70; Dennett, *Lincoln and the Civil War*, 131, 134 (December 9 and 10, 1863).

12. Sumner to Orestes A. Brownson, December 27, 1863, in Beverly Palmer, ed., *The Selected Letters of Charles Sumner* (Boston, 1990), 2:216–17.

13. Dennett, *Lincoln and the Civil War*, 112–13 (November 1, 1863).

14. Harris, *With Charity for All*, 1–2; LaWanda Cox, "Lincoln and Black Freedom," in Gabor S. Boritt, ed., *The Historian's Lincoln: Pseudohistory, Psychohistory, and History* (Urbana, Ill., 1988), 180. As Harris points out, historians have battled over what Lincoln's foremost purpose was in pushing wartime Reconstruction; I believe that he juggled wartime and postwar priorities while he struggled to come to terms with the nature of the postemancipation order.

15. Dennett, *Lincoln and the Civil War*, 73 (July 31, 1863); Lincoln to Alpheus Lewis, January 23, 1864, *CWAL*, 7:145–46; Lincoln to James S. Wadsworth, [January 1864?], ibid., 7:101. Several historians have debated the authencity of the Wadsworth letter; see Donald, *Lincoln*, 683, and Hans L. Trefousse, *The Radical Republicans: Lincoln's Vanguard for Racial Justice* (New York, 1968), 286. One may rightfully question the authenticity of the last section of the letter, where Lincoln believed reconstruction "must rest upon the principle of civil and political equality of both races," for it did not surface until 1893 (and the original letter is lost). However, Lincoln's comment about "suffrage on the basis of intelligence and military service" comports with his March 13, 1864, letter to Hahn.

16. Banks to Lincoln, December 30, 1863, and Lincoln to Banks, January 13, 1864, *CWAL*, 7:124; Belz, *Reconstructing the Union*, 190; Phillip Shaw Paludan, *The Presidency of Abraham Lincoln* (Lawrence, Kans., 1994), 276.

17. Paludan, *Presidency of Lincoln*, 276; LaWanda Cox, *Lincoln and Black Freedom: A Study in Presidential Leadership* (Columbia, S.C., 1981), 94–95.

18. Lincoln to Michael Hahn, March 13, 1864, *CWAL*, 7:243; Harris, *With Charity for All*, 182–84.

19. Paludan, *Presidency of Lincoln*, 277–78.

20. Lincoln to Quincy A. Gillmore, January 13, 1864, *CWAL*, 7:126; Dennett, *Lincoln and the Civil War*, 146 (December 28, 1863), 154 (January 13, 1864), 165 (March 1 [?], 1864); Lincoln to Frederick Steele, January 20 and 27, 1864, *CWAL*, 7:141–42, 154–55; Lincoln to Isaac Murphy, February 8, 1864, ibid., 7:173.

21. Paludan, *Presidency of Lincoln*, 279; Michael F. Holt, "Abraham Lincoln and the Politics of Union," in John L. Thomas, ed., *Abraham Lincoln and the American Political Tradition* (Amherst, Mass., 1986), 114.

22. Richard H. Sewell, *A House Divided: Sectionalism and Civil War, 1848–1865* (Baltimore, 1988), 189; David Donald, *Lincoln Reconsidered: Essays on the Civil War Era* (New York, 1956), 106–7.

23. Michael Les Benedict, *A Compromise of Principle: Congressional Republicans and Reconstruction, 1863–1869* (New York, 1974), 72; Hesseltine, *Lincoln's Plan of Reconstruction,* 101.

24. Holt, "Abraham Lincoln and the Politics of Union," 116.

25. Donald, *Lincoln,* 422, 488.

26. Ibid., 468–88 passim.

27. See John G. Nicolay to John Hay, June 5, 1864, and John Hay to John Nicolay, June 6, 1864, *CWAL,* 8:376–78; Dennett, *Lincoln and the Civil War,* 186 (June 6, 1864); John Nicolay and John Hay, *Abraham Lincoln: A History* (New York, 1890), 9:72–75; William O. Stoddard Jr., *Lincoln's Third Secretary: The Memoirs of William O. Stoddard* (New York, 1955), 215–16; Alexander K. McClure, *Abraham Lincoln and Men of War-Times* (Philadelphia, 1962 [1892]), 118–23; Hans L. Trefousse, *Andrew Johnson: A Biography* (New York, 1989), 177–78.

28. Benedict, *Compromise of Principle,* 73–79; Allan G. Bogue, *The Earnest Men: Republicans of the Civil War Senate* (Ithaca, N.Y., 1981), 240–47.

29. Dennett, *Lincoln and the Civil War,* 204 (July 4, 1864).

30. Ibid., 205 (July 4, 1864); Lincoln, Proclamation, July 8, 1864, *CWAL* 7:433–34.

31. Harold M. Hyman, ed., *The Radical Republicans and Reconstruction, 1861–1870* (Indianapolis, 1967), 137–47.

32. Paludan, *Presidency of Lincoln,* 282–83; Donald, *Lincoln,* 526–27; David W. Blight, *Frederick Douglass' Civil War: Keeping Faith in Jubilee* (Baton Rouge, La., 1989), 183–84.

33. Lincoln to Edward R. S. Canby, December 12, 1864, *CWAL,* 8:164. Eric Foner, *Reconstruction: America's Unfinished Revolution, 1863–1877* (New York, 1988), 55–56, offers a concise summary of Banks's policy.

34. Sumner to Lincoln, November 20, 1864, in Palmer, *Letters of Sumner,* 2:256.

35. Dennett, *Lincoln and the Civil War,* 245 (December 18, 1864).

36. Lincoln to Lyman Trumbull, January 21, 1863, *CWAL,* 8:207; Sumner to George Bancroft, February 28, 1865, and Sumner to John Bright, March 13, 1865, in Palmer, *Letters of Sumner,* 2:270, 273–74.

37. Harris, *With Charity for All,* 253–54.

38. Paludan, *Presidency of Lincoln,* 301.

39. Ibid., 299–302; Lincoln, Response to a Serenade, February 1, 1865, *CWAL,* 8:254.

40. Lincoln, Fourth Annual Message, December 6, 1864, *CWAL,* 8:151–52; Donald, *Lincoln,* 555–57.

41. Recently John Y. Simon has offered the curious claim that this incident and several other initiatives in early 1865 proved that "Lincoln rather than Grant pushed toward the goal of unconditional surrender," when in fact the two men agreed on war aims and worked closely together during the final months of the war. See Simon, "Grant, Lincoln, and Unconditional Surrender," in Gabor Boritt, ed., *Lincoln's Generals* (New York, 1994), 190–93; Brooks D. Simpson, *Let Us Have Peace: Ulysses S. Grant and the Politics of War and Reconstruction, 1861–1868* (Chapel Hill, N.C., 1991), 72–78.

42. Harris, *With Charity for All,* 238–39.

43. Lincoln, Second Inaugural Address, March 4, 1865, *CWAL*, 8:332-33; Donald, *Lincoln*, 565-68.

44. Simpson, *Let Us Have Peace*, 75-78, 84, 89.

45. *CWAL*, 8:152.

46. Cox, *Lincoln and Black Freedom*, 142-43.

47. *CWAL*, 8:399-405.

48. Gideon Welles to Andrew Johnson, July 27, 1869, Welles Papers, HL.

49. David Donald, ed., *Inside Lincoln's Cabinet: The Civil War Diaries of Salmon P. Chase* (New York, 1954), 268 (April 15, 1865).

50. Lincoln to Albert G. Hodges, April 4, 1864, *CWAL*, 7:282; Dennett, *Lincoln and the Civil War*, 146 (December 31, 1863).

CHAPTER 3. "THERE IS NO SUCH THING AS RECONSTRUCTION"

1. George L. Stearns to Johnson, May 17, 1865, *PAJ*, 8:83.

2. Hans L. Trefousse, *The Radical Republicans: Lincoln's Vanguard for Racial Justice* (New York, 1968), 307.

3. Ibid., 308.

4. James E. Sefton, *Andrew Johnson and the Uses of Constitutional Power* (Boston, 1980), 89, 96; Speech on Vice-Presidential Nomination, June 9, 1864, *PAJ*, 6:726; Speech on Restoration of State Government, January 21, 1864, ibid., 6:588; Johnson to Lincoln, May 17, 1864, ibid., 6:699.

5. George W. Julian, *Political Recollections 1840-1872* (Chicago, 1884), 257; Zachariah Chandler to wife, April 23 and 25, 1865, Zachariah Chandler Papers, LC.

6. Edward McPherson, *The Political History of the United States During the Period of Reconstruction* (New York, 1969 [1875]), 44; Howard K. Beale, ed., *The Diary of Gideon Welles* (New York, 1960), 2:291 (April 16, 1865).

7. E. McPherson, *Reconstruction*, 46-47.

8. John Cox and LaWanda Cox, *Politics, Principle, and Prejudice, 1865-1866: Dilemma of Reconstruction America* (New York, 1963), 51; Dixon to Johnson, May 5, 1865, *PAJ*, 8:31; Jacob Ziegler to Johnson, May 15, 1865, ibid., 8:75; Montgomery Blair to Samuel Barlow, May 13, 1865, Barlow Papers, HL.

9. Brooks D. Simpson, LeRoy P. Graf, and John Muldowny, *Advice After Appomattox: Letters to Andrew Johnson, 1865-1866* (Knoxville, Tenn., 1987), xiii-xiv; Julian, *Political Recollections*, 259.

10. David Donald, ed., *Inside Lincoln's Cabinet: The Civil War Diaries of Salmon P. Chase* (New York, 1954), 269 (April 18, 1865); Sumner to Wendell Phillips, May 1, 1865, and to Francis Leiber, May 2, 1865, in Beverly Palmer, ed., *The Selected Letters of Charles Sumner* (Boston, 1990), 2:298-300; Simpson, Graf, and Muldowny, *Advice After Appomattox*, 7.

11. Sumner to Leiber, May 2, 1865, in Palmer, *Letters of Sumner*, 2:300; Simpson, Graf, and Muldowny, *Advice After Appomattox*, 7. When Sumner proclaimed Johnson's support of black suffrage, Welles noted: "On this point I am skeptical. He would not oppose any such movement, were any state to make it" (Beale, *Diary of Welles*, 2:304 [May 10, 1865]).

12. Simpson, Graf, and Muldowny, *Advice After Appomattox*, 9-11, 14; Salmon P. Chase to Edwin M. Stanton, May 5, 1865, in Stanton Papers, LC; Chase to Johnson, May 7, 1865, in Simpson, Graf, and Muldowny, *Advice After Appomattox*, 19.

13. Johnson shared with others his fantastic story about Lincoln's constitutional amendment in his famed Washington's Birthday address; see *PAJ*, 10:153.

14. Johnson, Speech at Knoxville, April 16, 1864, ibid., 6:674; Johnson to Lincoln, July 13, 1864, ibid., 7:30.

15. John F. H. Claibourne to Johnson, May 1, 1865, ibid., 8:4.

16. Thaddeus Stevens to Johnson, May 16, 1865, ibid., 8:80; Michael Les Benedict, *A Compromise of Principle: Congressional Republicans and Reconstruction, 1863–1869* (New York, 1974), 105–6.

17. Benedict, *Compromise,* 106; Speed to Johnson, May 1, 1865, *PAJ*, 8:13.

18. Johnson, Proclamation, May 29, 1865, *PAJ*, 8:128–30.

19. Johnson, Proclamation, May 29, 1865, ibid., 8:136–38.

20. *Washington Morning Chronicle,* July 1, 1865, ibid., 8:154.

21. Joshua Hill to Johnson, May 10, 1865, ibid., 8:55; Christopher Memminger to Johnson, September 4, 1865, ibid., 9:22.

22. I. Welden to Elihu B. Washburne, August 21, 1865, Elihu Washburne Papers, LC; Hans L. Trefousse, *Andrew Johnson: A Biography* (New York, 1989), 236; Johnson to George H. Thomas, September 4, 1865, *PAJ*, 9:26; Thomas to Johnson, September 9, 1865, ibid., 9:57; Clinton B. Fisk to Johnson, October 3, 1865, ibid., 9:176.

23. Johnson, Reply to Delegation of Black Ministers, May 11, 1865, *PAJ*, 8:62; October 10, 1865, New York *Times,* October 11, 1865; interview with Alexander McClure, [October 1865], *PAJ*, 9:311; Cox and Cox, *Politics, Principle, and Prejudice,* 153–54.

24. Sefton, *Johnson,* 98.

25. C. Clara Cole to Johnson, August 15, 1865, and Johnson, endorsement to Oliver O. Howard, August 16, 1865, *PAJ*, 8:603; Johnson to Howard, August 24, 1865, ibid., 8:648; ibid., 9:310.

26. North Carolina Freedmen to Johnson, May 10, 1865, ibid., 8:57–58.

27. Petition from South Carolina Blacks, June 29, 1865, ibid., 8:317; Joseph Noxon to Johnson, May 27, 1865, ibid., 8:119.

28. William Johnson to Johnson, June 6, 1865, ibid., 8:190; J. Rhodes Mayo to Johnson, June 17, 1865, ibid., 8:252; J. G. Dodge to Johnson, June 20, 1865, ibid, 8:263; Carl Schurz to Johnson, June 6, 1865, ibid., 8:192; George Leslie to Johnson, June 24, 1865, ibid., 8:286.

29. Lewis D. Campbell to Johnson, May 8, 1865, ibid., 8:47; Henry Flanders to Johnson, May 31, 1865, ibid., 8:152; James A. Stewart to Johnson, August 12, 1865, ibid., 8:579; Harvey Watterson to Johnson, July 8, 1865, in Simpson, Graf, and Muldowny, *Advice After Appomattox,* 58.

30. Johnson to William L. Sharkey, August 15, 1865, *PAJ*, 8:599–600.

31. See Chapter 2 for Lincoln's position on black suffrage. Lincoln had included veterans but had said nothing about property holders; Johnson's suggestion complied with New York's suffrage provisions.

32. Sharkey to Johnson, August 20, 1865, *PAJ*, 8:627–28.

33. Cox and Cox, *Politics, Principle, and Prejudice,* 157; Boston *Evening Journal,* June 27, 1865, quoted in Michael Les Benedict, "Preserving the Constitution: The Conservative Basis of Radical Reconstruction," *Journal of American History* 61 (1974): 70.

34. Carl Schurz to Johnson, June 6, 1865, *PAJ*, 8:192; Cox and Cox, *Politics, Principle, and Prejudice,* 137; Trefousse, *Johnson,* 233; Sumner to Francis Leiber, October 8, 1865, in Palmer, *Selected Letters,* 2:336.

35. Johnson to George H. Thomas, September 8, 1865, *PAJ*, 9:48–49; Johnson to James Gordon Bennett, October 6, 1865, ibid., 9:196; Mrs. John A. Jackson to Johnson, September 2, 1865, ibid., 9:15; Orville Eastland to Johnson, September 3, 1865, ibid., 9:17–18.

36. Johnson, Speech to Southern Delegation, September 11, 1865, ibid., 9:64–67; Remarks, September 11, 1865, ibid., 9:66. As evidence of his consistency, he called on an old associate to forward an excerpt from an 1855 speech stating his position on the powers of the federal government over suffrage qualifications; Johnson to Edward H. East, September 21, 1865, ibid., 9:107.

37. James B. Campbell to Johnson, September 18, 1865, ibid., 9:94.

38. Johnson to Benjamin F. Perry, October 28 and 31, 1865, ibid., 9:299, 314; Johnson to William L. Sharkey, November 1, 1865, ibid., 9:325; Dan L. Carter, *When the War Was Over: The Failure of Self-Reconstruction in the South, 1865–1867* (Baton Rouge, La., 1985), 82–85.

39. William W. Holden to Johnson, October 20, 1865, *PAJ*, 9:260; Johnson to James Johnson, October 28, 1865, ibid., 9:299; Benjamin Perry to Johnson, November 1, 1865, ibid., 9:324; Johnson to Benjamin Humphreys, November 17, 1865, ibid., 9:397; Carter, *When the War Was Over*, 69, 72.

40. Carter, *When the War Was Over*, chap. 8; Eric Foner, *Reconstruction: America's Unfinished Revolution, 1863–1877* (New York, 1988), 199–205; Johnson to Benjamin Humphreys, November 17, 1865, *PAJ*, 9:397; Johnson to Benjamin Perry, November 27, 1865, ibid., 9:441; Johnson to Andrew J. Fletcher, December 9, 1865, ibid., 9:500.

41. Albemarle County citizens to Johnson, September 20, 1865, *PAJ*, 9:101; ibid., 9:102.

42. Trefousse, *Johnson*, 232; New York *Herald*, July 30, 1865, quoted in Simpson, Graf, and Muldowny, *Advice After Appomattox*, 86–87; William W. Holden to Johnson, *PAJ*, 9:487; E. R. S. Canby to William T. Sherman, October 5, 1865, William T. Sherman Papers, LC; Manning F. Force to father, December 3, 1865, Force Papers, University of Washington.

43. James L. Dunning to Johnson, July 2, 1865, *PAJ*, 8:339; James A. Stewart to Johnson, October 13, 1865, ibid., 9:239.

44. Sam Milligan to Johnson, September 1, 1865, ibid., 9:10–11; Orville Eastland to Johnson, September 3, 1865, ibid., 9:17; A. R. Wynne to Johnson, September 8, 1865, ibid., 9:51; Johnson to Lewis E. Parsons, September 1, 1865, ibid., 9:12; Johnson to James Johnson, November 5, 1865, ibid., 9:346; Johnson to Carl Schurz, August 30, 1865, ibid., 8:683; Johnson to George H. Thomas, September 8, 1865, ibid., 9:48–49.

45. Interview with George L. Stearns, October 3, 1865, ibid., 9:179.

46. Cox and Cox, *Politics, Principle, and Prejudice*, 155–56, 159; Washington *Evening Star*, June 26, 1865.

47. James Dixon to Johnson, October 8, 1865, *PAJ*, 9:205–6.

48. John Hogan to Johnson, June 19, 1865, ibid., 8:259; Duff Green to Johnson, June 25, 1865, ibid., 8:290; L. R. Marshall to Johnson, June 26, 1865, ibid., 8:296; Daniel S. Dickinson to Johnson, August 19, 1865, ibid., 8:615; Lewis D. Campbell to Johnson, August 21, 1865, ibid., 8:630; Hendrick B. Wright to Johnson, June 19, 1865, ibid., 8:261; Thomas Cottman to Johnson, June 5, 1865, ibid., 8:182; R. Weakley Brown to Johnson, October 16, 1865, ibid., 9:245; George W. Morgan to Johnson, September 14, 1865, ibid., 9:80; Cox and Cox, *Politics, Principle, and Prejudice*, 57; Montgomery Blair to Samuel Barlow, December 9, 1865, Barlow Papers, HL.

49. *PAJ,* 9:309.

50. Cox and Cox, *Politics, Principle, and Prejudice,* 74, 89, 101.

51. Sumner to Johnson, November 11, 1865, *PAJ,* 9:374; Andrew Armstrong to Johnson, November 8, 1865, ibid., 9:356; Henderson Crawford to Johnson, November 5, 1865, ibid., 9:345.

52. Whitewater (Wis.) *Register,* October 13, 1865; Joseph Medill to Johnson, September 15, 1865, *PAJ,* 9:82.

53. Cox and Cox, *Politics, Principle, and Prejudice,* 166; Alexander N. Wilson to Johnson, November 25, 1865, *PAJ,* 9:431; William W. Holden to Johnson, December 6, 1865, ibid., 486.

54. Johnson to Thaddeus C. Bolling, September 18, 1865, *PAJ,* 9:90; Benjamin F. Perry to Johnson, October 5 and November 27, 1865, ibid., 9:191, 441; Johnson to Perry, November 27, 1865, ibid., 9:441; Johnson to James Johnson, November 26, 1865, ibid., 9:432; Johnson to James B. Steedman, November 24, 1865, ibid., 9:434; Benedict, *Compromise,* 129.

55. Carter, *When the War Was Over,* 94; Charles Hening to Johnson, October 7, 1865, *PAJ,* 9:199.

56. Abel Anderson to Johnson, December 3, 1865, and Findlay Y. Clark to Johnson, December 4, 1865, *PAJ,* 9:458–60, 463–64; Joseph C. Bradley to Johnson, November 15, 1865, ibid., 9:388; Benjamin F. Perry to Johnson, December 2, 1865, ibid., 9:456.

57. Cox and Cox, *Politics, Principle, and Prejudice,* 164.

58. Ibid., 129–34.

59. Johnson, First Annual Message, December 4, 1865, *PAJ,* 9:466–72.

60. Ibid., 9:473–75.

61. Schurz to Johnson, August 21, 1865, and notes, in Simpson, Graf, and Muldowny, *Advice After Appomattox,* 103–5.

62. David H. Donald, *Charles Sumner and the Rights of Man* (New York, 1970), 237–38.

63. Simpson, Graf, and Muldowny, *Advice After Appomattox,* 216–17.

64. Oliver P. Morton to Johnson, December 7, 1865, *PAJ,* 9:492; Harry C. Page to Johnson, December 22, 1865, ibid., 9:532–34; Ransom Balcom to Johnson, January 2, 1866, ibid., 9:559–61; New York *Times,* December 29, 1865.

65. Benedict, *Compromise,* 147–52, 155; Brooks D. Simpson, *Let Us Have Peace: Ulysses S. Grant and the Politics of War and Reconstruction, 1861–1868* (Chapel Hill, N.C., 1991), 127–30.

66. Bennett to Johnson, February 1, 1866, *PAJ,* 10:7; Sherman to Johnson, February 2, 1866, ibid., 10:20–21; interview, February 7, 1866, ibid., 10:41–48; Joseph S. Fullerton to Johnson, February 9, 1866, ibid., 10:64–69; interview, February 10, 1866, ibid., 10:75–79; New York *Times,* February 11, 1866; Simpson, *Let Us Have Peace,* 130–32.

67. Johnson, Veto of the Freedmen's Bureau Bill, February 19, 1866, *PAJ,* 10:120–27.

68. Benedict, *Compromise,* 156.

69. Johnson, Washington's Birthday Speech, February 22, 1866, *PAJ,* 10: 145–57.

70. David Davis to George Davis, March 11, 1866, Davis Papers, CHS; Benedict, *Compromise,* 158–59, 162–63.

71. Earl M. Maltz, *Civil Rights, the Constitution, and Congress, 1863–1869* (Lawrence, Kans., 1990), 61–70.

72. Benedict, *Compromise,* 144, 149; Cox to Johnson, March 22, 1866, *PAJ,* 10:286–88.

73. John Sherman to William Stanton, March 21, 1866, William Stanton Papers, HL.

74. Benedict, *Compromise,* 138, 164–65; Cox and Cox, *Politics, Principle, and Prejudice,* 197; Johnson, veto of the Civil Rights Bill, March 27, 1866, *PAJ,* 10:312–20.

75. Cox and Cox, *Politics, Principle, and Prejudice,* 227; David W. Bowen, *Andrew Johnson and the Negro* (Knoxville, Tenn., 1989), 138.

76. Bowen, *Andrew Johnson and the Negro,* 122, 142; Cox and Cox, *Politics, Principle, and Prejudice,* 177, 203.

77. Johnson, Proclamation, April 2, 1866, *PAJ,* 10:349–52.

78. New York *Times,* May 14, 1866; Johnson, Speech to Soldiers and Sailors, April 18, 1866, *PAJ,* 10:422–28.

79. Cox and Cox, *Politics, Principle, and Prejudice,* 175.

CHAPTER 4. "DAMN THEM!"

1. Michael Les Benedict, *A Compromise of Principle: Congressional Republicans and Reconstruction, 1863–1869* (New York, 1974), 188.

2. Eugene Berwanger, *The West and Reconstruction* (Urbana, Ill., 1981), 67.

3. See Earl M. Maltz, *Civil Rights, the Constitution, and Congress, 1863–1869* (Lawrence, Kans., 1990), for a solid account of the framing of the amendment that stresses the compromises Republicans made; see also Joseph B. James, *The Framing of the Fourteenth Amendment* (Urbana, Ill., 1956).

4. Daniel Richards to Lyman Trumbull, May 7, 1866, Trumbull Papers, LC.

5. Hans L. Trefousse, *Andrew Johnson: A Biography* (New York, 1989), 255–57; Albert Castel, *The Presidency of Andrew Johnson* (Lawrence, Kans., 1979), 77–78.

6. Howard K. Beale, ed., *The Diary of Gideon Welles* (New York, 1960), 2:535 (June 21, 1866).

7. Trefousse, *Johnson,* 253–254; Benedict, *Compromise,* 196–97.

8. Eric Foner, *Reconstruction: America's Unfinished Revolution, 1863–1877* (New York, 1988), 262.

9. Patrick W. Riddleberger, *1866: The Critical Year Revisited* (Carbondale, Ill., 1979), 196–97.

10. Ibid., 197–98.

11. James E. Sefton, *Andrew Johnson and the Uses of Constitutional Power* (Boston, 1980), 139.

12. Orville H. Browning to James R. Doolittle, October 13, 1866, Doolittle Papers, State Historical Society of Wisconsin; Castel, *Presidency of Johnson,* 90; Trefousse, *Johnson,* 264.

13. Castel, *Presidency of Johnson,* 91.

14. Ibid., 93; Brooks D. Simpson, *Let Us Have Peace: Ulysses S. Grant and the Politics of War and Reconstruction, 1861–1868* (Chapel Hill, N.C., 1991), 150–51.

15. Trefousse, *Johnson,* 267–68; John Cox and LaWanda Cox, *Politics, Principle, and Prejudice: Dilemma of Reconstruction America, 1865–1866* (New York, 1963), 108–9.

16. Castel, *Presidency of Johnson,* 98.

17. Benedict, *Compromise,* 246.

18. Castel, *Presidency of Johnson,* 100–104.

19. Simpson, *Let Us Have Peace,* 166.

20. Trefousse, *Johnson,* 273–75; Mark E. Neely Jr., *The Fate of Liberty: Abraham Lincoln and Civil Liberties* (New York, 1991), 176. Neely's claim that the decision "had little impact on history" (184) is belied by an examination of it in the context of Reconstruction.

21. Benedict, *Compromise,* 221, 231–32.

22. Trefousse, *Johnson,* 276.

23. Ibid., 277; Castel, *Presidency of Johnson,* 112–13; Benjamin P. Thomas and Harold M. Hyman, *Stanton: Lincoln's Secretary of War* (New York, 1962), 523–27.

24. Trefousse, *Johnson,* 277–78.

25. Ibid., 279; Benedict, *Compromise,* 239.

26. Benedict, *Compromise,* 240; Francis P. Blair Sr. to Johnson, February 24, 1867, *PAJ,* 12:59; Montogmery Blair to Johnson, February 26, 1867, ibid., 12:67.

27. Benedict, *Compromise,* 214.

28. Ibid., 245.

29. Ibid., 244; Simpson, *Let Us Have Peace,* 179–85.

30. Simpson, *Let Us Have Peace,* 185–87; Benedict, *Compromise,* 254.

31. Sefton, *Johnson,* 157–58; Trefousse, *Johnson,* 290–91; Benedict, *Compromise,* 253.

32. Simpson, *Let Us Have Peace,* 192–201.

33. Trefousse, *Johnson,* 300.

34. Robert D. Sawrey, *Dubious Victory: The Reconstruction Debate in Ohio* (Lexington, Ky., 1992), 123; Georges Clemenceau, *American Reconstruction, 1865–1870* (New York, 1928), 102–3.

35. Sawrey, *Dubious Victory,* 100–117.

36. Orville E. Babcock to Elihu B. Washburne, October 9, 1867, *PUSG,* 18:325.

37. Trefousse, *Johnson,* 268, 299; Castel, *Presidency of Johnson,* 152.

38. Trefousse, *Johnson,* 300, 303; Benedict, *Compromise,* 283.

39. Castel, *Presidency of Johnson,* 155.

40. Simpson, *Let Us Have Peace,* 228–30. See Trefousse, *Johnson,* 306–7, for an account that accepts without question Johnson's version of events.

41. Simpson, *Let Us Have Peace,* 230–36.

42. Beale, *Diary of Welles,* 3:284 (February 21, 1868).

43. Trefousse, *Johnson,* 313; Castel, *Presidency of Johnson,* 178.

44. Edward McPherson, *The Political History of the United States of America During the Period of Reconstruction* (New York, 1969 [1875]), 270.

45. Castel, *Presidency of Johnson,* 184–85.

46. Ibid., 185–86.

47. Ibid., 187–88.

48. Trefousse, *Johnson,* 327.

49. Simpson, *Let Us Have Peace,* 247–48.

50. Ibid., 249–50; Castel, *Presidency of Johnson,* 205–6; Trefousse, *Johnson,* 333.

51. Clemenceau, *American Reconstruction,* 96.

CHAPTER 5. "LET US HAVE PEACE"

1. "General Ulysses Simpson Grant," *Edinburgh Review* 129 (1869): 230–69.

2. Brooks D. Simpson, *Let Us Have Peace: Ulysses S. Grant and the Politics of War and Reconstruction, 1861–1868* (Chapel Hill, N.C., 1991), 214, 245.

3. For a contrary view on Grant's interest in the presidency, see William S. McFeely, *Grant: A Biography* (New York, 1981), 160–64, 169–70, 263–66.

4. Grant to Joseph R. Hawley, May 29, 1868, *PUSG,* 18:263–64; First Inaugural Address, March 4, 1869, ibid., 19:139–42.

5. Michael Perman, *Emancipation and Reconstruction, 1862–1879* (Arlington Heights, Ill., 1987), contains the best explication of this dilemma.

6. Richard H. Abbott, *The Republican Party and the South, 1855–1877* (Chapel Hill, N.C., 1986), 204–5.

7. William Gillette, *Retreat from Reconstruction, 1869–1879* (Baton Rouge, La., 1979), 15.

8. Augustus Garland to William A. Graham, November 9, 1868, and Garland to Alexander H. Stephens, November 9, 1868, in Max R. Williams, ed., *The Papers of William A. Graham* (Raleigh, N.C., 1984), 7:625–29; Percy S. Flippin, *Herschel V. Johnson of Georgia: States Rights Unionist* (Richmond, Va., 1931); John Rangeley to William P. Fessenden, February 1869, William P. Fessenden Papers, LC; Henry L. Webb to Hamilton Fish, March 19, 1869, Fish Papers, LC; George S. Merriam, *The Life and Times of Samuel Bowles* (New York, 1885), 2:125.

9. William C. Harris, *William Woods Holden: Firebrand of North Carolina Politics* (Baton Rouge, La., 1987), 252–53; New York *Independent,* March 11, 1869.

10. Jack P. Maddex Jr., *The Virginia Conservatives, 1867–1879: A Study in Reconstruction Politics* (Chapel Hill, N.C., 1970), 59; Grant to Congress, April 7, 1869, in James D. Richardson, ed., *Messages and Papers of the Presidents* (Washington, D.C., 1912), 6:3965–66.

11. Cox to James A. Garfield, July 26, 1869, quoted in William B. Hesseltine, *Ulysses S. Grant: Politician* (New York, 1935), 182; Richard Lowe, *Republicans and Reconstruction in Virginia, 1856–70* (Charlottesville, Va., 1990), 177–79.

12. Thomas B. Alexander, "Political Reconstruction in Tennessee, 1865–1870," in Richard O. Curry, ed., *Radicalism, Racism, and Party Realignment: The Border States During Reconstruction* (Baltimore, 1969), 71–79; Allan Nevins, *Hamilton Fish: The Inner History of the Grant Administration* (New York, 1937), 290–91.

13. New York *Independent,* July 29, 1869; Horace Porter to Adelbert Ames, September 1, 1869, Lloyd Lewis Notes, Ulysses S. Grant Association, Southern Illinois University; William C. Harris, *The Day of the Carpetbagger: Republican Reconstruction in Mississippi* (Baton Rouge, La., 1979), 218–63; Carl Moneyhon, *Republicanism in Reconstruction Texas* (Austin, Tex., 1980), 106–7, 112–16; William L. Richter, *The Army in Texas During Reconstruction, 1865–1870* (College Station, Tex., 1987), chap. 10; Richter, "'We Must Rub Out and Begin Anew': The Army and the Republican Party in Texas Reconstruction, 1867–1870," *Civil War History* 19 (1973):334–52.

14. Grant, First Annual Message, December 6, 1869, in Richardson, *Messages and Papers,* 6:3983; Washington (D.C.) *National Republican,* January 1, 1870; Hesseltine, *Grant,* 187–88.

15. Washington (D.C.) *National Republican,* February 8 and March 11, 1870.

16. Washington (D.C.) *National Republican,* April 25, 1870, quoting the New York *Evening Post;* Washington (D.C.) *National Republican,* March 19, 1870. .

17. See William Gillette, *The Right to Vote: Politics and the Passage of the Fifteenth Amendment* (Baltimore, 1969).

18. Grant to Elihu B. Washburne, January 28, 1870, in James G. Wilson, ed., *General Grant's Letters to a Friend* (New York, 1897), 64–65; George Sinkler, *The Racial Attitudes of American Presidents* (New York, 1972), 163; Grant to David Butler, November 23, 1869, Grant Papers, LC; Gillette, *Right to Vote,* 157; Washington (D.C.) *National Republican,* February 18 and March 11, 1870; Nevins, Fish, 293; John Eaton, *Grant, Lincoln, and the Freedmen* (New York, 1907), 288.

19. Washington (D.C.) *National Republican,* March 4, 1870; Henry Adams, "The Session," in George Hochfield, *The Great Secession Winter and Other Essays* (New York, 1958), 205; Allan Peskin, *Garfield* (Kent, Ohio, 1978), 332; *Nation,* April 28, 1870; Manning F. Force to John Sherman, June 7, 1870, John Sherman Papers, LC; New York *Times* quoted in Washington (D.C.) *National Republican,* March 24, 1870.

20. Grant to Elihu B. Washburne, January 28, 1870, in Wilson, *Letters to a Friend,* 64; Hamilton Fish Diary, March 15 and April 15, 1870, Fish Papers, LC.

21. Andrew D. White, quoted in *Responses to a Toast at a Banquet Given by Members of the Union League in Commemoration of the Seventy-Fourth Anniversary of the Birth of General Ulysses S. Grant, Philadelphia, April 27, 1896* (Philadelphia, 1896), 40–41; Daniel Ammen, *The Old Navy and the New* (Philadelphia, 1891), 509; see also Ithaca (N.Y.) *Journal,* April 30, 1896.

22. M. G. Norman to Hamilton Fish, October 2, 1869, Fish Papers, LC.

23. Mark W. Summers, *The Era of Good Stealings* (New York, 1993), 189–91; William S. McFeely, "Amos T. Akerman: The Lawyer and Racial Justice," in J. Morgan Kousser and James M. McPherson, eds., *Region, Race, and Reconstruction: Essays in Honor of C. Vann Woodward* (New York, 1982), 395–415.

24. Hesseltine, *Grant,* 224–37; David Donald, *Charles Sumner and the Rights of Man* (New York, 1970), 467–76.

25. David J. Rothman, *Politics and Power: The United States Senate, 1869–1901* (New York, 1969), 12; Schuyler Colfax to Henry B. Anthony, August 7, 1870, Colfax Papers, LC; Michael Perman, *The Road to Redemption: Southern Politics, 1869–1879* (Chapel Hill, N.C., 1984), 17–18.

26. Perman, *Road to Redemption,* 20–21; Hesseltine, *Grant,* 207. William E. Parrish, *Missouri Under Radical Rule, 1865–1870* (Columbia, MO., 1965), chaps. 11 and 12, offer helpful information.

27. Hesseltine, *Grant,* 220–21.

28. New York *Standard,* June 30, 1870; Xi Wang, *The Trial of Democracy: Black Suffrage and Northern Republicans, 1860–1910* (Athens, Ga., 1997), 58–67, offers a detailed description of the framing of the May 1870 legislation.

29. Horace W. Raper, *William W. Holden: North Carolina's Political Enigma* (Chapel Hill, N.C., 1985), 162–64; Harris, *Holden,* 288–89; Wang, *The Trial of Democracy,* 54.

30. Harris, *Holden,* 284–91; Raper, *Holden,* 167, 171; Gillette, *Retreat from Reconstruction,* 90–91.

31. Harris, *Holden,* 292, 298–99.

32. Ibid., 295–96; Raper, *Holden,* 191–94.

33. Harris, *Holden,* 296–97, 307, 310–11; Raper, *Holden,* 229.

34. Washington (D.C.) *National Republican,* March 11, 1871; *Army and Navy Journal,* March 11, 1871; J. R. West to Henry Clay Warmoth, March 2, 1871, Warmoth Papers, Southern Historical Collections, University of North Carolina; Michael Les Benedict, *The Fruits of Victory: Alternatives in Restoring the Union, 1865–1877* (Lanham, Md., 1986), 54; Donald, *Sumner,* 421.

35. Fish Diary, February 24, 1871, Fish Papers, LC; Hesseltine, *Grant,* 242–44; James A. Garfield to Burke Hinsdale, March 23, 1871, in Mary L. Hinsdale, ed., *Garfield-Hinsdale Letters* (Ann Arbor, Mich., 1949), 171; Washington (D.C.) *National Republican,* March 24, 1871; George F. Hoar, *Autobiography of Seventy Years* (New York, 1906), 1:205–6.

36. Hesseltine, *Grant,* 246–47; New York *Evening Post,* quoted in Washington (D.C.) *National Republican,* March 31, 1871; Gillette, *Retreat from Reconstruction,* 52–53.

37. Baltimore *American,* quoted in the Washington (D.C.) *National Republican,* April 4, 1871; Alfred Wilkenson to Andrew D. White, January 16, 1871, White Papers, Cornell University; Hesseltine, *Grant,* 248.

38. Brooklyn (N.Y.) *Union,* April 3, 1871; Everett Swinney, "Enforcing the Fifteenth Amendment, 1870–1877," *Journal of Southern History* 28 (1962):203; Hayes to John Sherman, April 1, 1871, John Sherman Papers, LC.

39. Amos T. Akerman to E. P. Jacobson, August 18, 1871, and Akerman to R. A. Hill, September 12, 1871, Akerman Letterbooks, UVa.

40. Robert K. Scott to Grant, March 9, 1871, Department of Justice, Letters Received, 1871–1884, South Carolina, RG 60, NA (microfilm 947); Richard Zuczek, *State of Rebellion: Reconstruction in South Carolina, 1865–1877* (Columbia, S.C., 1996), 79, 91; Grant, Proclamation, March 24, 1871, in Richardson, *Messages and Papers,* 6:4088–89; Grant, Proclamations, October 12, 17, November 3, 10, 1871, ibid., 6:4089–95; G. Pillsbury to Robert K. Scott, October 14, 1871, Scott Papers, Ohio Historical Society; Washington (D.C.) *National Republican,* October 19, 1871. Eventually Grant withdrew Marion County, then added Union County to the list of counties where he suspended the writ of habeas corpus.

41. Zuczek, *State of Rebellion,* 99–105; Lewis Merrill to Amos T. Akerman, November 27, 1871, Department of Justice, Letters Received, 1871–1884, South Carolina, RG 60, NA (microfilm 947).

42. Amos T. Akerman to H. P. Farrow, November 25, 1871, Akerman to Foster Blodgett, November 8, 1871, Akerman to J. R. Parrott, December 6, 1871, and Akerman to Benjamin Conley, December 28, 1871, all in Akerman Papers, UVa.

43. Grant, Third Annual Message, December 4, 1871, in Richardson, *Messages and Papers,* 6:4104–5, 4107.

44. Benjamin Conley to Grant, November 24, 1871, Grant Papers, HPC; Fish Diary, December 1, 1871, Fish Papers, LC; Zuczek, *State of Rebellion,* 103; Hesseltine, *Grant,* 261–62.

45. Joe Gray Taylor, *Louisiana Reconstructed, 1863–1877* (Baton Rouge, La., 1974), 208–19; Gillette, *Retreat from Reconstruction,* 106–10; Washington (D.C.) *National Republican,* August 24, 1871, January 16, 1872, and February 26, 1872; Ted Tunnell, *Crucible of Reconstruction: War, Radicalism, and Race in Louisiana, 1862–1877* (Baton Rouge, La., 1984), chap. 8. Gillette blames Grant for not acting more vigorously in support of the customhouse faction, although he also points out that the earlier use of federal force to protect Casey and company sparked heavy criticism in northern newspapers.

46. Wang, *The Trial of Democracy,* 87; James R. Doolittle to David Davis, February 21, 1872, [?] to Lyman Trumbull, February 26, 1872, and Trumbull to John M. Palmer, April 8, 1872, Davis Papers, CHS; Nelson Cross, *The Modern Ulysses, LLD* (New York, 1872), 181.

47. William R. Thrall to John Eaton, April 27, 1872, Eaton Papers, University of Tennessee.

48. Washington (D.C.) *National Republican,* January 11, 1872; Donald, *Sumner,* 531–39, 545–47.

49. Grant to Thomas Settle, June 10, 1872, James G. Wilson, *The Life and Public Services of General Ulysses Simpson Grant* (New York, 1885), 86.

50. Grant to Gerrit Smith, July 28, 1872, Smith Papers, Syracuse University.

51. Washington (D.C.) *National Republican,* July 19, August 2, August 8, August 22, 1872.

52. Grant, Fourth Annual Message, December 2, 1872, in Richardson, *Messages and Papers,* 6:4138–59; Second Inaugural Address, March 4, 1873, ibid., 6:4175–77.

CHAPTER 6. "UNWHIPPED OF JUSTICE"

1. George C. Rable, "Republican Albatross: The Louisiana Question, National Politics, and the Failure of Reconstruction," *Louisiana History* 23 (1982):112–15; William Gillette, *Retreat from Reconstruction, 1869–1879* (Baton Rouge, La., 1979), 111–12.

2. Gillette, *Retreat from Reconstruction,* 96–99, 136–37. Gillette implies that in Louisiana, Alabama, and Arkansas, Democratic claims were at least as good if not better than those presented by Republicans.

3. Gideon Pillow to Grant, March 21, 1873, Special Collections, University of Tennessee; Fish Diary, February 21, 1873, Fish Papers, LC.

4. W. D. Porter to George H. Williams, July 30, 1873, and D. T. Corbin to George H. Williams, March 28, 1874, Department of Justice, Letters Received, 1871–1884, South Carolina, RG 60, NA (microfilm 947); Everett Swinney, "Enforcing the Fifteenth Amendment," *Journal of Southern History* 28 (1962): 206–7.

5. Henry Wayne to Hamilton Fish, September 11 and November 24, 1873, Fish Papers, LC; William H. Trescot to Hamilton Fish, August 16, 1874, ibid.

6. New York *Herald,* January 18, 1874; see the comments of George S. Robeson in the New York *Tribune,* September 13, 1885.

7. John Scott to James L. Kemper, November 18, 1873, Kemper Papers, UVa; Michael Perman, *The Road to Redemption, 1869–1879* (Chapel Hill, N.C., 1984), 162–63; Alfred Morton et al. to Grant, August 1, 1875, Fish Papers, LC.

8. Perman, *Road to Redemption,* 163; Carl H. Moneyhon, *Republicanism in Reconstruction Texas* (Austin, Tex., 1980), 191–94.

9. Washington (D.C.) *National Republican,* November 28, 1872; Barnas Sears to Robert C. Winthrop, January 4, 1874, in J. L. M. Curry, *History of the Peabody Education Fund* (Cambridge, Mass., 1898), 64–65.

10. Fish Diary, March 27, 1874; Fish Papers, LC; Joel Williamson, *After Slavery: The Negro in South Carolina During Reconstruction, 1861–1877* (Chapel Hill, N.C., 1965), 399–405.

11. William M. Heath to George H. Williams, October 24, 1874, J. C. Winnsmith to Ulysses S. Grant, October 5, 1874, and R. M. Wallace to George H. Wallace, September 18, 1874, Department of Justice, Letters Received, 1871–1884, South Carolina, RG 60, NA (microfilm 947).

12. Gillette, *Retreat from Reconstruction,* 136–44; Fish Diary, May 5, 1874, Fish Papers, LC. Gillette's treatment of this episode resembles the "damned if you do, damned if you don't" approach. He criticizes Grant for failing to crush Brooks's coup at the outset but later claims that after supposedly encouraging Republican hopes by tolerating Brooks, he eventually "shattered them with a blow from which the state party was not to recover" by recognizing Baxter.

13. Fish Diary, November 17, 1874, Fish Papers, LC.

14. Elihu B. Washburne to Hamilton Fish, March 4, 1874, ibid; Joe Gray Taylor, *Louisiana Reconstructed, 1863–1877* (Baton Rouge, La., 1974), 279–95.

15. Rable, "Republican Albatross," 115–17; Grant, Proclamation of September 15, 1874, in James D. Richardson, ed., *Messages and Papers of the Presidents* (Washington, D.C., 1912), 6:4230–31; Fish Diary, September 16, 1874, Fish Papers, LC; George Spencer to William E. Chandler, September 17, 1874, William E. Chandler Papers, LC; Henry Brinkerstaff to George H. Williams, September 1874, Department of Justice, Letters Received, 1871–1884, Louisiana, RG 60, NA (microfilm 970);

William B. Hesseltine, *Ulysses S. Grant: Politician* (New York, 1935), 348; Jewell to Elihu B. Washburne, September 19, 1874, Washburne Papers, LC; Taylor, *Louisiana Reconstructed*, 294–97.

16. R. M. Wallace to George H. Williams, September 17, 1874, Department of Justice, Letters Received, 1871–1884, South Carolina, RG 60, NA (microfilm 947); George Spencer to William E. Chandler, September 17, 1874, Chandler Papers, LC; Elihu B. Washburne to J. C. B. Davis, September 20, 1874, Fish Papers, LC.

17. Gillette, *Retreat from Reconstruction*, 214–15, 217, 221–22, 227–28, 251.

18. James L. Camp to Elihu B. Washburne, November 9, 1874, Edward B. Warner to Washburne, November 10, 1874, and Marshall Jewell to Washburne, December 5, 1874, all in Washburne Papers, LC; Perman, *Road to Redemption*, 141.

19. Grant, Sixth Annual Message, December 7, 1874, in Richardson, *Messages and Papers*, 6:4250–53.

20. Grant to James G. Blaine, December 22, 1874, ibid., 6:4258; Hesseltine, *Grant*, 353.

21. Grant, Proclamation, December 21, 1874, in Richardson, *Messages and Papers*, 6:4276–77.

22. Taylor, *Louisiana Reconstructed*, 302–6.

23. Ibid., 306; James A. Garfield to Burke Hinsdale, January 7, 1875, in Mary L. Hinsdale, ed., *Garfield-Hinsdale Letters* (Ann Arbor, Mich., 1949), 309.

24. Charles C. Tansill, *The Congressional Career of Thomas Francis Bayard, 1869–1885* (Washington, D.C., 1946), 92; James A. Garfield to Burke Hinsdale, January 11, 1875, in Hinsdale, *Garfield-Hinsdale Letters*, 311; New York *Times*, January 12, 1875; Frederic Bancroft, ed., *Speeches, Correspondence, and Political Papers of Carl Schurz* (New York, 1913), 3:125.

25. William Mitchell to Edwin H. Staughton, January 14, 1875, Stoughton Papers, HPC; New York *Times*, January 9 and 10, 1875; Hesseltine, *Grant*, 358.

26. Benjamin H. Bristow to E. D. Force, January 11, 1875, Bristow to G. C. Wharton, January 14, 1875, and Bristow to John Harlan, January 11, 1875, all in Bristow Papers, LC.

27. New York *Times*, January 13, 1875; Grant, Message to the Senate, January 13, 1875, in Richardson, *Messages and Papers*, 6:4259–68.

28. Grant, Message to the Senate, January 13, 1875, in Richardson, *Messages and Papers*, 6:4259–68.

29. Ibid.

30. Edwards Pierrepont to Hamilton Fish, January 15, 1875, Fish Papers, LC; Henry Dawes to Samuel Bowles, February 2, 1875, Bowles Papers, Yale University; J. R. Sherwood to John Sherman, February 1, 1875, John Sherman Papers, LC; Joseph Medill to James G. Blaine, February 14, 1875, Blaine Papers, LC.

31. Grant, Message to the Senate, February 8, 1875, in Richardson, *Messages and Papers*. 6:4273; John M. Harlan to Benjamin H. Bristow, February 17, 1875, Bristow Papers, LC.

32. Gillette, *Retreat from Reconstruction*, 287.

33. Ibid., 288.

34. John R. Lynch, *The Facts of Reconstruction* (New York, 1913), 135.

35. Gillette, *Retreat from Reconstruction*, 208, 256, 273–74; John Eaton, *Grant, Lincoln, and the Freedmen* (New York, 1907), 260–62; Wade to his wife, February 27, 1875, Wade Papers, LC.

36. New York *Independent*, January 6, 1870; Swinney, "Enforcing the Fifteenth Amendment," 211–13.

37. Swinney, "Enforcing the Fifteenth Amendment," 207–8; Robert J. Kaczorowski, *The Politics of Judicial Interpretation: The Federal Courts, Department of Justice, and Civil Rights, 1866–1876* (New York, 1985), 177–84, 202.

38. W. W. Dedrick to Edwards Pierrepont, June 21 and September 8, 1875, George T. Swann to Joseph P. Bradley, September 9, 1875, and R. A. Hill to Dedrick, September 9, 1875, Department of Justice, Letters Received, 1871–1884, Mississippi, RG 60, NA (microfilm 970).

39. George S. Boutwell to Hamilton Fish, September 19, 1873, Fish Papers, LC; Gillette, *Retreat from Reconstruction,* 187.

40. Charles Nordhoff to Rutherford B. Hayes, June 10, 1875, Hayes Papers, HPC; Carl Schurz to Charles Francis Adams Jr., July 22, 1875, in Bancroft, *Speeches,* 3:158; Mark W. Summers, *The Press Gang: Newspapers and Politics, 1865–1878* (Chapel Hill, N.C., 1994), 191–206.

41. William C. Harris, *The Day of the Carpetbagger: Republican Reconstruction in Mississippi* (Baton Rouge, La., 1979), 459–80, 634–49.

42. Blanche Ames Ames, *Adelbert Ames, 1835–1933: General, Senator, Governor* (North Easton, Mass., 1964), 415; Harris, *The Day of the Carpetbagger,* 657.

43. Adelbert Ames to Blanche Ames, August 31, 1875, in Ames, *Ames,* 419; Harris, *The Day of the Carpetbagger,* 660–68; Ames to Grant, September 8, 1875, Grant to adjutant general, September 8, 1875, and Grant to C. C. Augur, September 9, 1875, all in Edward McPherson, *A Hand-book of Politics for 1876* (Washington, D.C., 1876), 40–44; James W. Garner, *Reconstruction in Mississippi* (New York, 1901), 390–91.

44. John L. Cadwallader to Hamilton Fish, August 7, 1875, Fish Papers, LC; Edwards Pierrepont to Alphonso Taft, June 29, 1875, William Howard Taft Papers, LC; Grant to Washburne, August 23, 1875, in James G. Wilson, ed., *General Grant's Letters to a Friend* (New York, 1897), 75; Ames to Blanche B. Ames, September 7, 1875, in Ames, *Ames,* 423; Ames to Pierrepont, September 11, 1875, ibid., 427–28.

45. Grant to Edwards Pierrepont, September 13, 1875, Pierrepont Papers, Yale University.

46. Edwards Pierrepont to Hamilton Fish, September 10 and 11, 1875, and draft of proclamation, September 11, 1875, Fish Papers, LC; Edwards Pierrepont to Adelbert Ames, September 14, 1875, and Ames to Blanche Ames, September 17 and October 8, 1875, in Ames, *Ames,* 429–30, 432; W. W. Dedrick to Edwards Pierrepont, September 10 and 27, 1875, Department of Justice, Letters Received, 1871–1884, Mississippi, RG 60, NA (microfilm 970). Others offered a different opinion on the persistence of terrorism: see R. A. Hill to W. W. Dedrick, September 9, 1875, ibid.

47. Adelbert Ames to Blanche Ames, October 12 and 15, 1875, Ames to Edwards Pierrepont, October 16, 1875, Edwards Pierrepont to Adelbert Ames, October 23, 1875, and George K. Chase to Edwards Pierrepont, October 27, 1875, all in Ames, *Ames,* 434, 439–41, 444. Gillette and other scholars mistakenly assert that Grant's refusal to intervene in September was "final"; see Gillette, *Retreat from Reconstruction,* 157.

48. Gillette, *Retreat from Reconstruction,* 161–63; Lynch, *The Facts of Reconstruction,* 152–53.

49. Eaton, *Grant, Lincoln, and the Freedmen,* 270–71.

50. Brooks D. Simpson, "This Bloody and Monstrous Crime," *Constitution* 4 (1992):45–46; Gillette, *Retreat from Reconstruction,* 301.

51. Gillette, *Retreat from Reconstruction,* 305.

52. Grant to Chamberlain, July 26, 1876, Grant Papers, LC.

53. Grant, Message to the Senate, July 31, 1876, in Richardson, *Messages and Papers*, 6:4329–30.

54. Alphonso Taft to Rutherford B. Hayes, August 23, 1876, Hayes Papers, HPC; New York *Times*, October 5, 1876; Grant, Proclamation, October 17, 1876, in Richardson, *Messages and Papers*, 6:4350–51; Charles Nordhoff to Hayes, October 15, 1876, Hayes Papers, HPC.

55. Ulysses S. Grant to William T. Sherman, November 10 and 11, 1876, Grant Papers, HPC; New York *Times*, November 11 and December 17, 1876; Allan Nevins, *Abram S. Hewitt* (New York, 1935), 326; Joseph G. Dawson III, *Army Generals and Reconstruction: Louisiana, 1862–1877* (Baton Rouge, La., 1982), 236; Dee Brown, *The Year of the Century: 1876* (New York, 1966), 319; Allan Nevins, *Hamilton Fish: The Inner History of the Grant Administration* (New York, 1937), 844.

56. Daniel H. Chamberlain to Grant, November 25, 1876, and John B. Gordon, B. T. Johnson, Wade Hampton, and A. G. Magrath to Grant, November 27, 1876, Grant Papers, HPC; Nevins, *Fish*, 845–48; Grant to Ruger, December 3 (two letters) and 4, 1876, and Ruger to Grant, December 3, 1876, Grant Papers, HPC; Brown, *The Year of the Century*, 321; Chicago *Tribune*, November 13, 1876; William A. Russ, "Was There a Danger of a Second Civil War During Reconstruction?" *Mississippi Valley Historical Review* 25 (1938):39–58; Pillow to Tilden, November 18, 1876, in John Bigelow, ed., *Letters and Literary Memorials of Samuel J. Tilden* (New York, 1908), 2:489.

57. Nevins, *Hewitt*, 338–40.

58. Harry J. Brown and Frederick D. Williams, eds., *The Diary of James A. Garfield* (East Lansing, Mich., 1967–81), 3:420–21 (January 19 and 20, 1877); Grant to J. D. Cameron, November 26, 1876, and William T. Sherman to Thomas Ruger, December 5 and 7, 1876, in Edward McPherson, *A Hand-book of Politics for 1878* (Washington, D.C., 1878), 77, 79.

59. Grant to Cameron, November 23, 1876, and to Ruger, December 4 and 7, 1876, Department of Justice, Letters Received, 1871–1884, South Carolina, RG 60, NA (microfilm 947); Nevins, *Fish*, 844–49; New York *Times*, December 11, 1876; Virgil Carrington Jones, *Ranger Mosby* (Chapel Hill, N.C., 1944), 298–99; Dawson, *Army Generals and Reconstruction*, 243–49; Chicago *Tribune*, January 8, 1877; McPherson, *A Hand-book of Politics for 1878*, 57, 64–65; Brown and Williams, *Diary of Garfield*, 2:415 (January 14, 1876); Vincent P. DeSantis, *Republicans Face the Southern Question, 1877–1897* (Baltimore, 1959), 53; Hamilton Fish Diary, January 7, 17, and 27, 1877, Fish Papers, LC; Longstreet to Grant, January 4, 1877, Grant to Augur, January 14, 1877, and Cameron to Augur, January 16, 1877, McPherson, *A Hand-book of Politics for 1878*, 61, 64–65; *House Misc. Documents*, no. 31, 45th Cong., 3d sess., 3:614.

60. Hamilton Fish Diary, January 17 and 27, 1877, Fish Papers, LC; New York *Times*, December 25, 1876.

61. New York *Times*, December 25, 1876; Keith Ian Polakoff, *The Politics of Inertia: The Election of 1876 and the End of Reconstruction* (Baton Rouge, La., 1973), 277; George W. Childs, *Recollections* (Philadelphia, 1890), 78, 80; A. M. Gibson, *A Political Crime: The History of the Great Fraud* (New York, 1885), 28; New York *Times*, December 2, 1876; Willard L. King, *Lincoln's Manager, David Davis* (Cambridge, Mass., 1960) 290.

62. Charles Fairman, *Five Justices and the Electoral Commission of 1877* (New York, 1988), is a close study of the commission and an extended defense of Bradley.

63. Hamilton Fish Diary, February 18 and 19, 1876, Fish Papers, LC; Nevins, *Fish*, 856; Brown and Williams, *Diary of Garfield*, 3:420–21 (January 19 and 20, 1877); DeSantis, *Republicans Face the Southern Question*, 53; McPherson, *A Handbook of Politics for 1878*, 67; New York *Times*, February 26, 1876; *House Misc. Documents*, no. 31, 45th Cong., 3d sess., 3:617–29. Those who doubt that the primary consideration of the Louisiana Democrats was home rule should read the telegrams reprinted in the House document.

64. Packard to Grant, March 1, 1877, and C. C. Sniffen to Packard, March 1, 1877, HPC; Chicago *Tribune*, March 3, 1877; Ari Hoogenboom, *The Presidency of Rutherford B. Hayes* (Lawrence, Kans., 1988), 49; DeSantis, *Republicans Face the Southern Question*, 53; New York *Times*, March 4, 1877; C. Vann Woodward, *Reunion and Reaction: The Compromise of 1877 and the End of Reconstruction* (Boston, 1951), 202; Harry Barnard, *Rutherford B. Hayes and His America* (Indianapolis, 1954), 420; Polakoff, *Politics of Inertia*, 317; Dawson, *Army Generals and Reconstruction*, 255; *House Misc. Documents*, no. 31, 45th Cong., 3d sess., 3:629–30; Ella Lonn, *Reconstruction in Louisiana After 1868*, (Gloucester, Mass., 1967 [1918]), 515; Watt Marchman, ed., "The Memoirs of Thomas Donaldson," *Hayes Historical Journal* 2 (1979):196–97

CHAPTER 7. "THE GREAT PACIFICATOR"

1. Hayes to Murat Halstead, February 2, 1866, and to Sardis Birchard, February 28, 1866, in Charles R. Williams, *The Diary and Letters of Rutherford B. Hayes* (Columbus, 1922–1926), 3:16, 18; Charles R. Williams, *Life of Rutherford B. Hayes* (Columbus, 1914), 1:283–87; diary, May 15, 1866, and Hayes to Lucy Hayes, May 16, 1866, in William, *Diary and Letters*, 3:25. See George Sinkler's discussion of Hayes's racial attitudes in *The Racial Attitudes of American Presidents from Abraham Lincoln to Theodore Roosevelt* (Garden City, N.Y., 1972), 197–242.

2. C. Williams, *Life of Hayes*, 1:293–321; diary, July 9, 1868, Hayes to Sardis Birchard, March 7, 1869, and to Charles Nordhoff, March 13, 1871, diary, March 16, 1871, and Hayes to Guy M. Bryan, December 24, 1871, in C. Williams, *Diary and Letters*, 3:54, 59, 134, 135–36, 180; T. Harry Williams, ed., *Hayes: The Diary of a President, 1875–1881* (New York, 1964), 2 (March 28, 1875); Hayes to Bryan, January 2 and July 27, 1875, in C. Williams, *Diary and Letters*, 3:262, 286.

3. T. Williams, *Diary of a President*, 10–11 (October 17, 1875); Ari Hoogenboom, *The Presidency of Rutherford B. Hayes* (Lawrence, Kans., 1988), 14.

4. Hayes, letter of acceptance, July 8, 1876, Edward McPherson, *Hand-book of Politics for 1876* (Washington, D.C., 1876), 212–13; Vincent P. DeSantis, *Republicans Face the Southern Question: The New Departure Years, 1877–1897* (Baltimore, 1959), 55; Hayes to Carl Schurz, June 27, 1876, in C. Williams, *Diary and Letters*, 3:329.

5. Hayes to Joseph H. Barrett, June 30, 1876, Hayes to James A. Garfield, August 4, 1876, and Hayes to John Sherman, August 7, 1876, Hayes to Schurz, August 9, 1876, and Hayes to Garfield, August 10, 1876, in C. Williams, *Diary and Letters*, 3: 332, 338, 339, 340, 343.

6. Hayes, diary, September 18, 1876, in T. Williams, *Diary of a President*, 37–38; Hayes to William H. Smith, October 5, 1876, ibid., 40; Stanley P. Hirshson, *Farewell to the Bloody Shirt: Northern Republicans and the Southern Negro* (Bloomington, Ind., 1962), 24; DeSantis, *Republicans Face the Southern Question*, 34, 61; Charles Nordhoff to Hayes, June 22, 1876, Hayes Papers, HPC.

7. Hirshson, *Farewell to the Bloody Shirt*, 24.

8. Hayes to William Henry Smith, December 24, 1876, January 3, 1877, in C. Williams, *Diary and Letters,* 3:393, 399.

9. John Tyler Jr. to Hayes, February 17, 1877, Hayes Papers, HPC.

10. William D. Kelley to Hayes, December 17, 1876, in C. Vann Woodward, *Reunion and Reaction: The Compromise of 1877 and the End of Reconstruction* (Boston, 1956), 37; Jacob D. Cox to Hayes, January 31, 1877, Joseph Medill to Richard Smith, February 17, 1877, and Charles Nordhoff to Charles Foster, February 15, 1877, all in Hayes Papers, HPC; James Longstreet to Ulysses S. Grant, February 17, 1877, Grant Papers, HPC.

11. James A. Garfield to Hayes, December 12, 1876, Hayes Papers, HPC.

12. Jacob D. Cox to Rutherford B. Hayes, January 31, 1877, Hayes Papers, HPC; Hirshson, *Farewell to the Bloody Shirt,* 25; Lewis Hanes to Hayes, February 14, 1877, Hayes Papers, HPC.

13. T. Williams, *Diary of a President,* 74–75 (February 18, 1877); Hayes to Carl Schurz, February 4, 1877, in C. Williams, *Diary and Letters,* 3:412–13.

14. DeSantis, *Republicans Face the Southern Question,* 71, 80; J. C. Winsmith to Hayes, January 13, 1877, and Joseph Medill to Richard Smith, February 17, 1877, both in Hayes Papers, HPC.

15. C. Williams, *Life of Hayes,* 2:4.

16. William Gillette, *Retreat from Reconstruction, 1869–1879* (Baton Rouge, La., 1979), 335–36.

17. Hayes, Inaugural Address, March 5, 1877, in James D. Richardson, ed., *Messages and Papers of the Presidents* (Washington, D.C., 1912), 6:4394–99.

18. DeSantis, *Republicans Face the Southern Question,* 74; T. Williams, *Diary of a President,* 79 (February 27, 1877); Hoogenboom, *Presidency of Hayes,* 51–52.

19. See Ari Hoogenboom, *Rutherford B. Hayes: Warrior and President* (Lawrence, Kans., 1995), 301–4.

20. T. Williams, *Diary of a President,* 81, 83, 84, 85 (March 14, 16, 20, and 23, 1877).

21. DeSantis, *Republicans Face the Southern Question,* 125; T. Williams, *Diary of a President,* 83 (March 16, 1877); Terry L. Seip, *The South Returns to Congress: Men, Economic Measures, and Intersectional Relationships, 1868–1879* (Baton Rouge, La., 1983), 13; Hoogenboom, *Presidency of Hayes,* 57–58, 62.

22. T. Williams, *Diary of a President,* 84 (March 20, 1877); Hoogenboom, *Presidency of Hayes,* 64–65.

23. Gillette, *Retreat from Reconstruction,* 340; Hoogenboom, *Presidency of Hayes,* 63–64.

24. Hoogenboom, *Presidency of Hayes,* 66–67.

25. T. Williams, *Diary of a President,* 86–87 (April 22, 1877); Hayes to William D. Bickham, April 22, 1877, in C. Williams, *Diary and Letters,* 3:431.

26. Harry J. Brown and Frederick D. Williams, eds., *The Diary of James A. Garfield* (East Lansing, Mich., 1967–1981), 3.45, 46, 47 (March 11 and 27, 1877); Hirshson, *Farewell to the Bloody Shirt,* 27–28, 34.

27. Brown and Williams, *Diary of Garfield,* 3:469 (April 3, 1877).

28. Woodward, *Reunion and Reaction,* 218; T. Williams, *Diary of a President,* 79–80 (March 14, 1877); New York *Tribune,* March 13, 1877, and *Harper's Weekly,* March 31 and May 26, 1877, in DeSantis, *Republicans Face the Southern Question,* 24–25, 36.

29. Gillette, *Retreat from Reconstruction,* 336; Michael Perman, *The Road to Redemption: Southern Politics, 1869–1879* (Chapel Hill, N.C., 1984), 269; T. Williams, *Diary of a President,* 86–87 (April 22, 1877).

30. Brown and Williams, *Diary of Garfield,* 3:469 (April 3, 1877); Hayes to William D. Bickham, May 3, 1877, in C. Williams, *Diary and Letters,* 3:432; Watt P. Marchman, ed., "The 'Memoirs' of Thomas Donaldson," *Hayes Historical Journal* 2 (1979):164 (May 19, 1877).

31. Hirshson, *Farewell to the Bloody Shirt,* 35–39.

32. T. Williams, *Diary of a President,* 95 (August 26, 1877); Rayford Logan, *The Betrayal of the Negro* (New York, 1968 [1954]), 32–38; Hirshson, *Farewell to the Bloody Shirt,* 39; Hoogenboom, *Presidency of Hayes,* 69–70.

33. T. Williams, *Diary of a President,* 96, 101 (September 6 and November 3, 1877); Brown and Williams, *Diary of Garfield,* 3:535 (October 26, 1877); Hoogenboom, *Presidency of Hayes,* 63.

34. Brown and Williams, *Diary of Garfield,* 3:532 (October 19, 1877); Hirshson, *Farewell to the Bloody Shirt,* 40–42.

35. Marchman, "Memoirs of Donaldson," 169, 176, 181 (October 17 and November 27, 1877, and March 2, 1878).

36. Ibid., 167–68 (October 17, 1877).

37. DeSantis, *Republicans Face the Southern Question,* 78, 91–92.

38. Ibid., 98–99.

39. T. Williams, *Diary of a President,* 100 (October 24, 1877); Marchman, "Memoirs of Donaldson," 168 (October 17, 1877).

40. T. Williams, *Diary of a President,* 125–26 (March 12, 1878).

41. Theodore C. Smith, *The Life and Letters of James Abram Garfield* (New Haven, Conn., 1925), 2:665; Hirshson, *Farewell to the Bloody Shirt,* 43–44; Allan Peskin, *Garfield* (Kent, Ohio, 1978), 426–27.

42. Marchman, "Memoirs of Donaldson," 182 (March 6, 1878); Hoogenboom, *Warrior and President,* 324.

43. Smith, *Garfield,* 2:664.

44. T. Williams, *Diary of a President,* 141, 142 (May 14 and 19, 1878); C. Williams, *Diary and Letters,* 3:484; Smith, *Garfield,* 2:666; C. Williams, *Life of Hayes,* 2:155. In later years Hayes recalled his words more strongly: "Mr. Tilden will be arrested and shot. He cannot attempt to take possession of the White House without a fight. That means civil war, and in that event we shall whip them badly" (C. Williams, *Diary and Letters,* 3:484).

45. Hirshson, *Farewell to the Bloody Shirt,* 46; T. Williams, *Diary of a President,* 164, 167 (October 5 and 26, 1878).

46. DeSantis, *Republicans Face the Southern Question,* 100.

47. T. Williams, *Diary of a President,* 168, 170 (November 6 and 12, 1878); Marchman, "Memoirs of Donaldson," 208 (June 4, 1879); Hirshson, *Farewell to the Bloody Shirt,* 49; Garfield quoted in E. W. Winkler, ed., "Hayes-Bryan Correspondence," *Southwestern Historical Quarterly* 27 (1924):323.

48. McPherson, *Hand-book of Politics for 1878,* 3–4; Hayes to Bryan, December 13, 1878, January 10, 1879, in Winkler, "Hayes-Bryan Correspondence," 323, 324–25; T. Williams, *Diary of a President,* 175, 178 (December 4 and 25, 1878).

49. Hoogenboom, *Presidency of Hayes,* 73–74; Hoogenboom, *Warrior and President,* 382–83.

50. T. Williams, *Diary of a President,* 193 (March 18, 1879); Hoogenboom, *Presidency of Hayes,* 73–75; Hoogenboom, *Warrior and President,* 392–94. See also Frank P. Vazzano, "President Hayes, Congress and the Appropriations Riders Vetoes," *Congress and the Presidency* 20 (1993): 25–38.

51. Ibid., 193–94 (March 18, 1879), 196–97 (March 21, 1879), 197–98 (March 22, 1879), 198–202 (March 23, 1879).

52. Ibid., 210 (March 31, 1879); Garfield to Hinsdale, April 9, 1879, in Mary L. Hinsdale, ed., *Garfield-Hinsdale Letters* (Ann Arbor, Mich., 1949), 403–4; Hinsdale to Garfield, April 27, 1879, ibid., 409.

53. T. Williams, *Diary of a President*, 204 (March 27, 1878); 216 (April 26, 1879), 217 (April 30, 1879); Brown and Williams, *Diary of Garfield*, 4:223 (April 26, 1878).

54. Marchman, "Memoirs of Donaldson," 202–3 (May 7, 1879), 204 (May 16, 1879); T. Williams, *Diary of a President*, 219 (May 11, 1879); Brown and Williams, *Diary of Garfield*, 4:231 (May 12, 1879).

55. Marchman, "Memoirs of Donaldson," 205 (May 16, 1879); James A. Garfield to Burke Hinsdale, May 20, 1879, in Hinsdale, *Garfield-Hinsdale Letters*, 417.

56. Marchman, "Memoirs of Donaldson," 206 (May 29, 1879), 210 (June 26, 1879); T. Williams, *Diary of a President*, 226 (June 4, 1879); 232–33 (June 27, 1879); Hoogenboom, *Presidency of Hayes*, 77; James A. Garfield to Burke Hinsdale, June 23, 1879, in Hinsdale, *Garfield-Hinsdale Letters*, 426.

57. C. Williams, *Life of Hayes*, 2:203–5. This contest was revived in 1880, but after another Hayes veto on May 4, the Democrats abandoned even this shadow of a victory and made appropriations to pay the fees of marshals and deputies.

58. C. Williams, *Life of Hayes*, 2:205 n. 2 (quoting the New York *Herald*, July 3, 1879); Peskin, *Garfield*, 442.

59. Marchman, "Memoirs of Donaldson," 220 (January 5, 1880); T. Williams, *Diary of a President*, 217 (April 28, 1879); Brown and Williams, *Diary of Garfield*, 4:247, 252–53 (June 11, 20 and 23, 1879).

60. Hayes, speech, Youngstown, Ohio, September 12, 1879, HPC.

61. Brown and Wiliams, *Diary of Garfield*, 4:309–10 (October 14, 1879) and note; T. Williams, *Diary of a President*, 253 (November 26, 1879).

62. DeSantis, *Republicans Face the Southern Question*, 96.

63. Ibid., 94–96.

64. T. Williams, *Diary of a President*, 142–43 (May 19, 1878); Marchman, "Memoirs of Donaldson," 212 (July 23, 1879).

65. T. Williams, *Diary of a President*, 221 (May 24, 1879); William Johnston to Hayes, March 29, 1879, Hayes Papers, HPC.

66. T. Williams, *Diary of a President*, 278, 288–89 (June 5 and July 21, 1880); Hayes to William Henry Smith, June 18, 1880, in C. Williams, *Diary and Letters*, 3:606.

67. T. Williams, *Diary of a President*, 269–70 (April 11, 1880).

CONCLUSION

11. John Russell Young, *Around the World with General Grant* (New York, 1879), 2:362–63.

BIBLIOGRAPHICAL ESSAY

The literature on the historiography of Reconstruction has grown to such an extent that it alone is worthy of historiographical analysis. What follows is a selective bibliography, highlighting the works that proved most useful in the preparation of this book. Rather than reiterate the various traditional, revisionist, and subsequent cycles of scholarship, this essay emphasizes recent work, mentioning older works when appropriate.

The most comprehensive overview of Reconstruction is Eric Foner, *Reconstruction: America's Unfinished Revolution, 1863–1877* (New York, 1988). Shorter and dated but still useful is Kenneth M. Stampp, *The Era of Reconstruction, 1865–1877* (New York, 1965); John Hope Franklin, *Reconstruction: After the Civil War* (Chicago, 1961), has been partially updated but not replaced by a 1994 edition. On the racial attitudes of the presidents, George Sinkler, *The Racial Attitudes of American Presidents: From Abraham Lincoln to Theodore Roosevelt* (Garden City, N.Y., 1971), presents a point of departure. Especially useful for my purposes were Michael Perman, *Emancipation and Reconstruction, 1862–1879* (Arlington Heights, Ill., 1987), and Michael Les Benedict, *The Fruits of Victory: Alternatives in Restoring the Union, 1865–1877* (Lanham, Md., 1986). Included in C. Vann Woodward, *The Future of the Past* (New York, 1989), is the most recent of a series of essays that criticizes northern efforts during Reconstruction (in the process minimizing the contributions of white southerners to that outcome), but "Reconstruction: A Counterfactual Playback" ironically makes the case that perhaps critics of Republican policy makers expect too much of their subjects. Offering sound advice on how to approach the study of Reconstruction is Gerald N. Grob, "Reconstruction: An American Morality Play," in George A. Billias and Gerald N. Grob, eds., *American History: Retrospect and Prospect* (New York, 1971), and John Hope Franklin, "Mirror for Americans: A Century of Reconstruction History," in his *Race and History: Selected Essays, 1938–1988* (Baton Rouge, La., 1989).

It is essential to assess specific policies in broader political, institutional, and constitutional contexts. Toward that end, Morton Keller, *Affairs of State: Public Life in Late Nineteenth Century America* (Cambridge, Mass., 1977), and Stephen Skowronek, *Building a New American State: The Expansion of National Administrative Capacities, 1877–1920* (Cambridge, 1982), have much to say about the Reconstruction state. So does Richard Franklin Benzel, *Yankee Leviathan: The Origins of Central State Authority in America, 1859–1877* (Cambridge, 1990). Three explorations of the intersection of politics, policy, and constitutionalism are Herman Belz, *Emancipation and Equal Rights: Politics and Constitutionalism in the Civil War Era* (New York, 1978); Earl M. Maltz, *Civil Rights, the Constitution, and Congress, 1863–1869* (Lawrence, Kans., 1990); and Harold M. Hyman and William M. Wiecek, *Equal Justice Under Law: Constitutional Development, 1835–1875* (New York, 1982). Joel H. Silbey, *The American Political Nation, 1838–1893* (Stanford, Calif., 1991), establishes a larger framework. Two books by James M. McPherson, *The Struggle for Equality: Abolitionists and the Negro in the Civil War and Reconstruction* (Princeton, N.J., 1964), and *The Abolitionist Legacy: From Reconstruction to the NAACP* (Princeton, N.J., 1975), explore how abolitionists sought to shape emancipation and Reconstruction.

LINCOLN

Roy P. Basler and his associates compiled *The Collected Works of Abraham Lincoln* (New Brunswick, N.J., 1953–55) in eight volumes plus an index; supplementary volumes appeared in 1974 (published by Greenwood Press) and 1990. The sixteenth president has been well served by his biographers, led by David Donald's masterful *Lincoln* (New York, 1995). Two other biographies well worth examining, in part because of their contrasting views on Lincoln and Reconstruction, are Benjamin P. Thomas, *Abraham Lincoln* (New York, 1952), and Stephen B. Oates, *With Malice Toward None: The Life of Abraham Lincoln* (New York, 1977).

Phillip Shaw Paludan, *The Presidency of Abraham Lincoln* (Lawrence, Kans., 1994), offers the best extended treatment of the Lincoln presidency, although there is still much of value in James G. Randall, *Lincoln the President* (New York, 1945–1955; volume 4 with Richard N. Current). A succinct summary of Paludan's argument is to be found in his "Emancipating the Republic: Lincoln and the Means and Ends of Antislavery," in James M. McPherson, ed., *"We Cannot Escape History": Lincoln and the Last Best Hope of Earth* (Urbana, Ill., 1995). The literature devoted primarily to Lincoln's reconstruction policy is far more extensive than one might expect in light of Lincoln's rather limited achievements in this area. William B. Hesseltine, *Lincoln's Plan of Reconstruction* (Tuscaloosa, Ala., 1960), correctly reminds us that Lincoln juggled several approaches, while LaWanda Cox, *Lincoln and Black Freedom: A Study in Presidential Leadership* (Columbia, S.C., 1981), points out that he was committed to emancipation. It is remarkable that John Hope Franklin, *The Emancipation Proclamation* (Garden City, N.Y., 1963), remains the leading work on the subject of its title, a tribute to Franklin's scholarship. Peyton McCrary, *Abraham Lincoln and Reconstruction: The Louisiana Experiment* (Princeton, N.J., 1978), and William C. Harris, *With Charity for All: Lincoln and the Restoration of the Union* (Lexington, Ky., 1997), hold opposing views on what Lincoln sought, with McCrary emphasizing the advancement of black rights and opportunities and Harris stressing Lincoln's desire for conciliation.

Michael F. Holt, "Abraham Lincoln and the Politics of Union," in John L. Thomas, ed., *Abraham Lincoln and the American Political Tradition* (Amherst, Mass., 1986), 111–41, is a characteristically provocative if perhaps overstated and overargued reassessment of Lincoln's relations with congressional Republicans grounded in their differing political priorities, highlighting Lincoln's concern with extending Republicanism southward. Herman Belz, *Reconstructing the Union: Theory and Practice During the Civil War* (Ithaca, N.Y., 1969), emphasizes institutional and constitutional concerns. A fuller discussion of Senate Republicans can be found in Allan G. Bogue, *The Earnest Men: Republicans of the Civil War Senate* (Ithaca, N.Y., 1981).

JOHNSON

The best collection of Andrew Johnson's papers is held at the Library of Congress; they are being made accessible in a letterpress edition, *The Papers of Andrew Johnson,* edited by LeRoy P. Graf, Ralph W. Haskins, and Paul Bergeron (fourteen volumes to date [Knoxville, Tenn., 1967–]). The best biography, grounded in modern scholarship, is Hans L. Trefousse's *Andrew Johnson: A Biography* (New York, 1989). Much shorter and more favorable to Johnson is James E. Sefton, *Andrew Johnson and the Uses of Constitutional Power* (Boston, 1980). David W. Bowen provides a thoughtful assessment of Johnson's racial attitudes in *Andrew Johnson and the Negro* (Knoxville, Tenn., 1989).

Much of the revolution in Reconstruction scholarship in the last generation commenced as a reassessment of the Johnson administration; perhaps the
most influential of the books that came under scrutiny was Howard K. Beale,
The Critical Year: A Study of Andrew Johnson and Reconstruction (New York,
1930). George Fort Milton, *The Age of Hate: Andrew Johnson and the Radi-
cals* (New York, 1934), offers a more extended treatment grounded upon the
assumption that Johnson was basically pursuing the correct policy. Both Eric
L. McKitrick, *Andrew Johnson and Reconstruction* (Chicago, 1960), and
LaWanda and John H. Cox, *Politics, Principle, and Prejudice 1865–1866* (New
York, 1963), present reinterpretations of Johnson's first year in office, with
McKitrick emphasizing matters of personality and political dynamics while the
Coxes reaffirm the importance of racial attitudes in a broader political con-
text. William R. Brock, *An American Crisis: Congress and Reconstruction,
1865–1867* (New York, 1963), and David H. Donald, *The Politics of Reconstruction, 1863–1867* (Baton Rouge, La., 1965), build upon earlier recogni-
tions of the divisions among congressional Republicans, a process greatly
refined and elucidated in Michael Les Benedict, *A Compromise of Principle:
Congressional Republicans and Reconstruction, 1863–1869* (New York, 1973).
Patrick W. Riddleberger, *1866: The Critical Year Revisited* (Carbondale, Ill.,
1979), contains a useful overview. Johnson's dealings with the army and its
general in chief can be followed in Brooks D. Simpson, *Let Us Have Peace:
Ulysses S. Grant and the Politics of War and Reconstruction, 1861–1868*
(Chapel Hill, N.C., 1991). Donald G. Nieman, *To Set the Law in Motion: The
Freedmen's Bureau and the Legal Rights of Blacks, 1865–1868* (Millwood,
N.Y., 1979), is essential to an understanding of Johnson as obstructionist.
On impeachment, see Michael Les Benedict, *The Impeachment and Trial of
Andrew Johnson* (New York, 1973), and Hans L. Trefousse, *Impeachment of
a President: Andrew Johnson, the Blacks, and Reconstruction* (Knoxville, Tenn.,
1975).

The role of southern whites in reconstruction policy during Johnson's first
two years in office is outlined in Dan T. Carter, *When the War Was Over: The
Failure of Self-Reconstruction in the South, 1865–1867* (Baton Rouge, La.,
1985); in turn, Michael Perman, *Reunion Without Compromise: The South and
Reconstruction 1865–1868* (New York, 1973), emphasizes the problems raised
by seeking the cooperation of southern whites. That Andrew Johnson was more
or less dead set to do what he did in any case is the implicit assumption in
Brooks D. Simpson, LeRoy P. Graf, and John Muldowny, eds., *Advice After
Appomattox: Letters to Andrew Johnson, 1865–1866* (Knoxville, Tenn., 1987),
which documents and discusses several fact-finding missions.

GRANT

It is one of the puzzling lacuna in Reconstruction historiography (and that of political history in general) that no satisfactory study of the Grant presidency exists, which is all the more startling in light of the willingness of many scholars to pass judgment on it. One place to start is by looking at biographies of the eighteenth president. Although most studies of Grant are limited to his military career, a few full-length studies do explore his years in the White House. Alone in giving emphasis to Grant's political career is William B. Hesseltine, *Ulysses S. Grant: Politician* (New York, 1935), while Simpson, *Let Us Have Peace,* discusses why Grant decided to run for president. Two other studies, William S. McFeely, *Grant: A Biography* (New York, 1981), and John A. Carpenter, *Ulysses S. Grant* (New York, 1970), offer contrasting perspectives on the general/president. Geoffrey Perret, *Ulysses S. Grant: Soldier and President* (New York, 1997), presents an unsatisfactory, uninformed, and incomplete treatment of Grant and Reconstruction. Allan Nevins, *Hamilton Fish: The Inner History of the Grant Administration* (New York, 1937), contains a wealth of information, despite the author's willingness to adopt Fish's own perspective. Richard N. Current, "President Grant and the Continuing Civil War," in *Arguing with Historians: Essays on the Historical and the Unhistorical* (Middletown, Conn., 1987), points the way to revising our understanding of Grant's reconstruction policy. *The Papers of Ulysses S. Grant,* edited by John Y. Simon and his associates (Carbondale, Ill., 1967–), promises to offer more extensive documentation of the Grant presidency.

Taken together, William Gillette, *Retreat from Reconstruction, 1869–1879* (Baton Rouge, La., 1979), and Michael Perman, *The Road to Redemption: Southern Politics, 1869–1879* (Chapel Hill, N.C., 1984), offer hardheaded explanations of reconstruction policy grounded upon political priorities. Unfortunately, Gillette, after making the case that Grant was rather limited in the options available to him to respond to rather difficult if not confounding circumstances, nevertheless holds him responsible for much of what happened. Both historians, however, take Grant seriously as a politician. One learns much about why southern Republicanism collapsed in Terry L. Seip, *The South Returns to Congress: Men, Economic Measures, and Intersectional Relationships, 1868–1879* (Baton Rouge, La., 1983). The essays by Lawrence N. Powell, J. Mills Thornton, William S. McFeely, and Vincent P. DeSantis in J. Morgan Kousser and James M. McPherson, eds., *Region, Race, and Reconstruction: Essays in Honor of C. Vann Woodward* (New York, 1982), highlight themes important to an understanding of Republican reconstruction efforts in the 1870s.

William Gillette, *The Right to Vote: Politics and the Passage of the Fifteenth Amendment* (Baltimore, 1969), assesses the political motivations behind the constitutional proposal; enforcement legislation is examined in Xi Wang, *The Trial of Democracy: Black Suffrage and Northern Republicans, 1860–1910* (Athens, Ga., 1997), and Everette Swinney, *Suppressing the Ku Klux Klan: The Enforcement of the Reconstruction Amendments, 1870–1877* (New York, 1987). A most thoughtful treatment of corruption as both theme and reality is contained in Mark Wahlgren Summers, *The Era of Good Stealings* (New York, 1993). Brooks D. Simpson, *The Political Education of Henry Adams* (Columbia, S.C., 1996), illustrates one reformer's lack of interest in Reconstruction; Michael Les Benedict, "Reform Republicans and the Retreat from Reconstruction," in Eric Anderson and Alfred A. Moss Jr., eds., *The Facts of Reconstruction: Essays in Honor of John Hope Franklin* (Baton Rouge, La., 1991), offers a broader treatment of the same issue. Two other essays in the Anderson and Moss collection—Carl H. Moneyhon, "The Failure of Southern Republicanism, 1867–1876," and Michael Perman, "Counter Reconstruction: The Role of Violence in Southern Redemption"—present insightful overviews of their subjects.

HAYES

The best collection of Rutherford B. Hayes's papers can be found at the Rutherford B. Hayes Presidential Center in Fremont, Ohio. Edited versions of the president's diary and correspondence include Charles Richard Williams, ed., *Diary and Letters of Rutherford Birchard Hayes*, 5 vols. (Columbus, 1922–1926), and T. Harry Williams, *Hayes: The Diary of a President, 1875–1881* (New York, 1964). The best biography of the nineteenth president is Ari Hoogenboom, *Rutherford B. Hayes: Warrior and President* (Lawrence, Kans., 1995), but one can still gather information of value in Charles Richard Williams, *The Life of Rutherford B. Hayes*, 2 vols. (Columbus, 1914), and Harry Barnard, *Rutherford B. Hayes and His America* (Indianapolis, 1954). Less useful is H. J. Eckenrode, *Rutherford B. Hayes: Statesman of Reunion* (New York, 1930).

On the election of 1876, see Keith Ian Polakoff, *The Politics of Inertia: The Election of 1876 and the End of Reconstruction* (Baton Rouge, La., 1973), and C. Vann Woodward, *Reunion and Reaction: The Compromise of 1877 and the End of Reconstruction* (Boston, 1951), still venerable if no longer invulnerable. Several scholarly articles have done much to shape our understanding of the compromise negotiations, including Allen Peskin, "Was There a Compromise of 1877?" *Journal of American History* 60 (1973): 63–75; Michael Les Benedict, "Southern Democrats in the Crisis of 1876–77: A Reconsideration of *Reunion and Reaction*," *Journal of Southern History* 46 (1980): 489–524; and George C. Rable, "Southern Interests and the Election of 1876: A Reappraisal," *Civil War History* 26 (1980): 347–61.

On the Hayes presidency, one should turn first to Ari Hoogenboom, *The Presidency of Rutherford B. Hayes* (Lawrence, Kans., 1988), which supersedes Kenneth E. Davison, *The Presidency of Rutherford B. Hayes* (Westport, Conn., 1972), and John W. Burgess's little-known *The Administration of President Hayes* (New York, 1916). Most valuable for understanding the politics of the Hayes administration are *The Diary of James A. Garfield*, edited by Harry James Brown and Frederick D. Williams, 4 vols. (East Lansing, Mich., 1967–1981), and Allen Peskin, *Garfield* (Kent, Ohio, 1978). On Hayes's southern policy, see Gillette, *Retreat from Reconstruction*, Stanley P. Hirshson, *Farewell to the Bloody Shirt: Northern Republicans and the Southern Negro, 1877–1893* (Bloomington, Ind., 1962), and Vincent P. DeSantis, *Republicans Face the Southern Question: The New Departure Years, 1877–1897* (Baltimore, 1959). Frank P. Vazzano, "President Hayes, Congress, and the Appropriations Riders Vetoes," *Congress and the Presidency* 20 (1993): 25–37, explores a critical episode.

OTHER STUDIES

Otto H. Olsen, ed., *Reconstruction and Redemption in the South* (Baton Rouge, La., 1980), offers perceptive assessments of the fate of Reconstruction in six states; Richard O. Curry, ed., *Radicalism, Racism, and Party Realignment: The Border States During Reconstruction* (Baltimore, 1969), suggests why Republicanism struggled in that region. Mark W. Summers, *Railroads, Reconstruction, and the Gospel of Prosperity: Aid Under the Radical Republicans, 1865–1877* (Princeton, N.J., 1984), demonstrates why efforts to ground southern Republicanism on a foundation of economic growth failed. Richard Abbott, *The Republican Party and the South, 1855–1877: The First Southern Strategy* (Chapel Hill, N.C., 1986), concentrates on the pre-1869 period. Armstead Robinson, "Beyond the Realm of Social Consensus: New Meanings of Reconstruction for American History," *Journal of American History* 68 (1981): 276–97, is suggestive on the fate of southern Republicanism.

Explorations of politics in several southern states highlight the difficulties Republicans faced in extending the party southward. They include Richard

Lowe, *Republicans and Reconstruction in Virginia, 1856–70* (Charlottesville, Va., 1991); Joe Gray Taylor, *Louisiana Reconstructed, 1863–1877* (Baton Rouge, La., 1974); Ted Tunnell, *Crucible of Reconstruction: War, Radicalism, and Race in Louisiana, 1862–1877* (Baton Rouge, La., 1984); Jack P. Maddex Jr., *The Virginia Conservatives, 1867–1879: A Study in Reconstruction Politics* (Chapel Hill, N.C., 1970); William C. Harris, *The Day of the Carpetbagger: Republican Reconstruction in Mississippi* (Baton Rouge, La., 1979); Carl H. Moneyhon, *Republicanism in Reconstruction Texas* (Austin, Tex., 1980); and Elizabeth S. Nathans, *Losing the Peace: Georgia Republicans and Reconstruction, 1865–1871* (Baton Rouge, La., 1968).

Establishing a context for the limits of the possible in northern politics is Dale Baum, *The Civil War Party System: The Case of Massachusetts, 1848–1876* (Chapel Hill, N.C., 1984); Phyllis F. Field, *The Politics of Race in New York: The Struggle for Black Suffrage in the Civil War Era* (Ithaca, N.Y., 1982); James C. Mohr, *The Radical Republicans and Reform in New York During Reconstruction* (Ithaca, N.Y., 1973); Robert D. Sawrey, *Dubious Victory: The Reconstruction Debate in Ohio* (Lexington, Ky., 1992); Erwin S. Bradley, *The Triumph of Militant Republicanism: A Study of Pennsylvania and Presidential Politics, 1860–1872* (Philadelphia, 1964); Frank B. Evans, *Pennsylvania Politics, 1872–1877: A Study in Political Leadership* (Harrisburg, Pa., 1966); and James C. Mohr, ed., *Radical Republicans in the North: State Politics During Reconstruction* (Baltimore, 1976). More extensive examinations of northern politics, especially in the 1870s, are needed.

George C. Rable, *But There Was No Peace: The Role of Violence in the Politics of Reconstruction* (Athens, Ga., 1984), highlights the pervasiveness of violence in southern politics, while Allen W. Trelease, *White Terror: The Ku Klux Klan Conspiracy and Southern Reconstruction* (New York, 1971), offers a full examination of one particular wave of political terrorism. Charles Fairman, *Reconstruction and Reunion, 1864–1888* (New York, 1971), and Robert J. Kaczorowski, *The Politics of Judicial Interpretation: The Federal Courts, Department of Justice, and Civil Rights, 1866–1876* (New York, 1985), highlight the fate of enforcement initiatives. Taken together, Richard Zuczek, *State of Rebellion: Reconstruction in South Carolina, 1865–1877* (Columbia, S.C., 1996), and Lou Falkner Williams, *The Great South Carolina Ku Klux Klan Trials, 1871–1872* (Athens, Ga., 1996), examine the interrelationships between terrorist violence and federal policy in one state, although each slights the broader contexts of federal policy.

Several biographies of political leaders shed light on presidential policy. David Donald, *Charles Sumner and the Rights of Man* (New York, 1970), is especially useful on the decline of Reconstruction during the Grant administration. Hans L. Trefousse, *The Radical Republicans: Lincoln's Vanguard for Racial Justice* (New York, 1969), is a sympathetic portrayal; so are his individual biographies, from *Ben Butler: The South Called Him Beast* (New York, 1957), to *Benjamin Franklin Wade: Radical Republican from Ohio* (New York, 1963), and *Carl Schurz: A Biography* (Knoxville, Tenn., 1982); his *Thaddeus Stevens: Nineteenth-Century Egalitarian* (Chapel Hill, N.C., 1997), appeared too late for use in this study, although it should complement Fawn Brodie, *Thaddeus Stevens: Scourge of the South* (New York, 1959). Richard N. Current, *Those Terrible Carpetbaggers: A Reinterpretation* (New York, 1988), awaits a complementary study of southern-born white Republicans, while Howard N. Rabinowitz, ed., *Southern Black Leaders of the Reconstruction Era* (Urbana, Ill., 1982), offers a starting point for its subject. For the opposition, see Joel Silbey, *A Respectable Minority: The Democratic Party in the Civil War Era, 1860–1868* (New York, 1977), and Jean Baker, *Affairs of Party: The Political Culture of Northern Democrats in the Mid-Nineteenth Century* (Ithaca, N.Y., 1983).

Models of presidential leadership employed by political scientists are of limited use in assessing the performance of presidents in the nineteenth century, primarily because they reflect examinations of twentieth-century chief executives. Indeed, based as they are on selective syntheses of prevailing scholarship and the need to derive principles from case studies, one wonders if perhaps the whole enterprise of creating social scientific models should give way to a more disciplined form of historically grounded analysis. Moreover, the rating games in which many historians and political scientists participate ultimately tell us little, for they fail to take into account numerous variables that do much to determine presidential reputation or to define achievement and performance in meaningful ways. If anything, they help us understand the climate of opinion in which the polls are taken and the resulting reputation enjoyed by individual presidents among scholars and students. Of some use, however, were Richard E. Neustadt, *Presidential Power and the Modern Presidents* (New York, 1990), a revision of a classic; Fred I. Greenstein, ed., *Leadership in the Modern Presidency* (Cambridge, Mass., 1988); and especially Stephen Skowronek, *The Politics Presidents Make: Leadership from John Adams to George Bush* (Cambridge, Mass., 1993).

INDEX